A

BOOK

The Philip E. Lilienthal imprint
honors special books
in commemoration of a man whose work
at University of California Press from 1954 to 1979
was marked by dedication to young authors
and to high standards in the field of Asian Studies.
Friends, family, authors, and foundations have together
endowed the Lilienthal Fund, which enables UC Press
to publish under this imprint selected books
in a way that reflects the taste and judgment
of a great and beloved editor.

D0916134

The publisher gratefully acknowledges the generous support of the Philip E. Lilienthal Asian Studies Endowment Fund of the University of California Press Foundation, which was established by a major gift from Sally Lilienthal.

Haunting Images

Haunting Images

A Cultural Account of Selective
Reproduction in Vietnam

Tine M. Gammeltoft

UNIVERSITY OF CALIFORNIA PRESS
Berkeley · *Los Angeles* · *London*

University of California Press, one of the most
distinguished university presses in the United States,
enriches lives around the world by advancing scholarship
in the humanities, social sciences, and natural sciences. Its
activities are supported by the UC Press Foundation and
by philanthropic contributions from individuals and
institutions. For more information, visit www.ucpress.edu.

University of California Press
Berkeley and Los Angeles, California

University of California Press, Ltd.
London, England

Library of Congress Cataloging-in-Publication Data

Gammeltoft, Tine, author.

    Haunting images : a cultural account of selective
reproduction in Vietnam / Tine M. Gammeltoft.
        pages   cm.
    Includes bibliographical references and index.
    ISBN 978-0-520-27842-4 (cloth : alk. paper)
    ISBN 978-0-520-27843-1 (pbk. : alk. paper)
    ISBN 978-0-520-95815-9 (ebook)
    1. Abortion—Moral and ethical aspects—
Vietnam.   2. Abortion—Social aspects—Vietnam.
I. Title.
    HQ767.5.V5G36   2014
    179.7′609597—dc23   2013038507

Manufactured in the United States of America

23 22 21 20 19 18 17 16 15 14
10 9 8 7 6 5 4 3 2 1

In keeping with a commitment to support
environmentally responsible and sustainable printing
practices, UC Press has printed this book on Natures
Natural, a fiber that contains 30% post-consumer waste
and meets the minimum requirements of ANSI/NISO
Z39.48–1992 (R 1997) (*Permanence of Paper*).

For Anna and August

Contents

Illustrations

Acknowledgments

Books can be seen as products of their authors' belonging, or strivings to belong, to social collectives of conversation and collaboration. The process of writing this book has placed me in profound debt to a variety of such collectives and their individual members. First of all, I am indebted to my co-researchers in Vietnam. With me through three years of intense fieldwork, through lively meetings, inspired discussions, and nourishing lunches at our *bún ngan* restaurant in Hanoi's La Thành street has been a group of ten researchers: Bùi Kim Chi, Đỗ Thanh Toàn, Hoàng Hải Vân, Nguyễn Hoàng Oanh, Nguyễn Huy Bạo, Nguyễn Thị Hiệp, Nguyễn Thị Thanh, Nguyễn Thị Thuý Hạnh, Nguyễn Trung Kiên, and Trần Minh Hằng. Without you, this project would not have been possible. Our teamwork has enriched my life tremendously, and it forms the social, moral, and intellectual backbone of this book. I also extend my deepest thanks to the Hanoian women and their families who received us in their homes with such hospitality and shared a significant and difficult time of their lives with us. Further, I am grateful to physicians, nurses, and midwives at Hanoi's Obstetrics and Gynecology Hospital—and particularly to Đặng Thanh Vân, Nguyễn Công Nghĩa, Nguyễn Hoa Phương, Nguyễn Thị Nguyệt, Phạm Ngọc Bình, and Trần Kim Dung—for sharing their experiences, visions, and medical ambitions with us and for tolerating our presence, in the midst of demanding day-to-day work, with patience, humor, and generosity.

This project was funded by the Danish International Development Agency (Danida) and conducted under the auspices of REACH (Strengthening Reproductive Health Research in Vietnam), a long-term Danida-funded project for building research capacity, involving Vietnamese and Danish researchers. I am grateful to Danida for funding REACH and other research partnership projects in Vietnam; to the Vietnam Commission for Population, Family and Children (VCPFC) (Ủy Ban Dân Số, Gia Đình và Trẻ Em) for hosting the project; and to researchers and administrators involved in REACH for their enthusiasm and commitment. Special thanks for long-term collaboration in connection with REACH go to Nguyễn Đình Anh, Nguyễn Mỹ Hương, Nguyễn Quốc Anh, Nguyễn Thị Mai, Nguyễn Thị Minh Hảo, Nguyễn Thị Ngọc Lan, Nguyễn Thu Nam, Phạm Hương Thảo, Thiều Văn Nghinh, Trần Thu Thủy, and Trần Văn Chiến, and also to my Danish colleagues Dan Meyrowitsch, Hanne Overgaard Mogensen, Karen Fog Olwig, Lise Rosendahl Østergaard, and Vibeke Rasch. I thank the VCPFC and Hanoi's Health Authorities (Sở Y Tế Hà Nội) for granting us research permissions to conduct this project.

In Denmark, I am grateful to students and colleagues at the Department of Anthropology, University of Copenhagen, for day-to-day academic sustenance. Special thanks to Susan Reynolds Whyte for the example she sets, to Anne Line Dalsgaard for her creativity and generosity as a friend and colleague, to Ayo Wahlberg for his careful and constructive reading of this book manuscript at an early stage, to Inger Sjørslev and Heiko Henkel for being wonderful neighbors in the departmental community, and to Oscar Salemink for friendship and support. Another academic community to which I am indebted consists of Vietnam studies researchers across the globe. Over the years I have learned much from conversations with Annika Johansson, Christina Schwenkel, Christophe Guilmoto, Christophe Robert, Danièle Bélanger, Diane Fox, Froniga Greig, Harriet Phinney, Hoàng Tú Anh, Khuất Thu Hồng, Jennifer Hirsch, Lê Minh Giang, Lê Thị Nhâm Tuyết, Melissa Pashigian, Michael DiGregorio, Nguyễn Đức Hinh, Nguyễn Thu Hương, Nguyễn Tuấn Anh, Pauline Oosterhoff, Phạm Kim Ngọc, Philip Taylor, Victoria H. Luong, Vũ Quý Nhân, and Vũ Song Hà. Another scholarly collective that I am indebted to emerged at the Wenner-Gren Symposium No. 144, "The Anthropology of Potentiality," held in Teresopolis, Brazil, in 2011. The academic generosity at this event was immensely encouraging, and I am particularly grateful to Adriana Petryna, Bob Simpson, Jianfeng Zhu, Karen-Sue Taussig, Klaus Høyer, Mette Nordahl Svendsen, Michael Montoya, Sahra Gibbon, Sharon Kaufman, Stefan Helmreich, and Stefan Timmermans for ideas, suggestions, and critical questions. Very special thanks to Lynn Morgan for wisdom and for being there. At the University of California Press I am grateful to Stan Holwitz for believing in this book from the beginning, to Reed Malcolm for critical comments that contributed significantly to its final form, to Steven Baker for attentive copyediting, and to Chalon Emmons for careful guidance through production. I owe many thanks to Diane Fox and Lynn Morgan, who reviewed the manuscript for the University of California Press, offering helpful advice and thoughtful comments. Matthew Carey and Menaka Roy helped with English editing and offered perceptive counsel on much more than language.

Last but not least, I would like to thank friends and family members for patience, care, and support. I am particularly indebted to Rolf, Anna, and August for companionship and love. Our life together has deepened my sense of the wonders and complexities of belonging.

Prologue

Haunting Decisions

On an early morning in February 2004, four weeks after the lunar New Year (Tết Nguyên Đán), my colleague Hạnh and I drove in a rented car along bumpy rural gravel roads leading to Quyết Tiến, a village located in the Red River delta, a few kilometers from Vietnam's capital, Hanoi.[1] On this morning, the flooded rice fields were a calm ocean, the water reflecting the gray of the sky. At this time of the year, farmers usually began transplanting their spring seedlings, moving them from the nurseries in the village into the open fields. Had this been an ordinary spring day, twenty-five-year-old Tuyết would probably have been among the women standing in the paddy fields, her trousers and sleeves rolled up, pushing seedlings of vivid green into the clayey soil. Today, however, she was lying at home in bed, recovering from an induced abortion.[2]

Hạnh and I had first met Tuyết ten days earlier. A 3D scan performed in the maternity hospital where we did fieldwork had found that there was fluid on the brain of the child she was expecting. Today, following Tuyết's instructions, we asked villagers for directions to her home. Like many other women, she lived in an extended family, sharing a house with her parents-in-law, her husband, Huy, and their five-year-old son. As in other Red River delta hamlets, the houses in Quyết Tiến were clustered closely together. Tuyết's house was built of brick and had white plastered walls; it was surrounded by a lush green garden with banana and star fruit trees. A flock of squawking chickens was running around the yard, and from the neighboring houses floated the sounds of children's voices. As we approached, an elderly man came out to receive us, a toddler at his knees. This turned out to be Tuyết's father-in-law. He wore black pants and a white, meticulously ironed shirt that suggested he was expecting our visit. Inside, he invited us to sit in the solid wooden chairs in front of the ancestors' altar. On the altar were leftovers from Tết celebrations—branches with faded pink peach flowers, a box of Choco Pie cookies, and the remains of incense sticks stuck into a small pot. Appearing from a small bedroom adjacent to the main room, Tuyết came in and sat down with us, silent.

Her father-in-law immediately began to tell us the story of Tuyết's pregnancy. When she went for the ultrasound scan in Hanoi, Tuyết had been nearly 29 weeks pregnant and everyone in the family was happily anticipating the birth of a new child. The scanning result therefore confronted Tuyết and her relatives with a tormenting decision: should they keep this pregnancy or not? Everyone knew that an abortion at this stage of gestation could have fatal consequences for the mother; at stake, therefore, were the lives of both Tuyết and her child-to-be. To help his son and daughter-in-law to come to a decision, Tuyết's father-in-law had convened the kin group's male elders for a family meeting. The involvement of both maternal and paternal relatives in this life-and-death decision, he hoped, would help to prevent blame and accusations from arising later in case things went awry. Eventually, her father-in-law told us, based on "the collective spirit of the family," a decision to terminate Tuyết's pregnancy had been reached:

> The children [Tuyết and her husband, Huy] said that the doctors encouraged us to terminate the pregnancy. So we did that. In a case like this, if the child is born, it will not become complete (*hoàn chỉnh*). . . . Our elders said, "We are simple people, we cannot imagine what this fetus is like. So first of all, we have to trust the experts. If the experts have given their opinion, we should believe them." . . . This is what we say in a rural area like this. We cannot see beyond the flesh, so we cannot know. . . . The children discussed this with me, and then they made the decision. They are children. They do not dare decide about this on their own, they must rely on me. And I must rely on the collective spirit of the family, on many opinions, many people. . . . If we had kept this child, there would have been water on the brain. This child would not have become a person (*thành người*). . . .
>
> We discussed this a lot. Would it be immoral or not to terminate the pregnancy? But in reality, this fetus had not yet become a person. One of our elders said that it is not a person yet, it has not yet seen the light of day (*chào đời*). So it is better to nip it in the bud (*bỏ từ trứng nước*). To allow it to be born only to live with a deformity is not good. It is not good for the child, and it is not good for our family. We believe that children who are born

defective, their brains will never become good. We have seen many cases. . . . This is something we keep within the family. We do not want people outside to know about it. When people outside ask, we say it was a miscarriage. It is normal for a girl to miscarry. We prefer to use a word that makes it normal.

What constitutes a human being, a person, a livable life? These were the kinds of questions that Tuyết's family confronted. To place these philosophical questions in the more concrete context of the family's experiences with disability, I asked Tuyết's father-in-law if he knew of any children in the village who had been born disabled. "Yes," he said. "Tuyết's younger brother, Phúc. His father has made all efforts to find treatment for him and to get him to school. For years, he carried him to school every single day on the back of his bike and picked him up again in the afternoon. Still this boy has not become a complete person."

At this point in the conversation, Tuyết's father arrived. He was tall and very thin, the skin covering his cheekbones seemed stretched to its limit. He limped slightly as he walked from the door to our table. He knew, he told us, what water on the brain of a child meant: "When I heard my son-in-law say that the doctors say it is hydrocephalus, I immediately said that we could not keep it. Our grandfather asked for my opinion, and I said, I know what this is. In Vietnam, family feelings are very important, feelings of attachment. . . . Love between mother and child . . . [silence] But we still had to terminate it. We all agreed on that." I asked Tuyết's father to tell us more about his son. He began Phúc's story by telling us about his own years as a soldier in the "American war," during which he was exposed to the herbicide dioxin nicknamed Agent Orange:

> I spent five years in Quảng Trị [one of the most heavily sprayed provinces], from December 1967 to December 1972. When I returned, I had four daughters; the first was born in 1975. Today they have all married and moved to live with their husbands. When my wife was thirty-six, we had a fifth child. He was born too early, on the nineteenth day of my wife's seventh month of pregnancy. At birth he was purple all over, and we took him to a hospital in Hanoi. . . . After we got back home, his legs became more and more bent as each day passed, and I realized that he suffered from curved bones (*cong xương*). Now all of his bones are sticking out, even the bones of his face. . . . This year my son is twenty-two years old, but I feel very sad. I think there is no hope that he will become a person. Perhaps at some point he will not be able to breathe anymore. To be honest, I do not think that he will live for very long.

Along with seven other families from their village, Tuyết's father and brother had been recognized by local authorities as Agent Orange victims and received a monthly allowance from the state. While being grateful for the support, Tuyết's father still felt uncertain about the impact of Agent Orange on human health. He appealed to us: "I live nearby. If you are interested in this, can you come with me and meet my son? I do not know if Agent Orange is the cause or not. You see, at that time, we did not know how poisonous Agent Orange was. No one announced that to us. If they had told us, many of us would have gone home. We would have been very scared. If we had known, both the American soldiers and our people would have run away. But we did not know. Not even the Americans knew."[3]

We accepted the invitation and accompanied Tuyết's father to his home, a few lanes away. When we arrived, Phúc was lying in a large bed in the main room of the house, covered by a red and blue cotton blanket. A television set was placed on a shelf above his bed, and he was watching a quiz program for students. Staring intently at the television, Phúc ignored our greetings, hardly reacting as we entered the house. Tuyết's father offered us green tea, made from fresh tea leaves. Behind him, on Phúc's bed, his father sat leaning on a stick; he looked very old and fragile. Tuyết's father began the story about his son with these words: "Every day, when I look at him, I feel so sad. His life is full of suffering. He can do many things; he can wash himself and eat by himself. But he is not intelligent. I don't think he will ever become a person. I keep speculating about him. You can see how thin I have become . . ." While his father talked, Phúc got up and hobbled across the room, using the crutches his father had made for him. His height was approximately that of a ten-year-old, and his legs looked strangely curved and bent, like the roots of an old tree. He greeted us, then slipped silently out into the yard.

His mother joined us, turning the conversation to another topic: Tuyết's pregnancy termination. The abortion had, Tuyết's mother told us, been a harrowing experience. It took place at night and proceeded faster than anticipated. At 4:30 A.M. Tuyết was in unbearable pain and her mother went to wake up the attending doctor. Yet she refused to help:

> She said, "Oh, but she will not give birth until 6 or 7 A.M.," and then she went back to sleep. Then I saw the head coming out and I ran for help. I was trembling, and I called, "Please doctor, this is so painful. The child is coming, it is coming, please come and help my child." But no one came and at 5 A.M. my daughter gave birth. . . . It was so painful to see her giving birth in such a messy and sloppy (lôi thôi) manner. If we had not been lucky, if she

had hemorrhaged, she would have died. It was early morning and very cold and they just let her lie like that. . . . A few days later I went to see the doctor again. I said to her: "You should not attend to other people's children in that way. You should not disregard people from the countryside. Even though we are poor, you must value people like us. People must be able to come to this hospital and trust their doctors; doctors should be like loving mothers.[4] It was wrong of you to intimidate (*quát nạt*) our family the way you did." . . . When I got outside again, I found myself crying. It was so painful. I wish this child had been born in a decent manner; I wish my daughter had not been so cold and dirty during her delivery.

The respect that Tuyết's mother demanded, the moral worth of human beings that she insisted on, resonated with her and her husband's struggles to turn their disabled son into "a person" and with their choice of a painful and hazardous pregnancy termination for their daughter in a situation in which they doubted that the child she expected would ever achieve full personhood. In other words, at issue for Tuyết's family were fundamental questions regarding how to define, protect, and uphold morally valuable human existence. What, they asked, constitutes a person, a human being? What does it mean to "see beyond the flesh" through technological means? When can a mother-to-be justify—to herself, to others—the denial of life to the child she is expecting? How can parents support a disabled child in his or her efforts to attain personhood and social recognition? How has the herbicide dioxin known as Agent Orange, sprayed by the U.S military over Vietnam during the Second Indochina War, affected human health in general and human reproduction in particular? These questions, as Tuyết's family represented them, were matters of collectivity and belonging; problems that arose and were resolved through intimate human engagements. In this book, I seek to understand the social shaping of the questions that Tuyết and her relatives were struggling with, while I also ponder the analytical challenges that such questions—of knowledge, power, intimacy, choice, and belonging—raise for anthropology as a discipline.

Introduction

Choice as Belonging

It was the moral weight of the decision that burdened Tuyết and Huy. Sitting in the makeshift café outside Hanoi's Obstetrics and Gynecology Hospital, Tuyết folded her arms around her pregnant belly in a protective gesture. "I'm scared," she said. "I am scared of having to have an abortion. I don't understand this. Everything seems normal—it has arms and legs, everything looks so fine. There is only this problem with the brain. Having an abortion now would be wrong. But if it is not well, keeping it means suffering. Our child will suffer and I will suffer. We just have to trust the doctors." A tiny, elderly woman walked by. Heading for the taxis at the other side of the hospital yard, she held a tightly bundled infant in her arms. A young couple followed close behind her, carrying two brightly colored bags. Tuyết fell silent, following the small procession with her eyes. "Here you are," the café owner said, placing three cups in front of us, Dilmah tea for Tuyết and coffee for Huy and me. Huy heaped several spoonfuls of sugar into his cup. Tuyết did not touch hers. She looked into the distance, her eyes dark. His elbows on his knees, his hands folded under his chin, Huy looked deeply uncomfortable, as if he wanted to be anywhere but here.

On this February day in 2004, Tuyết was nearly 29 weeks into her pregnancy. The ultrasound scan she had just undergone had revealed that there were large amounts of fluid on the brain of her fetus. One scanning image showed the face of the fetus. Another depicted the fetal brain seen from above; three large black blots filled nearly the entire head. Sitting in the café outside the hospital, Tuyết and her husband, Huy, were scrutinizing the images, pondering how to act on the information they offered. During the ultrasound scan, the physician had told them only that there was water on the brain of their fetus, and that the decision regarding how to act on this information was theirs. Yet as Tuyết and Huy described it to me, this decision was not their own, but one that they must make together with others. "We must talk to the doctors again," Tuyết said in a low voice. "After all, they are the experts." "What do *you* think?" Huy appealed to my colleague Hằng and me. "Have you ever seen a problem like this before?" Sensing the drama of the situation, the café owner—who turned out to live in the same Red River delta village as Tuyết and Huy—sat down at our table, venturing that in *her* opinion they should have this pregnancy terminated. A child with water on the brain, she claimed, would *never* be any good. She had seen cases like this before. Tuyết should be grateful that new technology had revealed this problem at an early stage, while something could still be done. Three other women in the café joined the conversation, one advocating for an abortion, another suggesting further examinations at another hospital, and the third offering to contact a physician she knew for advice. In the end, Huy closed the discussion by saying that they would have to return to their village and talk to their elders. This decision, he said, demanded the entire family's participation. But while emphasizing the collective nature of their plight, Huy also made it clear that, ultimately, the moral responsibility for this decision was his and his wife's. Looking me in the eye, he said, "This is a question of conscience. No matter what we do, this decision will haunt us forever." This tension between the moral solitude of the individual and communal lives led in association with others forms a core theme in this book.[1]

Across the globe, advancing technologies for selective reproduction place increasing numbers of women in situations where they must make excruciating decisions about the outcomes of their pregnancies.[2] For anthropology, this development raises thorny questions about risk, knowledge, power, and choice; at issue are moral questions about the meaning and value of particular human lives and political questions regarding how such questions are posed, answered, and acted upon. In what has come to be called "the West," contemporary health care policies and programs define human reproduction largely as a matter of individual autonomy and choice, underscoring pregnant women's rights to make their own decisions.[3] This seems to confirm Nikolas Rose's observation (1999:87) that in advanced liberal societies, people are not merely free to choose but *"obliged to be free*, to understand and enact their lives in terms of choice" (emphasis in original).[4] Yet in other parts of the world, as this book shows, prenatal examinations are deemed essential for the welfare of family, community, and nation; rather than in terms of individual choice, selective reproductive technologies are framed as questions of collectivity, responsibility, and shared national fates. In other words, the sociopolitical terrains in which advancing biomedical technologies are put to use vary in significant ways across countries and world regions (cf. Lock 2009).

This is a study of the use of ultrasound imaging for prenatal screening in Hanoi, Vietnam. In the chapters that follow, I offer an ethnographic account of the moral doubts and uncertainties, the dizzying possibilities, and the unsettling prospects that women and their relatives wrestled with when a prenatal diagnosis confronted them with the existential *extrema* of birth, death, and love. The overall analytical concern of the book is to explore how women and men in Hanoi handle the decisions that selective reproduction entails. I develop two main propositions. First, I suggest that life-and-death decisions place people in situations where they are forced to consider not merely what to do but also who they themselves are. Existentially extreme predicaments conjure questions of ethical subjectivity. Second, I argue that it was through the enactment of social belonging that people in Hanoi forged moral selves in the confrontation with ethically demanding circumstances. Finding themselves adrift in a sea of decision-making possibilities, people such as Tuyết and Huy seemed to strive to anchor themselves within the moral communities that made up their day-to-day life worlds, thereby regaining a sense of attachment, meaning, and orientation. Rather than acts of freedom, their reproductive choices were acts of belonging; they were ways of responding to and seizing others. This observation has led me to believe that there is reason for anthropology to pay closer attention to human quests for belonging; to the ways in which people strive to tie themselves into relations with others, thereby becoming part of something larger. With this, I do not intend to depict belonging as a simple or taken-for-granted immersion of the individual in a sea of communality. On the contrary, my material from Vietnam suggests that belonging must be understood as an intensely precarious accomplishment, as an uncertain, unstable, and emergent cultural identity. Human strivings for belonging, I contend, are articulated in particularly poignant ways in the realm of pregnancy and childbearing, where new individuals are brought into being, intimate interhuman connections are forged, and the fundamental sociality of human existence is made manifest.[5] In situations where parenthood departs from conventional paths—such as when new children arrive in unexpected ways or forms—the dependencies and vulnerabilities that characterize human existence as such often stand out with particular clarity.

On that February day in 2004, Tuyết had, as she described the situation herself, two options. She could either keep her pregnancy, thereby throwing herself and her family into suffering, or she could terminate it, thereby ending the life of the child she was expecting. This placed her among the women that Rayna Rapp (1999:3) has termed moral pioneers: individuals who "are forced to judge the quality of their own fetuses, making concrete and embodied decisions about the standards for entry into the human community." Tuyết found herself in this painful dilemma as a consequence of the ultrasound scan she had undergone a few days earlier in her local health clinic: like most other pregnant women in her Red River delta village, she had obtained this examination as a routine part of antenatal care. In Vietnam, as in many other countries, ultrasonography has now become a habituated tool of pregnancy care, a device used both for obstetric purposes and to screen children-to-be for physiological anomalies.

SEEING AND SELECTING: PRENATAL ULTRASOUND AS A SCREENING TECHNOLOGY

In global biomedical practice, obstetrical ultrasound scanning is the most widely used tool for prenatal diagnosis.[6] In the course of their pregnancies, women in most Western countries are offered one or two ultrasound scans, and in many low-income settings, ultrasonography is becoming an increasingly routinized part of antenatal care. Ultrasonography thus contributes significantly to accelerating the global routinization of prenatal screening technologies. The expansion of prenatal ultrasound seems to have happened with particular force and rapidity in Asia; in Vietnam, as in many other Asian countries, prenatal ultrasounds are widely available and eagerly used (see chapter 1). The desire to determine the sex of the fetus seems to have played a prominent role in the spread of this technology; in countries such as China, India, and Vietnam, the preference for male offspring is strong and the increasingly skewed sex ratios at birth are attributed partly to the use of ultrasonography in combination with second-trimester abortion.

Ultrasound works through high-frequency sound: a transducer emitting sound waves is inserted vaginally or placed on the pregnant woman's abdomen. The information gained from the reflections of the sound waves produces the sonogram, an image that is shown on a monitor and can be printed for the woman to take home. In addition to the initial 2D scans, 3D and 4D scans are now available: 3D scans produce three-dimensional images that facilitate detection of certain fetal anomalies and offer appealing photos of the face of the child-to-be; 4D scans—also known as live, dynamic, or motion 3Ds—add a time dimension, thereby producing a "movie" of the fetus. Obstetrical ultrasound differs from other prenatal screening techniques in several important respects. First, it provides instant results: the fetus is—sometimes in dramatic ways—rendered visible before the eyes of health providers and expectant parents. Second, it is considered noninvasive and medically safe, requiring neither blood tests nor amniotic fluid samples.[7] Third, it blurs the boundaries between screening and testing: across the world, ultrasonography is increasingly used as a routine tool in pregnancy care, regardless of the woman's age or risk status. It is, in other words, used as a screening technique, often with the aim of finding markers of problems that require further diagnostic investigations. Yet ultrasound scans may also provide definitive information regarding structural malformations in the fetus, and in this sense they are testing tools.[8] Fourth, obstetrical ultrasound scanning costs the least of all techniques for prenatal diagnosis; this is what gives the technology such a powerful potential for global diffusion.

Developed during World War I as a sonar device to detect underwater submarines, ultrasound began to be used in pregnancy care in Europe and North America in the 1960s. Initially, prenatal ultrasound served mainly obstetric purposes: measuring the fetus, determining gestational age, locating the placenta, assessing amniotic fluid volume, and identifying multiple pregnancies. Recently, with the development of higher-quality images and more refined diagnostic capabilities, screening for fetal anomalies has become a more prominent purpose. Since the possibilities for biomedical treatment of the fetus are limited, the most frequent intervention when an anomaly is found is an induced abortion.[9] As a German obstetrician told Susan Erikson (2007:209), "Prenatal diagnostic ultrasound is the only routine scan in all of medicine for which the only treatment is death. There is no cure but abortion for what we find. This makes ultrasound very strange and very special."[10] Notably, in many countries, the expanding use of ultrasounds has taken place against professional advice. In the United States, for instance, professional guidelines recommend ultrasound scanning only when clinically indicated; the World Health Organization notes that routine use of ultrasonography in early pregnancy is not warranted in low-income settings, as its benefits in terms of improved pregnancy outcomes have not been documented; and at the time of this research, Vietnam's Ministry of Health recommended that ultrasound scanning be used only in cases of pregnancy complications.[11] These gaps between policy and practice raise numerous questions, including, What forces are driving the expanding use of this technology? What roles do state policies play in the diffusion of ultrasonography? What, in practice, does ultrasound do for pregnant women, families, health care providers, and policy makers?

SELECTIVE REPRODUCTION: QUESTIONS OF CHOICE

"You know, the *last* thing we want is state interference in these things," an official of the Danish Board of Health explained to me in a telephone conversation in May 2003. I had called him to inquire about the ongoing restructuring of Danish antenatal care, and he took the opportunity to remind me of the emphasis that was placed in this process on "women's own choice."

The research behind this book has been an exercise in comparative thinking. In 2003, when I began this project, Danish prenatal screening was in the process of a comprehensive restructuring, and the principles behind this reorganization have formed an implicit point of comparison during my fieldwork in Vietnam.[12] This is not an investigation of health care provision in Denmark, and it is not an explicitly comparative study, but the Danish case does form an important backdrop to the research that this book presents. In the new guidelines on prenatal diagnosis that the Danish Board of Health issued in 2004, *informed choice* was defined as the aim of prenatal screening. In the old system, which the above official characterized as belonging in "Jurassic Park," prenatal testing had been offered only to women who were considered at risk, either due to their age or due to a known probability of having a child with a genetic problem. With the new guidelines, this paradigm of prevention was replaced by a new paradigm of self-determination: prenatal screening was now to be offered to all women, regardless of their risk situation. The aim of this shift was, the Board of Health emphasized, to enhance individual choice, whereas the old program was more crudely focused on preventing the birth of children with disabilities. Before they were issued, the Danish Parliament discussed the new guidelines and put forth the following statement: "The aim of prenatal testing is—within the juridical framework of Danish Law—to assist a pregnant woman, if she wants such assistance, to make her capable of making her own decisions. Neutral and adequate information is a necessary condition to this end. . . . The aim of prenatal testing is not to prevent the birth of children with serious diseases or handicaps."[13]

This emphasis on women's own decisions and on neutral and adequate information illustrates a more general tendency in Western societies to give primacy to individual self-determination and choice in the realm of reproduction. In Europe and North America, health care policies and clinical guidelines emphasize principles of autonomy, defining respect for individual rights as an ethical and political precondition for the use of selective reproductive technologies.[14] In reproductive counseling, therefore, *nondirectiveness* is a paramount principle. Rather than offering directive advice or imposing certain reproductive agendas, health care providers are expected to support patients to come to their own decisions (see chapter 4).[15] This emphasis on noncoercion and individual self-determination must be seen against the background of the dark history of selective reproduction in this region; the ideal of nondirectiveness in medical counseling emerged as a direct response to the eugenics movement and World War II (Wertz and Fletcher 2004:36). In northern Europe and North America, thousands of individuals were sterilized under twentieth-century eugenics legislation, and in Nazi Germany, initiatives arising from eugenics included euthanasia programs directed at people with disabilities. In Denmark, eugenic practices were integral components of the development of the welfare state, and sterilizations on social grounds were carried out even as recently as the 1970s (Broberg and Roll-Hansen 2005). When Danish parliamentarians underscored the importance of individual reproductive choice, then, they sought to distance present-day selective reproduction from a problematic past.[16]

The primacy of individual choice in the domain of reproduction must be seen also in the context of the liberal assumptions that currently underpin policy making in many parts of the world. Liberal conceptions of politics are based on certain assumptions about human nature, including the conviction that human desires for freedom outweigh other human needs such as the quest for companionship or the urge to belong or to be taken care of (cf. Mahmood 2005). Similar suppositions regarding the human desire for freedom form the basis for claims to the extension of reproductive rights and individual autonomy made by women's and civil rights movements across the globe. Particularly since the 1994 UN Conference on Population held in Cairo—which replaced previous population control discourses with a new language of sexual and reproductive health and rights—principles of self-determination and autonomy have been at the center of political struggles in the realms of sexuality and reproduction. The right of women to control their own bodies has been formally recognized in numerous international documents and is actively pursued on a global scale, forming a shared basis for feminist movements around the world.

This political emphasis on freedom and autonomy is often repeated in social science studies of reproductive experiences and practices; there is, as Meredith W. Michaels and Lynn M. Morgan (1999:7) have observed, a marked tendency to theorize reproduction from the perspective of liberal individualism. In studies of prenatal screening and testing, questions of choice and autonomy figure particularly prominently. Among the issues that researchers have typically addressed are, How do pregnant women come to choose—or not—to make use of selective reproductive technologies?[17] What decisions do women imagine they would make in case a fetal problem were detected?[18] What decisions do women *actually* make when finding themselves in this situation?[19] Existing research has often come to the conclusion that the very offer of technologies for prenatal diagnosis tends to mandate certain kinds of choices, pushing women toward taking up new technologies and acting on the knowledge that they generate. The provision of prenatal screening as a routine part of pregnancy care can, in other words, be seen as an indirect insistence on the need to prevent certain kinds of children from being born. This has led numerous scholars to claim that what we see today is a new form of eugenics; a laissez-faire, backdoor, private, liberal, voluntary, neo-, soft, or flexible eugenics.[20] As Rose (2007:51) has rightly argued, however, today's more subtle politics of life differs significantly from the crude authoritarianism of the past. Assuming that history simply repeats itself may therefore blind us to the particularities of contemporary biopolitics, rendering it difficult to capture the specific and varying ways in which knowledge and power play out in the realm of selective reproduction.[21] Rather than defining the current emphasis on individual choice as a new variant of old-school eugenics, I have therefore found it more productive to reconsider the liberal assumptions on which present-day reflections on selective reproduction tend to rest. This demands, first of all, critical scrutiny of the notion of reproductive choice itself.

QUESTIONING QUESTIONS OF CHOICE

"No matter what we do," Huy said, "this decision will haunt us forever." In the conversation we had in the café outside the obstetrics hospital, Huy made it clear that he and his wife were facing an unbearable decision, one that threatened to trouble them for the rest of their lives. Many other people I met represented their plights in similar terms. The detection of a fetal anomaly, they suggested, placed them in a morally fraught situation where they had to reconsider fundamental values, pondering the meanings of good and evil, life and death, personhood and humanity. Thirty-year-old Bích, for instance, was 19 weeks pregnant when an ultrasound scan found that the ventricles in the brain of her fetus were dilated. Reflecting on the decision that she and her husband had to make, she said: "This gives us the opportunity to choose, either to keep it or to give it up. If the diagnosis is correct, this is an advantage for us. But it also pushes us into a situation where we must do something evil, evil to our own child." When Xuyến's fetus was diagnosed with a large umbilical hernia 22 weeks into her pregnancy, she and her husband, Quang, decided to opt for an abortion. Looking back on their decision a couple of months later, Quang told me about the profound moral doubts that had suffused this time of their lives. No matter what they did, he said, they had felt that it was wrong: "In terms of good and evil (*thiện ác*) or in terms of human morality, finding ourselves in this situation, we felt very sad and very uncertain. Should we keep it or not? If we decided to give it up, then according to Vietnamese people it means killing a person. But if we had kept it, our child would have suffered."

But although my interlocutors themselves often spoke in a language of choice and individual decision making, drawing such local languages into anthropological analysis demands certain measures of caution. First, the concept of choice is, in many respects, empirically misleading; it tempts us to overemphasize people's freedom to shape their world as they want to. The discrepancies between theoretical principles of choice and the realities of reproductive lives are well documented: bringing pregnancies and new children into being is rarely a matter of free individual choice, but events that are socially, economically, and politically conditioned in powerful ways.[22] The language of choice, therefore, risks concealing the structural forces and inequalities that shape reproductive decisions in all human societies. In the realm of selective reproduction, the power of such forces tends to intensify. For many people, as for Tuyết and Huy, carrying an affected pregnancy to term is not a realistic option. In most societies, not least in low-income parts of the world, the birth of a severely disabled child confronts parents with care-giving and economic demands that they must meet on their own, with very limited societal support. Under these conditions, defining pregnancy decisions in terms of choice risks grossly misrepresenting the human predicaments at issue. The second problem with the concept of reproductive choice concerns the burdens of responsibility that it places on individuals. The rhetoric of choice that permeates both biomedicine and feminism risks privatizing reproductive responsibilities, transforming biomedical knowledge into intensely individual dilemmas. The personal costs of this are vividly documented in Rapp's New York City research (1999), which shows how pregnant women must enact reproductive decisions that reach far beyond their own individual lives, compelling them to define where the human community should begin and end. Further, existing research shows that the privatization of reproductive responsibilities often leads to mother-blaming when pregnancies go awry; if the mother-to-be had made better choices, dominant moral opinion will often suggest, her pregnancy might have fared better.[23] Third, the notion of reproductive choice has significant theoretical limitations: it assumes the existence of a bounded subject who chooses, yet the existence of such a subject can be questioned.[24] Perhaps more clearly than any other social domain, the realm of reproduction reveals how we are always already connected with other human beings in intimate ways, being tied into social worlds and obligations not of our own choosing. Reproductive decisions emerge through embodied coexistence, yet the scholarly tendency to focus on individual choice in a more narrow sense tends to render this intersubjective being analytically invisible.

A closer examination of social science research on selective reproduction in Western settings, however, reveals a reproductive ethos that bears striking resemblance to the one I encountered in Vietnam: beneath the loud rhetoric of individual rights and informed choice, a more subdued discourse of responsibility, care, and collectivity can be found. In the West, too, people are encouraged to act responsibly by participating in public health initiatives aiming to ensure the birth of nondisabled children, though the obligations that are placed on them are expressed in more subtle ways. In the West, too, it can be questioned whether ideals of informed choice adequately capture how reproductive decisions are made in practice. When grappling with the ethical challenges that new technologies of pregnancy confront them with, prospective parents in Europe and North America, like their counterparts in Vietnam, often seek to share moral burdens and responsibilities with others, drawing health care professionals and relatives into their decisions.[25] This suggests, then, that an overemphasis on individual choice may lead us to ignore important aspects of human reproductive experiences. The language of rights, choice, and self-determination—though politically important—may be neither analytically productive nor ethnographically fruitful.

THE GLOBALIZATION OF SELECTIVE REPRODUCTION: CHALLENGES TO LANGUAGES OF CHOICE

In the global arena, the liberal reproductive ethos so predominant in the Western world does not go unchallenged. Many Asian governments, for instance, hold state interference in reproduction to be morally and politically appropriate—China's one-child policy being perhaps the most poignant example. During fieldwork in Hanoi, I was often struck by the fact that official Vietnamese framings of selective reproduction were characterized by a nearly complete absence of reference to choice or individual preference. Instead, as I describe in more detail throughout this book, selective reproductive technologies were represented in terms of collectivity, compassion, reciprocity, and responsibility. In newspaper articles, television programs, and health care encounters, pregnant women were told in relatively straightforward terms that as mothers and citizens, they were expected to undergo prenatal screening and to act on the results. In a typical statement, made in an article in the state-run journal *Family and Society* (*Gia Đình và Xã Hội*), Dr. Cường, a renowned obstetrician-gynecologist who often appeared on national television, proclaimed his enthusiasm in these words:

> Prenatal diagnosis has a very important function for pregnant women. Common disabilities such as Down syndrome, physical abnormalities (such as lack of arms or legs, lack of brain, abdominal malformations, umbilical hernia), or abnormalities of the heart, nervous system, curved legs, curved arms, can be detected early on, so that selections can be made. In each individual case, the doctors will offer the pregnant woman advice or appropriate directions. The aim is to significantly reduce the risk of abnormal children

being born who will become burdens for family and society. All pregnant women can and should use this diagnostic service. (Thảo Nguyên 2006:14)

In China and Vietnam, present-day population policies focus on the improvement of population quality (*suzhi* in China; *chất lượng dân số* in Vietnam).[26] In both countries, an important element in this biopolitical endeavor is the effort to improve pregnancy outcomes through enhanced antenatal care, including prenatal screening (see chapters 1 and 2). In 1994, China's new Law on Maternal and Infant Health Care set forth a range of measures intended to reduce the national prevalence of disability through premarital testing and prenatal screening. This led several commentators to argue that eugenics in the twentieth-century sense of state coercion was alive and well in this part of the world. Frank Dikötter, for instance, a Dutch historian, claimed that in China, as in the interwar period in Europe, "eugenics provides an overarching rationale for a range of reproductive and demographic concerns which are constrained by a policy which prioritises the needs of broad collectivities of interests such as 'the state,' 'the economy' or 'future generations' over the possible desires and choices of individuals" (1998:123). The labeling of certain reproductive health policies and practices as eugenic may, however, as mentioned above, not be very productive. The term *eugenics* is tied to particular twentieth-century events that took place mainly in Europe and North America and that continue to haunt people in this part of the world. Use of this term, therefore, may lead us to overlook the fact that in other parts of the world, other historical events may demand remembrance and response, and that state policies may be guided by other kinds of public memory. In Vietnam, for instance, I soon realized that people's eager embrace of new technologies for selective reproduction must be seen in the context of the country's history of toxic warfare (see chapter 1).

Problems with the term *eugenics* aside, the varying ways in which contemporary states intervene in the reproductive lives of their citizens do seem to demand more concerted anthropological attention. At present, little is known about how today's increasingly sophisticated selective reproductive technologies are put to use in regions such as Asia, Africa, and Latin America, as most existing anthropological research on selective reproduction has been conducted in Western societies.[27] Yet advancing biomedicine is not restricted to Europe or North America; as the case of obstetrical ultrasound shows, new biomedical technologies possess a powerful potential for diffusion to settings beyond the world's wealthy urban centers. Today, technologies for selective reproduction not only are used in New York City or Copenhagen but have become integral and routinized parts of the everyday lives of women living in low- and middle-income countries across the world. A basic assumption behind this book is that expanding anthropological investigations to include the study of high-tech reproduction in a wider range of settings offers possibilities for producing new anthropological understandings of human being and knowing. Such studies, I contend, not only are ethnographically important but may also present significant challenges to the liberal conceptions of human ontology that currently dominate scholarly thinking about the social implications of new reproductive technologies.

FORMATIONS OF SUBJECTIVITY: CHOICE AS BELONGING

What kind of person will I become, Tuyết seemed to ask, if I decide to end the life of the child I expect? The confrontation with ethically demanding decisions such as the one faced by Tuyết and Huy compels people to consider who they are and who they want to be; they are arenas for the making of subjects. For anthropology, practices of selective reproduction raise questions such as, How are the moral identities of parents-to-be and health care providers formed in encounters with advancing biomedical technologies? How, in making decisions about affected pregnancies, do prospective parents forge particular selves? How do some fetuses come to be seen as potential children and family members—and others not? What technologies of power are involved when lines are drawn between valuable and expendable forms of human life?

Questions of subjectivity and power have received increasing attention in anthropology over the past few years. After decades of deconstruction, the time seems to have come to reassemble the subject (cf. Humphrey 2008) and reconsider how subjectivity can be conceptualized in a post-post-humanist era.[28] In this context, morally fraught decisions—such as those that people must grapple with in the realm of high-tech reproduction—seem to offer particularly privileged starting points for anthropological analyses. Recent social science studies of the forging of selves in reproductive arenas have often taken Foucauldian approaches, describing how pregnant women, by adopting specific norms, turn themselves into autonomous subjects of choice and self-determination.[29]

Seen in this perspective, pregnancy care becomes an ethical practice through which both maternal and fetal subjectivities are produced. Although I too see pregnancy care as a matter of subjectivity formation, my experiences in Vietnam have compelled me to interpret my material along other lines than those laid out by Michel Foucault and his followers. As Tuyết and Huy articulated it, choice was less a question of what an individual prefers to do than a matter of with whom he or she belongs, a question of what demands are placed on him or her.[30] Although they certainly indicated that they found themselves in an acutely painful situation of choice, the prospective parents I met in Hanoi did not represent the decision they faced as a matter of freedom. Rather, they defined it as a question of social attachments and obligations—to their relatives, to other community members, and to the nation. Striving to find their bearings in an excruciating and morally disorienting situation, parents-to-be such as Tuyết and Huy looked toward others, considering the opinions of physicians, family members, and acquaintances; in enacting their decision, they also enacted social belonging. To comprehend how subjectivities were formed in this painful situation, therefore, we must attend to the interhuman experiences and sensibilities involved, paying attention to the push and pull of social relations, responsibilities, and demands.

To belong, according to the *Oxford Dictionaries Online*, means to be the property of, to be a member of, or to be rightly placed in a specified position. It is a notion, in other words, that connotes ownership and membership. In this book, I employ the term *belonging* to capture the sense of attachment that people in Hanoi articulated when describing the ties of mutuality that bound them together with others and into larger social communities. To capture this sense of attachment, I have searched for concepts that can help us to place human vulnerabilities and interdependencies at the center of analysis. In this endeavor, I have found inspiration in the philosophy of Emmanuel Levinas and other thinkers who place primacy on sensibility, defining knowledge, morality, and subjectivity as questions of embodied human interconnections. Levinas's main phenomenological claim is that subjectivity is structured in a relation of responsibility to the other; whether or not we accept this responsibility, it is there, imposed on us, haunting us, preceding our freedom.[31] Being sensible, vulnerable, exposed to wounding, pain, and caress, we come into being through the other's intervention; we are exposed to others before coming to ourselves, involved before we can make reasoned decisions. Along Levinasian lines, then, choice can be seen as an act of belonging in the sense that the decisions we make, the avenues of action we take, always arise in response to other human beings; individuals to whom we are always already obliged, exposed, and connected.

It was fieldwork in Vietnam that led me to this Levinasian perspective on subjectivity. Living in Vietnam, I have always been struck—sometimes annoyed, sometimes disturbed, sometimes comforted—by the ways in which people interfere in each other's lives.[32] In Denmark, if a person faces an unusually difficult decision, people are likely to tell her that "this is such a hard decision—only you can make it." In Vietnam, in contrast, people will say, "This is such a hard decision—you cannot make it on your own." Most people I know in Hanoi seem to take it as a basic premise of life that we cannot let each other be; that often we must act on behalf of and for others, taking charge of them even if this means setting aside their autonomy.[33] But what first led me to Levinas was the attention that I noticed people in Hanoi paid to the human face. By reading someone's face (*xem tướng*), people claim, one can determine his or her character and destiny; the face, in other words, opens one to others. In Vietnam, the face figures prominently at most life transitions: traditionally, betrothal arrangements have included a visit by the prospective groom's relatives to the family of the prospective bride in which they would see the face (*xem mặt*) of their new daughter-in-law; when ultrasound scans are performed, getting a good picture of the face of the fetus is often of primary importance to women, relatives, and health care providers; at funerals, beholding the face of the deceased person is a central element in people's leave-taking; and graves are usually adorned with tombstones displaying an image of the deceased person's face. This consistent cultural attention to the face resonates with the emphasis that Levinas places on the face as the primary site of ethicality. The face-to-face meeting, Levinas (1985a:96) contends, exposes us to the claims that the other person makes on us: "Since the Other looks at me, I am responsible for him, without even having *taken* on responsibilities in his regard; his responsibility *is incumbent on me*" (emphasis in original). Even prior to knowledge, awareness, and reflection, Levinas claims, we stand in an ethical relationship with the other person; ethics is precultural in the sense that our existence as social beings is always preconditioned by the presence of the other (cf. Scheper-Hughes 1992:23).

FIELDWORK

This book is based on nearly three years of ethnographic fieldwork conducted in Hanoi, Vietnam. Together with my husband and our children, then aged two and four, I arrived in Hanoi in September 2003 and stayed until April 2006.[34] Prior to this period, I had been involved in reproductive health research in Vietnam for more than a decade. I first visited Vietnam in February 1992 and returned to conduct fieldwork in a rural community in the Red River delta in 1993–94. Since my family and I left Hanoi in 2006, I have returned once or twice each year to do follow-up research or to teach.[35] The present research project is, in other words, embedded in a longer-term engagement with Vietnam. I conducted the fieldwork in close cooperation with a group of ten Vietnamese researchers. To begin with, our research team comprised five local researchers: Nguyễn Thị Thuý Hạnh and Đỗ Thị Thanh Toàn, both medical doctors and teachers at Hanoi Medical University, and Nguyễn Thị Hiệp, Bùi Kim Chi, and Trần Minh Hằng, social scientists with backgrounds in sociology or anthropology. Later, the team was extended to include five additional researchers: Nguyễn Huy Bạo, Hoàng Thị Hải Vân, Nguyễn Thị Thanh, Nguyễn Trung Kiên, and Nguyễn Hoàng Oanh; the first two are medical doctors, the last three social scientists. While I could devote most of my time to this project, my Vietnamese colleagues had numerous other commitments, and they therefore took turns accompanying me in the field. We conducted all research in Vietnamese and tape-recorded most of the conversations held in people's homes. The entire group shared all field notes and interview transcriptions, and in bimonthly seminars we discussed preliminary findings and drafted our first articles for publication.[36]

In designing this research, I was inspired by the extended-case method approach developed by Max Gluckman and other anthropologists of the Manchester school. In an effort to capture the social processes out of which societies are made, this methodological approach revolves around the intensive study of specific incidents or, in Gluckman's terminology, *trouble cases*. Through the detailed study of concrete cases as they evolve over time and across different situations, the extended-case method aspires to grasp social life as it is lived, thereby producing "a more complex, less rigid, less highly interconnected picture" of culture and society (Gluckman 2006 [1959]:17). By focusing on specific incidents and on the open-endedness of the situations in which people find themselves and the variable ways in which they handle their predicaments, this approach seeks to place the emergent character of social life at the center of analysis. As T. M. S. Evens (2006:58) puts it, "To grasp a social situation primarily in view of its temporal process entails ultimate focus not on the fixed and explicit principles of the social order but on the tacit ones, the principles that are chiefly lived rather than predicated categorically. Put differently, such principles are found in the saying instead of the said." In a world where the global and the local form complex assemblages that often challenge conventional methodological approaches (cf. Erikson 2011), the case study method suggests pathways for anthropological research that allow us to examine the concrete ways in which more general social principles of morality, power, and authority are enacted as people grapple with day-to-day predicaments.

Our fieldwork in Hanoi began in December 2003 in the 3D scanning room at Hanoi's Obstetrics and Gynecology Hospital (Bệnh Viện Phụ Sản Hà Nội). This hospital offers a variety of reproductive health services, including infertility treatment, family planning, abortion services, and antenatal and delivery care.[37] In August 2003, the hospital purchased a new piece of equipment: a 3D scanning machine imported from Japan. Room 15 on the hospital's first floor was allocated for this new machine, staffed by a nurse and a sonographer. It was this social space that formed the starting point for this fieldwork: we took the performance of each 3D scan to be an incident in Gluckman's sense, a concrete situation connected to a range of other situations within and outside the hospital. To begin with, my Vietnamese colleagues and I conducted semistructured interviews with one hundred women coming in for a routine 3D scan, in combination with day-to-day observations and informal conversations with women waiting their turn. We were interested in hearing about the women's motivations for seeking the scan and the expectations they invested in it. To bring this project into conversation with existing research, we included in the semistructured interviews a set of questions that aimed to explore how women imagined they would react if a fetal problem were found. This topic, however, turned out to be nearly impossible to talk about: the idea that their fetus might not be normal was more unsettling to the women than I had anticipated, causing massive and visible awkwardness and discomfort. It seemed ethically problematic, therefore, to pursue the questions that we had developed before beginning the fieldwork, and we had to reconsider our entire approach. It was through these methodological challenges that I first came to note the paradoxical presence of the malformed fetus in the

3D scanning room. On the one hand, this fetus was a powerfully present specter; on the other, pregnant women struggled to act as if it were not there. Approximately half a year after our first encounter with them at the hospital, we visited sixteen of these women in their homes. By this time, they had given birth to their children, and this status as mothers of healthy infants made it easier for many to talk about the images that had haunted them during their pregnancies (see chapter 3).

Each week, two or three of the scans performed in the 3D scanning room revealed a fetal problem. When this happened, the sonographer informed the woman of our research and asked if she was willing take part in it. Of the first forty-five women we contacted, nine declined, two were excluded as their fetus had died in utero, and four were excluded as their homes were located more than one hundred kilometers from Hanoi. Thirty women were enrolled in the research and became our core cases. At the moment when we met them, then, these women found themselves in an ethically tense situation fraught with uncertainty. Like Tuyết, whose story opens this chapter, they had to come to terms with a shocking medical message and to decide how to act on it. Like Tuyết, all the women expressed a need to consult others, and these others included not only their physicians and relatives but also my Vietnamese colleagues and me. This turned the research into more than a study of other people's moralities; we also had to constantly reflect on the ethics of our own conduct.[38] At the hospital and during visits to the women's homes, we engaged in intense conversations with them and their relatives about the many questions they confronted; questions about causal ontologies, about moral responsibilities, about whom to trust in this existentially fraught situation. Later, we accompanied the women back to the obstetrics hospital for further examinations, abortions, or deliveries; and after the pregnancy had ended, we visited them again in their homes. In some cases, especially when the pregnancy resulted in the birth of a live child, we kept in contact with the family, and still do. When we met them, the women were aged twenty to forty-four and were 14 to 38 weeks into their pregnancy. They lived either in Hanoi or the outlying rural provinces of Hà Tây, Vĩnh Phúc, and Ninh Bình, nineteen in a nuclear and eleven in an extended family. Most of the women were factory workers, farmers, or traders, but the sample also included teachers, officials, and office assistants (see the appendix). Of the thirty women, thirteen carried the pregnancy to term, while seventeen had an induced abortion. Several of the fetuses were found to suffer from multiple malformations (đa dị tật); according to the scan

FIGURE 1. Nguyễn Thị Thuý Hạnh and the author at the café of Hanoi's Obstetrics and Gynecology Hospital, November 21, 2004.

results, the main problems were the following: dilation of ventricles in the brain/hydrocephalus (11), hydrops fetalis (4), abdominal/umbilical hernia (4), anencephaly (2), heart defects (2), abdominal anomalies (2), curved arms/legs (2), prune belly syndrome (1), cleft lip (1), and twins with a shared spine (1) (see appendix).

While working in the 3D scanning room, we also talked on a day-to-day and informal basis with doctors and nurses. When a fetal problem was found, we followed the woman around in the hospital—to the antenatal care room where a physician counseled her, and later to either the delivery department or to A4, the hospital's department for reproductive disorders, where abortions for fetal anomaly were performed. This brought us into contact with physicians who worked in these departments, undertaking antenatal and delivery care and performing abortions. We had particularly frequent conversations with five doctors: two sonographers, Dr. Tuấn and Dr. Nhung, who served in the 3D scanning room; two obstetricians, Dr. Lương and Dr. Lan, who spent much of their working time in A4; and a pediatrician, Dr. Nga, who worked in the neonatal department. During these conversations, we talked to physicians about the plights of individual patients, about the medical and moral challenges that prenatal screening posed, and about the social and economic implications of childhood disability in a low-income country such as Vietnam. In addition to this, we also conducted formally arranged interviews and focus group discussions with physicians at the hospital, and a series of interviews with obstetricians and sonographers working in other health facilities in Hanoi.

Another important component of this research was the study of documents: during and after the fieldwork period, we collected and studied policy papers on population and reproductive health, unpublished research reports on population quality and prenatal screening, and articles in local academic journals. We also conducted a mass media study: from December 2004 to April 2005, we collected articles from ten different newspapers and recorded programs broadcast on national television on the topics of pregnancy, disability, and prenatal screening. We also talked informally to state officials about how to interpret population policy documents. Our counterpart on this research was the Vietnam Commission for Population, Family, and Children (VCPFC) (Ủy Ban Dân Số, Gia Đình và Trẻ Em), the government institution that develops and issues national population policies.[39] This brought us into frequent contact with state officials working within the population sector and offered numerous opportunities for informal conversations about the ambitions and anxieties that suffused population policies. In addition to our day-to-day conversations with VCPFC staff, we also conducted two interviews with Ministry of Health officials.

The last part of this research was a substudy on childhood disability that we conducted in Mễ Trì, a semiurban commune located on the southern outskirts of Hanoi, three kilometers from the obstetrics hospital. During fieldwork at the hospital, we talked to both patients and physicians about what they imagined would be the social implications of childhood disability. In the spring of 2005, we set out to learn more about what life with a disabled child actually implied, as described by parents, grandparents, and disabled children themselves. We worked in Mễ Trì from June 2005 to February 2006, getting to know thirty-two families with disabled children, as well as pregnant women, new mothers, and local health care and family planning cadres (cộng tác viên). We also talked to a handful of people who were active in local disability groups in Hanoi; some were engaged in clubs for parents of disabled children, others in the Bright Future Group, one of the first grassroots organizations formed by people with disabilities in Vietnam.

OUTLINE OF THIS BOOK

"How can we understand someone else without sacrificing him to our logic or it to him?" asks Maurice Merleau-Ponty (1964 [1960]:115). In this book, I seek to bring Western debates about prenatal screening into engagement with the concerns expressed by individuals and state authorities in Vietnam. In doing so, I have tried to find a mode of writing that allows me to frame the issues in a way that is close to how they were represented by people in Hanoi, rather than forcing them into the frameworks of interpretation established by public debates in Europe and North America. The chapters that follow are therefore structured largely according to the questions that the people I met in Hanoi struggled with.

The first chapter presents the setting of the research, Vietnam's capital of Hanoi, and offers a brief examination of the social forces that have turned obstetrical ultrasonography into such a widely used tool of pregnancy care in this city. Chapter 2 explores how current quality-oriented population policies devised by the Vietnamese party-state involve specific and historically grounded subjectivity templates, articulating models for subjectivity that place primacy on social belonging, collectivism, and mutual moral commitments. In chapter 3 I turn to the 3D scanning room at Hanoi's Obstetrics and Gynecology Hospital, approaching routine antenatal ultrasound as a site where the subjectivities of both fetuses and mothers are produced. I show how pregnant women obtained repeated ultrasound scans as a part of their efforts to gain full membership in families and local communities, and how, ironically, these quests for belonging seemed to deepen women's awareness of the contingency of their own and their children's attachments to social collectives. Chapter 4 investigates how doctors at Hanoi's Obstetrics and Gynecology Hospital defined their own roles as health care professionals in the ethically charged realm of selective reproduction. Rather than aiming to set women free to make their own decisions, I show, these physicians strove to care for their patients by taking responsibility for them. Chapters 5, 6, and 7 focus on the plight of women who were informed in the 3D scanning room that the child they expected was anomalous. In this situation, the first question that women and their relatives asked was *why:* what forces had made this pregnancy go awry? I begin my analysis in chapter 5 from this question, exploring how long-standing cosmological ideas of interhuman responsibilities and connections were reconfigured in this realm of high-tech medicine.

The next question that women and their relatives pondered was, If we keep it, what kind of child will this become? This question is at the center of chapter 6, where I examine how, in their search for answers, women and their relatives drew on local knowledge of the moral challenges posed by childhood disability. This chapter charts the social processes of inquiry through which prospective parents came to realize that this child, if born, would undo them, placing them in a position of permanent moral marginality within local social communities. The decisions that these couples came to were, this chapter shows, markedly less medicalized and less individualized than those described in studies from Europe or North America. In chapter 7 I focus on the decision-making processes that pregnant women and their relatives went through. At issue in this situation were not only questions of *why* this happened or *what* kind of child this was, but also questions of *who* the women themselves were—questions of ethical subjectivity. Who am I, women asked, to take the life of my own child? Or, What kind of person will I become if I bring this compromised child into the world? To answer these questions, women and their husbands placed themselves within national and familial communities, enacting belonging to the nation-state and to their kin group. Yet the persistent presence of the fetus they lost, this chapter shows, complicated the enactment of belonging that pregnancy decision making entailed. In the final chapter I conclude by summarizing the general arguments I have made and outlining the contours of an anthropology of belonging.

Sonographic Imaging and Selective Reproduction in Hanoi

"Beautiful, right!" Dr. Tuấn exclaimed, pointing to the 3D image of a fetus on the monitor in front of him. Despite the routine character of his work—as the hospital's most senior sonographer, he performed hundreds of scans every week—Dr. Tuấn seemed equally fascinated by every single scan he did. He praised each fetus for its beauty, its agile movements, its fine facial features, the perfect roundness of its head, and the balanced dimensions of its limbs. His wonder at the capacities of the machine he operated, and the pregnant woman's visible relief and delight when the scan went well, turned each of these medical encounters into emotionally powerful events.

This was my first day of fieldwork in the 3D scanning room at Hanoi's Obstetrics and Gynecology Hospital. The waiting rooms and corridors were busy, crowded with women at all stages of pregnancy and health staff in white uniforms striding from one room to another. Although it was relatively small, approximately three by five meters, the 3D scanning room served as a clinic and a waiting room at the same time: the scanning machine and examination bed were placed at one end, and at the other were seven blue plastic chairs along the walls. Each ultrasound scan was, in other words, a public performance involving not only the pregnant woman, the sonographer, and the nurse but also the women who were waiting for their own turn.[1] At the end of the day, Dr. Tuấn told me that he appreciated our research: the hospital had only recently invested in this 3D scanning machine, and he and his colleagues expected a lot from it. 3D scans, according to Dr. Tuấn, have strong popular appeal: "2D pictures are not very clear; only professionals like me can interpret them. But everyone can see a 3D image. People like you can see it too. You see, pregnant women like to see if their child is beautiful or ugly, and they want to see if it has any problems. 3D images give a clear and true picture. Ultrasound scanning is very useful, it is highly necessary in antenatal care."

In this chapter I introduce the reader to Vietnam's capital, Hanoi, and offer a brief description of the political context in which obstetrical ultrasound scanning has come to be considered a practically mandatory part of pregnancy care. I place obstetrical ultrasonography within four terrains of Vietnamese politics: the politics of health, abortion, disability, and population. At the beginning of the twenty-first century, I argue, the problem complex named *Agent Orange* affected these political terrains in profound ways. For ten years during the Second Indochina War—from 1961 to 1971—U.S. troops sprayed massive amounts of herbicides over Vietnam in order to defoliate jungles and rural lands, thereby depriving Việt Cộng guerillas of cover. Containing dioxin, one of the most toxic chemicals known to science, the herbicides—nicknamed Agent Orange—caused wide-ranging environmental damage. At the time of our fieldwork, this herbicide dioxin played a significant role in the politics of reproductive health in the country. In this chapter I therefore also present a brief account of the assumed public health consequences of wartime herbicide spraying and discuss the role played by Agent Orange in the uptake of prenatal screening. To begin with, I shall briefly introduce the setting of the research: the city of Hanoi.

HANOI: PUBLIC-PRIVATE SPACES

Vietnam's capital Hanoi traces its foundation to the eleventh century: according to historians, King Lý Thái Tổ of the Lý dynasty established Hanoi in the year 1010. Its name, Hà Nội, "the inside of the river," refers to its location on the western bank of the Red River, a calm reddish-brown river that sometimes swells into violent floods during the rainy season. In 1873, French forces occupied Hanoi, and in 1902 it became the capital of French Indochina. During the August Revolution of 1945, Việt Minh forces took control of the city, and on September 2,

Ba Đình square became the scene of one of the most momentous events in the history of socialist Vietnam: in the presence of a large gathering of people and in an exuberant atmosphere, Hồ Chí Minh read the Declaration of Independence of the Democratic Republic of Vietnam (cf. chapter 2).[2] In 1946, however, the French returned, and in 1954, after nine years of anticolonial resistance, Hanoi became the capital of an independent North Vietnam, the Democratic Republic of Vietnam. During the Second Indochina War (1959–1975), the city was the target of numerous attacks by U.S. air forces; Mễ Trì, the commune in which part of this research was conducted, was particularly heavily bombed due to its proximity to a radio transmitter. When the last U.S. troops left Vietnam on April 30, 1975, national victory and reunification were celebrated in the streets of Hanoi. Yet, according to today's Hanoians, postwar existence did not match the dreams and expectations that had animated the fight for independence. In his autobiographical novel, *The Sorrow of War,* Bao Ninh (1993:138) describes the collision between a guerilla fighter's wartime imaginings and 1975 realities: "Post-war Hanoi, in reality, was not like his jungle dreams. The streets revealed an unbroken, monotonous sorrow and suffering. There were joys, but those images blinked on and off, like cheap flashing lights in a shop window. There was a shared loneliness in poverty, and in his everyday walks he felt this mood in the stream of people he walked with."

In 1986, after a decade of persistent poverty and failed development efforts, the planned economy was officially abolished and Vietnam embarked on the economic reforms known as *đổi mới* (renovation). With *đổi mới,* a partial marketization has taken place, but politically Vietnam remains a one-party socialist state ruled by the Communist Party.[3] The country's integration into the global capitalist economy accelerated in 1994, when the U.S.-led trade embargo was lifted, and achieved further momentum in 2007, when Vietnam became a member of the World Trade Organization (WTO). As an element in its economic reforms, the Vietnamese state has withdrawn much of its support for health care, education, and social protection, and considerable economic disparities now exist between subgroups of the population. At the same time, however, economic growth rates have been high since the reforms began: the official poverty rate fell from 58 percent in the early 1990s to 14.5 percent by 2008, and in 2012 the country's economy was four times larger than in the early 1990s (World Bank 2012). In 2010, Vietnam escaped the low-income country category and was defined as a lower-middle-income country.[4]

Over the years that I have lived in Hanoi, these economic changes have left their mark on the city. In the early 1990s, Hanoi was a dense assemblage of villages; a city of bicycles, cyclos, and tree-lined avenues, of men dressed in green army clothes, women in dark trousers and conical hats, and children in school uniforms with red scarves around their necks. In the makeshift markets scattered across the town, vendors sold locally produced goods: green bean candy; jasmine soap; fish from local rivers and ponds; beef, pork, poultry; and a variety of rice, flowers, and fruit. In winter, there were miniature green apples, bananas, and guavas dipped in salt and chili pepper; in summer, mango, longan, durian, and lychee. On cool winter days in drizzling rain, or on summer days under a torrid sun, the city seemed calm, quiet, and self-contained. Today's Hanoi is different. A city of around three million people in the early 1990s, Vietnam's capital now numbers over six million inhabitants. In 2008, large parts of the surrounding provinces of Hà Tây, Vĩnh Phúc, and Hòa Bình were incorporated into the city of Hanoi, and rapidly expanding new urban zones now cover the suburban areas where rice fields used to stretch. The streets of today's Hanoi are packed with motorbikes and cars, shop windows display fashion clothes, and commercial advertisements for beauty products compete with official party-state posters and banners for the public's attention. Economic growth and the increasing integration into the global economy have expanded consumer options dramatically: whereas before the *đổi mới* period it was a luxury for people in Hanoi to own a Chinese bicycle or a bar of perfumed soap, today's middle-class citizens find it hard to imagine an existence without smartphones, motorbikes, and cars. Consumer goods that were unavailable as recently as the 1990s now fill stores, streets, and middle-class homes, and an expanding market for products associated with pregnancy and child care has emerged. Items for sale include toys, strollers, disposable diapers, formula milk, pregnancy manuals, and child care literature. Glossy magazines celebrate the joys of family life and motherhood, accentuating, implicitly as well as explicitly, parental—especially maternal—responsibility for child health and well-being. Within this consumer economy, children have become objects of investment in historically unprecedented ways, and middle-class parents have unprecedented amounts of money to spend on their care and upbringing.

Yet despite the city's growth and internationalization, in some ways Hanoi seems to have retained its villagelike character. At the time of our fieldwork, the city was divided into fourteen districts, of which nine were defined as inner-city (*nội thành*) and five as outer-city (*ngoại thành*) areas. Each urban district consisted of several smaller villages (*làng* or *thôn*) with their own communal houses, temples, and guardian spirits. Often, the inhabitants of these urban villages would express pride in the fact that local histories stretched centuries back in time. Village identities and close neighborhood relations, in other words, tend to persist in Hanoi, defying conventional distinctions between urban and rural forms of sociality. As houses in Hanoi are often cramped, many day-to-day activities are undertaken outside: people washing their hair, brushing their teeth, feeding their children, drinking tea, quarrelling, and engaging in love affairs in the public spaces of streets, alleys, and parks. Silence is rare, the normal backdrop to life being the roar of traffic, tapestries of human voices, dogs barking, roosters crowing, and the sounds of radios, televisions, and CD players. In many respects, then, lines between public and private tend to be blurred in Hanoi, as intimate life spills into public spaces and public stirrings reach into private homes. The areas around the city's two large maternity hospitals—the National Hospital of Obstetrics and Gynecology and Hanoi's Obstetrics and Gynecology Hospital—are among the sites where this merging of the intimate and the public happens in particularly graphic ways: around these hospitals, numerous private ob-gyn clinics advertise their services through the display of large images of fetuses, cervixes, and semen. Here, women's wombs are turned inside out, their contents rendered visible and public. If fetuses have, as Michaels and Morgan (1999:2) note, "become a regular, almost unremarkable feature of the public landscape" in the United States, this seems to be the case in Hanoi as well.

Hanoi's Obstetrics and Gynecology Hospital is located in Ba Đình district, between inner- and outer-city areas. The hospital was established in 1979, funded, its director told me, by an international women's organization as a gesture of solidarity with the women of Vietnam. At the time of our fieldwork, the hospital had three floors, its several buildings surrounded by a spacious yard in which tall eucalyptus trees offered shade to motorbikes and cars. In and around the hospital, Vietnam's increasing social differentiation was highly apparent: there were dramatic differences, for instance, between the economic means of patients coming from outlying rural areas on rented motorcycle taxis (*xe ôm*) and those of senior doctors who would arrive in shining cars with tinted windows. In the 3D scanning room, some women wore jeans and expensive leather jackets, while others had bare feet in rubber sandals. During the first months of fieldwork, I was struck by the intensive social exchanges that unfolded in this medical site. While waiting for examinations, women would often confide in each other, sharing intimate stories of reproductive difficulties and of family pressures and expectations. The hospital staff, too, engaged in constant and lively exchanges: while performing ultrasound scans, the sonographer in the 3D scanning room would often chat and joke with doctors in the adjacent 2D scanning room; as the walls did not reach all the way to the ceiling, people could hear each other across separate physical spaces, and news and rumors spread quickly within the hospital.[5] "Hospitals," note Sjaak van der Geest and Kaja Finkler (2004:1995), "both reflect and reinforce dominant social and cultural processes of their societies." Daily life in this Hanoian maternity hospital—the walls that did not really separate people, the lively exchanges of sentiments and stories, the constant presence of other people, talking, looking, touching, asking, acting—seemed to index the socially dense and communal character of everyday lives in Vietnam. In this medical facility as in day-to-day lives, there were always others around. In birth and death, in crises and routines, each individual would find herself accompanied by others; by people who would have an opinion, people who might help her or undo her, people on whom her existence would depend.

THE COMMERCIALIZATION OF ULTRASONOGRAPHY IN ĐỔI MỚI VIETNAM

In the course of one or two decades, practices of pregnancy care have changed dramatically in Hanoi. In 1993–1994, when I did my first fieldwork, antenatal care services consisted of basic physical examinations, while ultrasonography was used only under special circumstances. In 2004, a questionnaire study that my colleagues and I conducted among four hundred newly delivered women at the maternity department of Hanoi's Obstetrics and Gynecology Hospital showed that each woman had obtained an average of 6.6 ultrasound scans in her most recent pregnancy. A fifth of the women had had 10 scans or more; and we encountered some who had had 30 scans in one pregnancy. Ultrasonography had, it seemed, become a routine and unquestioned part of antenatal care. As one woman remarked: "You cannot go to an ob-gyn clinic and say, 'I don't need an ultrasound scan.' When you come in, the doctor tells you to lie on the bed and he will combine the antenatal examination and the ultrasound scan into one." Although some women

FIGURE 2. Private ob-gyn clinics outside Hanoi's Obstetrics and Gynecology Hospital.
Photo by the author, 2009.

expressed uncertainties about its safety, the vast majority seemed to take the use of this technology for granted.[6] The question was not whether or not to obtain ultrasounds, but how many, of what kind, and from which health care provider. How, then, did this rapid transition in pregnancy care practices come about?

To find answers to this question, I consulted half a dozen senior obstetricians identified by doctors at Hanoi's Obstetrics and Gynecology Hospital as pioneers in the introduction of obstetrical ultrasonography in Vietnam. According to these physicians, the first ultrasound scanning machines arrived in northern Vietnam in the early 1970s as donations from other countries, international organizations, or manufacturing companies.[7] In the beginning, ultrasonography was used only in highly specialized medical facilities and, in pregnancy, only when there were complications. The trend toward more widespread use of this technology began in the late 1980s when health sector reforms were initiated, and accelerated in the mid-1990s when the international trade embargo against Vietnam was lifted. By the late 1990s, ultrasonography was offered by all public hospitals and by a host of private ob-gyn clinics across Hanoi while also being available in provincial and district health facilities in rural areas. The routinization of obstetrical ultrasound scanning in urban northern Vietnam has, in other words, occurred at the same time as market economic reforms have taken hold in the country. As an element in Vietnam's economic transition, comprehensive health sector reforms have been undertaken: in 1989, user fees for health care services were introduced, and private medical practice legalized. In the years that followed, public spending on health dropped significantly, reaching its lowest level in 2006. At present, the share of out-of-pocket payments for health care remains high, accounting for around 55 percent of total health expenditure (Trần Văn Tiến et al. 2011). Furthermore, wages in the health sector are low and corruption rampant.[8] The consequence is inequity. For those who can afford it, access to high-tech health care has improved significantly over the past few decades, but for the country's poor, disease and disability can have catastrophic economic consequences.[9] For health care providers, the underfunding of the health sector creates strong incentives to gain additional income through the supply of revenue-generating services; and ultrasonography is, as Dr. Tuấn pointed out, among the services that have particularly strong consumer appeal.[10] Prenatal ultrasounds are offered by private ob-gyn clinics as well as by public health institutions; in the rapidly expanding health care market that had emerged in Hanoi by the time of our fieldwork, not only 2D but also 3D and 4D scans were offered. The price for a 2D scan was equivalent to US$1.30–2.00; for a 3D scan US$5–6; and for a 4D scan US$13–20. These prices were affordable for most women living in urban areas, but for rural women they were often prohibitive.

In short, the proliferation of ultrasonography in Hanoi must be seen in the context of health care sector liberalization; in Vietnam as in many other countries with privatized health systems, overuse of medical technology makes economic sense for health care providers and institutions. Yet while acknowledging the importance of revenue motives, the obstetricians I met also insisted that the adoption of this technology had been fueled by a profound professional fascination. Ultrasonography, they maintained, has brought remarkable benefits for antenatal care, allowing women in Vietnam to receive pregnancy care of a quality that matches that offered in more affluent countries. Dr. Tuấn, for instance, told us that he had worked with ultrasonography since 1988, when he attended a training course at Hanoi Medical University. "When you first encountered this technology," my colleague Hằng asked him, "what was your impression?" Dr. Tuấn responded promptly:

My first thought was that ultrasound brought a revolution to antenatal care. It was as if a great dream of mine came true. Before we had ultrasound, it was very difficult to diagnose in antenatal care. So this was something we had hoped for. I immediately said, "Now, this is something that is endlessly good for women and for our patients." Today, I still think so. I think this is something great. It is very good. We can offer better examinations and the technology is entirely safe. I have been captivated since I first encountered this technology. I am completely bewitched (*mê mẩn*) by it. I like it very much.

Like Dr. Tuấn, practically all health care providers framed ultrasonography as a benevolent intervention that helps women to go safely through pregnancy and to experience the joy of seeing their child-to-be develop month by month. In a conversation we had in June 2004, Dr. Lương, an obstetrician-gynecologist, expressed his position on this technology in terms that reflected what I had heard from many other health providers:

> Dr. L.: I think ultrasound is very good. It is very useful. It enables people to see the child. Seeing the child and knowing that it is developing without problems makes both doctors and parents feel happy. This is endlessly beneficial. I don't think there is anything harmful about it. I simply think that this is something we need. In my opinion, we must extend the awareness of ultrasound even wider, to reach more doctors.

> TG: Many women have an ultrasound scan each month. What do you think of that?

> Dr. L.: I think it is normal. It is not too much. This must be up to the individual. Some think it is too much, but I think it is normal. The parents have a need to see how their child is developing and growing. Since we know that ultrasonography is absolutely safe, I don't see why we should not do that for people if they ask for it.

Like Dr. Tuấn and Dr. Lương, Hanoian physicians generally embraced this new technology with enthusiasm, praising the numerous advantages that it brought to antenatal care. A female ob-gyn, Dr. Hương, summed up its benefits: "In the first trimester, we can see if the fetus is properly placed in the uterus and if it is developing well. In the second trimester, we can detect if there are any malformations and check the fetus's position and development. In the third trimester, we can see the development of the fetus, its weight and position, the amount of amniotic fluid, the placenta."

In the United States and Europe, the use of ultrasonography for obstetrical purposes is usually considered uncontroversial, whereas its use for reproductive selection raises ethical problems. In Vietnam, in contrast, ultrasonography was considered beneficial *because* it enabled health care providers to detect and act on fetal anomalies; it was the capacity for selection that physicians and pregnant women alike defined as the main advantage of this technology. In the words of Oanh, a twenty-nine-year-old mother of two: "Today, if there is a problem, people will terminate the pregnancy. In the past people did not know anything. When a child was born disabled, they were astonished. But now, with modern science, people go for examinations and if there is a problem, they will give up the pregnancy." Selective reproduction was, in other words, generally embraced by people, framed as an element in an enlightened and modern way of life that reaps the benefits of scientific progress. The use of ultrasonography, then, rested on a key premise: if a severe fetal anomaly was found, the woman was expected to consider a termination of her pregnancy. This assumption is, of course, not unique to Vietnam. As Rapp (1999:129) points out in a U.S. context, induced abortion is "the barely hidden interlocutor of all prenatal testing." But two other characteristics are specific to Vietnam. First, no attempts are made to conceal this clinical-political agenda of reproductive selection; and second, national abortion laws are, seen in a global perspective, unusually liberal. While prenatal screening is relatively new in Vietnam, induced abortion is a well-established reproductive health intervention.

PREGNANCY TERMINATIONS IN VIETNAM

Limited information is available on the legal status of induced abortion in Vietnam in early postcolonial times, but some sources suggest that abortion was legalized in the Democratic Republic of Vietnam already in 1945.[11] From the early 1960s, family planning became a political priority, and contraception and abortion became increasingly available in public health services. In the 1960s and 1970s, birth control was officially represented as an element in efforts to create a modern socialist society, free from the entrenched gender inequalities, kinship hierarchies, and economic underdevelopment that had characterized the presocialist era (see chapter 4). In 1988, seeking to bring population growth rates under control, the government launched a one-to-two-child family planning policy. The new policy was modeled on China's one-child policy but implemented through less draconian means: through moral persuasion, cash incentives for sterilization, and economic sanctions, citizens were urged to limit the size of their families by stopping at two children. With the launch of this policy, fertility control was more vigorously promoted, and pregnancy terminations became routine medical procedures, performed in hospitals and clinics in urban areas and by mobile teams in rural districts.[12]

By the mid-1990s, global estimates found Vietnam to have one of the world's highest abortion rates. In the public sector alone, each woman in the country obtained an average of 2.5 abortions in her reproductive lifetime. Since the number of abortions performed in the private sector was estimated at one third the public sector total, this added up to a considerable number (cf. Henshaw et al. 1999). According to official reports, abortion rates have declined significantly since the 1990s, from 83 abortions per 1,000 women in 1996 to 26 in 2003 (Sedgh et al. 2007). It is, however, practically impossible to assess abortion trends in Vietnam, since private sector abortions are not registered. In the public sector, most pregnancy terminations are performed in the first trimester. In 2005, 77 percent of all recorded abortions were done at up to 8 weeks' gestation. The remaining were performed after week 9, but official data do not distinguish between later first- and second-trimester abortions (Bélanger and Oanh 2009). An increasing number of second-trimester abortions are performed on female fetuses; although sex-selective abortion has been illegal since 2003, growing numbers of women resort to this procedure in the hope of having a son in their next pregnancy.[13]

At the time of this fieldwork, the legal limit for abortion in Vietnam was 22 weeks' gestation. First-trimester abortions were affordable and easily accessible, offered by both public and private service providers, while second-trimester abortions were performed only at provincial and central hospitals. Abortions prior to 18 weeks' gestation were usually performed surgically: in the first trimester through manual vacuum aspiration (MVA) (*hút thai*) or dilatation and curettage (D&C) (*nạo thai*), and from week 13 to 18 through dilatation and evacuation (D&E). Abortions after 18 weeks' gestation (*phá thai to*) were performed either through a modified Kovac's method or through medical abortion.[14] These abortions were more costly—hospitals charged around 1.5 million Vietnamese *đồng* (US$100) per procedure—and more administratively cumbersome, requiring the presentation of identification documents. If a fetus was found to be anomalous, there was no legal upper limit for abortion, but the termination had to be approved by a professional board at the hospital where it was performed. At Hanoi's Obstetrics and Gynecology Hospital, abortions after week 18 were induced through use of the drug Cytotec (known generically as misoprostol). After the medication had been administered to the woman, the delivery would usually take place within twenty-four hours. Neither feticide nor fetal autopsies were performed.[15]

Existing research has shown that many people in Vietnam consider pregnancy terminations to be morally problematic interventions (see chapters 3 and 7). During the years when family planning was a key political priority, such concerns were articulated mainly in private and were shrouded in silence in the public sphere.[16] At the time of this field-work, however, moral skepticism toward abortion began to be articulated more openly. Under the headline "Abortion—Belated Tears," for instance, an article published in the official journal *Family and Children* asserted: "Abortions generate not only physical pain but also spiritual trauma for pregnant women" (Thùy Hương 2009:20–21). Defining induced abortion as an extremely dangerous procedure, the article told heart-wrenching stories of women who had suffered profoundly when having their pregnancies terminated. One story portrayed a couple that decided to opt for a sex-selective abortion in the wife's 18th week of pregnancy. On this occasion, the husband cried for the first time in his adult life. The journalist commented: "Thinking of the bloody scene and the innocent little creature who had not had the chance to live, all he could do was to cry."

In public discourse, however, abortions for fetal malformation were represented as categorically different from other kinds of pregnancy termination. The pain of this particular kind of abortion, official accounts suggested, is modest in comparison with the suffering that the birth of a severely disabled child would have caused; unlike abortions that aim to select for sex, selection against disability was represented as entirely morally appropriate. At the time of this fieldwork, newspaper stories, government reports, and population policy documents all depicted the prospect of childhood disability as a serious threat to individuals, family, and society. As one government report warned: "Congenital defects still threaten severely the lives of the next generation" (National Committee for Population and Family Planning 2001:9). To contextualize such statements, I now briefly consider the social and political connotations of the notion of disability in present-day Vietnam.

"THE WHOLE LEAF SHALL PROTECT THE DAMAGED ONE": DISABILITY IN VIETNAM

The government of Vietnam prides itself on a long tradition of compassion and support for people with disabilities. Socialist Vietnam's first

Constitution, issued in 1946, stated that "old and handicapped persons (*người tàn tật*), incapable of working, shall receive assistance." All subsequent constitutions (1959, 1980, 1992) have explicitly guaranteed social protection of the nation's disabled people. In official discourse, measures to protect the disabled are often represented with reference to a longstanding cultural tradition in Vietnam of mutual care and protection, as captured in sayings such as "The whole leaf shall protect the damaged one" (*Lá lành đùm lá rách*) or exhortations to "love others like yourself" (*thương người như thể thương thân*). Despite this, there is no national disability registration system in Vietnam, and estimates of disability rates vary. In an effort to enhance evidence-based policy making, questions on disability were included in two national surveys: the 2006 Vietnam Household Living Standards Survey and the 2009 Vietnam Population and Housing Census. The 2009 census found that among Vietnam's 78.5 million persons aged five years or older, almost 6.1 million, or 7.8 percent, lived with one or more disabilities in seeing, hearing, walking, or cognition. Of this population, 385,000 were categorized as persons with severe disabilities (UNFPA 2011a). In 2005, the Vietnamese Ministry of Labor, Invalids, and Social Affairs (MOLISA) estimated that around 3 percent of all children were born with congenital disabilities (Government of Vietnam 2006:13). According to MOLISA statistics, in 2007, the number of people with disabilities who received regular support from the state was 487,384 individuals (UNFPA 2011a). The remaining individuals either supported themselves or were supported by relatives.

Initially, in Vietnam as in many other countries, disability policies were aimed primarily at the provision of support for war veterans. In the words of a 1994 government ordinance: "The Fatherland and its people will be forever indebted to those who have made sacrifices to the revolutionary cause for national liberation and the defense of the Fatherland. Caring for the material and spiritual life of these people and their families is the responsibility of the State and the entire society" (Maarse 2000:33). In the 1990s, however, under the influence of international organizations, disability policies began to include a broader group of people, targeting disabled children (*trẻ khuyết tật*) in particular. The 1992 Constitution states that "the State and society shall create the necessary conditions for disabled children to acquire general knowledge and appropriate training"; and the 1998 Ordinance on Disabled Persons expressed extensive state commitment to the enhancement of the political, economic, cultural, and social rights of people with disabilities. In the wake of this ordinance, several laws concerning education and employment have included protections for people with disabilities, and a variety of projects and programs have been launched to enhance educational and employment opportunities for the disabled, thereby increasing their inclusion in community and society (*hòa nhập với cộng đồng, xã hội*). The effectiveness of these measures is, however, not clearly documented. Findings from existing research indicate that social protection of the disabled remains limited; that disability and poverty are closely linked; and that Vietnam's disabled people continue to face enormous problems in accessing education, health care, and employment.[17]

At the time of our fieldwork, disability statistics and stories figured prominently in the mass media. On a daily basis, the citizens of Hanoi were confronted with television programs and newspaper accounts that offered personal stories of disabled individuals and their families, portraying the plights of mothers who must leave their severely disabled children unattended for hours while they went to work; of fathers who engaged in desperate searches for medication, spending fortunes on futile therapeutic journeys; and of unhappy children who spent their days lying in one place. These mass-mediated stories were always told with great pathos, detailing the pain (*nỗi đau*), suffering (*nỗi khổ*), and unhappiness (*bất hạnh*) of disabled individuals and their families. Newspaper articles were often accompanied by heart-wrenching photographs of crying children, of young adults who spent their days on a straw mat on their parents' living room floor, of worn-out parents and grandparents. Many stories ended with appeals to their readers to offer financial contributions that could help the disabled to achieve a life like everyone else's. The special moral obligation of the national mass media was explicitly set forth in an editorial in the Ministry of Health's journal *Health and Life* on the occasion of the International Day of Persons with Disabilities in 2004:

> Newspapers and mass media have an important role as bridges in this area. In the past years, many newspapers have organized help and support directly. The voices of newspapers and journals, of public opinion, are extremely important means of calling on conscience and responsibility. And next, together, schools, families, and mass organizations are places where charity and charitable deeds can be cultivated. Our country is still poor, but in Vietnam we have a one thousand–year-old history of human compassion (*lòng nhân ái*)! Together, let us offer people with disabilities more attention. (*Sức Khỏe và Đời Sống* [Health and Life] 2004)

In official discourse, it seemed to be taken for granted that disability equals suffering (see chapter 6). State messages suggested, moreover, that while treatment, rehabilitation, and social support are important for averting such suffering, the *prevention* of disability is a societal obligation too. In Europe and the United States, the use of prenatal screening to prevent the birth of children with disabilities has met strong criticism from disability rights advocates who claim that such measures cannot but convey the idea that people with disabilities are of less value than others. Martha Saxton (2006:108), for instance, writes that selective abortion must be resisted because "contributions of human beings cannot be judged by how we fit into the mold of normalcy, productivity, or cost-benefit. People who are different from us (whether in color, ability, age, or ethnic origin) have much to share about what it means to be human. We must not deny ourselves the opportunity for connection to basic humanness by dismissing the existence of people labeled 'severely disabled.'"

During fieldwork in Hanoi, I very rarely heard anyone express opinions of this kind.[18] The disability movement in Vietnam is still nascent, and there is no national organization that advocates for disabled people. Over the past decade, an array of local self-help disability groups has emerged, including groups for parents, students, women, and groups of people with specific impairments.[19] To date, however, none of these groups have expressed criticism of the use of prenatal screening and selective abortion; rather, there seems to be nearly complete social consensus that these are useful and beneficial medical interventions. When I talked to activists in local disability groups, I found to my surprise that nearly everyone condoned prenatal screening. Rather than seeing this medical intervention as an indication of discrimination, they depicted it as a privilege, their main concern being whether women with disabilities could get as easy access to screening as others. On February 22, 2006, for instance, my colleague Toàn and I met with forty-nine-year-old Phương, who was mobility impaired and an active disability support group member. We visited Phương in her home in a spacious house near the Red River where she lived with her husband and twenty-year-old son. Her tricycle was parked inside the gate, covered with a plastic sheet to protect it against the winter rain, and the yard was full of luxuriously green potted flowers. Inviting us in, Phương opened the conversation by telling us about her own childbearing experiences. "Before I had my son," she said, "*nobody* had imagined that I was able to have a child. At that time, people thought that a disabled person would never get married, have children, or take a job." When I asked Phương what she thought of the new technologies for prenatal screening that are now available in Vietnam, she replied: "I think this is something very humane. To have a child like that means suffering. The child will suffer, the family will suffer, even society will suffer. Of course, it is very difficult (*ái ngại*) for the parents to find out that something is wrong with their child and to undergo an abortion. But in my opinion, if one finds out that the fetus is not normal, it is best to have an abortion. It is better to feel pain for a short while than for an entire life."

These relatively homogeneous views of disability and prenatal screening must, I contend, be seen in the context of the social problems associated with the herbicide dioxin known as Agent Orange. Given that physicians and pregnant women found prenatal screening so necessary, that policy makers emphasized the need for systematic interventions to prevent disability, and that disability was equaled with suffering even by disability movement members, this must all be seen in the context of the agony associated with Agent Orange. At the time of our fieldwork, the nation's Agent Orange victims (*nạn nhân chất độc da cam*) were the objects of intense mass media attention. The editorial in *Health and Life* mentioned above concluded with these words: "The war in our country ended thirty years ago, but many of the nation's beloved children, and their children, grandchildren, and families, must still bear the bitter consequences of war; the consequences of Agent Orange, of infirmity and disease. . . . They sacrificed their blood and bones in order to win back independence, freedom, and peace for our country."

"AGENT OF AGONY": HUMAN CONSEQUENCES OF WARTIME HERBICIDE SPRAYING

Between 1961 and 1971, U.S. airplanes sprayed 11 to 12 million gallons of herbicides over Vietnam in order to defoliate forests and mangroves presumed to be used by the Việt Cộng for cover. The spraying caused massive environmental destruction, devastating large areas of land, and affected between 2.1 and 4.8 million Vietnamese people directly (Stellman et al. 2003).[20] The herbicide mixture most often used has become known as Agent Orange, named for the orange stripes on the barrels in which it was shipped. Agent Orange contained dioxin, a highly toxic chemical that is very persistent in the environment and in human tissue. "Dioxins are of concern," notes a WHO fact sheet, "because of their highly toxic potential. . . . Once dioxins have entered the body, they endure a long time because of their chemical stability and their ability to be absorbed by fat tissue, where they are then stored in the body" (WHO 2010).

During the years of our fieldwork, there was mounting concern in Vietnam about the long-term health effects of herbicide spraying. The Vietnamese Association of Victims of Agent Orange (VAVA) has estimated that more than 3 million citizens of Vietnam suffer from serious health problems caused by dioxin exposure (Martin 2009). The chemical has, advocacy groups claim, harmed the health of Vietnam's people in several ways. First, those who were directly exposed to Agent Orange during the war, or who live in areas with residual dioxin in soil and water, experience a much higher rate of certain diseases than other members of the population. Second, the children and grandchildren of individuals exposed to herbicide spraying are born with unusually high rates of congenital malformations or diseases, or both. According to Nguyễn Trọng Nhân, vice president of VAVA, the rate of severe congenital anomalies in herbicide-exposed populations in Vietnam is 2.95 percent, compared to 0.74 percent in non-exposed populations (Stone 2007:178). Like the WHO, Vietnamese researchers point to the uncanny persistence of dioxins in the human body and in the environment, arguing that dioxins not only may be transmitted from the exposed generation to the next, but may also skip a generation and manifest again in the grandchildren of those directly exposed (Hoàng Bá Thịnh 2006).[21] Internationally, questions of how dioxin exposure affects human health are steeped in uncertainty, as the impact of toxic chemicals on human beings cannot be easily gauged. The possible health consequences include "increased risk for cancers, adverse reproductive and developmental effects, immune deficiency, endocrine disruption, and neurological damage including cognitive and behavioral damage from in utero exposure, and other health effects" (Schechter et al. 1995:520). There is firm evidence of association between exposure to dioxin and five illnesses: soft-tissue sarcoma, non-Hodgkin's lymphoma, chronic lymphocytic leukemia, Hodgkin's lymphoma, and chloracne. There is limited or suggestive evidence of association between dioxin exposure and a range of other ailments, including prostate and respiratory cancers, Parkinson's disease, Ischemic heart disease, Type 2 diabetes, and spina bifida in offspring of exposed individuals (Institute of Medicine 2009). To date, the actual consequences of dioxin exposure for the health of Vietnamese citizens remain a topic of intense scientific and political controversy (see D. Fox 2007). The impact on reproductive health is perhaps the most unsettling and contentious issue.

In Vietnam, concerns that dioxin exposure may cause birth defects were first raised in newspaper articles in Saigon in the 1960s. Since the

1970s, epidemiological studies conducted by Vietnamese researchers have found elevated rates of congenital malformations in children of men and women who have been exposed to the chemical.[22] In 1980, the Vietnamese government set up the 10–80 Committee (named for the month and year of its establishment) as the official body for Agent Orange research, and the consequences of herbicide spraying for human health and the environment were discussed at international scientific conferences held in Ho Chi Minh City and Hanoi in 1983 and 1993. Epidemiological research on herbicide spraying conducted by Vietnamese researchers has, however, rarely been published in international peer-reviewed scientific journals. The validity of this research has therefore been questioned, some scholars claiming that with the exception of spina bifida and anencephaly, the peer-reviewed literature does not offer convincing indications of connections between herbicide exposure and congenital malformations (Schechter and Constable 2006). The official U.S. standpoint is that there is no conclusive evidence that herbicide spraying has caused health problems among exposed Vietnamese individuals and their children.[23] In 2007, then–U.S. ambassador to Vietnam Michael W. Marine declared: "But honestly, I cannot say whether or not I have myself seen a victim of Agent Orange. The reason for that is that we still lack good scientific definitions of the causes of disabilities . . . that have occurred in Vietnam. . . . We just don't have the scientific evidence to make that statement with certainty" (Martin 2009:7). Despite this purported lack of evidence, five countries involved in the war—the United States, Vietnam, Australia, South Korea, and New Zealand—now offer their veterans compensations for diseases and congenital birth defects related to Agent Orange (D. Fox 2007:3). Meanwhile, victims in Vietnam have received no compensation from the U.S. government or the companies that produced the chemicals.[24]

"JUSTICE HAS NO BORDERS": CONTESTED RESPONSIBILITIES FOR HEALTH DAMAGE

In May 2005, I talked informally to a senior official employed at the U.S. embassy in Hanoi. When I mentioned that I found it noteworthy that U.S. veterans are offered compensations for health problems associated with Agent Orange while Vietnamese citizens are not, he responded: "Actually, you know, no one really believes that Agent Orange causes health damage. In the U.S., there were huge pressures for compensation from veterans' organizations, and it was felt that we had to give them something. But we never really believed that these things are linked." As represented by this official, in other words, the granting of compensation to U.S. veterans was a moral gesture made in recognition of the pain they had suffered; it was not, he claimed, an evidence-based acknowledgment of causality. His opinion echoed that expressed by Agent Orange manufacturers who emphasize the lack of proof of health damage. On its homepage, for instance, Dow Chemical Company (2013) states that the "very substantial body of human evidence on Agent Orange does not establish that veterans' illnesses are caused by Agent Orange." The U.S. decision to grant veterans compensations for health problems in spite of these controversies regarding the evidence must be seen against the background of a historic toxic tort lawsuit.

In 1984, a group of U.S. veterans filed a class action lawsuit against Agent Orange manufacturers. While denying any link between the chemical and veterans' health problems, seven companies settled the lawsuit out of court, agreeing to pay a compensation of $180 million. Seven years later, in 1991, the U.S. Congress passed the Agent Orange Act, making veterans who served in Vietnam eligible to receive treatment and compensation for certain conditions. It is likely, observers have noted, that the court case and its settlement contributed to the passage of this act (Martin 2009:24). No legal liability has, however, been admitted. In 1984, Judge Jack B. Weinstein, who presided over the court case, emphasized that given the scientific uncertainties at issue, there was no proof that Agent Orange had harmed veterans' health (Schuck 1986:185). Despite this denial of responsibility and despite the fact that the compensation that veterans received was financially modest, the 1984 settlement did constitute an important symbolic gesture. As Veena Das (1995:141–142) observes: "Courts became sites on which the Vietnam war and its hardships were symbolically re-enacted. The same law suit could also be seen as a cathartic drama in which war veterans gave public expression to annoyance at their dismal treatment at the hands of their society: the court case became an occasion to comment upon the moral problems of contemporary society." U.S. veterans have, in other words, been relatively successful in contesting companies' definitions of harm and in gaining moral recognition of their suffering. In this regard, Vietnamese victims have had less success.

In Vietnam, Agent Orange has only recently become a matter of public concern. Although the possible problems caused by Agent Orange were afforded some scientific attention in the decades immediately following the war, from 1975 to around 2000 there was a marked reluctance in both Hanoi and Washington to discuss the Vietnamese Agent Orange case in public. On Vietnam's part, this silence was due to intertwined economic and diplomatic concerns: officials feared that publicity around the Agent Orange issue could damage Vietnam's image internationally, making it harder to market agricultural and aquacultural products, while also hindering the normalization of diplomatic relations with the United States. It was not until the mid-1990s, therefore, that the fate of Agent Orange victims was brought to mainstream public attention. Vietnamese writers and artists played a key role in this process: in 1996, Trần Văn Thủy's film *A Story from a Corner of the Park* depicted a Hanoi family affected by Agent Orange, and in the nation's newspapers, writers and journalists began to tell victims' stories. In 1998, the Vietnamese Red Cross established an Agent Orange Victims' Fund; in 2000, the Vietnamese government set up its Agent Orange Central Payments Program, providing financial assistance to victims; and in 2001 the Vietnamese government launched a campaign for "poor disabled people, including those thought to be affected by Agent Orange."

In Hanoi, public attention to Agent Orange heightened in 2005 when three Vietnamese citizens filed a class action lawsuit in U.S. District Court in New York against Agent Orange manufacturers, demanding compensation for the injuries inflicted on them. Their claims were dismissed. The court ruled that since the herbicides were not intended to poison humans, their use was not a violation of international law; this could not be considered chemical warfare. Judge Weinstein—the same judge who presided in the 1984 court case filed by U.S. veterans—concluded: "The fact that diseases were experienced by some people after spraying does not suffice to prove general or specific causation. Proof of causal connection depends primarily upon substantial epidemiological and other scientific data" (Stone 2007:179).[25] The attempts made by Vietnamese victims to draw U.S. public attention to their grievances have, in other words, had limited effect; their lawsuit failed to achieve the moral and financial results gained by U.S. veterans. As observed in a petition issued by the Association of Agent Orange/Dioxin Victims of Ho Chi Minh City in July 2012: "The greatest injustice is that of all the victims of this monstrous chemical, only the American veterans have been compensated since 1985 whilst the Vietnamese victims have been discriminated [against] and ignored" (Gender and Society Research Center 2012).

At the time of our fieldwork, public demands for justice and U.S. acknowledgment of its responsibility were intensifying in Vietnam. In the months preceding the New York court case, the mass media unleashed a torrent of unsettling stories of Agent Orange victims, defining the lawsuit—a "suit for conscience and justice" (*vụ kiện vì lương tri và công lý*)—as a necessary response to this human suffering. When the victims' case was dismissed, the ruling was characterized as unjust, inhuman, and irresponsible—"a verdict that challenges the world's conscience," as one newspaper put it. Given the deep and perhaps permanent damage that has been done to the health of Vietnamese citizens, mass media reports asserted, U.S. manufacturers and authorities must be held accountable. Under the headline "The U.S. Must Take Responsibility," for instance, the daily newspaper *Hà Nội Mới* commented, "This pain will haunt (*ám ảnh*) the people of Vietnam from this generation to the next. The U.S., a country that always preaches loudly about human rights, must assume responsibility for Agent Orange victims in Vietnam" (Bích Thuận 2005).

In today's Vietnam, such demands for responsibility are articulated most vocally by nongovernmental organizations. The above petition, for instance, declares:

> The war has been over for 37 years but for the victims of Dioxin/Agent Orange the war has not ended. Every day of their lives, they endure physical pain and severe mental wounds. The consequences of Agent Orange are long term and [a] heavy burden on society. The pharmaceutical companies (Dow Chemical and Monsanto), the producers of the toxic chemical and the decision-makers who are responsible for the use of dioxin during the war in Vietnam remain unperturbed and avoid their responsibility for their own acts. . . . The reality is that more than 3 million AO Vietnamese victims are confronted with a daily struggle for life and enduring physical pain from the fatal diseases. Many died very young. Others, and in particular their children born after the war, are malformed and unable to care for themselves. Nor should we forget all the dead fetuses that did not see life. . . . We believe that it is high time for all of us to demonstrate our clear and simple message and demand that the U.S. pharmaceutical companies and the U.S. government take responsibility for their actions and alleviate the severe effects of the Dioxin Agent Orange in Vietnam. . . . Everyone in this world should be treated equally; justice has no borders. Agent Orange victims wherever they reside should be treated fairly. . . . The suffering of the victims is the common pain of all Vietnamese and, it can be even said, the pain of humanity. (Gender and Society Research Center 2012)

The demands set forth in such public calls for responsibility drew moral and emotional force from the harrowing stories of the plight of Agent Orange victims that have proliferated in the mass media since the beginning of this millennium. Depicting the day-to-day lives of families in which several generations suffered from devastating dioxin-related diseases and disabilities, these narratives paid particular heed to tragedies of a reproductive nature. One typical story, told in *Family and Society* under the headline "A Pain Bearing the Name Orange," introduced readers to a man named Phạm Hùng who lived in Phú Yên province. During his military service, Hùng worked in heavily sprayed areas. Since his return, he had suffered from frequent health problems, and three of his four children, Hường, Hoài, and Hoa, had been "crazy" (*điên*) from birth. None of them could talk, yet their shrieks could be heard far away. Hùng and his wife made their living from a small plot of land, and one of them always had to stay at home to watch their children; in a moment's lapse of parental attention any one of them could run out of the house and injure him- or herself. Meeting this family, the journalist wrote, she could not hold back her tears. Hùng too shed tears as he said: "We don't know what to do. We have given birth to them, so no matter what they are like, these are our children. We do our best. Even though we have only vegetables and rice gruel to eat, we get by day by day" (Nguyễn Xuân Hoài 2005).

Often, stories of Agent Orange victims' plights portrayed parents who had had one severely disabled child after the other, yet kept clinging to a desperate hope of having at least one healthy child. Reporting on her interactions with victims, for instance, the social researcher Phạm Kim Ngọc, from the nongovernmental Research Center for Gender, Family, and Environment in Development (CGFED), writes:

> We have heard heart-breaking stories of the destruction of health, particularly reproductive health. There were women who suffered unspeakably (*chết đi sống lại*), because each time they gave birth, the child was deformed. There were fathers who had to bury the bloody lumps of meat [when their children were born] inhumanly deformed. There were parents who had to swallow their own tears to look after children who had been born without intelligence and awareness, who could do nothing for themselves, who did not have the ability to learn, to think or to work. There were parents who thought they were living in happiness when suddenly their children got ill and nothing could be done to help them. . . . All those fathers and mothers, husbands and wives, always nourish a deep desire, although they know that it can never be fulfilled: *giving birth to a healthy and normal child.* (Phạm Kim Ngọc 2006:33–34; emphasis in original)[26]

Through stories conveyed in the mass media, Vietnamese citizens have become intimately familiar with images of children without arms or legs, with weirdly deformed limbs, or without eyes; children with enormous heads; children whose skin flakes off or whose bodies are

FIGURE 3. A three-generation "Agent Orange family" living in Nam Định province. Photo by Research Center for Gender, Family, and Environment in Development (CGFED), 2005.

covered with black hair or dark spots; children who are partly or completely paralyzed and spend their days on beds or in cagelike enclosures.[27] These images, I suggest, formed a vital substratum for people engaged in selective reproduction with the fervor I observed; at this moment in time, all citizens of Hanoi were keenly aware of the fact that human reproduction can go terribly awry. Partly in response to the agony associated with Agent Orange and partly in an effort to accelerate the country's economic development, Vietnamese policy makers have recently turned problems associated with the "quality" (chất lượng) of the nation's population into a central political issue. In this policy realm, emotional mobilization around the Agent Orange issue forms an important basis for political strategies and interventions.

ENHANCING POPULATION QUALITY: ULTRASONOGRAPHY AS A POLITICAL DEVICE

As I approached Hanoi's Obstetrics and Gynecology Hospital on a bright day in September 2009, I noticed that one of the private clinics outside its gates advertised its services in a new terminology. On the glass doors that separated the clinic from the street outside, large red letters now announced: "Prenatal screening. Screening for the factors that determine human quality (*chất lượng con người*). A chance to give birth to healthy children for every family." Next to the clinic entrance, a huge photograph, approximately two meters high, showed a child lying curled up inside the palm of a hand. This image, presented in an effort to attract customers, attested not only to the commercialization of reproductive health care in Vietnam, but also to the increasing political attention that this area of human life attracts. While human reproduction has long been an important terrain for the exercise of state power in Vietnam, at present the quality of future citizens is problematized in novel ways.

At the beginning of the twenty-first century, the Vietnamese government's efforts to control population growth seemed to have largely achieved their objectives: national fertility rates had dropped from an average of 5.7 births per woman in 1979 to 3.8 in 1989 and 2.1 in 2005 (Teerawichitchainan and Amin 2009). Political attention therefore began to turn toward questions pertaining to the quality of the country's population. The first official document that placed population quality on the political agenda was the national Population Strategy for the years 2001 to 2010, issued in 2001. In the years that followed, questions about what population quality means and how it can be measured were intensely debated in government policy papers and state-run journals. Often, officials would refer to UNDP's Human Development Index (HDI, which combines measures of life expectancy, literacy, educational attainment, and GDP per capita), regretting Vietnam's low ranking as compared with other Southeast Asian countries. But while making frequent reference to the HDI, government documents also defined this as a relatively simple index that "does not include the full complexity and multifaceted character of human development . . . and does not highlight all the challenges that a developing country must give priority to solving" (Ủy Ban Dân Số, Gia Đình và Trẻ Em 2003:135). One key dimension of human development that the HDI ignores, officials claimed, is the physical quality of the population.

At the time of this research, policy papers and the public press expressed intense concern regarding the physical deficiencies of Vietnam's citizens: young people, citizens were told, are too short in stature compared to their peers in the region; too many children are born at a low birth weight; the nutritional status of children under five is too poor; and the proportion of disabled people in the population is too large.

These deficiencies, officials maintained, hamper the competitiveness of the national workforce; if Vietnam is to compete with other nations in the global capitalist arena, the physical quality of the country's citizens must be enhanced. In a special issue of the state-run journal *Family and Children,* for instance, a high-ranking population official wrote:

> The low population quality hinders the development of our country and places us at risk of falling even further behind. We cannot yet meet the requirements for a high quality work force that can serve the industrialization and modernization of the nation. . . . It is necessary to extend preliminary models for technological intervention in the areas of prenatal and neonatal screening in order to detect and treat congenital diseases, neonatal disability, and genetic disabilities, and it is necessary to perform premarital health examinations and counseling. Step by step, through research and experimentation, we must develop models of intervention that can contribute to reducing the factors that weaken our stock (*giống nòi*), models for building cultured families,[28] safety, and social dynamics that suit a developing society, particularly as Vietnam joins the World Trade Organization. (Nguyễn Bá Thủy 2007:7)

If Vietnam is to benefit from the development opportunities arising from gaining membership in the World Trade Organization in 2007, officials argued, the physical quality of the population must be enhanced; to attain this goal, the number of children born with diseases and disabilities must be reduced. It is in this context of heightened biopolitical attention to the bodily quality of Vietnam's present and future citizenry that obstetrical ultrasonography has achieved its significance as a political device.

At the time of this fieldwork, prenatal genetic tests such as amniocentesis were used only at Hanoi Medical University and at the city's largest maternity hospital, the National Hospital of Obstetrics and Gynecology, and in both sites only on an experimental basis. According to the policy makers I talked to, general coverage of genetic examinations in pregnancy was not considered immediately realistic.[29] Due to its limited cost, in contrast, ultrasonography was seen as having the potential for more widespread use. The expectations that officials and physicians invested in this new technology were set forth with particular clarity in a talk that Dr. Lan, a senior ob-gyn, gave at a scientific conference on prenatal screening held at Hanoi's Obstetrics and Gynecology Hospital on March 31, 2006. Dr. Lan said:

> Abnormal fetuses pose large problems for our entire society. Across the world, numerous different methods have been used to detect abnormal fetuses, such as X-rays, amniocentesis, chorionic villus sampling, fetal tissue

sampling, umbilical blood sampling, maternal serum screening. These methods are very precise, but they intervene in the body and require time, equipment, and medical specialization. Therefore, they cannot always be used. Thanks to the rapid progress of science and technology, ultrasound scanning is now widely used.

At birth, children have the right to health, the right to play and to learn. The birth of sick and disabled children not only increases the risk of tragedies in terms of health, which make both the family and the disabled child itself tense and tired. Such children are also an economic burden for both family and society. The use of ultrasound scanning for early detection of fetal malformations is a simple and affordable method that can easily be used everywhere, at any time, even at basic health care service delivery points. Therefore, we need more research on this issue in order to eliminate fetuses with severe disabilities at an early stage.

Since the turn of the millennium, official appeals to the nation's citizens to make use of selective reproductive technologies have been made with increasing intensity. An article in *Family and Society,* for instance, told its readers that "methods for genetic screening and diagnosis bring benefits for women, families, and the community, improving the chances of having healthy children and reducing worries about having disabled children. At the same time, they reduce costs for families and society and contribute to improving population quality. . . . According to experts, if pregnant women undergo prenatal and neonatal screening, it is possible to eliminate up to 95% of all abnormal cases and ensure that healthy children come into being" (Hà Thư 2010c:6). Newspaper reports often expressed regret that rates of prenatal screening are too low in Vietnam. In Singapore, one article stated, 99 percent of all children are screened before birth; in Thailand this figure is 80 percent and in Australia 100 percent. In Vietnam, in contrast, only 1 percent of children were reportedly examined before birth (Hà Thư 2010d:6).

On December 3, 2004, I asked Đặng Văn Phòng, a senior official with Vietnam's Commission for Population, Family, and Children, how the concept of population quality had been introduced in Vietnam. Sitting at his desk, surrounded by stacks of research reports, policy papers, and other documents, he told me that examples set by other countries in the region had compelled Vietnamese policy makers to place questions of quality at the center of national development efforts:

> We noticed that several other countries in Asia placed population quality high on the agenda. Asian countries are often poor and underdeveloped, and many people have weak physiques and are very small. . . . So for these reasons, we had to take up the problem of population quality in order to par-

ticipate together with other countries in processes of modernization and industrialization. We also studied documents from other Asian countries, for instance from Japan, where they addressed the issue of population quality already around 1945, after the Second World War.[30] I read documents that stated that after losing in the war, Japan was a very poor country that encountered many difficulties. Therefore, Japan had to strive hard to reach the development level of other countries. Genetics programs were implemented, and policies were launched that encouraged scientists to have many children and allowed people to marry foreigners. . . . In Japan they thought that this could enhance the quality of Japanese people. They wanted to change the stock (*giống nòi*) of the Japanese in order to be able to engage with other countries.

If a country such as Japan had attained economic development by enhancing the fitness of the national labor force, Phòng and other officials reasoned, then Vietnam must leap out of its poverty and postwar deprivation in a similar manner. But, Phòng suggested, at the time that population quality became an object of political attention in Vietnam, more country-specific anxieties were at issue as well. In the 1990s, a national-level research project had been conducted on different aspects of population quality and, among a range of topics under consideration, the involved officials had decided to give priority to genetics. The government's interest in genetics, Phòng said, was directly associated with concerns about the long-term consequences of wartime herbicide spraying. As a part of efforts to enhance population quality, recommendations were made to extend the availability of genetic health care services, particularly to citizens exposed to Agent Orange. In Phòng's words:

> We must explain clearly to such people that this may affect their childbearing. If their parents lived in areas exposed to Agent Orange, this will be carried in their genes. Research conducted by Professor Cầu found that the chemical affected five generations, but in irregular ways: perhaps the children were not affected, but the next generation was. So it is very complicated, and we must tell these people the truth and encourage them to be careful in their reproductive practices. I have visited local areas together with the Ministry of Labor, Invalids, and Social Affairs and met people who do not know [about their genetic status], so they keep hoping that they can have a normal child. Therefore in some families they have three, four, or five children who are all disabled. It was so painful to witness this. It was like a disability camp (*cái trại bị dị tật*)—all the children were disabled. The entire family lived in misery. The kin group suffered too, because other family members such as aunts and uncles had to help. The village also had to help, so this became a very heavy burden for the entire society. Therefore, this problem is very complicated in Vietnam and we have not been able to solve it yet.

When Phòng contributed to the drafting of national population policies, he saw before him the suffering child victims he had encountered
during field trips. Such suffering can, he told me, be prevented: "I am
not saying that Agent Orange victims should not have children," he
emphasized, hinting at a conversation we had recently had about twentieth-century European eugenics. "What I say is that these people need
help from the health care system. If they lived in your country, they
would have access to genetic health care services. So why should we not
be able to offer Vietnamese people this kind of assistance?"

Numerous official documents, including the government's 2001 Population Strategy and the 2003 Population Ordinance, make direct reference to the population's exposure to toxic chemicals, linking the need
for expanded prenatal screening to this unsettling national history.
Reading these policy documents, I was often struck by the emotion and
empathy that animated them. Policy making in the realm of selective
reproduction seemed inflected with heartfelt distress, anxiety, and compassion.

When calling for more extensive use of prenatal screening, policy
makers would often, like Phòng, refer explicitly to the devastating consequences of dioxin contamination for human health and lives. In official discourse, the suffering of Agent Orange victims was represented as
iconic of the suffering that all severe disability induces; the horrors associated with Agent Orange seemed to spill over into the realm of disability in general. The following excerpt from an official document accompanying the government's 2003 Population Ordinance illustrates how
observations that alluded specifically to Agent Orange could slip into
more general statements about disability:

> At present, considerable numbers of children are born with congenital dis-
> abilities. Due to a lack of knowledge about reproduction, many families with
> disabled children still hope that their second, third, or . . . [later-sequenced]
> child will not suffer such consequences. This has led to a situation in which
> many families have three or four disabled children, causing suffering and
> difficulties for family and society. Congenital disabilities are very difficult to
> treat, the death rate is high, and the disabilities usually remain for the entire
> life of the disabled person. The life situation of people with congenital dis-
> abilities is very painful, and the lives of family members are very difficult and
> full of suffering. This places burdens on society too. (Ủy Ban Dân Số, Gia
> Đình và Trẻ Em 2003:140)

Existing analyses of East Asian population policies have often framed
state policies as rational and instrumental technologies of power that

are driven by faceless bureaucratic machineries (e.g., Sigley 2009). During fieldwork in Hanoi, however, I came to see Vietnamese state efforts to enhance population quality as a politics of proximity; that is, as a way in which intuitive reactions to the suffering of other persons were turned into a basis for policy measures and political claims (cf. Levinas 1998a [1985]:165). When policy makers in Hanoi strove to avert the suffering associated with severe disability, they seemed motivated not only by economic goals or national development ambitions but also by a sense of responsibility and solidarity, by feelings of compassion with fellow citizens whose family lives had been thrown off track by a war that ended decades ago. The words of policy makers such as Phòng draw our attention to these affective aspects of state policies, to the human anxieties and desires that animate biopolitical strategies.[31] Ignoring these dimensions of governance may, I contend, lead us to portray the actors who devise and implement state policies as less than human and to overlook the emotional forces that lie behind citizens' compliance—or complicity—with state demands.[32]

In today's Vietnam, as this chapter shows, state and citizen anxieties tend to merge in the realm of reproductive politics. The policy makers, pregnant women, and health care providers I met all expressed fears and concerns about the long-term consequences of herbicide spraying for human reproduction and an acute awareness of the risks that childbearing entails. During a conversation we had about selective reproduction, for instance, Dr. Tuấn said: "Vietnam is a country that has been through many wars. Many weapons have been used, including chemical ones. Their environmental effects are very long term and they affect the people of Vietnam. . . . But in the health care system there are things we can do. We can encourage women to get enough folic acid, and we can conduct prenatal screening. We can categorize the children in a scientific and effective way, to ensure that those that are born have good physiological indicators and are perfect (hoàn thiện)." When a disability movement activist such as Phương defined prenatal screening as a necessary and humane intervention, she too was associating disability with the deformation of human bodies caused by herbicide exposure. During our conversation, it soon became clear that when Phương talked about the disasters involved in having "a child like that," it was images of Agent Orange victims that were on her mind. When we asked her about the differences between severe and mild disabilities, she answered by pointing to the problems associated with Agent Orange: "Some Agent Orange families have four children and they are all disabled. This shows that there is a need for better communication. It is important to make such people understand that even if they have ten children, they will never have a complete (*lành lặn*) child. Sooner or later, the child will become sick. Such families suffer, and indirectly society suffers too. They keep hoping, but their hope is groundless. So there is a need for better counseling, to make these people understand."[33]

In sum, the human damage done by the spraying of toxic herbicides over Vietnam during the Second Indochina War is figured in public discourse in ways that render close surveillance of the pregnancies of the nation's women a social, political, and humanitarian necessity: official responses to the toxic aftermaths of war include biopolitical attempts to ensure the integrity of the national body through active promotion of selective reproduction. Yet present-day Vietnamese biopolitics differs, I contend, in significant respects from the forms of governance that unfold in advanced liberal societies where moral and political primacy is placed on individual decision making and choice. This is what I discuss in the following chapter.

CHAPTER 2

A Collectivizing Biopolitics

"Our principal goal for the future is to improve population quality. More concretely, this means improving the quality of the Vietnamese people's stock (*giống nòi*) by strengthening premarital, prenatal, and neonatal counseling and examinations. This will help produce a population that is healthy in physical, mental, and spiritual terms. . . . However, in our country prenatal and neonatal screening are new programs, which means that many couples have not realized their benefits, and many children are still born with disabilities that could have been prevented before or during pregnancy."

These are the words of Dr. Dương Quốc Trọng, a high-ranking party-state official and head of the Government Office for Population and Family Planning. In August 2009, he was interviewed at length in an article published in the state-run journal *Family and Society* (Hà Thư 2009a:6). Under the headline "Population and Family Planning Work in the Coming Stage: Great Difficulties," readers were informed of the significance of prenatal and neonatal screening. Linking the state of the national body directly to the reproductive behavior of individual women and men, the article expressed regret that, to date, adoption of new screening technologies remained limited in Vietnam. In a subsequent article published in the same journal a couple of weeks later, Dr. Trọng was interviewed again. This time, he emphasized that screening aims to enhance the national stock through voluntary means. "But," he added, "if couples receive careful counseling, they will make the decisions that are best for future generations in terms of health and heredity" (Hà Thư 2009b:6).

In this chapter I examine the rhetoric through which Vietnamese state policies of selective reproduction are set forth; I focus particularly on the ways in which official discourses on population enhancement project specific models for subjectivity, gender, and citizenship. In the discursive field constituted by official debates on population problems, reproduction is closely associated with identity—that of the nation (*quốc gia*) as a coherent unity over which the state exercises authority, and that of the family (*gia đình*) and the patrilineage (*dòng họ*).[1] Vietnamese state discourses on reproduction constitute, as this chapter shows, powerful ideologies of belonging; they tell people that as individuals, they are composites of larger social structures that exceed their own existence in time and space. This observation adds nuance to ongoing scholarly debates regarding whether, how, and to what extent present-day East Asian modes of governmentality can be characterized as neoliberal. In recent years, numerous observers have claimed that contemporary regimes of governance in late-socialist countries such as China and Vietnam work by stimulating processes of individuation, inducing citizens to self-manage according to neoliberal principles of competitiveness, discipline, and choice.[2] Yet although the turn to a market economy has clearly entailed state retreat from previous forms of welfare provisioning in both China and Vietnam, thereby to some extent encouraging individual self-responsibility and self-regulation, I find it important not to stretch the notion of neoliberalism too far.[3] Like the Chinese state, that of Vietnam continues to intervene in markets and investments in significant ways, and the influence of global neoliberal trends on the workings of the state apparatus appears to be relatively modest. Further, the decline in the state's biopolitical role that some scholars have posited is hardly universal; in countries such as China and Vietnam, the control of national bodies clearly remains central to modern forms of governance. I suggest, therefore, that we take a more cautious, and more ethnographically grounded, approach to the analysis of the identity making that population governance entails. Rather than assuming that contemporary governance and subjectivity formation unfold in homogeneous and universal ways across the globe, I find it important to trace the specific ways in which new forms of governance intertwine with long-standing cultural values and practices in particular social settings. I suggest, therefore, that we return to Foucault's thoughts on biopower, and particularly to his observation that the formation of subjectivities always takes place in locally specific ways: "If I am now interested in how the subject constitutes itself in an active fashion through practices of the self, these practices are nevertheless not something invented by the individual himself. They are models that he finds in his culture and are proposed, suggested, imposed upon him by his culture, his society, and his social group" (Foucault 2003b:34). Such models for the fashioning of subjectivity do not, presumably, change overnight; in East Asia, as some anthropologists have argued, contemporary biopolitical approaches to the management of life seem to draw on long-standing models for the making of selves.[4] I now turn to an examination of the terrain of reproductive politics in Vietnam and the subjectivity templates conjured in this realm.

ENHANCING THE QUALITY OF THE PEOPLE: A TWENTY-FIRST CENTURY POLITICS OF LIFE

Over the two decades that I have worked in Vietnam, I have often been struck by the continuities that characterize political rhetoric in the realm of population governance: the norms advanced by party-state discourses in this biopolitical terrain seem surprisingly stable and constant.[5] The introduction of market economic reforms in 1986 entailed a return to the household as a primary economic unit, and with this followed a renewed political focus on the family and on women's roles as nurturers and family caretakers.[6] In the *đổi mới* era, party-state intentions to curb and control population growth therefore blended with new forms of governance that centered on the family and the household, encouraging citizens to invest pride, passion, and labor in families rather than in agricultural cooperatives or work units. Beginning in the late 1980s, large-scale national campaigns were launched in which new norms for family life were set forth: for the sake of children, family, and nation, citizens were told, childbearing must be kept within a two-child limit. During the family planning campaigns (*chiến dịch*) held at regular intervals, grassroots cadres encouraged (*động viên*) couples to accept the two-child family model, mobilizing (*vận động*) women to adopt a modern method of contraception, preferably an IUD.[7] Graphic images displayed on posters and billboards contrasted the plump and attractive children of small-size families to miserable children in rags growing up in large, poverty-ridden households. The "happy family" (*gia đình hạnh phúc*) was introduced as a social ideal for couples to emulate and became a key image in party-state development efforts.[8] Slogans painted on village walls and city billboards read "a happy family, a prosperous country" (*gia đình hạnh phúc, đất nước phồn vinh*), informing people that "family planning is the key to family happiness" (*kế hoạch hoá gia đình là chìa khóa của hạnh phúc gia đình*). In present-day Vietnam, official discourse continues to tie family and nation closely together, representing both as timeless and enduring communities of loyalty and shared responsibility. An article authored by the chairwoman of the Vietnam Commission for Population, Family, and Children, for instance, described the Vietnamese family: "In the consciousness of the Vietnamese nation, the family is always a sweet home, a primary environment in which virtues are born and nurtured and the Vietnamese personality created. The precious traditional values of the Vietnamese nation such as love for the country, solidarity, industriousness and creativeness at work, resilience, undauntedness in overcoming difficulties [and] trials have been kept up and developed by the Vietnamese family throughout the history of national construction and defense" (Lê Thị Thu 2004:4). At present, the small-size family model envisioned in official discourse seems to have been adopted by most Hanoian citizens in a manner that confirms Foucault's observations regarding the ability of governmentality schemes to blend seamlessly with common sense, becoming absorbed into people's everyday practices and self-understandings. Most couples now themselves take the initiative to limit the size of their families, reasoning—along the lines laid out in family planning rhetoric—that they cannot afford to raise more than two children.[9] Since party-state population control targets have by now been largely met, government attention is increasingly directed toward another field of vital politics: that of population quality.

The concept of population quality is, as shown in the previous chapter, ambiguous and multivocal. This overall ambiguity aside, however, the bodily quality of newborns is intensively problematized in Vietnam at present, and, as we have seen, much is being done to convince the country's citizens of the need to enhance the quality of reproduction. At the time of our fieldwork, most bookstores in Hanoi offered their customers several meters of shelves carrying handbooks on pregnancy and childcare, some written by Vietnamese authors, others translated from Chinese or English. These publications emphasized that proper pregnancy care is an essential precondition for normal fetal development, and that the prospective mother, more than any other person, carries the primary responsibility for pregnancy outcomes. One book, entitled *Pregnancy, Delivery, and Care for the Little One*, claimed: "For sure, mothers who lack the necessary knowledge and culture will not have enough insight into all the things necessary to ensure the birth of healthy children whose intellects develop well and as we want them to. Only by raising the levels of scientific knowledge of women who are preparing to become mothers can we ensure that children are born healthy and intelligent and that they are raised to become useful people who can meet the requirements of a civilized and modern society" (Nguyễn Văn Đức et al. 2003:61). In publications such as this, the risk of birth defects was a prominent topic. To ensure that children were born healthy and normal, pregnant women were cautioned not to drink Coca-Cola, to stay indoors during cold weather, to avoid watching television, and to always feel happy. The public health messages that abounded in the mass media made similar points: public service announcements broadcast at prime time, for instance, showed images of children born severely disabled, encouraging women to obtain rubella vaccinations and regular antenatal care.[10]

At first glance, then, these biopolitical discourses seem to offer a perfect illustration of the responsibilization processes discussed by governmentality scholars. But a closer inspection, I contend, reveals that Vietnamese discourses of reproductive responsibility unfold in ways that differ significantly from those observed in advanced liberal societies. Rather than encouraging women to fulfill themselves through their own free choices, party-state discourses in Vietnam define child health and normality as an unambiguous political objective and a shared public value, as a goal that all citizens—as members of this national collective—are obliged to pursue. In other words, although discourses of responsibility seem to figure as prominently in reproductive politics in Vietnam as they do in many Western societies, these discourses are configured in locally specific ways. In Hanoi, concepts of responsibility are articulated as elements in discourses that center on national belonging and social obligations, while notions of individual autonomy, choice, and freedom seem to play less prominent roles.

In Foucault's terminology, "modes of subjectivation" (*modes d'assujettissement*) refer to the ways in which "people are invited or incited to recognize their moral obligations" (Foucault 2003a:111). During fieldwork in Hanoi I often noticed that when people were encouraged to accept certain moral obligations, such as the duty to produce healthy and normal children, the national past was routinely evoked. Three particular pasts were often projected: a mythic past of shared biology, a socialist past of collective struggles, and a wartime past of shared injustice.[11] Each of these pasts had significant implications for the ways in which subjectivities were imagined and fashioned in the realm of selective reproduction. Out of the mythic past of shared biology emerged biologized subjects of kinship connection; the socialist past generated national subjects of collectivity and shared struggle; and the wartime past produced present-day subjectivities of compassion and shared emotion.

A MYTHIC PAST: BIOLOGIZED NATIONAL SUBJECTS

When state officials in Vietnam call on citizens to make use of new technologies for prenatal screening, the biological metaphor of the national stock (*giống nòi*) is often invoked. Enhancement of the population's physical strength is, officials claim, vitally important for the realization of national development potential. In contemporary political discourse, in other words, "the nation" is tied closely to "the stock." This bionationalist framing of the links between individual and social bodies is not new: in the Declaration of the foundation of the new Democratic Republic of Vietnam, which Hồ Chí Minh read aloud in Ba Đình square in September 1945, the denunciation of the French colonizers included a sharp critique of their attempts to weaken the Vietnamese people's race or stock (*làm cho nòi giống ta suy nhược*):

> Throughout the last eighty years, the French imperialists, abusing the principles of "freedom, equality and fraternity," have violated the integrity of our ancestral land and oppressed our countrymen. Their deeds run counter to the ideals of humanity and justice.
>
> In the political field, they have denied us every freedom. They have enforced upon us inhuman laws. They have set up three different political regimes in Northern, Central and Southern Vietnam (Tonkin, Annam, and Cochinchina) in an attempt to disrupt our national, historical, and ethnical unity.
>
> They have built more prisons than schools. They have callously ill-treated our fellow-compatriots. They have drowned our revolutions in blood.
>
> They have sought to stifle public opinion and pursued a policy of obscurantism on the largest scale; they have forced upon us alcohol and opium in order to weaken our race.
>
> In the economic field, they have shamelessly exploited our people, driven them into the worst misery and mercilessly plundered our country.
>
> They have ruthlessly appropriated our rice fields, mines, forests, and raw materials. They have arrogated to themselves the privilege of issuing banknotes, and monopolised all our external commerce. They have imposed hundreds of unjustifiable taxes, and reduced our countrymen, especially the peasants and petty tradesmen, to extreme poverty.
>
> They have prevented the development of native capital enterprises; they have exploited our workers in the most barbarous manner.[12]

During anticolonial struggles, revolutionary nationalists made intensive efforts to encourage citizens to place love of the nation over other commitments and loyalties, including attachments to the patriarchal family (cf. Phinney 2008). One of them, Phan Bội Châu (1867–1940), suggested that if girls were asked, "Do you have a husband yet?" they should reply, "Yes, his surname is Việt and his given name Nam," thereby stressing their devotion and attachment to the nation. Somewhat ironically, however, revolutionary nationalists imagined the nation as an extended family, and images drawn from biological kinship were routinely used in anticolonial mobilization. Using the term *đồng bào* (lit., children of one womb) to describe compatriots, for instance, Phan Bội Châu urged Vietnam's people to stand united against the French colonizers. Similarly, characterizing himself as Uncle (*bác*) Hồ and addressing people with intimate kinship terms such as "dear brothers and sisters" (*anh chị em yêu quí*), Hồ Chí Minh spoke of the Vietnamese people as children of one family/home (*con của một nhà*).[13] In a 1955 address to the National Conference of Health Care Cadres, Hồ encouraged health care workers to feel compassion for their patients, considering them as "brothers and sisters of the same flesh as you" (*anh em ruột thịt của mình*).[14] The moral dictum "A good doctor must be like a loving mother" (*Lương y như từ mẫu*), which Tuyết's mother cited (quoted in the prologue of this book), is also ascribed to Hồ Chí Minh. Like many other political metaphors, this dictum places officials and cadres, including the health workers who enlist people in state-led projects of health care and population control, in a family-like relation to the people they target.

In present-day state discourse, narratives of reproduction and biological continuity over time continue to play key roles when the nation is imagined. Vietnam's origin myth, for instance, which is often reiterated in official rhetoric, defines national belonging as a question of shared ancestry, drawing a continuous line between the nation's ancestors and its contemporary citizens. This myth traces the nation's roots to the marriage between the dragon father Lạc Long Quân and the mountain fairy mother Âu Cơ. This union produced an egg sac out of which hatched one hundred human children, of whom fifty went to live in the mountains and fifty by the sea. One of them became the first of the Hùng kings, the royal dynasty officially celebrated as having founded the Vietnamese nation. This shared ancestry, official writings maintain, has produced the strong community spirit (*tinh thần cộng đồng*) that characterizes Vietnam's people. In an article entitled "Searching for the

Characteristics of the Traditional Vietnamese Family," for instance, the sociologist Đặng Cảnh Khanh (2009:132–133) states:

> Respect for communal life is not a characteristic possessed by Vietnamese society alone. But few other peoples in the world consider communal welfare to be the primary and highest standard of morality, as the principle law of existence for all individuals, all families, and the entire people. Knowledge of Lạc Long Quân and Âu Cơ teaches us that all members of our people were born from one original and single embryo, from one hundred eggs. . . . Therefore, we can say that the basic character of the Vietnamese people is the communal character (*nhân cách cộng đồng*). In relations between individual and society, the highest principle is that the individual must submit to the community.

In contemporary political imagery, nation and family merge: the term for nation, *quốc gia*, is a compound of the terms country (*quốc*) and family (*gia*); the word *dân tộc*, which can be translated as "people" or "ethnos," consists of the terms for people (*dân*) and family/clan (*tộc*); the term for fatherland, *tổ quốc*, refers to ancestors (*tổ*) and country; and the term for state (*nhà nước*) combines "house" and "country." By modeling the nation on kin relations, then, the state defines citizenship as a matter of physical intimacy, affective attachment, and communal belonging. This belonging is accorded spiritual connotations: in daily life and political discourse, childbearing is often defined as a sacred (*thiêng liêng*) endeavor or a heavenly mandate (*thiên chức*). By bearing children, this language suggests, one unites oneself with a larger universe, transcending the physical boundaries of the individual body and the time limits of individual existence. Translating the term *giống nòi*—which is usually translated as "race" or "stock"—as "the refined seeds of life," the philosopher Chánh Công Phan (1993:174) argues that procreative sex is held to be sacred in Vietnamese cultural tradition because it ties individuals into larger collectives: "The biological perpetuation of one's family line, which presupposes that of one's clan, and one's whole nation, is thus held to be spiritually sacred in one's own erotically ritualistic act of onto-biological procreation which is also popularly called 'performing the đạo of Heaven and Earth' (làm cái đạo Trời Đất)." Procreative sexual acts become, in this rendition, ways in which people enact and embody spiritual belonging to families, kin groups, and the nation.

Drawing on images of intimate family life, then, official notions of nationhood offer promises of protection, significance, and continuity, conjuring ideas of belonging that transcend individual lives and offer people a sense of solidarity with others. This grounding of individual existence within larger communities of being hinges on reproductive biology: it is through the bearing of children, official rhetoric states, that individuals tie themselves into families, kin groups, and the nation. Men's contributions to reproduction inhere in the seed (*giống*) they provide: among Vietnam's ethnic majority Kinh people, prescribed kinship is patrilineal and patrilocal, and the genealogical line (*giống nòi*) that ties together ancestors and descendants is assumed to run through men only (see chapter 3).[15] Without sons, therefore, family lines will perish.[16] Male seeds are, however, carried and nourished in female wombs, and, in day-to-day lives as well as in official discourse, gestation is defined as the crux of kin relatedness; it is through the nurturance offered by female bodies that families, lineages, and nation are generated and sustained.[17] In contemporary state discourse, motherhood is celebrated as *the* female duty par excellence; although the veneration of mothers is not new, political attention to maternity does seem to have intensified since the country's 1986 shift toward a market economy. Party-state rhetoric represents mothers as key providers of life, love, and nurturance; they not only reproduce the country's citizens but also safeguard its most sacred values of intergenerational intimacy, community coherence, and spiritual belonging. In an era when people's access to high-tech medicine is rapidly expanding, maternal obligations seem to take new forms, being extended to include the duty to make use of new technologies of pregnancy. An article in the online version of the official journal *Health and Life,* for instance, encouraged expectant mothers to obtain rubella vaccinations: "In physiological life, the creator has given the female sex an extremely miraculous mandate: the heavenly mandate of becoming a mother, of bearing a fetus for nine months and ten days, of giving birth to healthy and intelligent children. . . . However, quite a large number of couples are unlucky, and at birth, their children suffer from congenital disabilities that place burdens on family and society" (Trần Quốc Long 2009).

In sum, at issue in discussions of population quality are not only economic development and WTO membership but also the making and remaking of the Vietnamese nation as a biological community of intimately related individuals. When officials promote new technologies for prenatal screening, they not only define the nation's women as self-responsible subjects; they also tell them that by bearing children, they place themselves and their offspring within a larger familial community of ancestors and descendants, turning themselves into members of a close-knit sociobiological collective that stretches far back in time and continues into the future. While these biologized national subjects are conjured against the background of a perennial and mythic past, in their calls on women, state officials also draw on long-standing templates for a Vietnamese socialist subjectivity.

A REVOLUTIONARY PAST: SUBJECTS OF SOCIALIST STRUGGLE

In Vietnam, 1945 and 1954 were watershed years. With the 1945 August Revolution, the new Democratic Republic of Vietnam was founded, and following the French defeat in 1954, Hồ Chí Minh's government took control of the northern part of the country. As part of their efforts to establish a new social order, socialist revolutionaries mobilized citizens to join new political organizations and replaced family-based ownership systems with agricultural cooperatives and state-run enterprises. Among the first political steps taken by the socialist government after the revolution was the implementation of land reforms that aimed to redistribute land and property more equitably to villagers and to transfer economic and political power from kin groups to the state. Nationwide mobilization campaigns or movements (*phong trào*) were carried out that aimed to institute collective ownership, increase production, enhance health, abolish feudal and superstitious ritual practices, and promote literacy. The 1959 Law of Marriage and the Family outlawed polygamy, child marriage, and forced marriage, thereby aiming to replace the patriarchal family with family structures that supported the emancipation of women and the abolishment of private property. In the new collective morality set out by the socialist government, gender equality (*bình đẳng nam nữ*) took center stage. By taking part in public acts of community and nation building, women were to achieve social and economic equality with men and shift their loyalties from the patriarchal family to larger collectives.

The ethical regime imparted by the new socialist government included particular subjectivity templates. Criticizing the colonial moral order, Hồ Chí Minh wrote numerous treatises on the new revolutionary morality (*đạo đức cách mạng*) that was to guide the building of a socialist society. A theme that ran through these writings was that of collectivity (*tập thể*) or community (*đoàn thể*) versus individualism (*chủ nghĩa cá nhân*). Hồ encouraged people to place collective interests before individual ones, defining individualism as an enemy of socialism and emphasizing that "everyone must know how to care for that which is of the collective, and must carry out the work of the collective, just as they take care of the affairs of their family."[18] The new collectivist norms for human conduct were explicitly gendered: while insisting on women's equality with men in the public sphere, officials also defined a specific female morality, underscoring women's special responsibilities for the collectives they were part of. Selflessness, endurance, and compassion were defined as natural female virtues, and national campaigns such as the Five Goods campaign (1961–1965) and the Three Responsibilities movement (1965–1975) encouraged women to take "responsibility for production and work, responsibility for the family, responsibility for national defense."

In contemporary political narratives, the colonial era that gave rise to the revolutionary movement is depicted as a time of callous economic exploitation, an era of excessive political injustices that denied native citizens the rights and privileges enjoyed by their colonizers. The anticolonial movement that brought the Communist Party into power was, these stories emphasize, driven by a collective vision of another kind of society: one of humanity, justice, and equality. Animating the revolutionary movement was, according to Nguyễn Văn Huyền (2004), Vietnam's former minister of education, a profoundly humanitarian vision: ultimately, this was a struggle for justice and dignity and for the sacred goal of enabling human beings to lead fully human lives. When people in present-day Hanoi talk about the legacy of Hồ Chí Minh, they often cite a statement made by the late president in 1946: "I have only one desire, a most profound desire; that is how to make our country entirely independent, our people entirely free, and ensure that everyone has rice to eat, clothes to wear, and that all are able to receive an education."[19]

When studying population policy documents, I have often noticed the close rhetorical parallels between present-day discourse on population quality and the welfare ambitions set out by Hồ Chí Minh. Seeking to capture the elusive concept of population quality, for instance, one government document points to factors that bear striking resemblance to long-standing socialist development goals: "It is very complicated and difficult to measure and assess population quality. But its characteristics can be divided into five groups: (1) income and welfare; (2) health and nutrition; (3) education and intellectual development; (4) cultural and spiritual recreation; (5) living environment" (Ủy Ban Dân Số, Gia Đình và Trẻ Em 2003:131). A Ministry of Health document describes the government's efforts to improve population quality as a direct extension of previous struggles for national development:

Enhancement of population quality is "a basic state policy that aims to develop the country." . . . Consider again the road toward establishing, building, and defending the country through the revolution to abolish feudal and colonialist rule; to give back the land to farmers; to drive out the enemies that are hunger, ignorance, and illness; to liberate the people, unify the country, and conduct the process of renovation. We have taken this long, difficult road of adversity and suffering in order to build an independent, democratic, wealthy, equitable, and civilized Vietnam. (Bộ Y Tế 2008:5–6)

Anthropologists who have studied China have often linked the concept of population quality to the shift from Maoist mass-line socialism to capitalism and neoliberal forms of governance.[20] Like these scholars, Vietnamese government officials draw direct links between efforts to enhance population quality and the formation of a particular kind of society; but they do so through explicit critiques of neoliberal development models. As framed in official rhetoric, the society that today's policy makers envisage is one that continues the country's proud socialist traditions and emphasizes collective welfare. Vietnam's market economy with a socialist orientation (*nền kinh tế thị trường định hướng xã hội chủ nghĩa*), officials contend, aims to create a society based on humanity and morality (*tính nhân văn, nhân bản, đạo đức*), as opposed to "the primitive market economy that is simple, barbarous, and in which the bigger fish swallow up the small" (Nguyễn Quốc Triệu 2009:11). In a publication on population quality, a senior official deployed the notion of equity (*công bằng xã hội*) as a marker of moral difference between a socialist and a neoliberal market economy: "The division between rich and poor is concrete and vivid evidence of a poor population quality. Actual developments in countries that follow economic models of a free market economy, the prime example being the United States, show that efforts to develop the economy by sacrificing the common good of the majority of people have led to a series of difficult cultural and social problems" (Trần Thị Trung Chiến 2005:48). Framed in these terms, efforts to enhance population quality represent a twenty-first-century version of long-standing socialist struggles for an equitable and welfarist society in which the common good of the majority of people is placed at the heart of development efforts. The aim remains, officials claim, to ensure that "everyone has rice to eat, clothes to wear, and that all are able to receive an education." To offer people better health care and education, a stronger national economy is required; yet economic competitiveness and growth can be attained only if the workforce is healthy and well educated. In official rhetoric, in other words, attempts to raise population quality are linked to what party-state officials define as a key political challenge in the renovation era—namely, how to achieve economic growth while also ensuring social inclusion and equity.[21] To realize the nation's development potential, officials argue, the health of the country's children must be enhanced; reproductive health care therefore has a distinctly societal character (*mang tính xã hội*) (Hà Anh 2009:6). At stake, people are told, is not only the health of individual children but also the welfare of the larger social collectives into which they are born. In a conference presentation on the use of pre- and neonatal screening as a means to enhance population quality, Dr. Hoàn, a pediatrician at the National Hospital of Pediatrics, summed up this effort: "Population quality is an issue of prime importance in countries across the world. The aim is to ensure that children are born entirely healthy, intelligent, and normal in terms of mental and physical development, so that they can become citizens who are useful for society and family" (Nguyễn Thị Hoàn 2006:84).

This project of population enhancement, as we saw in the previous chapter, acquires increased urgency at a time when the long-term consequences of wartime herbicide spraying are at the forefront of public attention. At present, officials underscore, the social body is under threat, and there is, yet again, a need to stand united against the dangers facing the nation. In an article published in the state-run journal *Population and Development* in 2001, three physicians drew readers' attention to the intergenerational transmission of dioxin-related problems: "The war against the U.S. ended more than a quarter of a century ago. But we do not know when the long-term consequences of chemical warfare will end. . . . Chemical warfare has placed a considerable burden on Vietnamese society because three generations are affected" (Hoàng Đình Cầu et al. 2001:7–8). Discussing what means are available to remedy this situation, the authors concluded that not only the direct victims of Agent Orange but all the nation's citizens must be involved in "the social work of maternity (*công tác thai sản*)": "To reduce the percentage of children born with congenital malformations, all women should regularly go to the centers for reproductive health counseling, taking more initiative in maternity work."

In this political framing, the nation is, once again, portrayed as a homogeneous collective of biologically related individuals, and new technologies for selective reproduction are presented as elements in another collectivist movement aimed at the creation of a better society. The idea of society as a single, unified domain is repeated and reinforced, and as citizen-subjects, people are placed under the obligation to participate in social programs aimed at its development. Seen from this perspective, using selective reproductive technologies becomes a way of contributing to long-standing collective struggles for a better society, and a means of enacting and affirming national and communal belonging.

THE WARTIME PAST: SUBJECTS OF SUFFERING AND COMPASSION

In Hanoi today, the war against the United States and its South Vietnamese allies is commemorated in numerous ways. In museum exhibits, in films and novels, in newspapers and television programs, citizens are reminded of the war and the losses and sacrifices it entailed. In these acts of commemoration, some things are remembered with pride: the heroism, the collectivity, and the victory that brought the fighting to an end. Yet other aspects of this war-torn past are more unsettling—and particularly so are those experiences that refuse to remain in the past and that seep into and disturb the present. In the words of women's studies professor Lê Thi (2007:47): "Although the Vietnamese have done all they can to forget the past of war, hundreds of thousands of victims of Agent Orange are reminding us of the past of this horrible war, in which women and children are the worst hit."

During fieldwork, I noticed that in public discourse the Agent Orange issue was framed in two different, but co-constitutive languages. On the one hand, Agent Orange was represented as a matter of human rights and global justice. U.S. manufacturers and government administration, this discourse insisted, must take responsibility for wartime damage, compensating victims and cleaning up polluted environments. These demands were set forth with particular vigor by nongovernmental organizations (see chapter 1). In the domain of reproduction, for instance, the Research Center for Gender, Family, and Environment in Development (CGFED) defined Agent Orange as a human rights question: "Reproductive rights, human rights, and children's rights are being violated. . . . For the sake of peace and justice, for the human rights of men, women and children, we support the victims of Agent Orange/dioxin in their lawsuit against the American chemical companies" (CGFED n.d.). At the same time as it was defined as an international justice-and-rights issue, Agent Orange was also framed as a national humanitarian problem, as a human crisis that placed moral demands on all Vietnamese citizens. If the United States denies its responsibility and justice cannot be attained, this framing of the problem suggested, then Vietnamese citizens must step in, offering moral support and financial assistance; although the government of Vietnam offers some support for victims, much more is needed. This definition of the Agent Orange issue as a national humanitarian emergency has, I contend, turned the chemical into an important site of subjectivity-making in Vietnam.[22]

What is Agent Orange? asks Diane Fox (2003:73–74). She replies by pointing to the many different ways in which this problem is articulated in Vietnam:

> At times, it is a code name for a chemical, at times, a metonym for TCDD dioxin, or a generic term for all the chemicals used during the war in Vietnam, or a synecdoche for all the environmental damage that lingers from that war, or even more globally, for the consequences of war. At other times, it is the name of an illness: "My uncle's daughter is suffering from Agent Orange"; or "I know a man who can cure Agent Orange." In some popular uses it seems to serve as a synonym for "birth defect." The disabilities associated with it are sometimes taken as a sign of the workings of the law of karma, or of the hand of fate.

In addition to all this, Agent Orange is also a national political project and a terrain where subjectivities are forged. In Vietnam, the present-day politics of Agent Orange has at least three interrelated dimensions. First, it is a project of *moral recognition*. In a situation where U.S. authorities claim that scientific proof of the damage inflicted on Vietnam's population is lacking, Agent Orange images and narratives offer another kind of evidence, articulating the pain and acknowledging the plight of victims. Seen in this perspective, Agent Orange narratives constitute demands for moral acknowledgment in a context of U.S. denials of responsibility. Second, Agent Orange is a political project of *solidarity*. During our fieldwork, many newspapers ran special Agent Orange columns, offering moving portraits of Agent Orange families and collecting funds to assist them. Since no U.S. compensation has been granted to victims in Vietnam, and since the financial support that the Vietnamese government can offer this group of citizens is limited, television programs, newspaper stories, and research reports often form part of nationwide efforts to raise funds for victims. Third, Agent Orange is a project of *collectivity and national unity*. The Second Indochina War was divisive, tearing apart both individual bodies and the social body.[23] Agent Orange, in contrast, unites the nation in suffering that cuts across former military and political divides: although herbicides were sprayed only in the south, the exposed individuals include both southerners and soldiers from the North Vietnamese army. In the words of Vietnamese professor Khổng Diễn (2006:75): "Agent Orange/dioxin victims in Vietnam are not only from the Kinh but also ethnic minority groups. . . . They are not only those who were from the revolutionary armed forces but also civilians and personnel of the former Saigon puppet army and administration. . . . Agent Orange/dioxin victims are not only in southern provinces and cities but also in all northern provinces and cities." Paradoxically, therefore, the chemical to which such gruesome bodily damage is attributed promises to have healing social and political effects. Agent Orange ties together the nation in shared pain, a pain felt not only by the victims themselves but also by their compatriots. In this sharing of emotion, mass-mediated images play a significant role.

On January 7, 2005, over a cup of coffee in a café near Hanoi National University, my colleague Kiên handed me a videotape. In conducting the mass media component of our research, Kiên was collecting newspaper articles and television programs about pregnancy, prenatal screening, and disability. The evening before, he had recorded a live TV show featuring Agent Orange victims. Broadcast in an effort to raise money for victims, the show was entitled *Chung ta không vô cảm* (We are not without feelings). Kiên urged me to watch it as soon as I got home. "It is so sad to witness the plight of these people," he said, "last night, I spent the entire evening crying in front of the television." Kiên was probably not the only person crying in front of the television screen that evening. As Lori Allen argues in the context of the Israeli-Palestinian conflict, visual images have a powerful capacity to engage our passions; images afford sensual rather than cognitive forms of communication, creating "a sense of immediacy through the joining of emotion and objectivity, which occurs formally through realist, photographic images, as well as through affect-laden narrations and displays of destroyed bodies" (Allen 2009:172).[24] The mass media are, as Asad (2003:5) observes, not simply the means through which people come to imagine their worlds; "they *mediate* that imagination, construct the sensibilities that underpin it" (emphasis in original). In Hanoi, as Kiên's words suggested, images of Agent Orange victims often seemed to grip people in other and more immediate ways than words did. In publications on Agent Orange produced by researchers, journalists, and advocacy organizations, images of victims were always prominently placed. These accounts were accompanied by unsettling photographs of children with strangely malformed bodies, grieving parents, and worn-out grandparents. Through these images, Agent Orange has, as D. Fox (2007:253) notes, become a symbol of the suffering of innocents, "suffering that is intensified and perpetuated by the refusal of those who caused the suffering to take responsibility for their actions." In Vietnam, I contend, an important political effect of this display of unsettling images was the formation of a national subject united in collectively felt emotions of sadness, solidarity, and sympathy, in a joint conviction that something must be done.

In short, the politics of Agent Orange offers another example of the point that I make throughout this chapter: that twenty-first-century biopolitics can be associated with forms of subjectivity other than those commonly characterized as neoliberal. When high-ranking officials such as Dr. Trọng placed demands on prospective parents to contribute to collective national projects by making use of new biomedical technologies for reproductive selection, they also invited people to turn themselves into particular kinds of subjects. Yet the subjects these officials envisioned differed markedly from those projected by neoliberal imaginings: as the admonitions of this state official suggest, contemporary politics of subjectivity may work in ways that place individual actions and choices within a larger frame of communal attachments and obligations, thereby infusing notions of responsibility with more collectivist values and assumptions. These assumptions arise from the past: in official discourse, the national past—be it primordial and mythic, socialist, or tied up with the war—is evoked in ways that define subjectivity in terms of compassion, shared fates, physical intimacy, and communal belonging. In the realm of reproduction and beyond, state discourses stress the unity of the nation and its people, reminding citizens of their debts, obligations, and emotional attachments to the collectives they are part of. Individuals are enjoined to see themselves, above all, as socially responsible beings: as members of families toward which they have duties, and as citizens of a nation-state to which they owe respect and commitment. In Vietnamese government discourse, then, rather than being positioned vis-à-vis each other in freedom and independence, individuals are depicted as organically related social beings tied together through mutual commitments and blood-based obligations.

It is important to note, however, that although state discourses place demands on citizens to turn themselves into certain kinds of subjects, this does not ensure that people actually assume and accept these demands, nor does it explain through what social processes it becomes meaningful for people to align themselves with the expectations that state authorities place on them. Policy and subjectivity do not stand in any simple or unmediated relationship (cf. Kipnis 2011). In the following chapter I begin my ethnographic investigation of the ways in which physicians and prospective parents in Hanoi framed and handled questions of selective reproduction, thereby also, directly or indirectly, responding to the state's mobilization efforts.

CHAPTER 3

Precarious Maternal Belonging

> I think that in order to live, a child must be complete (*lành lặn*) like other children. If the child simply lies there, or sits there, or does not understand anything . . . then it means a lot of suffering (*khổ lắm*). Then it is better to be brutal right from the beginning. Of course, that will be very painful. But I still think it is better than letting the child live. It will lead a life of suffering. The child is the one who will suffer most. As a mother, you live only for a short while and then you die, but the child will suffer for much longer.

When we first met, on March 17, 2004, Oanh was twenty-nine years old and five months pregnant. Sitting on one of the blue plastic chairs lining the wall in the 3D scanning room, she folded her arms around her belly in the protective gesture that I had seen so many other women use. In a low voice, she said: "I had a cold when I was two months pregnant, so I considered having an abortion. I don't know what I would do if this child were not normal. . . . I so much want to erase this picture of a disabled child from my mind, but I can't." Like many other women that I met, Oanh looked forward to the birth of her child with joy and happy anticipation, but she also struggled with dark thoughts of how this pregnancy might end if her fetus did not develop as hoped for. During fieldwork, I heard many other women express similar anxieties; among people in Hanoi, it was generally taken for granted that a maternal cold could pose serious risks to fetal development, including physical or cognitive disabilities.[1]

In this chapter I explore Vietnamese women's experiences of obstetrical ultrasound scanning, focusing particularly on the ways in which this technology comes to operate as a site for the formation of ethical subjectivity. I begin with Oanh's story. In many respects, her predicament—the intense emotions she invested in her fetus, the anxious pregnancy care she undertook, her relatives' active involvement in her pregnancy, her eager use of prenatal screening, and her readiness to give up her fetus if it turned out anomalous—resembled the situation of many other women that I came to know in the course of this research. Hanoian women's pregnancy care practices were, I suggest, quests for identity and belonging; by caring meticulously for their pregnancies, they strove to gain socially valorized positions as mothers and citizens. The image of the fetus on the monitor in the 3D scanning room offered a glimpse of what pregnant women hoped awaited them: a culturally celebrated status as a loving and caring mother, a position as someone who belongs—with her child, her husband, her family, and her community. In the final part of the chapter, I show how prenatal screening, at the same time as it intensified them, also complicated these processes of identity-making and attachment. By confronting women with the hypothetical possibility that they might have to give up their fetuses, the biomedical practices by which they strove for belonging also threatened, paradoxically, to undermine this endeavor, bringing attachments into question and raising moral doubts about what maternal responsibility means and entails.

OANH

On October 5, 2004, Toàn picked me up on her motorbike, and we went to visit Oanh in her home. She lived in a two-story house located on a busy, dusty street on the banks of the Tô Lịch river. When we arrived, Oanh's husband received us at the door and helped Toàn to push her motorbike into the corridor. The apartment consisted of one room, sparsely furnished with a large wooden bed, a table, a television, and a gas stove in the corner. The floor tiles were cracked in the corners, and the faded green paint on the walls was stained from the damp. Even though the doors and windows were tightly shut, the noise from the traffic outside was overwhelming. Oanh's husband served us tea, then left, leaving the conversation to his wife. We sat on the large bed where

Oanh's baby daughter was fast asleep under a quilted blanket. Over the bed was a poster-size photograph of a chubby toddler with dimples.

With her full cheeks, lively eyes, and sports T-shirt and sneakers, Oanh looked younger than her twenty-nine years. But she engaged with us in the bold and confident manner that often came with successful motherhood. Knowing that we had come to talk about ultrasonography, she pointed to the photograph on the wall and said, "That's my son when he was little. When I was pregnant with him, I had only one scan during the entire pregnancy." "How many did you have this time?" I asked, nodding at her sleeping daughter. Oanh replied by describing the vulnerability she had felt during this pregnancy: "I had a cold early in my pregnancy. I did not have fever, but it was a really nasty cold, and I had to stay in bed for more than a week. Viruses are dangerous during pregnancy, so afterward I felt very burdened and worried. . . . So I had a lot of scans, perhaps fifteen or sixteen in all. I felt anxious and I wanted to see if my fetus had all its limbs or not. I decided that if it were not normal, I would have to give it up."

In her family and neighborhood everyone had encouraged Oanh to terminate the pregnancy, arguing that her cold might have harmed the fetus. Her husband and mother-in-law were particularly adamant, insisting that she could always get pregnant again later. Oanh shared their concerns: "If one has a mild cold, the child may be born with a cleft lip. If the cold is more severe, its limbs may not be normal, and in severe cases, its brain will be damaged. So I was very scared." Feeling attached to her fetus, however, Oanh eventually decided to disregard the advice she received. Instead of opting for an abortion immediately, she planned to have a detailed 3D scan done when she was four months pregnant. "I was gambling," she said. "Either I would have a decent (tử tế) child, or I would have to have an abortion. I thought my chances were fifty-fifty."[2]

Throughout her entire pregnancy, Oanh strove hard to protect the fetus growing inside her. She washed their vegetables more carefully than usual, dressed in warmer clothes, and rested more. When she needed to go somewhere, her husband would drive her on their motorbike rather than letting her drive it herself as she used to. She often looked at the large photograph of her son over their bed, hoping that her daughter would be born as healthy and complete (lành lặn) as him, that she would escape disease and disability. As in her first pregnancy, her mother-in-law would often come by, eager to help with her daily chores. Oanh appreciated her help, but she also felt that she was watching her, ready to judge and comment on everything she did. Her mother-in-law's supervision had, she said, been even more intense when she was pregnant with her first child. Until her son was born, her husband's siblings and parents had watched her closely, explicitly comparing her to the wives of his younger brothers—who had both given birth to healthy sons—and expressing doubts about her reproductive capacities. Her husband was the eldest of three brothers, so his son would be carrying on their family line. As a new daughter-in-law, Oanh felt, being accepted into this family hinged on her ability to produce two healthy and normal children of whom at least one was male: "If I had given birth only to girls, for sure there would have been a lot of complications with my husband's family," she said. "And if my daughter had not been normal, there would have been a lot of dissatisfaction in the family too." Oanh felt intensely happy and proud, therefore, when she brought home the 3D scanning image of her daughter: "When I came home, we all felt so happy (*mừng*), my husband and I, his family and mine. Our parents were so happy, oh, they were so very happy, and my husband and I were too." On that day, Oanh felt immensely relieved—to know that her fetus was developing normally, and to know that the lonely decision she had made seemed to have been the right one.

MORAL MOTHERHOODS: PRACTICING PROPER PREGNANCY CARE

Across the globe, ultrasonography has become an increasingly routinized antenatal care technology and an integral part of women's embodied experience of pregnancy. When women are offered an ultrasound scan, they rarely decline; and in many health care settings, ultrasounds are fervently used.[3] How can we account for the apparent appeal of this technology? What motivates women around the world to embrace it with such zeal? Previous studies suggest that women themselves tend to give three main answers to this question. First, many women indicate that they are eager to meet their baby, and the visual encounter with the fetus often predates other and more tactile confirmations of pregnancy, such as quickening. Second, prospective mothers want to ensure that their child-to-be is healthy and normal. Third, many women say that they simply do what others do, regarding ultrasonography as a routine part of pregnancy care.[4] In most settings, moreover, women's use of ultrasonography is embedded in a social environment in which the responsibility for reproduction lies firmly with the mother. Ethnographic studies conducted in a variety of different countries—ranging from the United States, Canada, Greece, and Israel to Ecuador, China, and Vietnam—show that the production of new persons is practically always considered a woman's responsibility.[5] Across the world, it seems, prospective mothers are held personally responsible for the outcomes of their pregnancies, and many resort to biomedical technologies that appear to offer help in this endeavor. The use of ultrasound scanning then comes to be considered as one way in which a woman can protect her pregnancy, turning herself into a good and responsible mother.

In the pregnancy stories that women in Hanoi told me, ultrasonography was merely one in a range of actions that they undertook in the hope of having a healthy child. Often, their elders admonished them to remember the old pregnancy precautions (kiêng) that are part of Vietnamese cultural tradition. These tell women, for instance, to avoid eating snails for fear that the child will drool, to avoid eating crabs to prevent breach births, to avoid attending weddings lest their child grow up lacking charm (vô duyên), and to avoid funerals, which are considered cold and dangerous for pregnant women. Such long-standing pregnancy taboos have now been supplemented by new biomedically based precautions that are advanced through the mass media and pregnancy handbooks. Some women insisted that they regarded their elders' pregnancy advice as mere superstition, but most said that they strove to strike a balance between old and new pregnancy care demands, taking both into consideration. This turned their daily lives into a careful balancing act: most women would engage in a meticulous process of self-supervision while they were pregnant, carefully monitoring their sleep, diets, moods, and physical movements. When pregnant, they asserted, one must be on guard (có thai thì phải giữ).

Feminist researchers have drawn attention to the risk discourses that surround pregnancies in the Western world; the anxieties that accompany childbearing have, these scholars suggest, intensified in the current era of high-tech medicine and increased pregnancy surveillance.[6] In Hanoi, I found such discourses of risk to be a permanent and pressing part of women's pregnancy experiences. In their day-to-day lives, pregnant women were incessantly reminded of the need to be careful and vigilant. On television, public service announcements called on them to remember their rubella vaccinations; mothers-in-law admonished them not to attend funerals or weddings; colleagues warned them of the fetal damage that too much work can cause; and husbands reminded them to eat a varied diet and get enough sleep. There seemed very little doubt about what constituted morally proper maternal behavior. During pregnancy, everyone seemed to agree, a woman should be mentally calm and balanced; avoid upsetting sensory experiences; eat a nourishing and varied diet; get plenty of sleep and rest; avoid exposure to wind, cold, and infections; and get regular medical checkups. By making repeated use of ultrasonography during her pregnancy, Oanh, then, was seeking to do everything right so as to produce a child that lived up to her own and others' expectations—a child who was healthy and complete. Like her, practically all the pregnant women I met expressed an intense sense of responsibility for the child they expected. When Chi asked Hiền, for instance, about the family's role in pregnancy care, she responded: "Of course the family is important. But I think the most important person is oneself. One must be determined to eat well, starting from the time when the child is still only an embryo. The moment at which the first cells form is particularly important for the brain and the health of the child. If one does not eat well, one will regret it later." If their child did not turn out as they hoped, women suggested, this would throw their lives off track socially, emotionally, economically, and existentially. When childbearing goes awry, their own and others' experiences told them, this has far-ranging consequences for the life of the mother, threatening to render her already vulnerable position in her family and kin group even more precarious.

HAPPY FAMILIES AND DEMANDING MOTHERHOODS: SUBDUED MORAL COSMOLOGIES

In Hanoi and nearby provinces, prescribed kinship is patrilineal and patrilocal.[7] Only men, people hold, can continue the family line (dòng họ); children are defined as belonging to their father's kin group, and upon marriage, a couple will usually reside with or close to the husband's family, supporting his parents in their old age and taking responsibility for ancestor worship. Kin relations are often described using spatial metaphors: the husband's relatives are called inside kin (họ nội), whereas the wife's side of the family is characterized as outside kin (họ ngoại). When a woman gets married, she achieves a new, and often highly vulnerable, social position as the daughter-in-law (con dâu) in her husband's household. Being new to this family, she has to prove her worth by behaving well and working hard, and by producing the heir who will carry on the patrilineage. Giving birth to a child, and preferably a son, therefore, secures a woman's position in her new family. Like Oanh, many of the women I met described in vivid terms how they felt that their membership in local communities of family and kin depended on their reproductive accomplishments. Their day-to-day lives were, they indicated, suffused by normative demands that defined successful childbearing as a key precondition for social belonging: a woman's entire social being hinged on her capacity to produce a healthy child and bring it up successfully into adulthood. Over the years that I have spent in Hanoi, I have often been struck by the passionate attention that children are afforded. Usually the eating habits, growth, and behaviors of each child are intensely observed, monitored, and commented upon by parents, relatives, and neighbors. Most mothers know exactly how much their child weighs and how tall it is, and my inability to provide this information for my own children was often met with mild skepticism and surprise.

When a woman is pregnant, in short, much is at stake: not only the coming-into-being of her child but also her own coming-into-being as a member of local moral communities. If her child turns out healthy and normal, this will win her recognition, respect, and a secure place in her new household. Yet if the pregnancy goes awry, this can undermine her social existence, placing her on the margins of her family and community. In the day-to-day conversations and gossip that tie together families and neighborhoods, I found, reproductive misfortune was often blamed on maternal mistakes, being associated with the mother's carelessness; with her inadequate use of antenatal care, her having taken too cold showers, her obsession with her work, or her having exposed herself to cold winds and harsh weather. While neighborly relations were often supportive and caring, the unfriendly gossip that sometimes circulated in closely knit neighborhoods could also be existentially devastating, undermining people's self-confidence and sense of worth. One woman who told me in particularly vivid detail about other people's inclination to blame the mother was Lê, whose fifteen-year-old son had been born with a cleft lip and palate. As we sat on the hard wooden couch in her living room, Lê recalled the time after she gave birth to her son, her first child. His birth threw the entire extended family into moral turmoil. "Whose fault is this?" everyone seemed to ask. Among members of her husband's family, Lê said, the answer was clear. "My husband's elder sister said: 'You eat but you can't give birth. The child you have given birth to is like a goose. How must you have lived to have given birth like this? . . . She was pecking at me like that, saying it was my fault. I had to accept that. I cannot place the fault on anyone else. I was the one who gave birth to him. I must admit that, the mother must always admit that."

This tendency to blame the mother is not new. For generations, Vietnamese proverbs and sayings have placed responsibility for the quality and character of her offspring on the mother. One frequently cited proverb says, "Children are spoilt by their mother; grandchildren are spoilt by their grandmother" (*Con hư tại mẹ, cháu hư tại bà*). Another states, "Happiness and virtue derive from the mother" (*Phúc đức tại mẫu*). Since the term *phúc* (happiness or luck) refers to forms of fortune that are the cosmologically mediated results of morally good behavior, this expression points to intergenerational sharing of karmic luck, suggesting that a mother's moral behavior has consequences for the life of her child (see chapter 5). As one dictionary of Vietnamese proverbs explains: "Whether a child grows up to become a decent person with a good life depends on whether the mother has lived with virtue (*ăn ở nhân đức*)" (Vũ Dung et al. 1993:523). When a birth goes well, people often proudly declare that "the mother is round, the child square" (*mẹ tròn con vuông*). This refers to the cosmological connotations that childbearing carries: in Vietnamese cultural imagery, round refers to Heaven and square to Earth, and a successful birth indicates a harmonious relationship between humanity and higher powers. In the past, people suggested, pregnant women would try to align themselves with Heaven by living with virtue (*ăn ở có đức*), and whether or not childbirth went well was thought to depend on the mother's moral standards. Elderly women in particular stressed this connection between maternal morality and reproductive outcomes in explicit terms. When seventy-six-year-old Bà Vinh, for instance, told me about her first childbirth—which took place in 1946—she described this successful birth as an indicator of her own and her family's high moral standards:

> When the pain of birth was over, and I saw that my child was chubby and square, I felt so happy, happier than I can describe in words. His face was round like a plate, his body plump. . . . Our elders taught us that we must live with virtue. Some women gave birth to children with too many fingers or with cleft lips or lacking arms or legs. I found that very scary. But thanks to Heaven and Buddha, there was nothing wrong with any of my children and all my grandchildren are complete too. We lived with virtue, so I was not afraid. Heaven forms the child (*ông trời bẩm sinh*).

In today's Vietnam, allocations of blame are configured in new ways; now, it seems, maternal misbehavior may also consist in a failure to take advantage of the new opportunities for pregnancy surveillance that mothers-to-be are offered. Twenty-six-year-old Ngân, one of the prospective mothers we met in the 3D scanning room, talked with particular vigor about the expectations placed on women to participate in modern and medicalized pregnancy care. Expressing her ideas in unusually sharp terms, she said: "If a child is born disabled, this has to do with parental ignorance. It means that the parents have not paid enough attention to the fetus and therefore the child is born disabled. If you pay attention to your health in the first three months, it is possible to have an abortion if needed and to have another child later." In associating congenital disability with parental ignorance, Ngân re-interpreted long-standing associations between morality and reproduction, placing them in the new terrain of advancing biomedicine. It is wrongdoing on the part of parents, she suggested, that causes children to be born defective. High-tech pregnancy care, in other words, seems to have cosmological connotations, becoming part of what it means to live properly as a modern mother-to-be (see chapter 5).[8]

Living in a social environment where reproductive problems have far-reaching moral implications, the women I met sought to protect themselves by resorting to medical technologies that offered the promise of reproductive success. Practically all the women in our sample embraced ultrasonography with enthusiasm. This new technology is, they asserted, scientific (*khoa học*), progressive (*tiến bộ*), and modern (*hiện đại*); it works to the benefit of both mothers and children. Ultrasounds are accurate (*chính xác*), comprehensive (*đầy đủ*), effective (*có hiệu quả*) and concrete (*cụ thể*). They throw light (*ánh sáng*) into the dark space of the womb, illuminating it and bringing it into the sphere of human knowledge and control. Like many other women, Oanh associated the use of this technology with a modern and educated mindset. Speaking with language that brought to mind official representations of childbearing as a site of scientific modernity, she defined the routine use of new medical technology as evidence that Vietnam is finally catching up with other countries after grim years of war and deprivation: "In my opinion, it is good to have regular ultrasounds. They are very useful for mothers and children. . . . Vietnam is like other countries now. We have followed other countries. Our medical system has progressed. Scientists have developed these scanning machines, so I think that they are good. It is good that we have progressed so that we can meet today's needs for detecting, preventing, and treating diseases."

By obtaining frequent scans, then, pregnant women sought to optimize their chances of having a healthy and complete child, while also demonstrating themselves to be modern mothers by living up to the moral demands placed on them by family members and health care

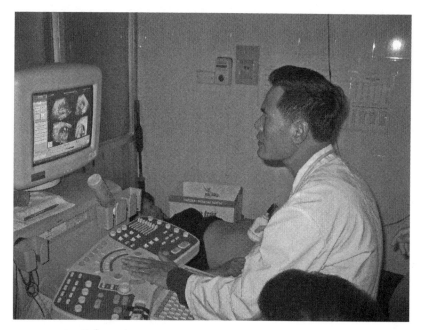

FIGURE 4. Dr. Tuấn performing a 3D scan. Photo by the author, 2004.

authorities. Their pregnancy care practices, in other words, seem to offer a perfect example of developments in subjectivity as described in the governmentality literature: taking upon themselves the responsibility for the planning of their own lives, they showed themselves to be knowledgeable citizen-subjects. Yet, on closer inspection, I found that processes of subjectivity formation were more complicated than this analysis suggests. First, I was often struck by the ways in which other people, too, claimed responsibility for the outcome of a pregnancy. Women's individual responsibility for the fetus seemed always embedded within larger networks of social obligation and support. When husbands, sisters, mothers-in-law, neighbors, and colleagues intervened in a woman's pregnancy care, they also defined the pregnancy as—to some extent—a joint social project. Being a mother, a sister, or a neighbor, they suggested, entails co-responsibility. Second, pregnant women were engaged in social relations with relatives and health care providers, but they also entered into an affective relationship with their fetus. Women's stories indicated that they defined the fetus that appeared on the monitor as already their child, investing it with intense—and intensely culturally celebrated—motherly love (tình mẫu tử). Nevertheless, reproductive selection was, as shown in the following section, placed at the heart of the ultrasound experience.

SEEING AND SELECTING: THE COMING-INTO-BEING OF FETAL SUBJECTS

"What number child is this?" Dr. Nhung inquired. "It's my second child," Trinh replied. "How old is your first?" "Three years old, doctor." While talking to Trinh, Dr. Nhung began performing the scan. She started by looking at the fetal head, measuring its circumference. To the nurse she said, "Lan *oi*,[9] there is one fetus. The head has not engaged yet." She then went on to examine the body, the heart, the stomach, and the legs of the fetus. While she did this, Trinh told her that she was very worried about this pregnancy. "In the first trimester, I was bleeding for twenty days." "How old was the fetus?" Dr. Nhung asked. "It was between the fifth and the eighth week." In a reassuring tone, Dr. Nhung said, "Your fetus is still developing. There is no problem." She then showed Trinh a series of graphs and said, "Look, all the measures are normal." She examined the fetus one more time, looking particularly closely at the head and the brain. To Trinh she said, "I'm looking closely this time, to see if there are any disabilities (*dị tật*)." Trinh asked, "Is it a girl?" and Dr. Nhung replied with a smile, "It's a boy, younger sister (*em ạ*)." She then focused on the face of the fetus, trying to get a good picture. When that proved impossible, she told Trinh, "The little one is lying with its face turned away, so I cannot take its picture. But you can come on another day and get a picture of the face. It will not cost you anything. That's all. We are finished for today. Your fetus is normal."

The nurse printed the scanning image and handed it to Trinh. The bottom line read, "Scan result: 1 fetus around 19 weeks and 3 days old. At this stage of pregnancy, the fetus is developing normally." Trinh did not look entirely happy. In a small voice she said to my colleague Hạnh, "At this age, they can only see the arms and legs of the fetus. So there are other things that they cannot know about. The fetus has to be bigger before they can see if there is a cleft lip or a cleft palate. I had this bleeding, so I am scared that there is something wrong."

Like pregnant women elsewhere in the world, prospective mothers in Hanoi described intense feelings of pleasure and joy at seeing the image of their fetus emerge on the monitor.[10] Now, they suggested, their child-to-be was real; the visualization offered proof that it was really there, living and lovable. Oanh's description of this event was typical: "I really liked seeing my child (*đứa trẻ*). I felt so delighted, so happy. I could see my child's face, its eyes and nose, its mouth. I even saw it move its hand. I liked that so much. I loved my child so." The scan, it seemed, turned pregnant women into mothers, asserting and confirming ties of mutual belonging between mother and child. Like Oanh, women often placed particular emphasis on the encounter with the face of the fetus; it was, they suggested, more than anything else the face-to-face meeting with their child-to-be that made them feel happy and content after a scan. Not only pregnant women and their relatives but also health care providers emphasized the face. As in Trinh's case, the woman would be offered a free 3D scan on another day if it proved impossible to get a good picture of the fetal face. But the fetus that came into being in the scanning room was not only a singular individual with a unique face; it was also a family member. Observing ultrasounds being performed at Hanoi's obstetrics hospital, I was often struck by the ways in which medical staff would routinely represent the fetus as a prospective family member, as a human being-in-becoming who was always already related to others. Before beginning the scan, the sonographer would usually ask the pregnant woman how many children she had already, thereby implicitly placing the mother and the new child within this existing network of kin. During the scan, the comments made by both medical staff and pregnant women often focused on similarities between the fetus and its parents, siblings, or grandparents. The fetus, in other words, was defined not only in terms of its potential as an individual person-to-be, but also, and primarily, in terms of its connections with others.[11]

In some respects, however, the interactions in the 3D scanning room in Hanoi differed from those described in other settings. Research conducted in the United States, Europe, and Japan has shown that health professionals tend to downplay the fact that an ultrasound scan may detect fetal abnormalities, and that although women are not unaware that a scan is also a prenatal test, they view it primarily as a benign source of reassurance, a procedure that allows them to see their child and confirm that it is healthy.[12] Still, the risk that something may be wrong is always there. As Janelle Taylor (1998:25) observes, reflecting on research conducted in the United States, "It is this dreaded possibility that lends such drama to the routine ultrasound examination—the agonizing suspense of waiting and wondering, the climactic moment of diagnosis, the joy (or despair) that follows." But although the risk of adverse findings was always present in the health care clinics she observed, Taylor notes, it remained silenced and suppressed in routine clinical encounters. In the 3D scanning room in Hanoi, in contrast, the risk that the fetus under inspection might not be normal was at the forefront of everyone's attention. Although the vast majority of fetuses were labeled normal, the abnormal fetus was always also present, as a latent, hypothetical, and frightening figure. As the following examples of conversations in the scanning room suggest, this figure was co-created by sonographers:

> *Sonographer to Thanh (31 weeks pregnant)*: You should have come earlier for the 3D scan. Earlier on it is easier for us to observe the fetus. At 22 weeks we can see everything very clearly, because all the limbs are complete. With a big fetus like yours, it is very hard. We can only check the amniotic fluid. Have you seen the face of the little one yet?
>
> *Thanh*: I have.
>
> *Sonographer*: The face is very normal. There is no cleft lip at all.
>
> *Sonographer to Hoa (21 weeks pregnant)*: What number child is this?
>
> *Hoa*: This is my first child.
>
> *Sonographer to nurse*: Lan ơi, the fetus has not yet engaged. Now, let's have a close look at the brain and see if the ventricles are dilated.

Like Oanh and Trinh, practically all the women were intensely preoccupied, not to say obsessed, with the normality of their fetus. When I asked her what she liked most about the scan she had just had, one woman emphasized in a sharp tone that this procedure was not undertaken for pleasure or entertainment: "I did not *like* anything," she said. "I had the scan to gain *knowledge (đi siêu âm cho biết)*." When I asked women in the 3D scanning room what had motivated them to come for a scan, the reply I usually received was: "I want to see how the little one is developing." This reply, I soon learned, indicated not only curiosity and joy at seeing one's child-to-be developing month by month, but also more sinister fears that something might be wrong. When women explained what, to them, made ultrasounds so useful, they emphasized that this technology—unlike all other technologies used in antenatal care—enables one to *see* the child. It took a while before I realized that a woman's emphasis on seeing indicated more than simply the pleasure of meeting the fetus face-to-face: most often, *seeing* meant seeing if the child-to-be had any disabilities. The ultrasound scan, as women in Hanoi represented it, was primarily a diagnostic test capable of detecting fetal abnormalities. As one woman said, "I think that the greatest benefit of ultrasonography is that people can give up children who are not normal. This can help everyone to have complete children. . . . In my case, my purpose was to have a healthy child, so I had to do what I could to make that happen."[13]

When reading Vietnamese newspapers, I was often struck by the ways in which the selective aims of ultrasound scans were explicitly articulated, being represented as necessary responses to risks of fetal malformations. In terms that expressed profound fascination with the capacities of this new technology, for instance, one article in the journal *Khoa Học và Đời Sống* (Science and Life) stated: "If they want to see clearly the eyes, nose, brow, chin, and the lovely mouth of the future child who is moving in their womb, pregnant women should obtain a 4D ultrasound scan. . . . You will see clearly the facial features, a face expressing pleasure or a face wrinkled in dissatisfaction when the fetus hears the sweet lullabies sung by its parents or their angry voices. . . . Scanning pictures offer expressive proof that the life of a human being does not begin at birth but inside the mother's womb" (Minh Thịnh 2004:9). Having established the fetus as a sentient and socialized being, the text continued by pointing to the selective purposes of ultrasound scans, stating that they help physicians to see "the skull, the joints, the fontanel, the height of the nose, the convex and concave parts of the face, so that it is easy to detect cases of cleft lip or palate; abnormalities of arms or legs (such as lacking or too short limbs, deformations), of the spinal cord (curved or crooked), or of the abdomen, urological system, or sexual organs."

Being aware that it served more than entertainment purposes, most women I met described the 3D scan as an intensely anxious experience. Hương, for instance, said, "When I went for the color scan and saw how far it had developed, arms and legs and all, I felt very worried. I was scared that it might not be developing normally, perhaps it lacked something, perhaps the brain was not developing normally, perhaps it lacked arms or legs, perhaps it was malformed." Similarly, Yến said, "I did not sleep the night before. We had decided to go for the scan early in the morning, and I spent the entire night awake, worrying that the fetus might be like this or like that." Although many women said that they found ultrasounds anxiety-relieving, their stories indicated that fetal images were also anxiety-producing. Each ultrasound scan confirmed what women already knew—that fetal development did not necessarily proceed as expected. Neither the birth of a complete child nor their own attachment to their families, women's accounts suggested, could ever be taken for granted; childbearing was a matter of contingency and acute vulnerability. The precarious nature of motherhood was, I found, epitomized in the 3D scanning room.

MALFORMED FETAL SPECTERS

One of the women I met in the scanning room was Thảo, a thirty-two-year old policewoman. On June 18, 2004, my colleague Hằng picked me up on her motorbike and steered us deftly though the busy inner-city traffic to Thảo's house. She lived together with her husband, two sons, and parents-in-law on a narrow street in Hanoi's old quarter, in a house that her husband's family had owned for generations. Rapidly rising real estate prices, she told us, had made this house worth a fortune, but since her husband's ancestors inhabited it, her parents-in-law would never consider selling it. In the future, her eldest son, Định Anh, would be living here with his children, taking care of the family's dead. "You know," Thảo said with a smile, "you may think that we are lucky to have two boys, but actually we are not. We must ensure that each of our boys has a house to live in when he gets married, but how can we ever afford buying a house like this for our younger son?" Despite her complaints, Thảo's bright smile revealed her pride in having produced two healthy male children; like Oanh, she comported herself with the self-assurance that only successful childbearing seemed to bring. During her pregnancy, she said, she had done all she could to ensure that everything went well. In the evening, she would often call in at a private ob-gyn clinic on her way home from work to have a scan and a checkup; in total she had had approximately twenty ultrasound scans. She had many reasons for getting frequent scans, she explained, but one was key: "Of course, every mother and father likes to see the face of the child; one is curious to see if it is beautiful or not. I really liked seeing his picture. It was very clear; his nose was big and he looked like his elder brother. . . . But for me, what was most important was to see if he was normal, if he was developing well. I wanted to find out if he was disabled. . . . That was what really mattered."

Thảo's last sentences point us to the submerged fetal bodies beneath the visible child-to-be in the scanning image. Into the joy that Thảo felt when seeing her fetus and imagining a younger brother for her son blended other kinds of imaginings: fears that her fetus might not be developing normally, that it might be born disabled or disfigured. This, Thảo said, was what really mattered. Like Trinh and Thảo, women saw what the sonographer pointed out to them: a normally developing fetus, a potential child, a new family member. Yet often they seemed to see more in the scanning image as well. Sonographers offered women facts about their fetus, telling them about its growth, physical dimensions, and facial features. In subtle ways, however, they also reminded women of the "what if" dimensions of the image, drawing attention to the other ways in which this pregnancy might end. On the printout of the scan, the bottom line nearly always read: "Conclusion: At this stage of pregnancy, the fetus is developing normally." This sentence pointed in two different directions: while establishing the normality of the fetus, it also left open the possibility that at later stages of pregnancy, normal development might be replaced by something else. A scanning image, in other words, opened imaginative vistas along which women envisioned themselves as socially acknowledged mothers, wives, and daughters-in-law. But it also raised the possibility that this pregnancy might end in unexpected and unwanted ways, placing them in positions of profound social vulnerability. When seeing a scanning image, then, women saw not only the normally developing fetus described by the sonographer, but also its invisible, imaginary opposite—the malformed fetus, the monstrous other of the son or daughter they looked forward to welcoming as their child.

This contingent and subjunctive side of the scanning image points to aspects of signification that existing studies on medical imaging have largely ignored.[14] Whereas much research has emphasized the capacity of medical imaging to generate factual representations of the human body, this material from Hanoi has compelled me to attend also to sensation and intuition, to the ways in which people come to know their worlds by being immersed in them, through a sensibility located "on the surface of the skin, at the edge of the nerves" (Levinas 2000 [1981]:15). Visual impressions are, as Merleau-Ponty points out, always generated within a larger perceptual setting; when we see things in certain ways, we do so against backgrounds generated by our prior life experiences. There is, therefore, always more to what we perceive than we know of, always something invisible in the visible, something unknown in the known, something strange in the apparently familiar: "To see is as a matter of principle to see farther than one sees, to reach a latent existence" (Merleau-Ponty 1964 [1960]:20).

In her research on ultrasonography in the United States, Sallie Han (2009) found that pregnant women associated scanning images with family photographs, seeing the fetus as they would see a child in a family photo. In Hanoi, women made dramatically different associations. Rather than being filled with homely family photographs, the visual field within which fetuses emerged was beset with unsettling images of severely disabled children. The public proliferation of images of suffering Agent Orange victims contributed, I contend, to placing latent images of monstrously deformed child bodies at the center of women's perceptions of the sonogram: by the time of this research, mass-mediated images of damaged human bodies had become a routine and inescapable part of day-to-day lives in Hanoi.

HAUNTING IMAGES

When reflecting on their own reproductive lives, the women I met would often refer to the plight of Agent Orange victims. In November 2004, for instance, Chi and I visited Yến in her home on the outskirts of Hanoi. While she was pregnant, Yến had told us about the anxieties that haunted her; now, she was proud to show us her five-month-old son fast asleep on their bed, chubby and healthy. When I asked her what she imagined that life with a disabled child would have been like, Yến immediately replied: "For sure it would be a miserable life. A life like that . . . I have seen pictures of Agent Orange [victims] on television. Their lives are miserable (khổ). A life like that would mean suffering, not only for the child but for the mother too. The mother would have to work very hard, and the child would not grow up; it would not develop normally." As Yến's words suggest, disability and Agent Orange were often conflated: the prototypical disabled child that people imagined was one who would spend its life lying in one place, its body weirdly malformed. The mental images that women and their relatives conjured seemed to closely resemble those circulated in the mass media. From newspapers and television, everyone was intimately familiar with Agent Orange–related disabilities. On a nearly daily basis, people were confronted with images of children with strangely curled limbs, black hair covering their bodies, bulging eyes, or enormous water-filled heads. In women's accounts, Agent Orange victims were described as human beings living on the edges and borders of social existence, as people in need of sympathy and support, and as frightening specters of human lives gone terribly awry. In this context, the capacity of visual images to disturb and obsess the viewer was a topic that people often brought up. The power of mental images seemed to them self-evident and had its own name: ám ảnh, being obsessed or haunted. "Don't you know what ám ảnh means?" Toàn blurted in disbelief when I first asked her about this term. "It means pictures that stay on your mind. No matter what you do to get rid of them, you cannot." A sensibility to unsettling images was, people suggested, something that everyone shared, but during pregnancy this openness to sense impressions was held to have particularly far-reaching consequences.

Theories of maternal impression have been reported across the world. When expecting a child, these theories suggest, a woman is open to external influences that may affect the developing fetus, shaping it according to the impression made on her. Moreover, the mother's moods may affect her child-to-be directly, causing it to feel depressed or happy depending on her state of mind. During our conversations, women in Hanoi would often express similar ideas: if they felt sad or anxious while pregnant, they suggested, this might harm their fetus. Women's fears often seemed exacerbated by popular pregnancy handbooks that conveyed messages of questionable veracity, such as the following: "Through scientific experiments and clinical observations of pregnant women, it has been found that if the mother is very worried, sad, or very irritable and angry, the child will often be born suffering from congenital malformations such as low weight, poor intelligence, poor development, cleft lip, cleft palate" (Nguyễn Văn Đức et al. 2003:58).[15] Knowing this, women told me, they strove hard to avoid upsetting sensory experiences and to think only of good and positive things. Their feelings of being open and vulnerable were particularly manifest in any confrontation with disability: many women said that while pregnant, they would look the other way if they met a disabled person in the street. In Mai's words: "Pregnant women are scared that if they think of frightening things such as disability, then when they give birth, the child will be like that. When you are pregnant you should think only about good and beautiful things. People say that whatever is on your mind, your child will be like that. Therefore, you should hang pictures of chubby children on the wall to look at, and you should not feel sad." If a mother-to-be looked at or imagined defective human bodies, women explained, this could affect the fetus in two ways: either directly, the sight being transported (vận) into the woman and marking her child-to-be, or indirectly, the mother's feelings of discomfort weakening her and, thereby, the fetus.

Although the imaginary malformed fetus was, as we have seen, a prominent figure in the 3D scanning room, it was also a specter that women tried hard to push to the back of their minds. In the conversations that we had with them while they were pregnant, very few women would, on their own initiative, bring up the topic of fetal abnormality. Oanh was, in this respect, unusually explicit. This issue, I soon learned, was so sensitive that it could usually be talked about only well after the child had been born and had proven itself healthy and complete. Thinking about the malformed fetus, women feared, would make it intrude upon them, etching itself into their bodies and minds (*in đậm vào mình*). As part of their effort to avoid unsettling sensory experiences, most women watched television with care during pregnancy, deliberately avoiding programs about disability. Many pointed to programs featuring Agent Orange victims as a particular source of worry. The memory of coming face-to-face with such images, they suggested, can continue haunting the spectator for a long time. Oanh said: "I was very scared of watching television while I was pregnant. Often, they broadcast programs about Agent Orange children, abnormal children with disabilities. I turned off the television or left the room, I did not want to watch that. I was afraid that the images would stay in my mind."

Instead of simply dismissing these conceptions of the open maternal body as pseudoscience or folklore, I want to explore the possibility that they may tell us something important about subjectivity. When women in Hanoi talked about the ways in which the damaged bodies of Agent Orange victims intervened in their bodies and minds, entering into their lives in ways they had difficulty protecting themselves against, they also set forth specific conceptions of what subjectivity entails. In exclaiming, "I so much want to erase this picture of a disabled child from my mind, but I can't," Oanh defined her own being as a matter of openness and vulnerability; she was exposed in ways that she could not herself control. Conceiving subjectivity in terms of such openness and exposure may, then, help us to comprehend how ultrasound scan sessions in Hanoi became so charged with affectivity and tension and how women came to feel so vulnerable in the encounter with this technology. Ethical subjectivity, these lines of analysis suggest, is formed not only through the active practices of the self described by Foucault and his followers, but also through a more passive exposure to the other.

PREGNANCY AS EXPOSURE: EXISTENTIAL APORIAS

Feminist scholars have often claimed that new technologies for prenatal screening render pregnancies tentative, as women hesitate to attach themselves to a fetus that they may not be able to keep (see Rothman 1993 [1986]). As described by the women I met in Hanoi, however, pregnancies were not tentative; from very early on, women enacted intense attachment to the child they expected.[16] Liên, who had her pregnancy terminated in week 14 due to a fetal anomaly, told me that it is part of Vietnamese cultural tradition to consider a new child as a family member (*một thành viên trong gia đình*) even before it is born: "Every day when my husband came home from work, he would massage my belly and say, 'My child, daddy is home now,' things like that. This is the tradition of Vietnamese people. I don't know what it is like in your country? Perhaps people there simply give birth to the child and take it home? In my country, people prepare carefully for the birth of a child." The fetus was, as described by women, another human being, a sentient *alter*, someone who intervened in their lives and to whom they felt attached and obligated. Oanh, for instance, told us that she resisted her relatives' demand that she undergo an abortion because she felt that her fetus placed demands on her too. As a little girl, she had felt neglected by her mother, and she wanted to offer her own children the love and protection that she herself had missed: "From when I was a little girl I have wanted to become a good mother, a better mother than my mother was to me. I felt that if I had given up this child, I would have been no better than my mother."

In an essay on the social recognition of new human life, Wendy R. James argues that potentiality is the *essence* of sociality. Potential human beings qualify as members of society, she suggests, because they have the capacity to be drawn into networks of anticipatory relations with others over time: "Foetuses, and even infants, may not be individually registered as jural persons, or holders of legal rights, or even given this or that specific status or legal protection in a particular social context. But they bear a relationship to others who may hold such rights and who are prepared to recognize and care for them, to confer a link on the model of 'I/Thou' with them" (James 2000:177). When an ultrasound scan was performed in Hanoi, expectant parents and health care providers conferred such links of recognition and care on the fetus, thereby turning it into a potential person, their child. During ultrasound scans, women's sense of connection with their child-to-be seemed to be reinforced: the fetus looked at them through the monitor, addressing them, and placing demands on them to love and to care for it. In experiential terms, this fetus was a subject-to-be, a human being-in-becoming to whom prospective mothers felt intimately connected. The scan often seemed to intensify women's feelings of love, obligation, and attachment. This child, they suggested, belonged to them, as they belonged to it; it was theirs to love, hold, and protect. The vulnerability that women described, then, arose from being for another; they were, in Levinasian terms, obsessed by their fetus, suffering from it, having charge of it, being in its place. These feelings of love and attachment came, however, into direct conflict with the selection agenda that drove the performance of 3D scans: if the scan found a defect in the fetus, everyone knew, this would place the expectant mother in a situation where she might have to end its life. The tense atmosphere in the scanning room seemed, then, to arise from the existential conflict that women experienced between the urge to love and protect their fetus and the necessity of taking its life in the event that a problem were to be found.[17]

The notion of unconditional maternal love must be seen, as anthropologists have argued, as an artifact of cultural politics rather than an essential female trait. But in order to grasp the existential drama at play in the scanning room in Hanoi, I contend, we must attend to the feelings of love and longing for their child that women described. Take for instance Hoa, a thirty-one-year-old mother of two children. In November 2004, when her youngest child was six months old, Toàn and I visited Hoa in her home in Hanoi's Thanh Xuân district. She told us that during her pregnancy she had felt very anxious and at the same time had tried not to think about these anxieties. "I was very worried that my child would be born with a disability," she said, "that at birth it would turn out to be abnormal." Toàn replied, "Luckily, both of your children are healthy. But if your fetus had had a disability, what do you think your attitude would have been?" Hoa responded by describing how she had felt torn between the urge to keep her fetus and her sense that if an anomaly had been found, a pregnancy termination might have been necessary:

> This is something that I can only think about now. When I was pregnant, it would have been difficult for me to talk about this. All I felt was "This is my child and I don't want to give it up." But if the fetus had had a defect (*khiếm khuyết*), an obstetrical intervention would have been better than letting it suffer in the future. . . . An early intervention is most humane (*nhân đạo*). Of course in terms of psychology, no mother wants to give up her child, not even if something is wrong with the child. This is about the feelings between mother and child (*tình mẹ con*). But in order to save the child from suffering, a medical intervention may be necessary if an abnormality is detected.

Imagining that their fetus might not be normal placed pregnant women in a hypothetical predicament of the kind that Michael Jackson (2007:xviii) has characterized as an existential aporia, *a-poria* in Greek meaning "without passage." No matter how one acts in this situation, women indicated, moral pain will result. It is wrong to terminate a pregnancy at a late stage of gestation, and it is wrong to give birth to a severely disabled child. As Trang summed up the problem: "I would feel that it was wrong (*tội*) to give it up. But keeping it would cause it to suffer." Those women who were able to talk about this predicament at all described the thought of having to terminate their pregnancy as nearly unbearable. Although many had undergone abortions themselves, they cast this medical intervention in terms such as heartless (*nhẫn tâm*), inhuman (*bất nhân*), evil (*ác*), and morally wrong (*tội*). Having an abortion, one woman said, means killing a human life (*giết một mạng người*). Yến described the abortion that she had had two weeks into her first pregnancy as an evil act. The fetus, she said, was "a drop of my own blood, my child." Telling Toàn and me about an abortion she had shortly after the birth of her son, Oanh said: "The fetus was only six weeks old, so it did not have a human form yet. But I still felt sad and to this day, I have not been able to forget it. So if one waits until the little one has become a fully formed child and *then* has an abortion, it will make one feel so much sadder."

Like Oanh, all the women I met considered second-trimester abortions particularly troublesome in both moral and emotional terms. First of all, they explained, such abortions pose risks to the mother's life and health.[18] Second, many women felt uncomfortable at the thought of ending the life of a human being-to-be.[19] In early pregnancy, they said, the fetus is still merely a drop of blood (*giọt máu*). But in the fourth or fifth month, when quickening has taken place and the fetus is fully formed, its moral status changes and it becomes an actor whose needs and claims must be taken seriously.[20] Therefore, most women concurred, if a fetus is diagnosed with a minor disability that can be surgically corrected, it is best to keep the pregnancy and seek treatment for the child after birth. But if the fetal problem is found to be severe, the most proper (*đúng đắn*) decision is to opt for a pregnancy termination. Since hardly any social assistance is offered to families with disabled children, women explained, a severely disabled child places a heavy burden of cost and care on its parents and siblings, and it is very difficult for the family to offer this child a good life. In the words of Thảo, the policewoman who lived in inner-city Hanoi:

> Today, medicine has developed. If the problem is not too severe, one can still overcome it. A cleft lip, for instance, can be operated on. But Down syndrome and other mental problems cannot be treated. In that case, you have to care for the child for its entire life. Giving birth to a child like that means suffering. And not just for one person; it means suffering for many people. . . .

In our case, if a problem like that had been found, I think we would have talked about it and agreed to opt for a termination. I think it is morally wrong (*tội*) to give birth to a child who is sick. For the family, it means that you have to buy a lot of medicine and you need one person to care for the child all the time.

Although prenatal screening can generate profound moral dilemmas, women suggested, it still helps people to avoid the even deeper dilemmas that arise if a child is born disabled. When I asked her if she saw any moral problems in selective abortions, Ngân turned my question around: "As I see it, the moral question is, Can you take care of this child? Can you give this child a happy life? That is what is important." When we talked about what life with a disabled child would be like, women practically always described this as an existence of constant frustration. Being unable to reciprocate all that it has been given, they suggested, a severely disabled child is doomed to a permanent existence on the margins of social collectives, living its life in dependency and isolation. No matter how hard the parents of such children struggle, women said, they cannot protect their child against hardship and suffering (cf. chapter 6). The possibility to abort a defective fetus was therefore described by most women as a privilege: although having to terminate a pregnancy that one has wanted and longed for is an agonizing experience, they suggested, it does prevent the much deeper moral quandaries that will arise if the pregnancy is carried to term.

PRECARIOUS MATERNAL BELONGING

By obtaining frequent ultrasound scans, women in Hanoi defined themselves as modern mothers and good citizens, while also seeking to enhance their chances of having a healthy and normal child who would help them to achieve full membership in their households and communities. Ultrasounds were, in this sense, quests for belonging and attachment; they were ways in which women strove to gain membership in already existing social collectives while also tying themselves into an affective relationship with the new child they expected. These quests for belonging unfolded in a moral terrain animated by intense feelings of hope, fear, dread, and anxiety. Practically all the pregnant women I met were haunted by mental images of disabled children; when looking at a scanning image, they saw not only the normal fetus that the sonographer pointed out to them but also its frighteningly malformed counterpart. Although women strove hard to erase such pictures from their minds, these images seemed to insist on being present, reminding prospective mothers of the risks and contingencies with which reproduction is fraught. The result of a pregnancy, like the course of a life, women knew, can never be taken for granted. No matter how hard one strives to shape one's life in certain ways, other forces may take over, thwarting intentions, desires, and ambitions.

In the 3D scanning room, everyone was acutely aware that a fetal problem, if found, would force the expectant mother into a tormenting choice between terminating her pregnancy or giving birth to a child whose anomalous body would render it impossible for her to achieve the secure social position she longed for. The scan, then, produced paradoxical results: on the one hand, it brought into being a new child and a caring mother, stimulating and sustaining feelings of love, obligation, and attachment; and on the other, it made it painfully clear that this mother might, in case her child were labeled defective, have to end its life. It was this dilemma, I suggest, that turned the malformed fetus into such a powerful yet elusive figure in the 3D scanning room. The social belonging that successful childbearing produced was, everyone knew, inherently precarious and unstable. What pregnant women confronted in the scanning room, therefore, was not only the technologically visualized fetus and its imaginary counterparts but also their own openness, exposure, and vulnerability as human beings.

CHAPTER 4

"Like a Loving Mother"

Moral Engagements in Medical Worlds

DR. TUẤN: "WE MUST HAVE A STRONG SENSE OF RESPONSIBILITY"

Dr. Tuấn usually talked about ultrasonography in enthusiastic terms. Yet in a conversation that my colleague Hằng and I had with him on May 19, 2004, he drew our attention to what he saw as the darker side of this technology: the human pain that resulted when a fetal problem was found. What Dr. Tuấn cherished about his job was to be able to reassure expectant mothers of the beauty and normality of their children-to-be, to share with them the happy future that this child body promised. The opposite situation was, I knew, one that he found difficult to bear. When I asked him about his role vis-à-vis the woman and her family in such cases, he responded promptly:

> I play a very important role for the patient and her family. People's happiness is their children. In the face of that responsibility, which is great and heavy, we must have comprehensive skills. We must have a strong sense of responsibility (*tinh thần trách nhiệm*) when making a diagnosis, and we must be very precise when assessing the condition of a child that is about to be born. When something abnormal is found in a child, we must feel deeply with people, encourage them, and support them spiritually. . . . The sonographer is the person who has the first contact with these people, so it is our responsibility to encourage (*động viên*) them by every means, to make them feel at peace, so that they can continue firmly along the road that they have to travel.

In this chapter, I examine the moral questions that practices of selective reproduction raised among the physicians I met in Hanoi; questions about how to care optimally for patients and about how best to fulfill their role as medical experts.[1] In official public health discourse in Vietnam, technologies for prenatal screening were, as the previous chapters show, defined as unquestionably benevolent and useful. In day-to-day clinical practice, however, moral matters became more complex. The physicians I met struggled with a variety of ethical and emotional challenges as they sought to determine where to draw the line, how to distinguish between fetuses that were to be selected for life and those that were not. Close ethnographic attention to the dilemmas faced by these physicians, I contend, allows us to open the state and its public health projects to anthropological scrutiny. As state-employed cadres (*cán bộ*), doctors at this obstetrics hospital embodied the state; in day-to-day practice, the task of carrying out national health care initiatives was assigned to them. My conversations and interactions with these health care professionals have led me to suggest that the state must be seen not as a closed system of administration and governance, but rather as an open and affective structure of mutual belonging. The state is, this material from Vietnam suggests, suffused with sentiment; rather than simply a locus of rational and bureaucratic practices, it is a site of vivid imaginings, fantasies, and desires (cf. Aretxaga 2003).

Conventional approaches to the state, however, render it difficult to bring this intertwining of power and passion into analysis. Despite recent deconstructions of the state as an integrated political entity, and despite reconceptualizations of states as powerful collective illusions, essentializing oppositions between state and society continue to prevail in anthropological analyses (cf. Ferguson and Gupta 2002). State-citizen divides tend to be sharply demarcated in research on the politics of reproduction; in many studies, the state is represented as an external agent of power and authority that encroaches on people's reproductive lives in fairly brutal ways.[2] The accounts of state-employed physicians such as Dr. Tuấn, however, invite us to reconsider these assumptions. The moral-emotional dilemmas that physicians described indicate that the medical world they inhabited was animated by intense interpersonal engagements that transcended conventional state-citizen dualities, revolving around what doctors described as a sense of responsibility (*tinh thần trách nhiệm*). In the above statement, Dr. Tuấn set forth this sense of responsibility in very explicit terms; yet I often found it to be articulated more indirectly, manifesting itself in the touch of a hand

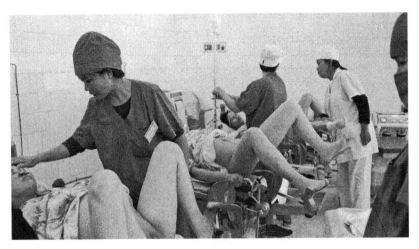

FIGURE 5. A communal birthing environment: the Delivery Department at Hanoi's Obstetrics and Gynecology Hospital. Photo by Ditte Bjerregaard, 2000.

during a difficult delivery; in eager attempts to persuade patients to opt for what physicians saw as the most proper decision; in angry and frustrated outbursts when a patient left a counseling session without having accepted the doctor's message; or in the caring tone conveyed by ending sentences with the words *em ạ,* "younger sister." What preoccupied physicians at this maternity hospital, I soon learned, were not primarily questions of how to enhance pregnant women's capacities for autonomous choice, but, rather, how society in general—and they as physicians in particular—could fulfill their responsibility to the women and their families. The ethical (self-)expectations that these physicians expressed were, I found, animated by national narratives of collective mobilization for health, drawing their moral force from widely shared stories about achievements accomplished since the 1945 revolution. To begin with, therefore, I offer a brief sketch of the history of public health care in socialist Vietnam.

FOR THE PEOPLE'S HEALTH: STATE MANAGEMENT OF PUBLIC HEALTH

In official accounts, the history of health care in socialist Vietnam is told as a story of revolutionary progress: a narrative of heroic and collective struggles to build and defend the nation. The socialist revolution served,

Vietnam's Ministry of Health reminds people, to "drive out the enemies that are hunger, ignorance, and illness" (Bộ Y Tế 2008:6). Under colonial rule, health conditions were, official accounts state, appalling. In 1970, Vietnam's former minister of health observed: "Twenty-five years ago, under French rule, our people were living in dire misery, a prey to terrible diseases. Cholera, smallpox, typhoid fever, poliomyelitis were raging, together with tuberculosis, leprosy, malaria, trachoma, syphilis, gonorrhea, which every year made thousands of victims. Perinatal mortality reached frightening proportions, especially in the countryside and the Highlands, where the rate was 300 and even 400 per thousand" (Nguyễn Văn Hương 1970:7). During the anticolonial resistance war, health promotion was closely connected to nationalist mobilization. Guerrillas serving with the Democratic Republic of Vietnam People's Army undertook not only military but also public health interventions, trying to persuade people to adopt new and scientifically based practices of health and hygiene (Trần Tuấn 1995).

When the socialist government came into power in 1954, public health care was afforded prime political priority. In the short period between the two Indochina Wars, a new national health care system was set up, aiming to be, in Hồ Chí Minh's words, scientific (*khoa học*), national (*dân tộc*), and popular (*đại chúng*). It was scientific, because it was based on modern methods of treatment and prevention; national, because it was funded and organized by the central government; and popular, because it was community based, was locally staffed, and incorporated traditional medicine. Health was defined as a basic human right, but also as strategically important for socialist nation-building and national defense. In Hồ Chí Minh's famous adage, *Each weak citizen causes the country to be weak; each healthy and strong citizen makes the entire country healthy and strong.* Beginning in the 1950s, and continuing during the war years, nationwide campaigns were conducted to improve sanitation and provide vaccinations; commune-level health stations were set up; an extensive network of grass-roots health care workers was established; and a system for referring people to curative services at clinics and hospitals was instituted. In this process, nationalism and health mobilization were closely linked. As one slogan went, *Hygiene is the love of one's nation* (*Vệ sinh là yêu nước*) (Craig 2002:56). In this era of collective mobilization for health, particular attention was paid to maternal and child health. Defining science as a universal agent of progress, the new socialist government organized a network of grassroots cadres who mobilized (*vận động*) women to follow the new scientific ways. Superstitious pregnancy precautions, they taught, must give way to modern antenatal care provided by trained health staff; the dangerous reliance on home births and traditional birth attendants must be replaced by institution-based deliveries; neonatal care was to be enhanced through better hygiene and infant vaccinations; and all children were to be immunized against infectious diseases. In 1979, a high-ranking official declared: "We are not satisfied with merely taking care of mothers and their babies. Our ambition is to give the young generation as much opportunity as young people in advanced countries have. We want to mould new, socialist men and women, and we must start in the cradle" (Vietnam Courier 1979:12).

These political efforts to establish a comprehensive health care network resulted in dramatic health gains. Between 1960 and the late 1980s, significant improvements in life expectancy and reductions in rates of infant mortality and maternal mortality occurred. Most observers ascribe present-day Vietnam's good health indicators to these early collective efforts for health.[3] The fact that the most impressive health care improvements were attained while the country was at war is no coincidence; mobilization for health blended with mobilization for national freedom and independence. In a 2009 comment on socialist Vietnam's health care achievements, Vice Minister of Health Trần Chí Liêm (2009:51) defined public health care as a key symbol of the socialist project: "As a whole, great emphasis was placed by the State on the building of material facilities for the Northern medical system since peace restoration, through the anti-US resistance war till the end of the 1980s. Though not yet modern, these models brought into the fullest play activities for preventing diseases, controlling epidemics, getting rid of dangerous contagious diseases (leprosy, tuberculosis, etc.)[;] this system was the symbol of the good, new socialist regime, the regime of equality and humanity."

Official accounts of the nation's history attribute much of the success of the socialist primary health care program to the efforts made by health professionals and grassroots cadres. Health care workers are usually represented as heroic individuals who, even during armed conflict, worked selflessly for the people's health, mobilizing local people to take part in nationalist movements for health, hygiene, and birth control.[4] Present-day newspaper articles and television programs often tell similar stories, celebrating the selflessness and community commitment of today's health care and family planning workers. A 2009 article in *Family and Society,* for instance, portrayed family planning cadres as "the people who struggle by day and night with work that requires devotion, enthusiasm, and perseverance. In order to achieve results in population work, they live near the people, understand the people, mobilize and convince the people through their own good reputation. They do all this not just for their own community, but for the future of the people (*dân tộc*), of the country (*đất nước*)" (Hà Thư and Hồng Sơn 2009:7).

The ways in which the past is invoked in Vietnam can be usefully compared with the situation in Japan, where Tsipy Ivry (2006) has found that prenatal screening tends to be pushed to a backstage realm and is practiced in highly discreet ways. To account for this cautious approach to screening technologies, she points to Japanese history, arguing that the historical weight of links between prenatal screening and the country's previous eugenic practices plays a significant role in deterring health providers from promoting these technologies.[5] The historical horizons within which new technologies of pregnancy care were inscribed in Vietnam, I found, differed markedly from those described by Ivry. In both settings, present-day reproductive challenges were shaped by national pasts. Yet in Hanoi, rather than being associated with a problematic history of eugenics, selective reproduction was incorporated within a proud socialist tradition of working collectively for the health of the entire people (*vì sức khỏe toàn dân*). Drawing comparisons with nationwide immunization programs, a 2010 article in *Family and Society* emphasized the need to convince the country's women of the benefits of prenatal screening: "Thanks to today's scientific developments, many disabilities can be detected at an early stage, while the fetus is still small. . . . To make mothers and their relatives understand the importance of prenatal and neonatal screening, and thereby to reduce the burdens on families and society, . . . what is needed most is information and counseling for the entire population, so that everyone accepts this as if it were an expanded immunization program" (Hà Thư 2010b:6).

In short, in official discourse, twenty-first-century biopolitical interventions are linked to older—and widely acclaimed—ones (cf. Wahlberg 2009).[6] New technologies of pregnancy care are presented as a direct extension of previous state efforts to care for the people's health (*chăm sóc sức khỏe nhân dân*) through public health programs of vaccination, nutrition, and hygiene. Within these narratives, technologies for selective reproduction are associated with courageous collective efforts to ensure the survival and welfare of mothers and children, and defined as the latest step on the long—and sometimes painful—journey toward a better and more humane society. It was in this context of shared commitment to collective population health that the physicians I met in Hanoi placed prenatal screening. When questions concerning the ethics of selective reproduction came up during our conversations, physicians pointed to two problem areas in particular: first, to the injustices that stem from Vietnamese women's unequal access to new reproductive technologies, and second, to the risk that, without proper guidance and support, women might make reproductive decisions that would throw their lives off track, causing deep human suffering.

MAKING ANTENATAL CARE AVAILABLE TO ALL:
HEALTH CARE INEQUITIES

Research on prenatal screening conducted in Europe and North America has paid much attention to the problem of whether women are free either to accept or refuse prenatal screening. Health care practitioners in Hanoi, however, drew attention to other kinds of questions. In the conversations that I had with physicians in the course of research, they rarely expressed concerns about patient freedom and autonomy. Rather, they spoke about equity, justice, and responsibility, asking whether there was equal access for all women in Vietnam to high-quality antenatal care.[7] In the current era of health sector liberalization and commercialization, they suggested, long-standing efforts to enhance people's health confront new challenges, and inequities in reproductive health care place some women at higher risk than others for unwanted reproductive outcomes.

One late afternoon in May 2004, Hằng and I talked to Dr. Tuấn. During hectic working days at the hospital, it was often difficult to talk to doctors at length, so today Dr. Tuấn had agreed to share his experiences with us after working hours. We met in the hospital's meeting room. Over a cup of strong green tea and a bunch of lychees that Hằng had bought from the vendors outside the hospital, Dr. Tuấn reiterated the numerous benefits that ultrasonography has brought to antenatal care. One advantage of this technology, he said, is that it has significant potential for geographical expansion: "With a neat and light technology such as this, we can serve women all over the country. It is light to carry, so health providers can bring it with them out to the communes and use it even in remote areas. For Vietnam, this is very important." This potential is, however, he regretted, not yet fully exploited: "We have not yet been able to ensure a full expansion. First, we lack money to buy enough machines, and second, we lack health care providers who have experience doing this kind of work. . . . In my opinion, we should give priority to remote areas rather than to urban areas. In the cities women pay for ultrasounds on their own initiative; there is no need for us to say anything. They have enough money. But in rural areas people worry about getting enough to eat. So for rural areas we need other kinds of policies."

In addition to problems of access, physicians such as Dr. Tuấn often pointed to problems of awareness (*nhận thức*): women living in rural areas, they said, often fail to recognize the importance of prenatal screening. They are not as well educated as urban women and have less access to public health information. As Dr. Hồng phrased the problem: "Not all women come for 3D scans. Not all women are aware that it is necessary. Only urban women get information about this; they are aware that one must examine the fetus to see if there are any problems. But in rural areas, where people are poor, it is good if they even get a simple 2D scan." These social disparities, health professionals said, place rural women at higher risk of giving birth to disabled children, thereby aggravating already existing social gaps between different segments of Vietnam's population. In Dr. Nam's words, "As soon as you go outside urban areas, there are many malformations, and rates of neonatal and maternal mortality remain high. We have not yet succeeded in broadening the scope of our work." As a consequence of access difficulties, doctors said, some pregnant women do not get the medical assistance they need. Dr. Nhung explained that if a fetal anomaly is detected at a district-level health facility, the physician often refers the woman to Hanoi. Yet by the time she arrives at the obstetrics hospital, the pregnancy may be so advanced that there is little physicians there can do to help her:

> This is a question of the intellectual level of our entire population (*dân trí*), it is not about one single individual. Even our health care providers lack awareness about this and they often refer patients to us when it is too late. . . . At 34 weeks, what can we do? At that stage the fetus lies curled up in the womb, and it is very big. It is hard to see arms and legs; one cannot see if it has five fingers or not, if the legs are curved, and if it is moving properly. There are many limitations at that stage, so there will be errors. But people don't understand this at all. We must make sure that our health care providers instruct women to come for at least three scans in each pregnancy.

Many doctors expressed similar concerns about fellow citizens' limited levels of education. Such statements can be interpreted in several ways.

From one perspective, they can be seen as rhetorical attempts to claim positions of expertise and privilege: by distancing themselves from patients and from colleagues practicing in rural provinces, these Hanoian physicians marked themselves as urban, modern, and well educated. Yet their statements can also be seen as calls for a more just society where medical privileges are distributed in an equitable manner; seen from this perspective, physicians' regrets repeat long-standing socialist visions of a better society, one that guarantees health for all.

Concerns about health care inequities were, in short, recurrent themes in our conversations with doctors. Although the vast majority of women in Vietnam do attend antenatal care, they observed, the country's deepening social inequalities produce significant differences in the quality of care that women can expect, and for those who live in rural areas, new technologies of pregnancy care such as ultrasonography often remain both geographically and financially out of reach.[8] Yet unfortunate pregnancy outcomes may also, physicians claimed, occur among women who *do* have access to new screening technologies. One never knows, they explained, how women and their relatives will interpret the information they obtain from an ultrasound scan, and there is always a risk that they will come to a decision other than the one physicians consider to be the most proper (*đúng đắn*).

PREVENTING DISABILITY: PHYSICIANS' MORAL OBLIGATIONS

What is the aim of prenatal screening? In the United States and Europe, prenatal screening is, as noted earlier, officially defined as an intervention that aims to enhance reproductive autonomy. The health care provider is therefore expected to offer the expectant parents the information they need, and then retreat, placing patients under minimal external pressure. Existing research has found that health care professionals involved in prenatal screening in Western settings often concur with these guidelines, finding it essential that prospective parents are allowed to make their own decisions. Health care practitioners in a study conducted in two English hospitals, for instance, claimed that the task of the health care provider is "to support the individual woman, whatever her choice" (Williams et al. 2002b:71).[9] The opinions expressed by physicians in Hanoi differed markedly from these positions. Practically all doctors I met seemed to hold that the primary aim of prenatal screening is not to enhance expectant parents' autonomy but to protect them by preventing them from undertaking actions that might result in the birth of a severely disabled child.

Dr. Mai Hương was one of the doctors whom I frequently met in the antenatal care room. A thirty-five-year old mother of two, she seemed eager to talk, asking questions about my children and comparing health care conditions in Vietnam to what she assumed was the situation in Europe. One day, when we talked about the tasks she performed in this maternity hospital, she summed up the ambition driving her work in two sentences: "You see, as an obstetrician I want women to give birth to children who are entirely healthy. I want that very much." Dr. Nam, a male colleague of Dr. Mai Hương who overheard our conversation, added: "It is our task to ensure that 'the mother is round, the child square,' that both mother and child are safe. . . . If that is not the case, it is the obstetrician's fault. It means that we have not exercised our professional skills properly. Children must be healthy in physical terms, but they must also be perfect (*hoàn thiện*) [i.e., nondisabled]."

Notably, when I asked physicians such as Dr. Mai Hương and Dr. Nam if they thought that ultrasound contributes to enhancing population quality, they would usually look puzzled, offering a one-word answer: *chịu* (no idea). In declaring their fascination with this new technology, then, physicians referred to its immediate clinical benefits rather than to national population policies; their day-to-day work, they implied, was oriented toward individual and family welfare rather than toward state-set demographic goals. Nevertheless, the opinions they expressed seemed to converge in significant ways with the political ambitions driving state efforts to enhance population quality. Like population policy makers, physicians defined severe disability as a heavy burden (*gánh nặng*) on family and society. Since childhood disability entails far-ranging societal costs, they claimed, reproductive decisions are not simply private questions that can be left to expectant parents alone. Rather, they are collective matters of vital importance for families, kin groups, and society at large. When a fetal problem was found, they said, they would therefore always encourage the woman to make her decision in consultation with her family. Dr. Yến, for instance, explained that because the woman depends on her relatives for support, she has to involve them in her decision: "If she keeps the child, she will have the family's sympathy (*thông cảm*). And if she terminates the pregnancy, she also has the family's sympathy." But although the family's opinion is important, doctors said, as health care professionals, they carry special, and more extensive, responsibilities. There are good and bad, proper and improper reproductive decisions, and it is the physician's responsibility to ensure that women reach decisions that are beneficial (có lợi) for them and their families. In Dr. Hồng's words, "We must have an opinion. We must tell them if they should keep this fetus or not."

When doctors at this maternity hospital placed themselves in protective positions vis-à-vis patients, they also took up subject positions offered by official discourse on national health care. Through decades of socialist mobilization for health, physicians have been charged with special responsibilities for the welfare of fellow citizens. Hồ Chí Minh, in his 1955 address to the nation's health care cadres (quoted in chapter 2), encouraged health care workers to show compassion for their patients, placing themselves in a kinlike position vis-à-vis their compatriots: "The patients entrust their lives to you. The government entrusts the treatment of your compatriots' (đồng bào) diseases and protection of their health to you. This is a very honorable responsibility. Therefore, health care cadres must love and care for their patients as for their own brothers and sisters, considering their patients' pain their own. 'The doctor must be like a loving mother'; this expression is quite true."

In short, although pregnancy care practices are changing in the current era of high-tech medicine, Hanoian physicians suggested, their task remains what it has always been: to enhance the health and protect the lives of mothers and children. Yet the availability of technologies for prenatal diagnosis, they indicated, has made this assignment more clinically and morally complicated than it was in the past. When prenatal screening is undertaken, boundaries must constantly be drawn— between more and less serious conditions, between disabilities that a child and its family can live with and those that they cannot. While other public health interventions, such as immunization programs, are implemented in a uniform and systematic manner across entire populations, prenatal screening demands constant assessments and decisions.

"I DO NOT WANT TO LET MY PATIENT KEEP SUCH A FETUS": STEERING PATIENTS TOWARD PROPER DECISIONS

How to draw the line—how to define which fetal conditions should be screened for, which conditions are severe, which problems give grounds for an abortion, and who should make these decisions—forms a contentious set of issues in prenatal diagnosis everywhere.[10] Yet unlike many health care professionals working in Western settings, the physicians I met in Hanoi did not hesitate to express their personal opinions on these matters. In conversations with my Vietnamese colleagues and me and in interactions with patients, they would often indicate in very direct terms what *they* thought were the right decisions for a woman and her relatives to make when a fetal problem was found. They distinguished between two kinds of fetal anomalies: those that are severe (*nặng*)—that is, incompatible either with life or with what they called a fully human life—and those that are mild (*nhẹ*)—that is, either surgically correctable or of minor consequence for the life of the child-to-be. Among the conditions that physicians placed in the first category were anencephaly (*vô sọ*), severe hydrocephalus (*não úng thủy*), large umbilical hernia (*thoát vị rốn*), large abdominal hernia (*thoát vị bụng*), hydrops fetalis (*dị sản bạch mạch*), and "frog belly syndrome" (*bụng cóc*). In the second category they placed problems such as cleft lip (*sứt môi*) and cleft palate (*hở hàm ếch*), small abdominal hernias, curved arms or legs, and missing or surplus fingers or toes.

If a fetus is found to suffer from a severe problem, physicians said, it is best for the woman to undergo an abortion, as carrying the pregnancy to term will be damaging for the life of the child, the parents, and the entire family. In Dr. Nga's words, "Letting such a child live is a much bigger moral problem than aborting it. Such children will suffer and bring pain to their parents and to other people too." Only if the problem was found during the very last weeks of the pregnancy, physicians claimed, should a severely impaired fetus be kept. In determining where to draw the line between severe and mild fetal problems, they often pointed to problems of social integration: the critical question was, they suggested, whether this child could be integrated into the community (*hoà nhập với cộng đồng*). If it seemed likely that the child would grow up to lead its life on the margins of society, unable to support itself and others, they explained, a pregnancy termination was the most humane (*nhân đạo*) solution. Dr. Trang, a thirty-four-year-old obstetrician-gynecologist, repeated the position taken by many other doctors when she said: "In my opinion, if the defect can be cured, the child should be allowed to live. But if the defect is severe, for instance, severe hydrocephalus, then I don't think the child will have a normal life like other children. The child will be unable to learn and to play. It will merely exist. I think this is a pity (*tội nghiệp*). It is better to allow the family to give up this child than to let it live in that way. Perhaps an abortion is most humane for both the child and the family."

Although new imaging techniques have made the detection of minor fetal anomalies increasingly possible, the problems detected during 3D scans at the obstetrics hospital were most often defined as severe. In such situations, physicians said, their primary obligation was to get the woman and her family to understand (*thông*) the necessity of a pregnancy termination. Usually, this concurred with the woman's own inclination: when hearing that something was wrong with their fetus, most women were, as Dr. Hồng put it, "immediately disposed toward an abortion" (see chapter 6). Dr. Lương explained this inclination by describing the economic-existential vulnerabilities that characterized his patients' lives: "Women are scared that this child will never be able to live independently, that they will have to care for it for their entire life. They know that society will not be able to provide for this child, that there are no welfare services. So the child will depend entirely on its parents. And when they get old, there will be no one to care for the child. It is these difficult prospects that people are thinking about. That's why they see it as a burden on the family. That's why they make a quick decision and opt for an abortion."

Doctors knew only too well, they told me, what life with a severely disabled child entails. In a country where economic insecurities are large and social welfare systems nearly nonexistent, the birth of a child with special needs places huge moral and financial demands on a family, posing challenges that are almost unimaginable for citizens of the world's wealthier countries. "In your country," Dr. Lan said in a sharp tone, "you have a lot of money, so it is different. Here, with a low income and a sick child, and one parent having to stay at home to care for the child the entire day, it is very hard. When the parents take the child to hospital it costs a lot of money, buying medicine, operations . . ." Also Dr. Trang drew attention to the ways in which economic conditions shape people's options for reproductive action. She had once worked at a hospital in France. There, she had noticed that women sometimes decided to keep fetuses with heart or kidney problems—fetuses that would instantly have been aborted in Vietnam: "In Vietnam it is extremely expensive for parents to cover treatment expenses for a child. The family has to cover all these expenses on its own. There is no help from the state or from society. So women think that if they have an abortion this time, the next time they can have a healthy child." The pressure to produce children who are entirely healthy and normal has, doctors said, intensified in the current era of low fertility: because people usually have only the one or two children that the population policy allows for, they place high expectations on their offspring. In Dr. Hồng's words, "Today people have few children and therefore they want them to be complete. They want children who are perfectly round (*tròn trịa*) [i.e., nondisabled]."

Another factor that compelled physicians to empathize with their patients was the karmic connotations that birth defects carry. In Vietnam, congenital malformations have traditionally been taken as signs that the child's parents or grandparents have acted immorally, thereby offending higher powers. If asked directly, most people will claim that such ideas are mere superstition and not to be taken seriously, yet in their day-to-day lives these notions often do seem to shape the moral judgments that are made when a child is born disabled. One day when I passed by the neonatal department, I found Dr. Nga bending over the crib of a newborn with hydrocephalus. "I feel so sorry for the parents of this child," she blurted. Assuming that as a foreigner I was unable to grasp the depth of the desperation the parents of this child must feel, she explained:

> You see, when people in Vietnam have a child who is born malformed (*quái thai*), they don't want to tell anyone. They wait for the child to die, and then the family will keep it secret. If the neighbors get to know about it, the old women in the neighborhood will say, "Oh Heaven, for sure people in that house have lived immorally (*ăn ở thất đức*)." "If you live properly, your life turns out well (*ở hiền gặp hiền*); if you live badly, your life turns out badly (*ở dữ gặp dữ*)." This makes it very difficult for such parents. . . . People are scared of what others will say [*miệng lưỡi thế gian*; lit., the tongues of the world].

When counseling their patients, physicians said, they took into account this moral environment into which the child would be born. Like their patients, they lived within close-knit communities where the birth of a defective child raises moral questions, exposing the parents to a public opinion (*dư luận*) that can be very hurtful. This knowledge of the sociomoral consequences of abnormal births often seemed to shape the ways in which doctors themselves regarded fetal anomalies; they too felt profoundly disturbed when a fetal anomaly was detected. Dr. Trang said: "In Vietnam, a fetal malformation has serious psychological consequences for the patient and her family. Other people will see them as something very terrible; they will look at them as if they are monsters, thinking, 'For sure they live indecently, or this would not have happened.' So that's why we must help the patient to solve such problems. . . . I don't think people should keep a child like that. If it happens in my department, I do not want to let my patient keep such a fetus."

All physicians insisted that abortions must always be voluntary (*tự nguyện*); no one, they emphasized, would ever force a woman to terminate her pregnancy against her will. Physicians would advise (*khuyên*), encourage (*động viên*), guide (*hướng dẫn*), explain (*giải thích*), and analyze (*phân tích*), but the final decision, they said, must be made by the woman in consultation with her relatives. In Dr. Nhung's words: "It always depends on the patient's opinion. People are very different. Some people cannot accept even a small disability. Others may keep a fetus with anencephaly or hydrocephalus. Even if we tell them to have an abortion, they still want to keep it. We have no right to change that; we cannot encroach on people." Yet despite this commitment not to encroach on people, doctors did not hide the fact that they would usually try to steer (*lái*) women toward what they themselves saw as the best solution. As Dr. Tuấn said, "It's the patient's decision. But it is the physician's task to steer people according to what is best for them. . . . We must analyze the problems carefully so that they understand and so that they can imagine the child's future and consider whether they can ensure that this child will have a good future." The counseling offered by physicians in Hanoi was, in other words, directive in ways that would be considered problematic in European or North American clinical settings. This observation resonates with research that has found systematic differences between East Asian and Western bioethical principles.

BETWEEN BIOETHICS AND MORAL EXPERIENCE

The moral ideals articulated by these Vietnamese physicians, while differing significantly from the ethical expectations set forth in clinical guidelines in the West, seemed to closely resemble those that researchers have observed in other East Asian settings. Renée C. Fox and Judith P. Swazey (1984), for instance, describe a Chinese medical morality that resonates with the one set forth by my interlocutors in Hanoi, one that emphasizes responsibilities, commitments, and emotional bonds while deemphasizing individual rights to self-determination. Similarly, based on a study of informed treatment decisions in Chinese hospital care, Mei-che Pang (1999:252) identifies protectiveness as a guiding principle in medical practice: "Health care professionals are expected to act as if they were patients' family members, protecting patients from harm, and bearing the patients' burdens of illness." Notions of protectiveness and responsibility, Pang argues, occupy a central place in ancient medical texts and continue to inform present-day medical practices in China.

Based on similar observations, bioethicists have often argued that in Asian medical settings, principles of beneficence tend to take precedence over principles of patient autonomy.[11]

From an anthropological perspective, however, attempts to interpret clinical dilemmas within bioethical frames of reference raise several problems. First, as R. Fox and Swazey (1984) have argued, bioethics assumes that selves are individuated and exist in ontological opposition to the collective, and this assumption makes it difficult to capture how social forces bring individuals into being rather than simply placing external constraints on them. Second, by giving explanatory priority to abstract ethical principles over concrete moral experiences, bioethics tends to gloss over the complexities and contradictions that always suffuse actual medical practice, thereby abstracting itself from the human sentiments and interactions that medical dilemmas entail.[12]

In order to include such sentiments in the analysis, I now turn to a more detailed examination of the social relations and events that informed Hanoian physicians' ethical deliberations. To comprehend how it came to seem self-evident to these health care professionals that direct interventions in their patients' decisions were necessary, we must attend to the day-to-day medical challenges that they confronted. The moral concerns they articulated evolved around what I have termed *critical junctures*: medical situations that were morally and affectively fraught. An exploration of these critical junctures allows us to expand the analysis of what happened in encounters between physicians and patients in this maternity hospital. On the one hand, doctors embodied the state, implementing its public health agenda in day-to-day medical practice; on the other, as we shall see, they also embodied their patients, engaging with their pain in intimate ways. To provide a sense of the situations in which patients and physicians found themselves, I begin with Bích's 3D ultrasonography. When I first met her, on February 9, 2004, Bích was thirty years old. She was a factory worker, the mother of a five-year old girl, and married to Hùng, a vegetable trader.

ENTERING BIOMEDICAL TERRAINS: BÍCH'S 3D ULTRASONOGRAPHY

Bích looked anxious. "I cannot believe this," she said. "I feel so scared. I did not sleep last night at all. My health is good, I have a good appetite, I am never sick—so why does this happen? Can you tell me?"[13] While waiting for her turn in the 3D scanning room, Bích told my colleague Chi that two days earlier, a doctor in a private ob-gyn clinic had informed her that something was wrong with her fetus. The doctor had been very curt. "This fetus is abnormal (*bất thường*)," he had said. "You will have to have an abortion right away." This message contradicted Bích's own sense of the situation: to her, this pregnancy had felt completely right. Her body heavy already, she was well into the second trimester, and she and her husband were eagerly awaiting this new child. "We have planned this pregnancy for years," she said, "we are ready to have another child now. Our daughter is five years old, we have paid off what we owe on our new house, our incomes are stable. . . . I cannot believe this."

When the nurse called out Bích's name, she lay down on the examination bed, her eyes fixed on the screen above her. The atmosphere in the room was tense. Relatives were normally not allowed to enter the 3D scanning room, but today Bích's husband was present too, looking as pale and uncomfortable as his wife. Dr. Nhung began the scan, then asked, "Have you had a cold during your pregnancy? Have you been ill?" Bích replied that she had had some slight bleeding when she was three months pregnant, but apart from that she had felt fine. Dr. Nhung focused on the fetal head, scrutinizing the image on the monitor. She concentrated for a while, then asked Bích how many weeks she was pregnant. Bích said sixteen or seventeen, but Dr. Nhung corrected her: "Your last menstrual period was September 26, so the fetus must be around 19 weeks now, right? This fetus is very small. It's developing too slowly. But the picture is not very clear. Perhaps you should go and drink some water." To Lan, the nurse, who was typing the scan result, Dr. Nhung said, "The ventricles are dilated. It is very hard to distinguish the different parts of the brain." Turning to Bích, she said, "Come back for another scan this afternoon. The result will probably be the same, but I would like to be on the safe side." In the afternoon, Dr. Nhung got the same result. She told Bích to return the following Saturday: "Small children (*trẻ nhỏ*) can change, so we must observe it for some time. Ten days from now is still not too late to make a decision."

When Bích and Hùng returned the week after, Dr. Nhung, Dr. Tuấn, Chi, and I were present in the scanning room. Dr. Tuấn performed the scan, looking closely at the brain of the fetus. The room was shrouded in silence, as if all the women awaiting their turn were feeling with Bích. From the 2D scanning room next door floated the sounds of doctors' voices; they were joking and laughing. Looking anxious, Hùng glanced from the monitor to Dr. Tuấn and back again. Finally Dr. Tuấn said to

Dr. Nhung, "They are still dilated. The lateral and the lower ventricles are dilated, for sure. There is not much amniotic fluid either. And the fetal body is very short." Bích was now sitting up on the examination bed, her husband standing next to her. Dr. Nhung looked her in the eye and said, "For sure, you will have to abort this fetus. You cannot keep it." Dr. Tuấn added, "The fetus is not even 22 weeks old, but the ventricles are *very* dilated. This means that the brain will be pressured." In a caring tone, Dr. Nhung said, "You should have an abortion, younger sister (*nên bỏ em ạ*)." In Bích's eyes, tears were welling up. She did not say anything. Dr. Nhung continued, "There is no brain, and the body is abnormal too. The bones are too short, and it is developing too slowly. Now, go and see the doctor in the antenatal care room." To me, Dr. Nhung said, "You know her, right? She should give up this fetus. The ventricles are much too dilated for a fetus this age."

The antenatal care room was crowded with women at different stages of pregnancy, some sitting on chairs along the wall, others walking in and out. Two doctors clad in white coats were performing examinations. Their faces closed, they seemed intensely concentrated on their work. Standing in a corner of the room, Bích looked lost. She gripped her antenatal care book tightly in her hand as she tried to attract the attention of one of the physicians. He ignored her, turning to another woman. After a while, a female doctor gestured to her to lie down on an examination bed. Without a word, she measured her blood pressure, listened to the heartbeat of the fetus, and wrote the results in the antenatal care book. At the bottom of the page she copied the scan result, "The ventricles of the brain are dilated. The fetus is developing too slowly," and noted, "Sent to A4." Without giving Bích any opportunity to ask questions, she handed her two forms, one for blood tests, the other for urine tests. Indicating that the session was over, she said, "When you have got the results from these examinations, you can register to go into hospital." A few hours later, Bích entered A4, the department for reproductive disorders. Three days later, the abortion was completed.

CRITICAL JUNCTURES

"A pregnant woman stands at the edge of the grave" (*chửa như ở cửa mả*), Vietnamese folk wisdom says. Although maternal deaths are relatively rare in Hanoi today, childbearing is still considered a hazardous endeavor. Pregnancies can take unforeseen turns, and childbirth is an unpredictable and existentially extreme event in which blood is spilled, insides are turned out, and intimate body parts are exposed. During fieldwork at this hospital, I was often struck by the intensity of doctors' emotional engagement with their patients in maternity care practices. When performing ultrasound scans, Dr. Tuấn beamed with pride and joy as he showed the woman the physical features of her fetus. Dr. Lan's interest in bringing down rates of children born with congenital disabilities was, she told me, grounded in the sadness and empathy she felt when witnessing parents' desperation at the birth of a disabled child. During counseling sessions, physicians' frustration when a woman failed to get the message they tried to convey often showed in angry gestures and an impatient tone of voice. And doctors' unease when patients came to decisions other than those that they had steered them toward was evident from their wrinkled brows and eager appeals to me to convince the women to follow medical advice. When talking about their work, physicians often focused on three critical junctures where affective stakes were particularly high: first, when an ultrasound scan revealed a fetal problem; second, when decisions about a pregnancy were made; and third, when second-trimester abortions were performed.

Sonographers such as Dr. Nhung and Dr. Tuấn often emphasized how difficult they found it to convey the bad news to a patient when a fetal anomaly was detected. This situation, Dr. Nhung told me, reminded her of a pregnancy loss that she herself had suffered years earlier:

> I find it terribly hard (*khó kinh khủng*). Often I prolong the examination because I don't know how to broach the issue. Sometimes I work very slowly, spending forty minutes on the examination because I don't know how to tell them. It is so painful. I feel so sad. . . . You see, the first time I was pregnant, I lost the child, and it was very painful for me. So I think that for sure this woman will also feel tormented when she hears this. Sometimes I wonder if I have to tell her. It is so tormenting, so difficult. In such situations I have sometimes consulted my former teacher, and he has said to me, "You *must* tell them, younger sister." That makes me feel confident in doing so. I think that getting to know early on makes it easier for them. But when we find a problem late in the pregnancy [too late for an abortion], it is very hard. Then I know that these people will always be haunted by the fact that their child was born like this. That's what I find hardest of all.

Many doctors told us that they had developed special strategies for conveying bad news as gently as possible. Dr. Lan worked in the hospital's department for reproductive disorders during the day, and after work she ran a private ob-gyn clinic where ultrasounds were a routine part of antenatal care. If a prenatal exam conducted in her clinic found a fetal problem, she said, she would never tell the patient straightaway. Instead, she would say to her that something *might* be wrong and that, to be sure, she should go for another scan somewhere else. This gradual process of coming to know, Dr. Lan assumed, would lessen the shock for the woman: "It is easier if she comes to accept the problem gradually. It does not matter if she carries the pregnancy for one or two more days. But it is important not to shock her by conveying the news to her too abruptly. Pregnant women cherish their pregnancies. They are elated when they come for the scan. It is so difficult to have to tell them that something is wrong."

The second kind of critical juncture was that of pregnancy-related decision making. When a 3D scan found a fetal anomaly, the woman would usually, like Bích, be referred to the antenatal care department, where a physician would read the result for her. Doctors working in this department often described how they felt a surge of compassion for their patient. Having to decide whether or not to terminate a wanted pregnancy was, they said, inhumanly hard for the woman and her relatives, and the difficulty of this choice also posed moral challenges for health care professionals. Dr. Mai Hương, for instance, talked at length about the demands she felt that her patients' distress placed on her as a medical provider: "Many patients are in shock. They don't understand what is wrong with the fetus or why this has happened. They ask many questions and they are *very* worried. Practically all women who come with such a result are crying. . . . Therefore, we try to explain very carefully so that they understand that the fetus is not normal, and we encourage them to opt for the solution that is best for them." While emphasizing that the final decision was always the woman's, doctors defined it as *their* task to care for her by giving her decision-making directions (*hướng quyết định*). Dr. Lan told me that she and her colleagues had attended numerous training courses conducted by international organizations on two-way or nondirective counseling. Yet their professional opinion continued to be, she said, that the physician has an obligation to get involved in more direct ways with the patient's decision making: "Ideally, the patients should make the decision. We should offer them information and they should make the decision themselves. But in some cases, we must help people to decide (*quyết định giúp người ta*). . . . In reality, in many cases, we do not just give information and let the patient decide." Doctors' responsibilities in this realm intensified, they said, when a patient ignored their advice, refusing to believe the medical message she was being given. One such patient was Tuyết, whose story opens this book. When Dr. Tuấn told her that there was water on the brain of her fetus, she refused to believe him and left the hospital. Telling me about this episode, Lan, the scanning room nurse, was visibly upset, and when Tuyết returned a few days later, she asked me to "give her some counseling"—that is, convince her that the condition of her fetus was severe and that an abortion was necessary. This was one of the situations that health practitioners feared the most; when women turned their backs on medical expertise, they said, there was nothing they could do to help them.

But the need to steer patients arose not only when the physician found an abortion necessary. Doctors also expressed intense frustration when pregnant women requested—and obtained—second-trimester abortions that health providers thought unwarranted.[14] Their moral unease particularly concerned sex-selective abortions and abortions obtained due to minor problems such as a cleft lip or palate.[15] Such abortions are, many doctors insisted, extremely immoral (vô nhân đạo quá). In Dr. Trang's words: "Cleft lips and cleft palates can be operated on. Still, some mothers opt for an abortion. No matter what we say to them, they don't listen. . . . I feel it is wrong to perform such abortions." When a scan found a fetal problem that they defined as minor, physicians would inform the woman that for this condition, an abortion was not necessary. Yet if she insisted on an abortion, they had to perform it. In her reflections on this, Dr. Thúy resorted to a language of rights: "In terms of decision making, we can give people directions (hướng), but the final decision is always the patient's. In my opinion, it is their right, the couple's right, to decide to have an abortion if they want to. We can give them information and directions, but it's the family's decision. Today, many families are very scared of having a disabled child. They are worried about public opinion and many other problems. So in many cases they prefer to give up this child and have another instead. This is their right." In sum, doctors suggested that when women and their relatives found themselves in the position of having to make a tremendously painful choice, the doctors faced special responsibilities; in order to care for their patients, they had to intervene and guide them in their decisions.

The third critical juncture that physicians evoked was the performance of late-term abortions. None of the doctors I met ever questioned the necessity of offering women access to induced abortion. But late-term pregnancy terminations were, they said, intensely troublesome emotionally: they felt sorry for the child-to-be who lost its

life and for the mother who lost her child. Since most pregnancy terminations for fetal anomaly took place after week 18, they were conducted at a stage of gestation when a delivery had to be induced. "I
don't know how men feel about this," Dr. Lan said. "But as a woman,
I feel so sorry for these women. They have been pregnant for a long
time, and the fetus is big. . . . When I see such fetuses I feel so pained
(*áy náy*). With a small fetus I feel lighter at heart. That's different. But
with a big fetus I feel very pained and sad."[16] At this hospital, physicians said, late-term abortions are conducted under safe circumstances;
but no matter how careful physicians are, there is always a risk of uterine rupture, hemorrhage, and maternal death. In physicians' accounts,
fears loomed large, therefore, of performing this intervention on the
basis of an incorrect diagnosis. In the early days of ultrasonography in
Vietnam, Dr. Lan told me, there had been cases in which fetuses that
the physician had declared dead in utero had turned out to be alive at
birth. With today's more sophisticated medical equipment, she said,
such crude mistakes no longer occurred, but the fear of making an
error of judgment remained, and many doctors felt both morally and
legally vulnerable. Dr. Nam shared Dr. Lan's opinion: "Making a diagnosis is difficult in itself," he said, "but making the decision to abort
the fetus is even more difficult. If we perform an abortion and there
turns out to be no problem with the fetus, we die. To tell you the truth,
we die."

At each of these critical junctures, then, Hanoian physicians played
key roles, exercising medical authority and entering into women's lives
in consequential ways. Throughout our conversations, they depicted
their own and their patients' existence as closely interconnected. Taking
Hồ Chí Minh's metaphor seriously, they described themselves as being
affiliated with their patients in kinlike relations of compassion, affect,
and care. Despite the status differences that separated them, they suggested, physicians and patients were implicated in each other's lives,
and it was this interpersonal engagement that generated the sense of
responsibility they described and that animated their efforts to ensure
that pregnant women "did the right thing." Rather than standing vis-à-
vis their patients in a relation of externality, doctors suggested, they
were open and exposed to them, involved in their plights. They were
vulnerable to their patients' vulnerability; if their patients suffered,
they suffered with them. This brings to mind Levinas's claim (1998c
[1982]:94) that suffering can be considered as the very nexus of human
subjectivity. Suffering is, Levinas says, in itself useless, for nothing. Yet

it can take on meaning by becoming a suffering for the other: one person's suffering places a moral obligation on the other, calling on him or her to respond. Suffering opens people to one another, showing that "no one can remain in himself" (Levinas 2006 [1970]:149). Their professional expertise, Hanoian physicians suggested, placed them under an obligation to respond, helping their patient by guiding her decision. To *not* do this, to take a more detached position and leave the decision to the woman, would be to let her down, to betray her. In Dr. Trang's words, "I think that when people find out that their fetus is malformed, it helps them to know that they are under the doctor's protection (*bảo trợ*). They need to know that the doctor watches over them and shows concern for them." Yet in day-to-day clinical practice, this inclination to respond to the patient's needs for support often seemed to come up against very concrete limits to the care that could be offered. I soon realized that, in practice, doctors did not always act in the committed and caring ways that they claimed as ideal. Often, the medical support that women received when a fetal problem was found was—in my eyes—disturbingly inadequate.[17]

MEDICAL CONNECTIONS AND DISCONNECTIONS

When a fetal anomaly was detected in the 3D scanning room, the woman was usually simply handed the scan result and told to go to the antenatal care room for more information. Interpreting the result, sonographers explained to me, was the task of the physician on duty there. The antenatal care room was, however, practically always crowded and hectic, and, as in Bích's case, even getting a doctor's attention was often a challenge for the woman. When she finally did manage to make contact with a physician, she would usually be offered minimal information and hardly any opportunity to ask questions. Doctors often seemed brusque and short-tempered, and patient-provider interactions would usually last only a few minutes, aiming, it seemed, primarily to make sure the woman got the message about how to act on the scan result. The following interactions were typical:

> Chung was 21 weeks pregnant. The ultrasound scan showed that the fetus was possibly suffering from abdominal hernia. The doctor in the antenatal care room told her: "Abdominal hernia can be operated on after birth. It is not among the conditions we do abortions for." Chung asked, "So it is not so serious?" The doctor did not reply, but returned Chung's papers to her, indicating that the session was over.

Hồng was 26 weeks pregnant, the scan showed anencephaly. The doctor said, "Oh heavens, are you aware that your child is disabled? We will admit you to the hospital for an abortion. If you keep this one, it will only mean hardship for you and hardship for your child. I will prepare the papers for you to go into hospital, if you are not ready today, then tomorrow. Today, go home and talk to your family." She filled out some forms; Hồng left without a word.

To Trâm, the doctor said, "This fetus has prune belly syndrome (bụng cóc). It is 19 weeks and 3 days old. What do you intend?" A younger doctor standing next to her exclaimed, "The fetus has prune belly syndrome; why don't you just send her for examinations [i.e., to prepare for an abortion]." Trâm asked, "What does prune belly syndrome mean?" The doctor replied, "It means the fetus is malformed. It cannot live. You are from Vĩnh Phúc province, so in principle we do not admit you here, but go and sign up to go into hospital. Now, next patient."

Numerous ethnographic studies have documented serious gaps in the quality of care provided in public hospitals in low- and middle-income settings. When health care providers act harshly toward patients, these studies suggest, this is most often because they themselves feel under pressure—from other professional groups, from patients, or from managers higher up in health system hierarchies.[18] When their professional position is threatened, in other words, health providers across the globe seem to react by exercising authority and enforcing control where they can, as in relations with patients. Often, studies have shown, assumptions of patient ignorance and inferiority tend to exacerbate these practices. To account for the discrepancies between the ideals articulated by Hanoian physicians and the actual antenatal care they provided, I suggest, we must take into consideration the professional pressures they were exposed to and the structural forces that shaped these pressures. As Sharon Kaufman (1997:4) notes, "Doctor-patient interactions, wherever they occur physically, are situated also in structural, political, and socio-economic environments which influence the construction of moral-medical problems. Sources of dilemmas are in many cases beyond the literal walls of hospital, clinic, home, and office and are located, more importantly, in poverty and social inequality, the organization of health care institutions, the perceived 'need' to act with the newest technologies available, and other normalizing features and strategies that shape the cultural field in which physicians practice."

Hanoi's Obstetrics and Gynecology Hospital was, as its name suggests, originally established to provide the inhabitants of Hanoi with reproductive health care services. At the time of this fieldwork, however, it also catered to people from outlying rural provinces. Underresourced provincial hospitals, patients and providers explained, could not provide the high-tech care and specialized medical expertise that central-level hospitals offered.[19] When pregnancy complications occurred, therefore, many women preferred to travel to Hanoi despite the inconvenience and the higher costs. Trâm was one of them. She should, as the doctor indicated, in principle have obtained care at her local provincial hospital, but went to Hanoi instead. This influx of patients resulted in a very high patient load at this maternity hospital, as women living as far away as the provinces bordering China chose to avail themselves of reproductive health care services here. Due to health sector liberalization, the hospital depended financially on revenue generated from patients' out-of-pocket payments; in this market-based system, therefore, there were strong economic incentives to receive as many patients as possible. As a consequence, hospital facilities were overstretched. From early morning until late afternoon, waiting rooms and corridors were crowded with women, many accompanied by their husbands or other family members. The atmosphere was busy and hectic as people walked up and down corridors and hallways, trying to find their way around, picking up results from blood or urine tests, paying fees, or waiting for their turn for services.

One late afternoon in October 2004, Dr. Lan and I were sitting in the doctors' room in A4, the department for reproductive disorders. She was filling out patients' files, and I was going over my field notes. After a while, she put aside the papers in front of her and asked me what I was writing. When I told her about my observations in the antenatal care room earlier that day, she nodded and said: "You know, we have so many patients. In one morning, a doctor has to see around fifty patients and there are hardly any breaks. Due to these time constraints, we have become used to not offering any counseling. Even if we have time, we don't offer counseling; this has become a habit. Our boss keeps instructing us to greet people and treat them carefully and examine them properly and so on. But time is so short and outside the patients are flocking. This makes providers tired, and often we don't give any counseling at all." Looking out into the corridor outside the doctors' room, I understood what she meant. This department was one of the quietest in the hospital, and still the corridor was full of people, the atmosphere nervous and chaotic. While Dr. Lan and I talked, pregnant women in red-and-white hospital gowns shuffled up and down the corridor, some of them looking introverted and in pain; relatives went in and out carrying extra clothes or trays of food; and doctors walked hastily through as if signaling that they had no time to spare. During antenatal care consultations, as Dr. Lan said, a similarly hectic atmosphere prevailed. Doctors seemed always conscious of the fact that they were working under pressure, almost racing against time, and that scores of women were waiting to get their attention.[20]

Witnessing doctor-patient interactions, I often speculated whether these stressful working conditions produced a sense of frustration and disempowerment that doctors then handled by exercising dominance and authority over patients. Was there, I wondered, also an element of self-protection at play in situations where doctors seemed impatient and rough? Being keenly aware that there were limits to the care they could provide, did health staff sometimes have to distance themselves emotionally in order to maintain self-comportment and professionalism? Might such emotional detachment be even more likely in cases of acute reproductive crisis—such as those of Chung, Hồng, and Trâm described above—where physicians themselves felt anguished and disturbed by their patient's predicament?

These were not, however, the explanations that doctors themselves resorted to when I presented my observations to them. Instead, they would most often focus on the clinical uncertainties that they struggled with in this new and professionally demanding field of reproductive health care.

CLINICAL UNCERTAINTIES: THE SOCIAL CONDITIONING OF MEDICAL MORALITIES

On May 14, 2004, I had a conversation with Dr. Lương, a thirty-eight-year-old obstetrician-gynecologist. On this day he talked in unusually explicit terms about the clinical uncertainties that he and his colleagues faced; uncertainties, he told me, that prevented them from offering pregnant women optimal counseling and care. We were sitting in the hospital's library, the table fan next to us running at maximum speed and carving pockets of coolness in the hot afternoon air. Dr. Lương told me that he had worked with ultrasonography since its introduction at the hospital in the early 1990s. But even though they worked with this technology on a day-to-day basis, he explained, he and his colleagues had attended only a relatively short training course on obstetrical ultrasonography. This course had focused mainly on the normal fetus, and he felt that as physicians, they were not adequately trained in the interpretation of abnormal ultrasound findings. He reminded me of the case of a woman named Lý (recounted fully in chapter 6), saying:

> Do you remember how we all felt unsure about what was wrong with Lý's fetus? To tell you the truth, her case is not unique. The reality is that we do not know much about these things. . . . Take prune belly syndrome (*bụng cóc*; lit., frog belly), for instance. This is a condition that is very easy to see [in the scanning image], and we call it prune belly syndrome. But actually, we don't know what it is. We don't know what it may imply, what kind of abilities the child will have, how it will develop, or if it can be treated. . . . If the physicians do not know anything about this, how can they counsel the parents? This means that the parents' understanding of their child's disease will be very vague and inexact. This is something very damaging (*thiệt*). It is not beneficial for the parents. They don't know if their child's disease is mild or severe, and if it can be treated or not. We say that the parents have the right to decide, but how can they decide if they are not offered any information?

There were fetal problems, Dr. Lương said, that he and his colleagues encountered relatively frequently and whose implications they felt certain about. Yet in cases of rare conditions, or when common conditions manifested in unusual ways, it was difficult for them to offer the woman a reading of the scan image and guidance on how to act on it. Drawing on their professional experience, they might be able to say with certainty that a fetus was not normal, but remain unable to define this abnormality in biomedical terms. This, Dr. Lương said, made physicians inclined to share their patients' view of the anomalous fetus as a strange and frightening creature: "People in Vietnam have a characteristic that I feel uneasy about. In Vietnam, even physicians think that congenital defects are something very severe. Always. Because we cannot determine which defects are minor and which ones are severe. So whenever we find a congenital problem we think that it is very severe and very difficult to overcome. That is why, in counseling, doctors' ideas are quite subjective when they say, 'You may as well give up this one,' for instance. This makes the patient inclined to feel that way too."

The clinical uncertainties that characterized their work with ultrasonography, doctors said, stemmed partly from the fact that they did not have access to genetic testing.[21] Regretting this lack of more sophisticated diagnostic technologies, Dr. Mai Hương described the powerlessness she felt in cases where her own insight into a fetal problem hardly surpassed that of her patient:

> If the diagnosis is clear, it is easy to talk to the patient. In that case I can describe to her what this diagnosis means. I know if this fetus will live or die

after birth. But with some malformations, it is very difficult for the doctor to picture for herself what their consequences will be. Our knowledge about such malformations may be very limited, and so all I can say is that according to the sonographer, this fetus is not normal. . . . Often, when I encounter a malformed fetus, there are many things that I want to understand better. I want to understand *why* this has happened and *what* the problem is so that I can answer the patient's questions. But this is very difficult, because we rely entirely on the scan result. We have no other means of making a diagnosis.

Before ending our fieldwork at the hospital, my Vietnamese colleagues and I held a group discussion with some of the doctors who worked with prenatal screening. At an early point in this discussion, Dr. Thụ, a senior obstetrician, said: "To be honest, one of our main problems in prenatal screening is that we lack equipment. Without proper equipment, it is often impossible to establish a diagnosis." Such diagnostic uncertainty is, he continued, often very painful for physicians, placing them in humiliating situations where they are unable to answer their patients' questions:

When the clinician relies only on the ultrasound scan result, it is not enough. Scientifically there is a need for more. But in Vietnam we do not have the conditions to do this, so we have to simply rely on our experience. So, for instance, if the patient asks me whether she should have an abortion or not, I can tell her to have an abortion. But if she asks what disease it is, I cannot reply. I can only say something very general based on my experience. I can say for instance that this disease may be genetic, and the fetus is not normal. But if she asks me what kind of genetic disease it is, I cannot tell her. I do not know.

Dr. Liên, another senior ob-gyn, supported Dr. Thụ's position:

Today people in Vietnam have a very high level of knowledge (*dân trí cao lắm*). In the past, all people could think of was how to get two meals a day. Today educational levels are higher, the economy has developed, and people have time to pay attention to other things. They read books, they watch television, and they know that colds, fevers, and intake of medicine can cause malformations. Then they ask, "I did not suffer from any of this, so why is my fetus malformed?" They ask a lot of questions. "If I keep this fetus, will the child live?" "Will this child be able to develop normally?" and so on. Often, it is very difficult for us to answer their questions.[22]

In short, as they engaged in novel forms of medical practice, Hanoian health care providers often found themselves in professionally challenging and personally troubling situations where the kinds of care they were able to offer were far from the ideals that they themselves set forth. Their ambitions to act as competent, compassionate, caring, knowledgeable, and responsible health care experts collided, in other words, with the socioeconomic conditions under which they worked. Day-to-day clinical realities often made it difficult to serve as the vanguard protectors of the people's health that they aspired to be.

STATES OF BELONGING

As this chapter shows, the ideas and sentiments that Hanoian health professionals expressed represent forms of ethicality that differ significantly from those that are placed at the forefront of clinical practices in the Western world. In medical settings in Europe and North America, nondirective counseling tends to be regarded as the most proper model for patient-provider interactions in ethically demanding situations.[23] This raises the question of how to interpret the medical practices I observed in Hanoi, practices in which health staff tried to steer their patients toward what *they* considered to be the right decisions. Hanoian physicians' preferences for directive counseling could be interpreted in several different ways—as expressions of East Asian medical paternalism, as attempts to claim privileged social positions within an increasingly competitive society, or as elements in state-led efforts to persuade people to conform with state-set norms for human quality. What I have argued, however, is that there is reason to take seriously the moral principles and affective sensibilities that underpinned these medical positions. Rather than seeking to realize liberal ideals of autonomy and self-determination, this chapter shows, health care practitioners in Hanoi placed emphasis on moral values of empathy, affiliation, care, and responsibility. Underlying day-to-day medical practice in this maternity hospital was a specific ontology of the human: a tacit assumption that rather than standing vis-à-vis each other in external confrontation, patients and providers are tied together in affective and morally binding relations, relations that compel physicians to take active part in patients' decisions. By offering pregnant women directive guidance, then, physicians articulated a sense of responsibility and belonging—to their patients and to established national public health projects involving mothers and children across the country. In practice, however, physicians in this maternity hospital often found it difficult to offer patients the motherly care and authoritative guidance that they defined as ideal. The social and economic conditions under which they worked set limits on the care they could provide, separating the professional roles that they rhetorically ascribed to themselves from day-to-day clinical practices.

These observations then also invite us to reconsider the ways in which state-society relations are configured in research on reproductive politics. The ethnographic findings that I present in this chapter suggest that conventional concepts of the state as a machinery of power that controls and disciplines people leaves important affective and interpersonal dynamics out of the analysis (cf. chapter 1). Anthropological analyses of state-citizen relations may, I suggest, demand more cautious avenues of interpretation; avenues that allow us to transcend state-citizen binaries. This chapter shows, first, that the moral parameters set forth by the state—including its visions of interhuman connections and responsibilities—are not restricted to laws, policies, and other official statements, but diffuse into everyday lives through the social practices that tie together physicians and patients, cadres and ordinary citizens. The obstetrics hospital in Hanoi was one site in which this diffusion of official rhetoric on care and responsibility took place in particularly poignant ways, entering into affective engagements with the life projects of patients and physicians. Second, not only do official expectations extend into everyday lives, but everyday lives also contribute to shaping state interventions. In Hanoian medical practice, as we have seen, the sentiments expressed by health care professionals resonated in striking ways with those of their patients. Although physicians would usually present themselves as possessors of privileged scientific knowledge, taking up positions of authority and certainty vis-à-vis their patients, they also expressed ideas and intuitions that closely resembled the imaginings of pregnant women and their relatives. Like their patients, physicians tended to react to the emergence of a malformed fetus on the monitor with terror and trepidation. They too did not understand why fetal development had gone awry, and they too knew how people in local communities react when children are born defective. Their professional stances were, in other words, grounded in a visceral, embodied awareness of the sociomoral implications of infant disability. As practiced on the ground, in short, the Vietnamese state's political project of population enhancement was embedded in ethically and emotionally charged interhuman engagements; rather than simply being implemented in a top-down process, it was animated by local moral sensibilities and by widely shared visions of human connections and interdependencies.

CHAPTER 5

"How Have We Lived?"

Accounting for Reproductive Misfortune

CHÚC: "WHY DO I MEET THIS MISFORTUNE?"

"In our family we don't have much expert knowledge. We do not understand this. Her husband has not been in the army. Can there be environmental problems in this area, as this has happened?" Định, Chúc's elder brother-in-law, looked bewildered.

On December 10, 2003, Toàn and I traveled to a rural village twenty-five kilometers from Hanoi to meet with twenty-seven-year old Chúc and her family. A few days earlier, an ultrasound scan performed at the obstetrics hospital had revealed that her fetus fell far outside the boundaries of the normal. Its legs were 40 millimeters long—this was defined as normal at 24 weeks gestation, but Chúc was 36 weeks pregnant. In the hospital, sitting on the bench outside the 3D scanning room, Chúc had briefly told us about the events that had brought her to Hanoi. One month earlier, she had been for an ultrasound scan at the district health center. When the doctor told her that something was wrong with her fetus, it was as if the ground vanished from under her. She could hardly take in his words. "This fetus is malformed (*dị dạng*)," he had said. "You must go to Hanoi for another scan." A few days later, Chúc's husband, Tuệ, drove her on the back of his motorbike to the obstetrics hospital in Hanoi. Here, Dr. Tuấn told her that the legs of her fetus were curved and much too short. Had she come two or three months earlier, he would have recommended a pregnancy termination. But since she was now seven months pregnant, he advised her to simply keep the pregnancy and hope for the best. A month later, when Chúc returned to the obstetrics hospital for another scan, she was informed that the legs of her fetus had not developed at all during the past month; they remained only four centimeters long. It was at this visit that I first met her.

When Toàn and I arrived, we found a group of around ten people, mainly women, waiting for us in the main room of the house. It was a chilly morning, and everyone was wearing a padded overcoat, so it took a few seconds for me to spot Chúc among all the other women. Although it was close to her due date, one could scarcely see that she was pregnant. Tuệ invited Toàn and me to sit in the heavy wooden chairs beneath the ancestral altar. Chúc was sitting next to us, her mother and mother-in-law opposite us, and Tuệ was standing behind the grandmothers, together with the women who turned out to be his sisters and his mother's sisters. We engaged in small talk for a while, about the weather and the crops, until Định arrived. A local official, he was tall and obese and a person who was clearly used to commanding respect. As soon as he sat down with us, his mother indicated that he should tell us the story.

He began by telling us of Chúc's reproductive history: this was her fourth pregnancy. No live children had come from her first two pregnancies: the first child had died at birth, the second too. Yet her third pregnancy had resulted in the birth of a son whose body was, as one of the women interjected, *lành*—complete. Định emphasized that nothing had been wrong with the first two children, except that the umbilical cord had been too short. Moreover, Chúc was strong and in good health. Defying the merciless sun in summer and the drizzling cold rain in winter, she worked in the family's fields of rice, corn, and sugarcane for hours each day. Unlike many other women in her village, she had a good relationship with her mother-in-law, who appreciated her gentle temperament and diligence at work. The family had, Định concluded, never before experienced a problem like this, and frankly he did not understand why this had happened. "Look at us," he said, pointing to Tuệ; "we are five brothers, all of us tall and strong. We have never had problems like this in our family. Our father was in the army, but he was only here in the north; he never went south [where herbicides were sprayed]." Chúc added: "In the hospital they asked if there is anyone in our family with a gene for dwarfism. I told them that there is not, on the maternal side there is no one, on the paternal side no one. We are all healthy. Husband and wife, grandparents, siblings, children, all are healthy. There was nothing wrong with my first three children, none of them was disabled." In a firm tone, her mother-in-law asserted: "Among all my five sons, not one is thin." Chúc looked me in the eye and said, "I ask: why do I meet this misfortune (*rủi ro*)? I feel so uncomfortable (*ngại*) about this."

REPRODUCTIVE MISFORTUNE

In every human society, people strive to cope with misfortune. In the realm of childbearing, such efforts tend to reach particular intensity, as the actual course of people's reproductive lives often differs dramatically from the normative expectations placed on the bearing and rearing of children. When women have difficulties conceiving, lose their unborn children through miscarriage or stillbirth, or give birth to infants whose bodies deviate from the expected, the resulting clashes with cultural expectations often produce profound human suffering.[1] In addition to such long-standing troubles, advancing biomedical technologies generate new kinds of reproductive problems, placing pregnant women and their supporters in challenging situations of uncertainty and disorientation such as the one in which Chúc and Tuệ found themselves.

In an essay on religion and suffering, Clifford Geertz (1993 [1973]) identified three kinds of situation in which taken-for-granted tenets of social life are breached and chaos threatens to erupt: when we find ourselves at the limits of our analytic capacities, at the limits of our powers of endurance, and at the limits of our moral insight. When a fetal anomaly was identified, the women I met found themselves in a predicament that condensed Geertz's three situations of threatening chaos. Their pregnancies deviated dramatically and uncannily from the expected course of a pregnancy; they suffered the painful loss of the child they had hoped to have; and they found themselves in an unprecedented moral situation, having to determine whether it would be good or bad, right or wrong, to keep a child that physicians had labeled abnormal. Hanoian women's emotional reactions in this existentially challenging situation resembled those reported in other studies. Research conducted in the United States and Europe shows that when receiving an adverse prenatal diagnosis, prospective parents are thrown into deep shock and acute grief, their reactions including "anger, despair, guilt, inadequacy, sleeping and eating difficulties" (Statham 2002:219). Most existing studies on prenatal diagnosis have found that it is not the fetal problem as such, but rather the abortion decision that throws women into an existential crisis. In Hanoi, by contrast, I found that the diagnosis in itself caused major moral and existential anguish. In Vietnam, child-bearing is, as earlier chapters show, an intensely moral terrain. An adverse prenatal diagnosis, therefore, confronts prospective parents with hard decisions, but also with moral doubts and accusations. When Chúc told us how uncomfortable she felt, and when her brother-in-law kept circling around the question *why*, they were implicitly hinting at the moral substratum to this medical event, defending themselves against the blame they assumed that others would place on them.

In this chapter, I explore the different configurations of responsibility that people's accounts of reproductive misfortune entailed, examining the formations of subjectivity that were involved when people considered different causal ontologies. In searching for explanations, I suggest, women asked not only, "Why did this happen?" but also, "What sort of person must I be for this to happen to me?" They and their relatives pondered wide-ranging etiological possibilities, bringing into consideration not only genes, germs, and toxic substances but also ancestral wrath and cosmic imbalances. As Dorothy Nelkin (2003:viii) observes, "People perceive risks through different 'frames' that reflect their values, world views, and concepts of social order. These frames can influence definitions of risk, allocations of responsibility and blame, evaluations of scientific evidence, and ideas about appropriate decision-making authority." In their reflections on questions of causation, Hanoian women and their relatives distinguished between two realms of powerful forces: that of science and the material (*duy vật*) and that of superstition and the spiritual (*duy tâm*). Beneath the material-biological body of the fetus there lay another, more subdued spiritual-cosmological body; and under the biological body of the mother, exposed to colds and toxins, was a collective and cosmological family body exposed to the wrath of gods and ancestors. Following women through their reflections on causation made it clear that prenatal screening as a novel practice of science was embedded within long-standing cosmological frameworks, articulating older concepts and concerns. In what follows, I first examine the biological bodies that emerged in women's encounters with ultrasonography. I then explore the cosmological bodies that were also present in the scanning room, placing these bodies in the context of East Asian philosophical traditions. Against this background, I analyze the social processes through which the people I met searched for answers to the question *why?* Whereas feminist scholars have offered important analyses of the politics of blame that unfolds when responsibility for the pregnancy is individualized and placed on the shoulders of the mother-to-be, the analysis I present shows that for women in Hanoi, explanatory models that placed the blame on individuals were often seen as the most attractive. Since explanations that defined individual human beings as members of larger moral-cosmological collectives tended to involve allocations of blame and responsibility that were wide-ranging, inchoate, and morally painful, women often sought relief in scientific frames of understanding, taking upon themselves the responsibilities that this entailed.

ENCOUNTERING THE ABNORMAL FETUS: BIOMEDICAL TERRAINS

On a shelf in the 3D scanning room, Lan, the nurse, had taped a sheet of paper on which she had printed the words: "Patients observe: The first day of your last menstrual period should be given according to the solar calendar (*dương lịch*)." When women overlooked this announcement and reported their last menstrual period according to the lunar calendar (*âm lịch*), as is common practice, particularly in rural areas of Vietnam, this made health staff visibly annoyed. Their annoyance seemed to stem not only from the practical problems that use of this calendar caused in calculating the due date, but also from the connotations of ignorance and backwardness that clung to this mode of calculating time.

When the socialist government came into power in 1954, it sought to establish a radically new social order in which superstitious beliefs and practices were abolished and an empiricist worldview prevailed. Science (*khoa học*) and superstition (*mê tín*) were pitted against each other. Science was associated with socialist modernity, with the striving for better lives than those led under colonialism, while superstitious practices engaging souls, spirits, and other supernatural beings of the "other world" were cast in opposition to modernity, rationality, and progress. The lunar calendar, which was associated with actions invoking the spirit world, was replaced by the solar calendar as the official tool for the calculation of time. Over the past two decades, ritual and religious practices have become more politically acceptable in Vietnam, but in daily lives and official rhetoric, a relatively sharp distinction is still maintained between the material and the spiritual, science and superstition, the realm of the living (*dương*) and that of the dead (*âm*), "this world" and "the other."[2] The lunar calendar remains associated with the other world, with the supernatural realm in which gods reign, spirits roam, and ghosts linger; while the solar calendar records time according to rational and this-worldly principles. Like most other human activities, childbearing spans this and the other world. While people in Hanoi usually talk about conception and gestation in terms of the biological models that health care providers and pregnancy handbooks promote, they also pay ritual respect to the twelve goddesses (12 *bà mụ*) who, according to Vietnamese tradition, are held to have shaped the child in the womb. When an infant turns one month old, most families organize a celebration (*cúng mụ*) to honor and thank the twelve goddesses, pleading to them to protect (*phù hộ*) the child so that it will live a long, fruitful, and happy life. Activities associated with the other world remain, however, tinged with the negative labels attached to them by the socialist authorities. When the people I met pleaded to higher powers, placing an amulet on a sick child or consulting a fortune teller, therefore, they often seemed to do so with a certain ambivalence.

The announcement that Lan had hung on the shelf in the 3D scanning room points us, then, to two different registers through which human existence could be interpreted in this medical setting. In insisting on the use of the solar calendar, health providers placed pregnant bodies firmly within a this-worldly realm of science, modernity, and the material. During scanning sessions, sonographers enacted this as a scientific procedure by dictating detailed fetal measures to the nurse in technical terms incomprehensible to laypeople, then turning to the pregnant woman and summing up what she needed to know: "Your fetus is developing normally." When an adverse diagnosis was made, questions of causation always seemed at the forefront of people's attention, and the sonographer would often ask the woman questions concerning forms of causation that were considered relevant from a biomedical point of view, such as "Have you had a cold during your pregnancy?" or "Have you worked with pesticides?"

Bích was, as we saw in chapter 4, 19 weeks pregnant with her second child when the sonographer found water on the brain of her fetus. On that day, I arrived at the hospital shortly after the scan had been performed. I found Bích and Chi sitting outside the scanning room, talking. Joining their conversation, I asked Bích what was wrong with her fetus. She replied: "I don't know what the problem is. As I understand it, there is a problem with the brain, but I am not sure. . . . I feel very perplexed. I don't understand why this has happened. Perhaps the fetus has been stressed? I work every day from 7:30 in the morning until 9 at night. Could that be the reason?" With this reply, Bích turned the conversation away from the topic that I had asked about—the biomedical nature of the malformation—and toward the topic most important to her: its cause. When Chi and I asked if we could visit her at home to talk more, she hesitated at first, but then accepted. But we must, she insisted, come after dark and enter her village in a discreet manner. She did not want her neighbors to know about her predicament.

A few days later, Chi and I drove on her motorbike along the banks of the Red River to Bích's home on the outskirts of Hanoi. Chi drove carefully in the dark, trying to avoid the deep potholes in the road. After half an hour we reached Bích's house, a white two-story building located at the edge of the village, facing a small green pond. As Chi parked her motorbike in the yard, Bích and her husband appeared in the doorway. Complimenting us for having been able to find the way on our own, they invited us in. Their five-year-old daughter, bright-eyed and with her hair in ponytails, greeted us politely, then disappeared upstairs. Bích seated us on the wooden sofa, poured hot water from the thermos into the teapot, and turned immediately to the question of causation:

> Can I ask you, why has this happened? I don't understand it. I don't understand why. What is most painful is that I don't understand why. We had prepared everything so carefully. Psychologically, economically, we were ready to have our second child. So truly, I don't understand why this has happened. Is it something I have eaten? We did eat a lot of chicken, and there was bird flu at that time. Or could it be because the fruit that my husband sells has been sprayed with pesticides? But I always wash and peel our fruit carefully. Or are there some changes in my body? . . . I so much want to know for what reason this has happened. Is it because of me or something else? Did it just happen accidentally to our family? Was it just bad luck?

Bích had, she insisted, done everything right—so why had her pregnancy gone wrong? While biomedicine made it possible to visualize the fetus and to assess its normality, science offered women few answers to the primary problem that haunted them: *Why?* When prospective parents pondered what might have caused a fetal malformation, they often brought up scientific factors first. Later in the conversation, however, other explanatory possibilities would often emerge.

BODIES OF COSMOLOGY: SUBDUED MORAL ACCUSATIONS

On the day when Toàn and I visited Chúc and her family, we spent the first couple of hours talking to the large group of relatives that had convened. The family meeting then dissolved, and, sitting in a smaller room adjacent to the main room of the house, we talked to Chúc alone. In this more private space, she again turned to the question *why?* Whereas her relatives had scrutinized the family body for biological faults, Chúc now talked about the moral-cosmological connotations that this situation implied. Although no one had said anything directly to her about this, she felt that her fellow villagers read moral fault into the body of the child she was expecting. Talking about the painful possibility that this reproductive mishap would alter her family's moral status in the local community, Chúc turned from biology to cosmology, from physical health to moral culpability. "This is so painful," she said. "I feel so sad. People here talk a lot. They keep asking me how I am. But that just makes me feel even sadder. We are both healthy, so why does this happen? We do live properly (*mình thì lành hiền*), we don't do anything wrong, we have never hurt anyone. Why do we meet this misfortune? This burdens my conscience; I feel so embarrassed."

Like Chúc, practically all women described feeling morally burdened by this event. This defective fetal body, they suggested, placed their own and their family's moral integrity in question. Explaining how difficult he had found it to accept the scanning result, Bích's husband said: "When the obstetrics hospital confirmed that there was something wrong with the fetus, we felt so troubled (*áy náy*). We are both healthy, we live honestly (*làm ăn lương thiện*), we have not done anything bad that could make our child suffer like this." Bích added: "We have never done anything evil. We are workers, we live honestly, we don't do anything bad." When Chi asked her if she thought that any events in the family's past could have brought this about, Bích replied in terms which indicated that personal reproductive misfortune could—though she rejected this in her own case—be interpreted as a consequence of family members' moral behavior. Alluding to the country's revolutionary past and the political divisions that had split the population, she said: "I would never blame my elders for this. None of my elders has ever done anything immoral that could have caused this. All of my elders have been farmers, none of them sided with the French, none have been bureaucrats in any position of power." Political affinities during the anticolonial resistance war could, Bích implied, have resulted in birth defects in later generations; supporting the wrong side in a political conflict could have far-reaching consequences for one's descendants.[3] Many of the people we met drew similar links between an individual's reproductive plight and the family's collective politicomoral habitus.

When Hồng's fetus was diagnosed with anencephaly, for instance, her brother-in-law told us: "If a child is born disabled, our elders used to say that this had to do with the family and its way of living. But to tell you the truth, at heart our family has always been good. Our elders, going back several generations, have been good people. We have always been poor farmers, and we have lived peacefully together with our neighbors. There have never been any problems."

Chapter 3 tells of Oanh's anxiety at the prospect of having a disabled child. This, she explained, would confront her not only with practical problems of child care but also with moral accusations: "People in Vietnam can be very condemning. If a child is born with even a small disability such as a cleft lip, and if there are people who don't like you, if they dislike you or have some problem with you, they will say that this happened because of the way you have been living. They will say that Heaven punishes you for living in an evil and heartless way, that your way of living affects your child." The relief that Oanh felt at her daughter's birth, then, not only concerned child health in a biomedical sense but stemmed also from being recognized as a morally proper person: her daughter's complete body offered protection against the moral accusations that she and her family might otherwise have faced. A reproductive mishap, in short, indicated moral fault, but this was an inchoate form of fault whose origins could be difficult to trace. At issue was the behavior not only of the individual mother-to-be but also that of the entire extended family going back over generations: moral wrongs done by family elders, people suggested, might have catastrophic consequences for present-day childbearing. Most of the people I met insisted that they did live in morally proper ways and that the reasons for this reproductive mishap were *not* to be found in the family's past. But in a few cases, women and their relatives identified sociomoral events that they thought could have affected their fetus. One of them was Phương, a twenty-year-old farmer living in Vĩnh Phúc province.

Hằng and I first met Phương on December 26, 2003, in the 3D scanning room. During the scan, the sonographer found fluid on the brain of Phương's fetus, and her mother, a worn-out-looking peasant woman, broke down sobbing, "I knew it, I knew it." Phương was eight months pregnant, so the physicians advised mother and daughter to keep the child. A few days later, Hằng and I traveled to Vĩnh Phúc province to visit Phương and her mother in the rural village where their families had lived for generations. They lived together with Phương's younger brother in a small house on the edge of the hamlet. On the mint green wall in the main room, Phương's mother had placed a wedding photo of her daughter on top of a 2002 calendar. Next to it was a poster showing Hồ Chí Minh tying a red scarf around the neck of a schoolgirl, the text beneath the image citing his words, "To reap a return in ten years, we must cultivate trees. To reap a return in one hundred years, we must cultivate people" (*Vì lợi ích mười năm phải trồng cây, vì lợi ích trăm năm phải trồng người*).

In tears, Phương's mother told us of the calamities that had hit their family, beginning the day before Phương's wedding. In accordance with tradition, the two families had arranged a large wedding celebration, inviting practically the entire village for the feast and purchasing large amounts of pork, beef, chicken, and vegetables. But the day before the wedding, Phương's maternal grandfather had died unexpectedly. This placed the two families in a moral conundrum: going through with the wedding would violate traditional moral principles of filiality that demanded that children observe a period of mourning after the death of a parent. But a cancellation would mean a considerable economic loss, as large amounts of fresh food had been purchased. Without consulting Phương and her husband-to-be, their elders decided to go through with the wedding. Soon after, Phương's mother suggested, higher powers struck back. Phương's first pregnancy ended in a spontaneous abortion. During her second pregnancy, her husband was killed in a motorbike accident. After that, his parents started to treat their new daughter-in-law in a cold and harsh manner. Depressed by the loss of her husband and by his parents' change of attitude toward her, Phương tried twice to take her own life by drinking pesticides. A few months after her suicide attempts, the 3D ultrasound scan revealed that her fetus was not normal. When we talked to Phương and her mother about these events, her mother suggested that the moral fault generating all this misfortune was the decision to go through with Phương's wedding the day after her grandfather's death. Although Phương and her husband could, in one sense, not be held responsible for this decision—which was taken by their elders—they were responsible nevertheless.

While claiming that they could not identify any events in their family's history that might have caused their misfortune, most of the women we met seemed to feel haunted by a past that they did not fully know. "How must we have lived," they asked, "to cause our children to suffer like this?" In this moral framing, the pregnant woman's responsibility reached far beyond her own body. Her child-to-be carried the trace of previous generations; as its mother, she was responsible for the deeds of family elders whom she might not even know. Placing individual fates within a larger collective history, the people I met located reproductive responsibility within the moral body of the family. Deeds done in the past by a child's parents, grandparents, or great-grandparents, they suggested, can directly affect its physiological development. This made individual women responsible for much more than antenatal care visits and appropriate diets, exposing them to a responsibility that exceeded their own here-and-now and placing on their shoulders, to paraphrase Levinas (2000 [1981]:116), faults and misfortunes that did not begin in their own freedom. Within this frame of understanding, not only biological factors such as viruses and toxicity but also the identity of the family as a moral collective became subject to scrutiny. This turned the human body into far more than a biological entity: the bodies of women such as Phương and Bích were not only their own biological and bounded bodies but open structures of susceptibility, exposedness, and passivity, sites in which selves were connected with others. Through their bodies, women were opened to others in ways that they themselves were unable to fathom or control. This sense of a wider-ranging moral responsibility reaching into an immemorial past points us to a different modality of subjectivity than the one outlined in current social science scholarship on responsibility and governmentality. Whereas this line of thinking assumes that subjects come into being through individual practices of freedom, self-formation can also be seen as a question of passivity, vulnerability, and attachment. The subject, as Levinas (2000 [1981]:104) says, cannot form itself: "It is already formed with absolute passivity. . . . This passivity is that of an attachment that has already been made, as something irreversibly past, prior to all memory and all recall." When people in Hanoi talked about the sphere of the spiritual and about supernatural causation, they evoked a universe in which individuals came into being in subjection, being responsible for others in ways that reached beyond cognition and consciousness. This spiritual world, they suggested, belongs to the part of Vietnamese cultural tradition that is rooted in ancient East Asian ethical philosophies.

SPIRITUAL WORLDS: THE TRIPLE RELIGION

Vietnamese spirituality is often described as a syncretic "triple religion" (*tam giáo*) that blends Confucianism (*nho giáo*), Buddhism (*phật giáo*), and Daoism (*lão giáo*). From 111 BCE to 938 CE, northern Vietnam was occupied by the Chinese Han dynasty. In this period, Confucianism,

Taoism, and Mahayana Buddhism spread from China to Vietnam. In the centuries following Chinese occupation, Buddhism was the official state religion, playing an important political role in the Lý and Trần dynasties.[4] By the end of the twelfth century, Confucianism became the official state ideology, and Confucian teachings and rituals acquired a central place in state governance. Although historians debate the extent to which Confucianism actually replaced Buddhism as the official orthodoxy, most scholars hold that Confucian philosophies have contributed in important ways to shaping moral, spiritual, and political orientations in Vietnam (cf. McHale 2004).

In contemporary Vietnam, the spiritual beliefs subsumed in the triple religion seem to play out with particular force in the realm of reproduction. In Confucian moral doctrines, childbearing is central; according to these teachings, people both demonstrate and acquire moral virtue by giving birth to healthy and normal children. The cardinal virtue in Confucianism, filial piety (*hiếu*), places moral demands on children to demonstrate love and respect for their parents, particularly by ensuring that the ancestral line is continued (*nối dõi tông đường*) and by offering parents care in their old age and after their deaths. Biological procreation, then, has a significant spiritual—or, as people in Hanoi say, sacred (*thiêng liêng*)—dimension, connecting each individual with ancestors and descendants, and binding together the living and the dead, this world and the next. But severely disabled children, people often suggest, may never achieve a place in this eternal chain of sociomoral connections. As the social researcher Phạm Kim Ngọc (2006:33) observes, children with severe disabilities cannot but fail morally: since they are unable to "perform their sacred responsibility of fulfilling duties to their parents and grandparents, looking after the worship of their ancestors," they will never attain the full personhood that is acquired by fulfilling filial obligations.[5] In asking the pained question, "How have we lived?" then, people also asked, "What has brought us into a situation where we are rendered unable to realize the important moral mission of honoring our parents and ancestors through the children we have and thereby turning ourselves into morally complete persons?"

Besides setting forth moral precepts for family and communal lives, classical Confucian thought also tied the parent-child nexus into larger cosmological schemes. Inspired by Daoist and other philosophies, Confucian thought in Han dynasty times represented the human organism as a microcosm closely aligned with larger macrocosmic processes. In the correlative cosmology formulated by Confucian philosophers, all things in the universe were tied together in a dense continuity of being that comprised Heaven, Earth, and its human inhabitants (Tu 1985). Within this world of intimate resonances, pregnancy and childbirth were represented as manifestations of the generative powers of Heaven, as the very embodiment of cosmic forces. The classical *Book of Changes,* for instance, modeled universal creation on sexual generation, stating that "Heaven and earth intermingle *qi* [cosmic energy] and all things are transformed thereby; man and woman intermingle essences [the human aspect of cosmic energies] and all things are born thereby" (Furth 1995:159). Seen from this perspective, the sexual act condenses the creative powers of the cosmos; human procreation becomes the analogue of heavenly creation.

This conception recalls the philosopher Chánh Công Phan's claim that, in Vietnamese cultural tradition, sexual intercourse is considered a sacred act that embodies "the đạo of Heaven and Earth (đạo Trời Đất)" (see chapter 2). When procreative sex is seen as blending human and heavenly forces, fetuses embody the cosmos. One text from the Han era explicitly defines Heaven as father and Earth as mother, and describes fetal development in terms of the cosmogony of the *Tao Te Ching.* At birth, this text states, the roundness of the infant's head imitates Heaven while its square feet imitate Earth, thus Heaven, Earth, and human beings form a trinity (Kinney 2004:156). Under China's Qin and Han dynasties, historians note, there was an important political dimension to such analogies between human and divine orders: the political order, like the human body, was seen as a structure that resonated with the ways of Heaven and Earth. If the state were governed in accordance with the Way of Heaven, birth defects would be prevented, while a ruler's abuse of power led to monstrous births (Kinney 2004:159). When people in present-day Hanoi proudly declare after a birth that "the mother is round, the child square," then, they also define this childbirth as a moral accomplishment, representing it as a site in which the parents' position within an ethically ordered world is made manifest. In this framing, reproductive success becomes an indicator of cosmic harmony, while reproductive calamities point to cosmic imbalances, suggesting a world out of joint.

Buddhist philosophies also draw intimate connections between cosmology, morality, and embodiment. These beliefs hold that an individual's life extends beyond the present incarnation, beginning before birth and continuing after death. According to laws of karma (*luật nhân quả*), everything we do contributes to shaping our destiny: bad deeds cause suffering, virtuous ones bring good fortune—if not in this life, then in the next. In Buddhist hierarchies of virtue, people with impairments are placed in lower positions than others, as bodily anomalies are regarded as forms of misfortune that manifest past karma.[6] Body and morality are, in other words, inseparably linked. Importantly, Buddhist philosophies represent karmic moral mechanisms as extending beyond individuals, as karma can be shared among several people. "Karma is," notes Wendy O'Flaherty (1980:28–29), "a metaphor for the effects that human beings have upon one another, in this life and even across the barrier of death." Karma sharing is particularly dense between sexual partners and between parents and children, and a person's life is therefore to some extent shaped by the karma of his or her parents, children, and lovers.[7] Due to its collective nature, karma presents a situation of existential indeterminacy entailing a burden of unknown past deeds; one can never fully know what forces and actions are impacting one's life. The concept of karma, then, also suggests a specific configuration of subjectivity: rather than as a bounded and autonomous individual, the human self is defined in Buddhist thinking as intimately connected with others. Our moral practices have far-reaching consequences, shaping not only our own lives but also those of our intimate others; things that I do in this life can harm the children that my children have. Buddhist ethical discourse, in other words, blurs the boundaries between self and other, between ethical agents and ethical patients (cf. Mrozik 2007:54).

In Hanoi, when misfortune occurs, people—particularly those of the older generations—often lay blame on the sufferer, commenting that "those who live with virtue will meet good fortune" (ở hiền gặp lành). Distributions of virtue and fortune are often held to take place across generations, and numerous sayings and proverbs tie the bodies of parent and child closely together, suggesting that faults in their offspring can be attributed to parental or grandparental misdeeds. "When the father eats salty things," people say, "the child will be thirsty" (Đời cha ăn mặn, đời con khát nước). The terminology that people in Hanoi use to designate anomalous human bodies also attests to these underlying linkages between bodily integrity and moral fault. In Vietnamese, people with disabilities are termed người khuyết tật or người tàn tật. These terms have double meanings, collapsing bodily and moral universes: according to the dictionary, tật means "physical defect," but also "moral fault," "blemish," or "shortcoming"; tàn is to expire, die out, wither. Khuyết is translated as "missing/lacking" or as "shortage/deficiency," and khuyết tật, like tàn tật, alludes to both physical defect and moral flaw.[8] The bodies of nondisabled individuals, in turn, are described in terms of intact-ness or completeness (*lành lặn, hoàn chỉnh, nguyên vẹn*). *Lành,* which can be translated as "intact," "good," "lucky," "gentle," or "benign," suggests not only bodily but also moral integrity and wholesomeness.[9]

In short, both Buddhist and Confucian philosophies place the physi-cality of the individual body within a larger moral universe of interper-sonal connections, responsibilities, and dependencies, tying individuals into dense sociomoral networks of mutual belonging. It seemed to be these intimate, but inchoate, associations between an individual's fate and the moral actions of his or her intimate others that compelled peo-ple in Hanoi to foreground the question *Why?* when reproduction went awry. In so doing, they claimed innocence and virtue, saying, "We are good people. No one in our family has committed the wrongs that this anomaly suggests." Although most people treated them with skepti-cism, spiritual ideas and explanations seemed constantly present, gener-ating a substratum of moral doubt and trepidation when reproductive misfortune occurred. In a typical statement, Hảo, a twenty-seven-year-old mother of one, reflected on fetal anomalies in these words: "In my opinion, such things happen due to genes or something like that, or because one does not eat a balanced diet. This may make the fetus develop abnormally. It is not because of how people live (*do ăn ở*) or other spiritual things at all. . . . But I don't know what people think, because if they think bad things, they would never say it aloud. Perhaps some people think like that." Beneath the firmness of Hảo's insistence on scientific explanations lurked, as always, uncertainties about whether *others* might place reproductive problems within a spiritual frame of interpretation and attribute them to unspecified actions on the part of the individual or her relatives. While many people claimed that they considered cosmological interpretations superstitious relics from the past that only their elders would take seriously, everyone seemed acutely aware that in other people's eyes, reproductive trouble *did* signify moral failure, exposing not only the mother but her entire extended family to unspoken accusations and blame.

There was, however, one interpretation of "the spiritual" that offered moral relief: when reproductive mishaps were attributed to fate (*số phận*), human beings were exempted from moral responsibility. In many cases, women and their relatives ended up deciding that their predicament must be attributable to the unpredictable forces that govern human lives. No one and nothing, they suggested, was to blame for this.

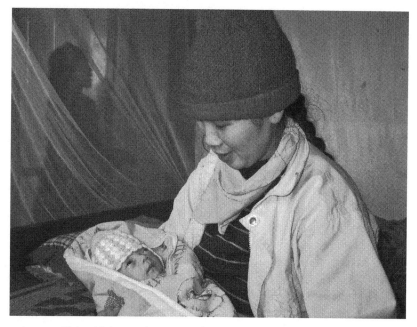

FIGURE 6. Chúc with her newborn son. Behind the mosquito net is her mother-in-law. Photo by the author, 2004.

"I DID NOT DO ANYTHING TO MAKE THIS HAPPEN": THE POWERS OF FATE

"In this pregnancy, I did not do anything that I can feel remorse for now. I did not do anything to make this happen. I was not ill. I did not do heavy work. My diet was healthy. So I just feel sorry that my fate has to be like this. I just have to accept this. Our elders say that people born in the year of the tiger often suffer this kind of misery. . . . To feel lighter at heart, I place responsibility for this on my fate."

Vietnamese notions of fate are, as Bích suggests here, associated with an astrological scheme in which each individual acquires a particular destiny by being born at a particular moment in time. This destiny can be predicted by fortune-tellers who analyze the individual's position vis-à-vis the cycles of the universe, calculating which days, months, or years will be particularly dangerous or beneficial for specific activities. Based on the lunar calendar, these calculations are often made to ensure the auspicious timing of important events such as house constructions, weddings, pregnancies, births, or bringing home a new child from the hospital.[10] In contrast to karmic ideas, which are categorized as super-stition, notions of fate are considered relatively respectable. As Charles Stafford (2009:123) observes in the context of China, concepts of fate "appear to describe, rather precisely, and through the use of calcula-tion, the mechanics of the universe and the place of people within it. . . . many people are attracted to this exactly because it seems equally scien-tific *and* religious (or metaphysical)" (emphasis in original). In several of the families we visited, relatives and community members had recourse to fate, seeking, it seemed, to free the couple from moral blame. For instance, emphasizing that nobody held her responsible for what had happened, Mây said, "Everyone encourages me, saying 'You have a hard fate (*số vất vả*), so you must bear that.' All they talk about is fate." People's talk about fate seemed to acknowledge the contingency that characterizes human existence. It is not always possible, they indi-cated, to hold human actors responsible when lives run off track. If a person's life projects fail, this may not be because she lacks talent or morality, but is simply something that fate has determined.

Hồng lived in a semirural area on the banks of the Red River in a house that she shared with her husband, daughter, mother-in-law, and brother-in-law and his family. Although she had been pregnant five times, she had only one child, a six-year-old girl. Three pregnancies had ended as either spontaneous abortions or very premature deliveries. Now she was pregnant again, but her fetus had been diagnosed with anencephaly. When Hằng and I visited the family on April 26, 2004, Chính, her eldest brother-in-law, took the lead in the conversation. Their family failed to understand, he said, why Hồng and her husband had experienced so much trouble in having children: "In the past, I worked in areas near the border that had been sprayed with chemicals and there were many bombs and mines. But my brother hasn't been away, he hasn't been in contact with anything like that. So we say it is due to fate. My brother and his wife are good people, and still they experience hardship." In a situation where no other explanations could be found, Chính said, the family turned to fate:

> We have to look to spiritual matters, to fate. Fate does not spare poor peo-ple. Fate is like a thief who steals from the poor. In our house we may have a rice bowl; to us it means much, but to rich people it is nothing. Still, the thief steals this rice bowl. He does not spare us because we are poor. My brother and his wife are very good people, and yet this misfortune comes to our house. . . . Our elders have always believed in fate. Sometimes Heaven makes its own arrangements and we must accept that. That's all.

Later Hồng's sixty-nine-year-old mother-in-law explained how, in her experience, emphasizing fate could help people to stay alive and sane in the wake of reproductive calamities or other forms of misfortune. She herself had lost two young children; one suffered a stroke (*bị trúng gió*) after a cold bath, and the other drowned in the village pond. She knew, therefore, the importance of handling such losses in ways that did not blame the bereaved but instead supported their will to live:

> In my opinion, this has to do first with the fate of the child, and second with the fate of the parents. In our family, no one suffers from hereditary diseases. We think in terms of spiritual matters. Fate did not allow this child to become a person, and the parents have a hard fate. That's all. I encourage them. I say, "No one can escape fate. To escape fate, you must know things beforehand. Or else, you just have to endure. Don't think. Don't feel sad. Don't do anything except keep working. We do feel sorry for our child. These feelings must cool off gradually. If you keep thinking, you cannot live, right? This child was not allowed to become a person; that's all, don't think any more about that."

Taking a sip of the strong green tea in the tiny cup in front of her, Hồng's mother-in-law concluded in a firm tone, "That's how we used to think in the old days. We thought in a feudal manner, that's why we talked like that. Now we hope that science can help our child." With these words, this elderly woman seemed to suggest that the readiness to accept one's fate that had prevailed in her generation might currently be replaced by other and more interventionist approaches to human existence.

"TODAY PEOPLE THINK IN OTHER TERMS": SHIFTING MORAL CONFIGURATIONS

The contrast between science and superstition, between biological and cosmological bodies, between officially accepted explanations and more spiritual frames of reference ran through most of our conversations. In Vietnam as in China, people seemed to know, as Stafford (2009:123) puts it, "that religion is supposed to be 'superstition' and that science is supposed to be truth." Often, our interlocutors would claim that only old people believe in spiritual explanations, whereas younger generations look to science instead. In a typical statement, Hương, the twenty-five-year-old mother of a newborn boy, claimed that there had been a shift from spiritual and collectivist explanations that involve entire families toward more scientific and individualizing modes of accounting for reproductive misfortune: "In the past, if a family had a child that was not normal, people would say that the parents lived immorally. Perhaps it would be difficult for the siblings of that child to get married. . . . But today people think in other terms. They think that things like that happen because the mother did not eat properly during pregnancy or because she had a cold—that's why she had an abnormal child."

Their country's experiences with toxic warfare, people in Hanoi suggested, had played a major role in creating this moral turn. Sim, for instance, the mother of a six-month-old girl, explicitly rejected the causal ontologies through which people of her parents' generation had ascribed meaning to reproductive misfortune. Agent Orange, she said, has made people think about these things in other ways: "Take the people who went to war for our country and were exposed to Agent Orange. When peace came, they returned home, married, and had children. But in bearing children, they experienced many difficulties and much suffering. They made a contribution to our nation, so how could that be a question of lacking virtue (vô phúc)?" The predicament of Agent Orange victims has, Sim suggested, made it abundantly clear to people that no simple causal links exist between moral virtue and reproductive outcomes; individuals who selflessly risked their health and lives for their country now suffer terrible reproductive plights. Similarly, Trâm's sister-in-law, who lived in a rural village in Vĩnh Phúc province, said:

In this area, Agent Orange has affected many people. Some children are missing fingers, some children suffer from spasms, some lie immobile on their beds for years, some are just stupid. In the past, village people did not understand, and they would despise families with such children. They said that the family had lived immorally and that the child was suffering the consequences. But one day people from the Department of Invalids and Social Affairs came and did examinations, and they concluded that these children were suffering from Agent Orange because of the U.S. Since that day, people have come to understand, and they don't despise them anymore. Now people know that the men who went to the front for our people were affected by Agent Orange. Our elders are wrong if they blame such problems on immoral living.

The public attention paid to wartime herbicide spraying seems, in other words, to have contributed to shifting the birth of anomalous children from a moral-cosmological realm into the sphere of science. Research conducted among Agent Orange victims in Vietnam has come to similar conclusions, showing that new scientific interpretations of reproductive misfortune have provided significant relief: when the human body is freed from cosmology, the moral burdens that disability places on a family tend to be diminished.[11]

By rejecting spiritual explanations and turning to science instead, women and their relatives seemed to do two things. First, they marked themselves as modern and educated by distancing themselves from what they considered backward and superstitious modes of thinking. Second, they resisted the inchoate and far-ranging moral responsibilities that explanations of a cosmological nature would imply. As Levinas (2000 [1981]:116) says, defining subjectivity in terms of passivity, susceptibility, and openness entails placing the weight of the universe on the shoulders of the individual, making her "responsible for everything." Such infinite responsibility is, my interlocutors suggested, too much for a person to bear. The explanations offered by science, in contrast, seemed to reduce the moral problems to something more limited and manageable. In the words of Trang, the mother of a five-month-old girl: "People's attitudes toward children with disabilities have changed. Today science and technology have developed and people hear a lot from the mass media, so they know what causes such things, toxic chemicals, for instance. This makes people feel less scared. If one understands the reason why the child is born disabled, one does not feel so scared." The family discussions of causation that we took part in would often end with the same conclusion: the fetal problem, women and their relatives claimed, must have been caused by a maternal cold. Although opting for the maternal cold as an explanation placed responsibility squarely on the shoulders of the individual woman who had not done enough to be "on guard" during her pregnancy, most women seemed to find this kind of moral burden more bearable than its alternatives. The case of Liên, a twenty-four-year-old journalist, may serve as an example.

Liên was 14 weeks pregnant when a 3D scan performed by Dr. Tuấn found that the spine of her fetus was curved and there was fluid in its abdomen.[12] He printed the scan result, handed it to Liên, and sent her to the antenatal care room for counseling. The physician glanced quickly through the printout. Then he asked: "Do you want to abort this one, or what do you want?" Liên replied, "I want an abortion," and the physician proceeded to take her blood pressure, saying, "I'll make sure you get all the necessary examinations done to get into hospital. Do you want to have the abortion immediately?" In a barely audible voice, Liên replied, "Yes. I'll have it immediately," and the consultation ended. Afterward, as my colleague Toàn accompanied Liên and her husband, Minh, to the department where blood tests were done, they bombarded her with questions. Minh asked, "With a fetus this age, how do they do the abortion?" "If we had not had the scan, what would have happened?" "What will be the consequences of this for Liên's health?" "How long do we have to wait before she can get pregnant again?" Liên insisted: "You work at the Medical University. So can you tell me *why* this has happened?"

On a misty morning in January 2004, Toàn and I visited Liên and Minh. They lived in the center of Hanoi, in a socialist-era apartment complex (*khu tập thể*) consisting of five-story houses painted in a faded yellow color. It was mid-morning; the children's playground was deserted, and the area quiet and empty. When we arrived at the apartment, Liên was sitting on a mat on the living room floor finishing her breakfast, a bowl of rice porridge. She looked pale, but greeted us with a big smile and gestured to us to sit down with her. Minh served tea and put a pillow behind Liên's back so she could sit more comfortably. He had taken the week off, he explained, in order to look after her. Sitting with her legs crossed and her back against the pillow, Liên told us that she had had her pregnancy terminated immediately after the scan. She was only 14 weeks pregnant, so the abortion was done through dilatation and curettage, and she had been able to go home the same evening. Liên again insisted that she did not understand *why* this had happened. She had looked forward so much to becoming a mother and had done all she could to care for herself during pregnancy, taking folic acid that Minh had bought for her when he was in the United States, resting a lot, eating well—particularly the kind of fish that people say gives the baby a round face and red lips—and playing Mozart for the fetus in the hope that it would become more intelligent. But, she said, she had wondered whether the lacquer that she had worked with when she was in art school a few years earlier could have damaged her fetus. Or could the cause be that Minh had once worked with radioactive materials? Although several explanations were possible, Liên and Minh had eventually decided to believe that the reason for the malformation must be the colds that Liên had had in early pregnancy. In Liên's words, "Between the first and the third month of my pregnancy, I had a cold several times. . . . I think this is the reason. The doctors thought so too. They said that next time everything will be fine. 'This fetus is not normal,' they said; 'it is better for you to give it up. You are still young. You can have another one. Next time it will be like other people.'"

Like Liên and Minh, many couples ended up attributing the reproductive trouble they had experienced to a maternal cold. Anxieties that a cold might damage the fetus were, as chapter 3 shows, fueled by the information that people received through television, newspapers, and pregnancy handbooks that a cold can cause severe damage to the fetus. A cold is, moreover, a benign cause in the sense that it is random, accidental, and temporary. If a cold was the causal agent, then it was, as Liên said, likely that future pregnancies would fare better. Another possibility that expectant parents often pondered was whether exposure to pesticides, herbicides, or other toxic substances could have made the pregnancy go awry. These were, like the maternal cold, factors that people placed within a scientific frame of reference.

TOXIC EXPOSURE: SOCIOECONOMIC FAULTLINES

On April 1, 2004, the firstborn son of Hoa and Khánh died at the children's hospital in Hanoi. On March 25, a few hours before his birth, an ultrasound scan had found that he was suffering from umbilical hernia. At birth, he was immediately transferred to the children's hospital. After spending the day at the hospital with the family, I went home, but at 9 P.M. Khánh called and asked me to come, as the physicians had said that they were planning to operate on the boy soon. I found Khánh outside the intensive care unit. With him were his mother, his aunt, and four colleagues from the factory where he worked. His mother, a small and fragile-looking elderly woman, was wearing a dark headscarf and a pair of rubber slippers that revealed she came from a rural area. She looked as if she had been crying for hours. Holding my hand tightly, she pleaded, "Do you think our child will survive?" We waited for a couple of hours in the corridor, amidst other groups of anxious relatives who were sitting on the benches, walking restlessly around, or sleeping on mats they had brought with them. At midnight, a doctor informed us that they were not going to operate on the child until tomorrow. One of Khánh's colleagues offered to drive me home on his motorbike, and as we walked through the corridors of the hospital, he said, "We all find this very unsettling. Khánh did not tell you this, but he works in an extremely toxic environment. No one else dares touch the chemicals he is working with. We can't breathe when we get near the room where he is working. He has been doing this job for eight years now. It is *very* toxic." I wondered aloud why Khánh had not said anything about this. While we waited outside the intensive care unit, his mother had kept asking me why this happened, and when we first arrived at the hospital, one of the doctors had inquired what kind of work Khánh and Hoa were doing. Yet none of them had mentioned Khánh's working conditions. The colleague looked embarrassed. Then he mumbled that he thought that Khánh did not want to deepen his mother's worry. She was so upset already. "Also," he said, "coming from a rural area, he is happy just to have a job."

Two months later, Hằng and I visited Khánh and Hoa in their home in Hanoi's Gia Lâm district. They lived close to the factory where they worked, in a small rented house that consisted of one room with a kitchen. The wall over their bed was adorned with a framed wedding photo and a large poster with a picture of a plump baby boy—the child, I thought, whom they had hoped to have. Khánh and Hoa were both migrant workers; they came from two different rural provinces and had met each other at the factory. When she was three months pregnant, Hoa had a cold. This had frightened her, she said, because she knew from television that a cold in early pregnancy can cause cleft lip and cleft palate. To strengthen her health, she bought some traditional medicine from a local healer. A dwarf himself, he had encouraged her to obtain frequent ultrasound scans, saying: "When my mother was pregnant with me, she had a cold. I was lucky not to be born mute or crippled." After this episode, Hoa had a scan each month. They all concluded that her fetus was normal, and it was not until she was about to give birth that the fetal problem was detected. In retrospect, Hoa and Khánh asserted, they thought that it must have been Hoa's cold that had damaged the fetus. When Hằng asked Khánh about his working environment, he replied, "I do work in a polluted place. But I don't think it is a problem, because the people I work with have not had any problems. Everyone has healthy children. There *are* toxic substances and a lot of dust and dirt. With the kind of work I do, I cannot avoid that. . . . But I don't think too much about my working environment."

In many of the conversations we had, people expressed anxieties about the growing pollution of food, air, and working environments in Vietnam. The price for the country's rapid economic growth, they suggested, is an increasingly toxic environment. Many compared their own to their grandparents' generation, observing that in the past, women would give birth to ten or twelve children easily, whereas today, producing just one or two healthy children seemed to pose difficulties for many. Infertility, spontaneous abortions, and birth defects, people claimed, are considerably more prevalent today than a generation or two ago, and today's practices of prenatal screening therefore respond to needs that did not exist to the same extent in the past. People often voiced particularly intense concern about the toxicity of foods, pointing to the widespread use of pesticides in Vietnamese agriculture. One of the women who feared that pesticide exposure might have harmed her pregnancy was Trâm, who lived in a rural village in Vĩnh Phúc province. Making their living mainly from rice farming, she and her husband, Thà, shared a small house adjacent to a larger house owned by his elder brother.

When we first met, on February 5, 2004, Trâm was twenty-two years old and 19 weeks pregnant. Her fetus was found to be suffering from prune belly syndrome (bụng cóc), and on February 12, she had her pregnancy terminated in the provincial hospital near her home. A week later, my colleague Hằng and I visited her. When we arrived, we asked villagers for directions to Trâm's house. We found it at the end of the hamlet, facing the rice fields. The house had a thatched roof and mud walls; an old bicycle with two large baskets was leaning against the wall. On a line strung across the yard, a worn-out shirt was hanging, gray from having been washed so often. Inside, we found a large group of people. Besides Trâm and Thà, Trâm's sister-in-law, aunt, grandmother, and a couple of other relatives and neighbors were also present and took part in our conversation. An elderly woman served us tea. She opened the conversation by saying that Trâm and Thà probably lived in more difficult circumstances than any other couple in the village; they had both been orphaned at a young age and had to struggle hard to make a living. Trâm's abortion had been an economic disaster: the cost, 1,000,000 Vietnamese đồng, had equaled the amount of money they earned from rice farming in an entire year.

Soon, our conversation turned to the question of causation, and Trâm told us that she had worked with several different kinds of chemicals during her pregnancy, both pesticides and fertilizers. Her aunt commented, "Stupid. Why didn't you ask your husband to do that? When you are pregnant, you must avoid that kind of work. People who carry those bottles die early. It is very poisonous. I *never* let my son do that work." Trâm's grandmother said, "Why didn't you pay someone to do the spraying? Renting someone costs only 2,000 đồng per bottle; that's what you can make in one day's work in the market." To me, she explained, "If we don't spray, the insects eat everything. They eat the flowers, the buds. They eat the fruits before they are ripe. We lose everything." Trâm showed us the pesticides she had worked with, and Hằng exclaimed, "I thought that brand had been prohibited from use because it is too toxic. Where did you get it?"[13] Trâm said that she had bought it from the local store and that everyone used it.

There were three women in her village, including herself, who had gotten married in July 2002, she said. One of them gave birth to a child without a head, the other to a child who was born prematurely and died shortly after birth, and now she herself had suffered reproductive trouble too. When I asked Trâm if she had been concerned about working with these chemicals, she replied:

> Yes, I was aware that working with pesticides can affect the fetus. But in the first month of my pregnancy I did not know that I was pregnant. When I found out, I continued the spraying because I had not finished it yet. In our family we have no one else who can do this. I did ask my husband to do it, but he was busy working—he has a job doing road construction to supplement our income. So I was the only one at home, and I had to do it. In our area it is difficult to hire someone to spray pesticides, because people say it is very poisonous, so nobody wants to do it.

The differences between women such as Liên and Trâm attest to the growing economic inequalities in renovation-era Vietnam. It is precisely people like Hoa and Khánh, Trâm and Thà—urban migrants and the rural poor—who are the most vulnerable in the current era of transition to a liberalized market economy. It is of course impossible to say if there was indeed any causal link between Khánh's working conditions and his child's umbilical hernia, but his determination to ignore this possibility was striking, and probably reflected a very realistic assessment of his own chances in the urban labor market. Coming from a rural area, he did not have much choice, just as Trâm did not have much choice when she continued working with pesticides because no one else could do it.[14]

Despite their different life conditions and varying chances of living up to the norms of self-responsibility that the public health authorities were propagating, the plights of women such as Liên, Hoa, and Trâm converged in one significant respect: they all took upon themselves the reproductive responsibility that others placed on them. At the time of our fieldwork, ideas that government, employers, or society as a whole could have a responsibility for creating the economic and social conditions that would enhance the health of mothers and children were strikingly absent, while individual responsibility for reproductive health was a high-profile topic in the media. Considered from this privatizing perspective, Liên and Hoa had failed in protecting their health properly against autumn colds; Khánh had, as his colleagues suggested, placed the life of his child in jeopardy by agreeing to work in toxic conditions; and Trâm had acted irresponsibly in not refusing to work with pesticides. The consequences of poverty and gender inequality for maternal and child health were, in other words, largely ignored in both private and public discussions, while individual mothers- or fathers-to-be were held personally accountable for the reproductive mishap that had shattered their family.

In some cases, however, the biological body whose weaknesses were scrutinized in family discussions was not that of the individual, but a more collective, family body. This was particularly the case in households where one or more family members had been exposed to herbicide spraying during the Second Indochina War.

BIOLOGICAL DAMAGE: BLEMISHED FAMILY BODIES

"Perhaps this is my fault. I was a professional soldier in Quảng Trị. Until 1979 I was a driver, working in Laos and Kampuchea. My son was born in 1976." His large hands folded in his lap, Ông Bình, Thu's father-in-law, had tears in his eyes. He was a dignified elderly man, dressed in a white shirt and well-kept black pants—normally, it seemed, a man of considerable composure. But on this April morning in 2004, sitting on the bench outside the 3D scanning room, Ông Bình looked fragile. Dr. Tuấn had confirmed what physicians in another hospital had found the day before: the child that his daughter-in-law was expecting was too small for its age, and its upper lip had a deep cleft. We were studying Thu's scan result—Thu, her husband, Ông Bình, my colleague Hạnh, and I, pondering how to interpret it. At this point a senior obstetrician passed us, striding down the corridor. Before the scan, Thu had told us that this doctor, an old friend of her father-in-law, had informed her that it was unlikely that she could keep this fetus. Now, he confirmed this. After glancing through the scan result, he said, "This is very clear. The palate has a cleft too, and there is a problem with the brain. You'll have to do as we talked about." He then handed Thu the scan result and left. None of us said anything. From Ông Bình's eyes, large tears were dropping. He took Hạnh's hand and said in a low voice, "I have a daughter who is affected too. She has a large tumor on her wrist. She has had five operations, but in vain. The tumor is still there. When she was pregnant with her, my wife did have a cold, but . . . She was born in 1980, after I got back from Kampuchea."

By mentioning his wife's cold, Ông Bình suggested that perhaps his daughter's health problems should not, after all, be ascribed to his military service in areas exposed to herbicide spraying. Yet he felt burdened by the possibility of a link between his own military past and the present-day health problems suffered by his daughter and daughter-in-law. In several of the families we visited, similar suspicions lingered. A few women in our sample—such as Tuyết, whose story opens this book—had a close relative, usually a brother or a brother-in-law, who was officially classified as an Agent Orange victim. In these families, Agent Orange loomed large when causes were considered. But fears hovered also in other families: if a grandparent of the child-to-be had served in areas that had been sprayed during the war, family members would always wonder whether this could be the reason for the malformation. Although Hanoi had not been exposed to herbicide spraying, many of its contemporary inhabitants still seemed to feel at risk when reproductive mishaps occurred. One of the families in which anxieties about the possible effects of Agent Orange lingered was that of Lan.

Lan was 37 weeks pregnant when an ultrasound scan found that the ventricles of the fetal brain were dilated. The child she was expecting, the physician in the antenatal care room explained, was likely to be born with severe hydrocephalus. "Now," he said, "there are two options. Either we can wait for you to go into labor normally. Or we can induce the delivery. This is up to you. You and your family must think this over carefully." Two days later, on February 13, 2004, Hạnh and I visited Lan in the village on the outskirts of Hanoi where she lived together with her husband, Anh, and his parents. Following local tradition, Lan had moved into the house of her parents-in-law when she and Anh had gotten married a year earlier. On the spring day when we visited the family, the weather was beautiful, yellow flowers lighting up the winter-tired fields along the road. When I think back on it, the brightness of this day stands in stark contrast to the sinister atmosphere that met us when we reached Lan's house. Shooing away the barking dog, her mother-in-law received us in the yard outside the house. She took Hạnh's hand and invited us in. Inside, a group of men were sitting in a circle on a straw mat on the floor. As if to grant the men the authority to decide what to do, Lan and her mother-in-law took more peripheral positions, sitting on a bed at the side of the room. Anh gestured to us to sit down with the men and introduced them to us. As usual when family meetings were held, both sides of the family were represented: the group included Anh, his father, and his brother-in-law, and Lan's father and eldest brother. Anh's father explained to us that he had invited representatives from Lan's family to join them that morning in order to have "a truly thorough discussion." The atmosphere was tense—not just, I realized, because of the hard decision that the family confronted but also because of lingering, and potentially divisive, uncertainties regarding which side of the family was to be held accountable for this reproductive mishap.

As the host of the meeting, Anh's father opened the debate in an authoritative fashion:

> There are two possible causes. The first is that the grandfather on the other side [Lan's father] was in the army during the war. He served in Quảng Trị and Huế from 1968 to 1976. Perhaps he was exposed to Agent Orange there. He had two children before joining the army and three children after he came back. Lan was born in 1979, after he returned. When people have served in the army, their children are often affected by Agent Orange. In our village, several families receive Agent Orange compensation. The children are disabled, they are lame or their legs are curved because their father was in the army. That's the first possibility. The second is that Lan had a cold during her pregnancy.

Lan's brother immediately objected, "Those are only suspicions. If our father had suffered from that, his children would have been affected too. But Lan and our younger siblings are all healthy." Anh supported him: "I do think it is because of the cold." Lan's brother-in-law chimed in: "Of course it's because of the cold." Her brother concurred, "Of course it's the cold. A lot of people here were infected by that cold." After a while, Anh ended the discussion by saying that only experts would be able to say what had actually caused the problem. A few weeks later, when we visited Lan again, her mother-in-law asked me if I could tell her what the reason was: "I don't understand it," she insisted. "In our families, everyone is healthy. Nobody has ever had problems like this before." When I could not offer an explanation, she ventured: "I think it is because Lan had that cold. She is often very careless. For instance, when she comes home from work, she washes her hair in cold water. She did not think about the fact that during pregnancy, this kind of behavior could affect her child."

Adriana Petryna (2002) and Matthew Kohrman (2005) have shown that, in Ukraine and the People's Republic of China, respectively, people struggle for disability status as a means of gaining social membership and access to state protection. The people I met in Hanoi, by contrast, were reluctant to be identified as Agent Orange victims. Although being classified as a victim brought economic benefits, it also involved biological stigma. The eagerness with which Lan's relatives blamed this reproductive mishap on her cold must be seen in light of the consequences in store for a family if a negative biological label is attached to it. In Vietnam, Agent Orange is, as shown in previous chapters, widely assumed to cause genetic problems that may haunt a family for generations, affecting not only the exposed individual but also his or her children and grandchildren. Annika Johansson's research among Agent Orange victims in Vietnam suggests that in some cases, this negative marking as an Agent Orange family has had dramatic consequences. Some young women, rumors say, have committed suicide because of fears that they carry their father's "Agent Orange genes." Both victims themselves and other community members, Johansson notes, are often of the opinion that individuals with suspected genetic problems caused by Agent Orange, even if healthy, should refrain from having children: "There seemed to be a generalized fear that the 'dioxin genes' might spread in the general population. This fear is fuelled by the increasing proliferation in the mass media of cases of 'third generation Agent Orange victims' where parents who were exposed to chemical spraying during the war get healthy children but their grandchildren are born disabled or develop strange diseases" (Johansson 2007:8).

In the families we visited, however, Agent Orange was always weighed against other possible explanations, and in most cases people ended up deciding *not* to believe that the fetal anomaly had been caused by wartime exposure to herbicides. Thu, for instance, told her father-in-law to stop thinking about the past. This reproductive mishap, she insisted, must have been caused by the cold she had in early pregnancy: "I hope this happened because I had a cold. If that is the case, then I will have an ordinary pregnancy next time. I don't want the reason to be that my father-in-law was in the army. In that case, it might happen again, if not in my life, then in the lives of my children." Nevertheless, Thu said, since she had her abortion, her father-in-law had cried a lot, pondering aloud if relations between the living and the dead within their family had somehow gone awry. He kept lamenting, "I don't know if there is something wrong with the ancestors in this house . . ."

Since Agent Orange is assumed in Vietnam to cause genetic problems that can persist for generations, individuals and families affected by herbicide spraying are placed in a situation structurally similar to those thought to suffer from hereditary diseases (*bệnh di truyền*). Within local neighborhoods, congenital disabilities were often assumed to be associated with the blood (*máu*) or genes (*gen*) that family members shared. One problem that arises if the stigma of hereditary disease is attached to a family, people explained, is that it becomes difficult for the children to find attractive marriage partners. In Bích's words, "I fear that when my daughter grows up, everybody will think that there is something hereditary in the family. No matter how pretty she is, if there is someone in the family like that, then of course [she will have trouble getting married.] . . . To be honest, if my daughter wanted to marry someone from a family that had such a child, I too would feel very scared. I would accept that marriage only if they truly loved each other deeply." In this sense, disability is, as Veena Das and Renu Addlakha (2001:512) point out in an Indian context, located not in individual bodies, but "'off' the body of the individual and within a network of social and kin relationships."[15] The detection of a fetal anomaly blemishes a family biologically, sowing doubts about the ability of its members to produce healthy children. This was the reason that it was so important for Lan's relatives to determine whether the problem was located on the maternal or the paternal side: this allocation of biological fault could have far-ranging consequences for junior family members. While offering relief from cosmology, then, scientific explanations produced other kinds of moral accusation, generating friction and mutual suspicion within families. As a consequence, women would often opt to take the blame themselves. Ngọc, for instance, said: "I tell my husband that I think this has happened because of me. I take the blame for it because I want to encourage him so that he does not have to worry so much. But actually, I don't see any reason why it should be because of me." By placing the fault on the individual maternal body, in other words, women such as Ngọc tried to free the family body from both biological and cosmological fault, attributing the fetal defect to their own failure to care properly for their health during pregnancy.

COSMOLOGICALLY INFLECTED SCIENCE: PROCESSES OF MORAL IMBRICATION

As this chapter demonstrates, people in Hanoi would often claim that new biomedical ideas and practices are currently replacing old approaches to human reproduction, shifting childbearing from the realm of superstition into a modern world of science. In one frame of interpretation, such a change toward more individualized and scientifically grounded explanations could be seen as an indication of a broader cultural shift toward neoliberal modes of accounting for human lives; with Vietnam's economic reforms has come, one might assume, an increased emphasis on individual self-responsibility. This ethnographic material points, however, to another mode of interpretation. Although

most of my Hanoian interlocutors insisted that the cause of their reproductive misfortune must be identified through the application of scientific principles, cosmological explanations always seemed to hover, animating family discussions and personal deliberations.[16] The experiences
that people placed within the realm of science were, as we have seen,
embedded in enduring frameworks of cosmological meanings, drawing
moral and emotional force from long-standing philosophies of body
and subjectivity. Rather than simply replacing existing visions and practices of procreation, therefore, new biomedical technologies were integrated with older cosmological ideas, soaking meaning and import from
them. I therefore suggest that these engagements between science and
superstition must be understood as a process of *moral imbrication*
through which cosmological configurations of blame, responsibility,
and accusation came to suffuse the realms of science and technology.

During our fieldwork, these processes of moral imbrication became
particularly evident when people discussed new biomedical technologies in terms that explicitly placed practices associated with the realm of
science within a frame of cosmological meanings. Trâm's grandmother,
for instance, told us that her daughter-in-law had some complications
during her pregnancy, yet at birth the child was fine: "She went to
Hanoi for examinations. First, thanks to the experts, second, thanks to
the family's ancestral good fortune (*phúc ấm*), the child was complete."
During family conversations, people would often define the fact that the
fetal anomaly had been detected as evidence of the family's cosmologically mediated good fortune (*phúc*). For instance, after Hồng's abortion, her brother-in-law commented: "Bringing up a child like that
would have meant suffering. We do have luck (*phúc*), since science
detected this, so we must extend our thanks to science." Similarly, Mai
said: "This shows that our family still has luck (*phúc*), so we got to
know about it early on. We could resolve it; we were lucky. I do have a
lucky fate." The physicians who delivered high-tech medical care at the
obstetrics hospital would often resort to a similar language of interhuman moral-cosmological connections. Dr. Nga, the pediatrician, for
instance, told me that when an infant was born disabled, the parents
would often reject the child, trying to leave it behind at the hospital. In
such situations, she would appeal to their conscience using Buddhist
language of moral responsibility rather than medical language of diagnosis and treatment, saying, "Do take this child home. A child like this
carries all misfortune, all calamity for the entire family. Do take it home
and it will watch over (*phù hộ*) you all." The term *phù hộ* is usually

used to describe the protection and support provided by spirits or ancestors. By employing this term, therefore, this physician drew the power of cosmological forces into clinical interactions, suggesting that science alone cannot account for human misfortune. Similarly, Dr. Trang, a thirty-six-year-old female obstetrician working in the antenatal care department told us that in counseling her patients, she would take into account the moral condemnation she knew they were likely to meet: "In Vietnam, if a mother gives birth to a disfigured child, everyone else will think that, for sure, in this house they are not good. They are bad, so Heaven punishes them. This is the heaviest psychological burden for the mother and the family."

In public health announcements, pregnancies and their outcomes were, as we have seen, placed firmly in the realm of modernity and science; fetal development, women were told, is a physiological process that depends on their capacity to act as modern mothers, practicing scientifically recommended pregnancy care. But since, in their day-to-day lives, the entire terrain of reproduction was suffused with moral-cosmological meanings, exhortations that referred to science and modernity seemed to operate by tapping into women's awareness of the larger and more infinite responsibilities they were charged with in this realm. The weight of the demands placed on them to participate in modern and medicalized pregnancy care were, in other words, reinforced by older cosmological links between reproductive misfortune and moral misbehavior. Although officially placed in the domain of science, the connections that people drew between parental actions and the state of an infant's body reiterated and reworked long-standing theories of more comprehensive interpersonal responsibilities. Within cosmological frameworks, reproductive misfortune was interpreted as the corporeal instantiation of the failure to behave correctly; in the present-day era of science, these moral links between parental behavior and pregnancy outcomes were drawn again, but in novel ways.

Hanoian women's eager use of obstetrical ultrasonography must, I suggest, also be seen in the light of these processes of moral imbrication. When women felt that they *had to* have numerous ultrasound scans, this urge seemed to be fueled not only by the neoliberal forces at play when health providers tried to sell this technology to their customers, or by state demands placed on women to produce high-quality child-citizens, but also by more subdued moral-cosmological dynamics—by women's awareness of the fact that if something went wrong, this would place an infinite moral responsibility on their shoulders. The fetal body that emerged on the monitor was not simply the biobody theorized by Foucault and his followers but also a cosmological body ordered by long-standing conceptions of the cosmic reverberations of human actions. Understood along these lines, child health concerned more than infections and immunizations; the biologically normal child body was also cosmologically complete, its physical integrity attesting to the moral integrity of families and the political legitimacy of government. Considered through an optic of moral imbrication, then, present-day political celebrations of the happy family and a high-quality population become instruments of governance that fuse new biopolitical strategies with long-standing cosmologies of order, balance, and ethicality.

CHAPTER 6

Beyond Knowledge

Everyday Encounters with Disability

MÂY: "I SAW BEFORE ME THE IMAGE OF MY FRIEND'S CHILD"

On October 27, 2004, my colleague Toàn received a phone call. In a soft voice, the woman on the other end introduced herself as Mây. The day before, she told Toàn, a 3D scan performed by Dr. Tuấn had found that her fetus was not developing normally. She read his conclusion aloud to Toàn. Then she asked, "Can you tell me, If I keep this fetus, what will my child be like?"

Three weeks later, on November 18, Hiệp and I went to Hanoi's Thanh Xuân district where Mây lived with her husband. When we reached their apartment, Mây was waiting for us on the porch outside, wearing a thick brown knitted hat. The porch was full of potted flowers and a little yellow canary was twittering in its cage. Given that she had just undergone a second-trimester abortion, I thought, Mây looked well; she was beautiful and bright-eyed and her cheeks rosy. Inside, we sat down on the straw mat on the living room floor, and Mây immediately blurted out: "I so much wanted to keep this child. I think it was wrong *(tội)* to give it up. But my husband and many other people encouraged me to have an abortion, so I did." These words seemed to capture the essence of what she wanted to talk to us about that day: her desire to have a child and the forces that had compelled her to terminate her pregnancy. On Sunday, October 24, Mây told us, she had obtained a 3D ultrasound scan at a private ob-gyn clinic near her home. The doctor told her that her fetus was soaked with water and that she would have to have an abortion. She and her husband then went to Hanoi's obstetrics hospital for another 3D scan. "They concluded that the fetus suffered from hydrops (*bạch mạch*). They said that with this condition, there was no way that I could keep our child. . . . Neither my husband nor I have much expert knowledge about issues like this. So we listened to what the doctors said and followed their advice. We discussed it a lot, but in the end we decided to give it up." At first, Mây said, she had insisted on keeping her pregnancy. "I'm not giving up this child," she had told her husband. "I have carried this child in my womb and I will not give it up." But her husband persuaded her that an abortion was the best solution. "This is my child too," he said, "and I too do not want this to happen. But we must listen to the doctors. What else can we do?"

Like most other couples receiving an adverse diagnosis, Mây and her husband claimed that in making their decision, they followed advice given by health professionals. Mây's resort to an abortion could therefore be interpreted as a mode of self-making in which she, by submitting to expert biomedical knowledge, took up the position of a modern citizen-subject, aligning herself with dominant truths and forms of authority. Women's stories indicated, however, that the expert advice they received achieved its moral force and social significance from concrete everyday experience rather than by virtue of embodying abstract authority. In Mây's case, the experiences of her friend Xuân Anh played a decisive role in shaping the decision that she came to. "I have a friend," Mây said.

> Her name is Xuân Anh. She was born in 1978 like me. Her son was born with brain damage. He died recently, at the age of four. He spent his entire life lying in one place (*nằm một chỗ*). He could not do anything at all. The doctors said that if I gave birth, there would be something wrong with the brain of my child. When I heard that, I saw before me the image of my friend's child and I felt scared. What would I do if my child were like that too? I felt that it was better to set it free. I decided to give it up. I would feel so sorry for my child. This child would have had a life of suffering. . . . Whenever I ponder whether I am a cruel person, I think of that little child and I feel a bit lighter at heart. Then I think that what I did was right.

Xuân Anh's son, Mây suggested, belonged to Xuân Anh and her husband. As the parents of this child, they were responsible for his well-being, and it was *their* task to ensure that he lived a good life. But spending one's days lying in one place was, she claimed, not the kind of life that a human being should lead. "In her heart," Mây said, "Xuân Anh was always sad. Because she knew that at four years of age, a child should be able to do this and that, but her child was merely lying in one place. She speculated constantly and could not feel happy. When people came to visit, they would always ask, 'What is wrong with your child?'" Mây imagined that if she had kept her pregnancy, she would have found herself in a similar position of powerlessness, unable to offer her child what she saw as a fully human life: "I think my child would have suffered. He would not have been able to enjoy the beauty of life. To be human means to be able to experience life, to love and to hate. But as the mother of a disabled child, you can only give him food, clothes, and medicine. You cannot give him all those emotional experiences. . . . Perhaps we did come to the right decision."

SELECTIVE REPRODUCTION: ENGAGEMENTS WITH SCIENTIFIC KNOWLEDGE

In the contemporary world, childbearing decisions are increasingly made under the aegis of science, informed by biomedical knowledge and supported by experts. This raises questions about the ways in which scientific knowledge is generated, communicated, and used in this ethically sensitive terrain and about what kinds of knowledge are pursued and how they are put into action. In recent decades, numerous ethnographic studies have investigated how scientific knowledge of human bodies is interpreted and integrated into everyday lives. There is, these studies note, often a gap between the biomedical information that people are offered and their own socially shaped perceptions and categorizations (cf. Rapp 1999). Biomedicine is always articulated and interpreted in locally specific ways, put into practice through concrete engagements with preexisting predicaments and long-standing ways of handling human existence.

In this chapter I begin from these insights, exploring how the anomalous fetus came into being for pregnant women in Hanoi as an object of knowledge and imagination, care and concern. How, I ask, did authoritative biomedical knowledge engage with local experiences and practices? Through what social relations was scientific knowledge incorporated into people's experiences of themselves and their worlds, shaping desires, decisions, and actions? How did biomedical claims about the real intersect with other claims to knowledge about human bodies and lives? Working with this material from Vietnam, I have come to take knowledge to be always experiential and intersubjective. As human beings we get to know our worlds by drawing on previous life experiences; and since all experience is generated out of social interaction, knowledge is by definition intersubjective, contextual, and situated. An investigation of how Hanoian women and their relatives came to know, therefore, demands that we go beyond what Levinas (1998b:151) calls the intellectualism of knowing and approach knowledge as a product of embodied, intuitive, and morally charged human relations.

Like Mây, all the women I met asked themselves and others what kind of child might emerge from their wombs. What would happen if they carried this pregnancy to term? What would happen if they did not? To come to the decision that they had to make, they needed to know what would be the consequences of taking one or the other path of action. Accompanied by their relatives, they embarked on an extensive process of inquiry that, as I show in this chapter, took them from the medical world of the obstetrics hospital into local communities and national worlds of moral distinction and evaluation. To grasp the social dynamics of knowing in ethically charged situations such as the one in which Mây found herself, this ethnographic material suggests, we must look beyond knowledge, attending to forces that resist our powers of conceptualization and conscious reflection: those that bind us into relations with one another.

VISUALIZING THE ABNORMAL FETUS: THE PRECARIOUSNESS OF BIOMEDICAL KNOWLEDGE

Looking at this picture, I don't understand anything at all. Looking at this is like looking at the wall. The doctor explained something, but I did not understand him. In the antenatal care room, all they asked was if there was anyone in our family with a gene for dwarfism. That was all. They could not help me at all. It was quite one-sided (*phiến diện*). . . . So I went to ask our doctor at the commune health station—he is my uncle. He said, "Only experts can understand this picture; I too don't know what it means." So how about us, how can we be expected to understand? But I can see his face. The eyes, the nose, I can see his face clearly. Here are the hands. My son said, "He looks like me."

When Toàn and I visited Chúc in her village in December 2003, she showed us a pile of scanning images of the child she was expecting. Looking anxious, she appealed to us for help. Could we help her to interpret these images? What was she to make of them? What kind of child could she expect to be giving birth to in two months' time? Leafing through the scans, I too found it difficult to see any defect in this fetal image; to me it looked just like all the normally developing fetuses that I had seen on the monitor in the 3D scanning room. Like so many other times in the course of research, therefore, my colleagues and I remained unable to offer firm answers to the questions that women and their relatives posed. Instead, we engaged with them in an extended social process of exploring possible answers and interpretations.

Chúc's characterization of the scanning image was typical: most women said that this image remained opaque to them and that they found it hard to understand how their fetus differed from a normal one. The first question that women raised was therefore, If this pregnancy feels right to me, and I see no abnormality in the scan, should I then believe this medical verdict, or not? In day-to-day lives in Hanoi, science was, as seen earlier in the book, associated with progress, with the good, and with truth. Yet when science brought devastating news, most people seemed to feel that there was reason to be skeptical. Bích's husband, Hùng, for instance, told us how, deeply distrustful of their 3D scan result, he had accompanied his wife to several private clinics for additional examinations. The existential anxiety and confusion he felt manifested itself as geographical disorientation when he found himself unable to find his way around normally familiar parts of Hanoi:

> The doctor said that we must give it up. So I felt that we had to have more scans, in order to be sure. I took my wife to several other places. We drove around until evening. I felt out of myself, so when my wife asked me to take her to Nhà Chung street, I could not find it, I drove her around aimlessly. I had lost all my bearings. I had no sense of direction anymore and could not find the way. I have often taken my wife to the obstetrics hospital, but on that day I could not find the way. It was as if my mind was haunted.

Like Bích, most women obtained ultrasound scans from several different health care providers before finally accepting the counterintuitive medical message they received. Although the biomedical labeling of the fetus as abnormal contradicted their own embodied sense of their pregnancies, a vast majority ended up accepting the doctors' conclusion and opting to place faith in expert biomedical advice. At first glance, this seems to illustrate how authoritative knowledge (Jordan 1997) is established in health care encounters; women's own experiential sense of their pregnancies was, it seemed, overridden by the hard scientific facts established by health professionals. On closer inspection, however, these biomedical facts were suffused with uncertainty and ambiguity, and in women's decision making, the information that health providers offered was woven together with embodied, experiential knowledge of the social implications of childhood disability.

Research conducted in European and North American settings has shown that when an adverse prenatal diagnosis is made, pregnant women are offered substantial amounts of biomedical information on the fetal problem at issue.[1] Despite this medical support, however, pre-natal diagnoses often tend to remain ambiguous. Based on her New York City research, Rapp (1999:229) observes that women's reactions tended to vary depending on the clarity of the diagnosis they received, "disorienting pain and intimate upheaval" being particularly pro-nounced when women received ambiguous diagnoses. The women I met in Hanoi struggled not only with the shock of learning that their fetus was not normal, but also with the uncertainty that stemmed from not knowing *in what way* it was not normal. They all left the obstetrics hospital feeling disoriented, anxious, and uncertain, asking, as Mây and Chúc did: "If I keep this fetus, what will my child be like?" As we have seen, the information that women received at the hospital was relatively limited: during most consultations, physicians would briefly indicate what part of the fetal body was affected (the brain, the heart, the stom-ach, the spine, and so on), yet usually without offering further detail on the condition or on the child's prospects if the pregnancy were car-ried to term. Most women therefore had to make their decision on the basis of relatively rudimentary biomedical information about the condi-tion of their fetus. This, to me, seemed ethically questionable. How, I thought, can health care providers find it acceptable to let a woman terminate a wanted pregnancy in a situation where no diagnosis has been provided and where she may not understand for what medical reason the abortion is being performed? Yet while *I* expected physicians to offer more information, this was rarely an expectation that the women and their relatives shared. Rather than demanding better care or more detailed explanations, most women seemed to accept the current state of medical affairs. How, then, did prospective parents come to know about the child they were expecting? To illustrate the social proc-esses through which parents-to-be sought to make sense of the informa-tion they received at the obstetrics hospital, I now present the case of twenty-five-year-old Lý and her husband, Nam. When we met them, Lý was 23 weeks pregnant, and she and Nam were employed as factory workers in the southern suburbs of Hanoi.

LÝ AND NAM

On January 29, 2004, just after Tết (the lunar new year), Lý's husband drove her on the back of their motorbike to Hanoi's obstetrics hospital to obtain a 3D scan. When the scan identified an anomaly in the fetus, the nurse called my colleague Chi, who reached the hospital half an hour later. In her field notes, Chi wrote this account of the situation:

> When I arrived in the scanning room, Lan [the nurse] took me out into the corridor. Here, a young couple was sitting, looking as if they were waiting for someone. . . . We began to talk. Lý said she had had four or five antenatal check-ups and everything had been normal. Today, she and her husband had not imagined that the scan would turn out like this. Looking hopeful, Lý's husband asked me if there was any way that they could keep their child. Lý cried. At that moment, they both looked so deeply disappointed, and I did not know what to say. I tried to console Lý, taking her hand and holding it very tight. I asked her what Dr. Tuấn had said, and she replied that all he had said was that the fetus was suffering from hydrops fetalis (*dị sản bạch mạch*). Lý asked me what hydrops fetalis was. Her husband said, "Please, can you help us? How can we keep our child? What should we do now?" They both looked at me with begging eyes. I asked them to wait and went into the scanning room to ask Lan about Lý. She said that this fetus was suffering from multiple malformations: water on the lungs, facial deformities, and a membrane around the fetal skull. This pregnancy would have to be terminated. Listening to our conversation, Dr. Tuấn said that it was one hundred percent certain that Lý would have to abort this fetus. She could not keep it. He then told me to ask Lý to go to the antenatal care room and get an explanation from the doctors there. In the corridor, Lý and Nam were still waiting, looking worried and anxious. I told them what Dr. Tuấn had said, and Nam replied that they had already been to the antenatal care room. But because the doctors had not said anything, they had come back here to ask the sonographer again. I said to them, "Let's go and talk to Dr. Tuấn," and we returned to the scanning room. When he saw us, Dr. Tuấn said, "Lý, you'll have to prepare yourself to go into hospital. Then the doctors will have a conference and find out what to do. If you have to give up this fetus, you must accept that. You should consider yourself lucky that you found out about this early on. If you had come a bit later, it would have much harder to solve this problem and much more damaging to your health. If you are not prepared to go into hospital today, tomorrow will be OK too." In a comforting tone, Lan said to Lý: "You are still young. Do take this calmly. Now, go home and have something to eat and drink, have a rest and when you come back into hospital, the doctors will have a conference. Don't worry. Many women go through similar things. This is just bad luck. Nam, you must try to encourage your wife." Lý was now crying openly, and Nam and I helped her to sit on one of the chairs outside.

The next Sunday, Chi picked me up on her motorbike, and we went to visit Lý and Nam accompanied by Hạnh, one of the medical doctors on our team. Lý and Nam lived in Hanoi's Cầu Giấy district where they rented a room in a house owned by Lý's uncle. The house was located far from the main road, in a maze of narrow alleys. Steering their motorbikes carefully around the corners, Chi and Hạnh followed the directions that Nam had given us. As it was the weekend, people were at home and children were playing in the alleys, their voices echoing off the walls. Outside the gate to their house, Nam was waiting for us. He guided us through a living room where a young man was sleeping, and showed us up the narrow stairs to their room on the first floor. The room was furnished with a bed and a small television, the walls adorned with numerous images of the Virgin Mary holding baby Jesus. As we entered, Lý got up from the bed. She was very pale. Nam explained that they came from a poor Catholic village in Nghệ An province where people barely had enough to eat. They were both the eldest children in large families, and since they had had difficulty earning a living from farming alone, they had moved to Hanoi to find work.

In a small voice, Lý told us about the reproductive difficulties she had experienced. Having known each other since they were children, she and Nam got married in 1998. Soon after their wedding, Lý got pregnant. After seven months, she went into labor and the child was stillborn. Soon afterward, she got pregnant again, but after two months she miscarried. Her third pregnancy ended in a preterm birth and the child died. Now, Lý's fourth pregnancy seemed to have gone awry too. Before going to Hanoi's Obstetrics and Gynecology Hospital, Lý said, she had had a scan at the National Obstetrics Hospital. Without offering any kind of explanation, the doctors there had simply said that this pregnancy must be terminated. Lý and Nam had then hoped that physicians at another hospital might come to a different conclusion. After their three previous pregnancy losses, they wanted to keep this pregnancy. "But," Lý said, "when we got there, it was still the same. So I thought, then we will have to accept this. If the doctors say so, then . . . We don't know anything, so we must listen to what the doctors say. This fetus is malformed. Perhaps the child will die, or perhaps it will eke out a miserable existence, spending its entire life lying in one place."

After I left Lý and Nam's house that day, I could still see Lý's pale face before my eyes. I imagined how trying the past years must have been—hopes dashed, dreams crushed, time and time again. For Lý and Nam, these events must have taken an enormous emotional toll—witnessing the deaths of two children, disappointing their parents, having to answer swarms of questions posed by curious neighbors, and living with the uncertainty about whether they would ever become parents. Like Lý and Nam, I felt haunted by the indeterminacy of their situation, wondering, as they did, *why* this had happened. What was wrong?

Would they ever be able to have a child? Could anything be done to help them? Early the next day, I met with them at the gate to the hospital. It was a cold and gray winter morning, and people passing through the gate were wearing thick winter jackets, hats, and gloves. In a hesitant voice that contradicted the resoluteness of his words, Nam said: "We will have to do as the doctors say." Hạnh joined us, and we went together to the antenatal care room. This morning it was nearly empty; there was only a young female doctor sitting at her table. Lý handed her the scan result. She took a quick look at it, then told Lý: "This fetus is malformed. You must go into hospital." Lý did not reply. I asked, "If she kept this fetus, what would the child be like?" but received no answer. Instead, a nurse began explaining to Lý what examinations she must undergo. Following her instructions, we went to stand in line to get the forms for blood and urine tests. While we were waiting, I studied Lý's face. She looked burdened, but calm, as if this was the course of events that she had prepared herself for.

A few hours later, when all the tests had been done, a nurse led Lý to A4, the department for reproductive disorders. The day after, I went to the doctors' office in A4. On the blackboard, Lý's name was written next to the following prescription: Cytotec 200 mcg: 1 pill at 10:00, 13:00, 16:00, 19:00, 22:00. Dr. Lương was sitting at his desk scribbling, a pile of patient case records next to him. I asked him if he could tell me about Lý's case. What had the diagnosis been? He replied that he did not know the English term for this condition, but that excessive amounts of fluid had accumulated in the fetal body and he did not believe that this child would be able to live for very long after birth. "But go and ask Dr. Thành," he said. "He has studied in France; he is an expert on these things." I found Dr. Thành in another department. A middle-aged man with gentle features, he invited me to take a chair. After studying Lý's ultrasound result carefully, he said, "This fetus is suffering from a lot of problems. In French, this condition is called *anasarque*. It means that there is oedema in the entire body of the fetus. If this pregnancy is carried to term, the child will die after birth. If the mother gets pregnant again, she should have an amniocentesis. Do you know if there are hereditary diseases in either of their families? Or was anyone exposed to chemicals during the war?"

In the evening, I went to A4 again. I found Nam walking up and down the corridor outside the department. Looking distressed, he told me that Lý had been taking medication all day, but nothing had happened yet. When I found Lý in the room that she shared with five other women, I noticed that she looked better and less burdened than earlier in the day. She gestured for me to sit on her bed and started talking, telling me about the large bed that they had ordered for her and the new baby and that they did not need now. Two days later, when I visited again, the abortion was over. Lý was lying under a red and white hospital blanket, her eyes vacant, her face pale. In the bed next to hers a woman was nursing a newborn infant.[2]

TURNING AN INDETERMINATE SITUATION INTO A DETERMINATE ONE: PROBLEMS OF KNOWLEDGE

The point I wish to make in telling Lý's story concerns knowledge. During the days when Lý and Nam were hovering in suspense, not knowing if they would be able to keep this pregnancy or not, I was assuming that access to biomedical knowledge might be able to dispel the uncertainties that they confronted. No matter how culturally constructed, collaborative, and multiple scientific knowledge may be, I felt, our best chances of finding help in this situation seemed to lie in the realm of biomedicine. Lý and Nam, however, were engaged in a different kind of knowledge project. Whereas I was looking for diagnostic closure, searching for the biological truth of the fetal condition, they were oriented toward an end—trying to find out what to do. In responding to their predicament, I leaned toward what John Dewey called a spectator theory of knowledge, trying to handle the uncertainty of their situation by transcending it through objective information. Lý and Nam, however, were looking for a sense of direction, trying to find out what course to steer.

Conventional models of knowledge, Dewey (1929:23) observed, rely on a separation between the knower and the object to be known, assuming that "what is known is antecedent to the mental act of observation and inquiry, and is totally unaffected by these acts." In his critique of this conception of knowledge, Dewey cautions us to replace our search for certainty with detailed attention to processes of inquiry, to the practical actions through which people seek knowledge in an effort to gain some measure of control over their world. This requires attention, he argues, to "the problematic situation" in which the quest for knowledge arises: inquiry always arises from doubtful, open-ended situations in which people grope through moments of disorientation and uncertainty. There is an important temporal dimension, then, to our attainment of knowledge; coming-to-know is a temporal and social process through which we move from confusion and indeterminacy to a position where we know how to handle the predicament in which we find ourselves. Knowing lies in a pragmatic ability to anticipate consequences; rather than in passive apprehension, knowledge consists of active dispositions that we achieve over time and apply with the future in mind. "Knowledge as an act is bringing some of our dispositions to consciousness with a view to straightening out a perplexity, by conceiving the connection between ourselves and the world in which we live" (Dewey 1968 [1916]:344).

For Lý and Nam, coming-to-know was a mode of experiencing. On the evening before her pregnancy was terminated—when Lý seemed relieved in spite of the painful procedure that she was undergoing—she and Nam had come to know in the sense that they had accepted the doctors' definition of the pregnancy as unviable and come to terms with the loss that they were facing. Terminating the pregnancy, they suggested, was a painful solution, yet less excruciating than losing another child or giving birth to a severely disabled child would have been. Lý and Nam had, in other words, turned the highly indeterminate situation in which they found themselves on the day when we first met into a more determinate one where they knew what to do. In this process, they wove biomedical information together with their prior knowledge, drawing on their own reproductive experiences and on the stories of lives with severe disability that they had heard from others.[3] When their fetuses were labeled abnormal, all prospective parents went through similar processes of experience-based information seeking. To come to their decisions, they listened to expert opinion, but they also drew on their own preexisting experiential knowledge of what bringing up a disabled child entails.

CHILDHOOD DISABILITY: PROCESSES OF INQUIRY

During fieldwork, I was often struck by the contrast between the ambiguity that seemed to characterize scanning images and the apparent clarity of women's mental visions of impaired children. Although the scanning image seemed vague, the mental images of suffering children that women conjured were stark, clear, and frightening. In Mây's case, for instance, the biomedical information she received did not make much sense to her, but the plight of her friend Xuân Anh evoked powerful images of the future that might lie ahead. When a fetal anomaly was found, in other words, the mental visions of disabled children that preg-

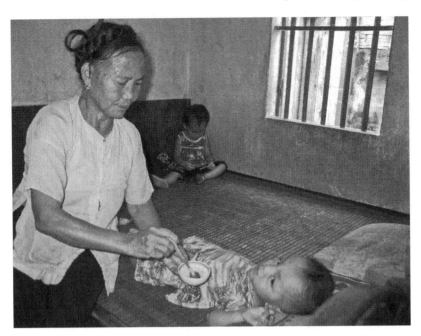

FIGURE 7. Labor of love. Chúc's mother-in-law feeding her grandson rice gruel. Photo by the author, 2010.

nant women would normally strive to steer clear of became impossible to keep away.

Disability is an integral part of day-to-day lives in Hanoi. In all the hamlets and neighborhoods I know, several households have disabled family members, many of them children. Some disabilities, such as Down syndrome (*bệnh Đao*) or cerebral palsy (*bại não*), are known by biomedical names, but physical and mental impairments are most often described in broad, general terms; a disabled person might be characterized as crippled (*què*) or as suffering from mental retardation (*chậm phát triển trí tuệ*). Rather than deriving from biomedicine, then, people's disability knowledge seems to be sensual, practical, and experiential. When imagining what their child might be like if they kept it, pregnant women and their relatives drew the experiences of relatives and neighbors into their deliberations, coming to know about their own potential child through already existing funds of shared social knowledge. When we visited her shortly before her son was born, for instance, Chúc drew up a detailed picture of the hardships she imagined that the future held in store for her. In her village lived a two-year-old boy named Dũng. His

FIGURE 8. Dũng and his grandfather. "We don't know what will happen. We care for our child day by day. We don't know what else to do." Photo by the author, 2004.

bones were brittle and broke very easily, and he could neither walk nor sit by himself. Although his grandfather helped with day-to-day care for him, Dũng remained, Chúc explained, a burden on his family. When Chúc's neighbors saw her scan, they declared that this fetus resembled Dũng.[4]

Imagining their life with this new child, Chúc looked to Dũng's family:

> This will be very hard for us as parents. In this village, people who are in a situation like this have to care constantly for their child. It is very expensive and very hard. . . . Healthy children can work and play; when they are four, they go to preschool. In school the teacher takes care of them, and the parents can work and earn money. But if the child is disabled, someone has to stay at home. Perhaps the parents can ask the grandparents to help. But if the parents have to stay at home, how can they earn enough to feed the child? . . . For sure it will be very hard, very difficult. I feel so worried. Since I came back from hospital, I have not been able to eat or sleep. The doctor said that if we had found out earlier, I could have had an abortion, but now it is too late and I must give birth. This is so hard. We cannot afford to have a child like this. But now we must do our best to manage.

Facing the prospect of having a child like Dũng, Chúc indicated, she knew what awaited her. She did not know how to interpret the scanning image of her own particular child-to-be, but she did possess more generalized knowledge of the social consequences of childhood disability. She knew how early Dũng's father had to get up to go to work in Hanoi, how late he returned home each day, and how an expression of hopelessness and exasperation seemed to have crept permanently onto his face. She knew of the mental instability, the mood swings, and the moments of insanity that had plagued Dũng's mother over the past few years. It was this knowledge that had kept Chúc awake at night during these last months before her son was born, disturbing her sleep and haunting her dreams.

Everyone I met seemed to possess this kind of experience-based knowledge of the social implications of childhood disability. When abortion decisions were made, women and their relatives drew this knowledge explicitly into their deliberations. When Chi and I talked to them during the weeks between diagnosis and decision, for instance, Bích and her husband referred repeatedly to the experiences of other people in their community. In an empathetic tone, Bích described the plight of one family:

> There's a child living in the house next door to my mother-in-law. He is eight years old now, but all he can do is eat and lie in the house. He can eat only if other people feed him. He cannot even chew by himself. His father has to chew the rice for him. He cannot go to the toilet on his own. He cannot walk. He lies in one place. He does not understand anything. To give birth to a child like that means suffering. . . . The child's grandparents are dead, and his mother goes to work at seven o'clock each morning and does not come back until nine in the evening. The father also has to work. He is a rice farmer. When they go to work, they often have to leave the child alone at home until noon. They don't have anyone to care for him. If he cries, they are forced to leave him to cry.

Bích's husband, Hùng, added, "When they leave, they put him in a cage, like an animal." To this, Bích objected, "Describing it like that makes it sound so harsh. It is more like a cot. You know the kind of cot that children sleep in so that they don't fall out. A cage. Who would have the heart to treat one's child like that. But when they go to work, they do have to put their child in something like a cage."

Bích's story of the neighboring family illustrates the expectations that are placed on parents within local moral communities: it is considered the duty of parents to provide for their children, ensuring that they are well fed and nurtured. The Vietnamese term for bringing up (*nuôi*) means "to feed" or "to nurture"; to belong to someone else as their child, in other words, means to be cared for through food. This requires resources. When imagining the prospect of childhood disability, people often emphasized the enormous strain that a severely disabled child places on the household economy. Some children need special diets or medications, both of which can be costly, and severely disabled children often need full-time care. Unless a grandparent can assist, this places parents in the impossible position of having to choose between leaving the child by itself at home—as Bích's fellow villagers did—or losing the income of one adult. The latter option will, in many cases, throw the family into poverty.[5] People explained how such financial difficulties, combined with emotional frustrations, often generate interpersonal tensions within households. In Bích's words: "It is impossible to live peacefully together if one has a child like that. It makes it harder for both parents and siblings to treat each other well. People in such families often scold each other, they feel depressed, sad, and pressured, and sometimes they just explode and shout at each other, blaming each other for this and that." A severely disabled child, moreover, demands lifelong care, not only from parents but also, particularly in the long term, from siblings. Prospective parents knew, therefore, that the decision they made now would have far-reaching consequences for their other children; a defect in the body of one child would affect the entire family body. Bích told us that what pained her most were the potential consequences of this decision for her daughter's life. As long as Bích herself lived, she would be able to care for the new child. But if the child outlived her, her daughter would have to manage these caregiving tasks. This would place a lifelong responsibility on her, thereby also reducing her chances of making a good and happy marriage: few men, Bích said, would be willing to marry a woman who brought this kind of burden along with her. While women who were mothers already often shared Bích's concerns, those who were pregnant with their first child usually expressed fears that no one would take care of their child when they themselves could no longer shoulder this task. Mây, for instance, said: "I think that a child like that will have a miserable life. As long as I am healthy, I can care for the child. But when I get old and die, nobody would care for my child."

Yet the processes of inquiry in which women and their relatives engaged did not always lead to the conclusion that the child they were expecting would shatter their lives and livelihoods. When physicians defined a fetal problem as mild (*nhẹ*), prospective parents often expressed hope that their child might be able to achieve a nearly normal life. Thuý's fetus, for instance, was found to be suffering from curved arms, a problem that, according to doctors, could be remedied through orthopedics after birth. On March 31, 2004, Chi and I visited Thuý, a secondary school teacher, in her home in a provincial town. The images of disability that she conjured differed markedly from those we had encountered elsewhere. It is, Thuý claimed, possible to lead a good life with a disabled child, provided that the problem is not severe. She based this assumption on the stories of two individuals. The first was her husband's younger brother: "He suffered from Down syndrome, but his condition was very mild. It was not severe at all. He could still understand. My husband's family sent him to school, but he did not like it, so he stopped. He died in 1990 from heart problems. Our family is still devoted to him. We take care to burn incense for him. The eighth day of the first month each year is the anniversary of his death. My husband's family does live with human sentiment (*sống rất tình cảm*)." I asked Thuý to explain in more detail what she meant by her last sentence. She replied that everyone lived closely together, loving each other—implying, it seemed, that in this family, the disabled child was offered as much love and care as other children. The second story that Thuý told us was about a neighboring family in which a girl had been born with curved legs. The family had sought treatment for her once she was a few months old, and the girl was now able to walk normally and about to finish tertiary school. "I look at that family," Thuý said, "and my husband tells me that their daughter is disabled too. Still, she can go to school. So my husband says that I should not worry. When our child is a few months old, we will take him to the children's hospital for orthopedics." In telling us the story of this girl, Thuý also conjured hope that the child they were expecting could grow up to become nearly normal.

Women who received an ambiguous diagnosis and no instructions from doctors regarding how to act on it often expressed similar hopes of normality. One woman in this situation was forty-four-year-old Loan. She was a secondary school teacher, her husband a government official. They had two daughters, aged nineteen and fourteen, and had embarked on this pregnancy in the hope of having a son. Loan's husband was his parents' only son, so they expected him to produce a son to continue their lineage. When a scan performed in week 16 informed Loan and her husband that the fetus was male, they were elated. From that day, Loan's husband took even better care of her than in her first months of pregnancy, buying delicacies for her to eat and taking over household chores. Yet another scan, done in week 23, found that their fetus suffered from an anomaly of the heart. Drawing on their social networks, they consulted a range of physicians, but none of them could say how this problem would affect the life of their child-to-be. Loan and her husband therefore had to make their decision in a situation of extreme indeterminacy. If their child turned out severely disabled, they said, this would alter their lives dramatically, throwing their daughters and themselves into suffering. On the other hand, they could not know for sure what this child would be like—and given Loan's age, their chances of having another son later on seemed small. They decided, therefore, to keep the pregnancy and hope for the best. Loan's husband remarked: "We hope . . . People in Vietnam feel that when something is not yet clear, not yet concrete, and you cannot yet know for sure, then you have a bit of hope. This fetus is still developing. We hope that at some point in its development, it will become normal."

Anticipating the hardships that the birth of a disabled child would entail, most women opted to terminate their pregnancy if they could. As Nga said, "It hurts now, but it saves mother and child from suffering. I am forced to accept this. I don't know what else to do." In our sample, seventeen women underwent an abortion, while thirteen gave birth to the child.[6] In most cases, the women who kept their pregnancies did so because physicians estimated that the pregnancy was so advanced that an abortion was not an option. Seven of these thirteen children survived. Three of them were born with negligible or no apparent disabilities, while four were considered severely disabled. The sons of Phương and Loan were born with Down syndrome, Lan's son with hydrocephalus, and Chúc's son with the rare condition arthrogryposis (cứng đa khớp bẩm sinh). When we met with them after their children had been born, these four women all expressed profound distress at the prospect of the lives that awaited them and their families. The task of caregiving they faced was daunting, as were the demands that this new child placed on their already tight household economy.[7] What seemed to pain them most, however, were the *moral* problems that they confronted; their children's anomalous bodies seemed to raise troubling questions regarding personhood, sociality, and moral value. These moral questions haunted not only those who became mothers of children with disabilities, but also the women who ended up terminating their pregnancies. In the following section I therefore examine more closely the everyday forms of moral knowledge that suffused women's experiences, informing their decisions to opt for an abortion.

"IF WE HAD KEPT OUR CHILD, IT WOULD HAVE SUFFERED": THE DISABILITY-SUFFERING EQUATION

When a fetal anomaly was detected, most women said that they found themselves faced with a troubling choice, one that raised wide-ranging moral questions. Is it right or wrong, they and their relatives asked, to take the life of this potential human being, our child-to-be? If we opt for a pregnancy termination, can we ever justify this to others and ourselves? Notably, the decisions that women came to always seemed to be made through concrete and pragmatic assessments of what course it was possible to steer rather than through a theoretical weighing of abstract moral principles. In their conversations with us, most women represented their decision in terms that suggested that they simply did what they had to do, either keeping their pregnancy, if they could, or giving it up, if they had to. Mai, for instance, said: "My child could not be cured, so my family and I made the decision [to terminate the pregnancy]." She then paused and asked, as if talking to herself: "Decision, what decision (*quyết định, quyết định cái gì*)?"[8] Mai's remark raises more general questions regarding how specific courses of action are generated in particular situations; in other words, what conditions the pragmatic assessments that people make when navigating complex moral terrains?

When Hanoian women and their relatives opted for an abortion, they nearly always insisted that they did so to save their child from suffering. If a child is born severely disabled, they said, it is destined to lead a miserable and painful life. Tuyết's comment on her abortion decision was typical: "A child that does not become a normal person will suffer. Now it was still a fetus, it was not yet a person (*người*), so this prevented my child and me from suffering." The suffering that childhood disability causes, people explained, stems from the child's inability to engage in the activities that other children are able to undertake; from the powerlessness of not being able to eat, walk, talk, and study like other children do. Huyền's husband, Trọng, put the problem in these words:

> Our child had water on the brain, so it would not have been normal. It would not be complete (*vẹn toàn*) as we are, not intelligent like others. When

the scan showed this, our family decided on an abortion. If we had kept our child, it would have suffered. So we thought it was better to let it go. But we were in so much pain (*khổ tâm*). This was our child. I felt as if I had cut a piece of my own flesh; it was very painful. But if we had not done that, our child would have suffered forever (*mãi mãi con nó đau khổ*). [Tine: In what way would your child have suffered?] It would have had a life of suffering. It would not have been complete. It would have suffered.

To Trọng, as to practically everyone I met, it seemed self-evident that a child whose body is not complete will suffer.

Most people took the link between disability and suffering as a fact in a way that brings to mind Pierre Bourdieu's (1977:169) concept of *doxa*: "that which is beyond question and which each agent tacitly accords by the mere fact of acting in accord with social convention." When I talked to Dr. Nam, an ob-gyn at the obstetrics hospital, about prenatal screening, he summarized what he saw as the most common patient reaction when a fetal problem was found: "At the district level, health staff usually simply tell the patient that her fetus is abnormal (*bất thường*). So when she comes here, all she asks for is an abortion. She doesn't need any counseling. She simply wants an abortion immediately." Similarly, Dr. Lương said: "Most women make the decision right away, right there. People in Vietnam have an inclination that I find very disturbing. Everyone, including the doctors, thinks that a congenital malformation is something very severe. Always. . . . In counseling, physicians have a certain inclination. They think it is better to give up the pregnancy, and this makes the patient disposed (*thiên về*) to do so too."

When prospective parents opted for a pregnancy termination, in other words, the disability-suffering equation was the taken-for-granted premise upon which their decisions rested. If they wanted to protect their child against suffering, they indicated, they had no other option than a pregnancy termination. As Hoa put it: "Giving birth to a disabled child means causing the child to suffer. The child will suffer because it feels inferior to others (*mặc cảm*). . . . Our child would have compared himself to others, and he would feel that he was not like them (*không được như mọi người*)." This equation of disability with suffering permeated everyday lives; in day-to-day conversations and interactions, people with disabilities seemed to be always considered inferior, explicitly categorized as burdens (*gánh nặng*) on family and society. In a typical statement, Thu, a thirty-two-year-old veterinarian and the mother of two nondisabled children, described the plight of one of her aunts whose husband had been exposed to Agent Orange:

My aunt has a child who has trouble talking and is not intelligent. He is stupid (*đần độn*). He does not know anything and my aunt has to care for him. Now he is twenty years old and all he can do is eat and go to the toilet. . . . My aunt has a hard life. To have a child that you bring up for nothing . . . then it is better to have an abortion. It is very hard to bring up a child who lives as a parasite (*báo cô*). The person who cares for the child will suffer and so will the child. It is especially hard for the mother. The child does not know anything, but the mother knows and she has to think a lot.

In the mass media, too, people with disabilities were usually portrayed as suffering, pitiful, and tragic figures (see chapter 1).[9] During fieldwork, I often felt uneasy in the confrontation with this consistent rhetorical framing of disability in terms of misery and suffering; yet in my interpretation of these statements, I have sought to attend to the everyday universes within which they became commonsensical and meaningful to people. Official as well as everyday reflections on childhood disability must, I suggest, be considered both in the context of the material conditions under which people live and against the background of socially shared and cosmologically inflected notions of personhood, humanity, morality, and responsibility. At the same time that the lives and personhood of people with disabilities were thrown into doubt in day-to-day discourse, I noticed, all the women in our sample defined the fetus as a human being-in-becoming and as their child.[10] It was in this terrain of tension between the certainty of the humanity and the uncertainty of the personhood of their child-to-be that the crux of their moral dilemma seemed located: is it right or wrong, women and their relatives asked, to take the life of a human being who is unlikely to ever become a full person?

"TO BECOME A PERSON ONE MUST MAKE A CONTRIBUTION": CHILDHOOD DISABILITY AS MORAL TRAGEDY

"Each society," note Beth A. Conklin and Lynn M. Morgan (1996:657–658), "must determine how its youngest will come to achieve the status of persons, how they will be recognized and granted a place within a human community. . . . In all societies, the complexities and contradictions in normative ideologies of personhood are heightened during the transitional moments of gestation, birth, and infancy, when personhood is imminent but not assured." Personhood and humanness, this and other ethnographic studies tell us, do not always coincide; an individual may be considered human without being recognized as a person, and personhood may be attributed to nonhuman entities.[11] The imprecision of lines between humans and spirits, persons and nonpersons, is often revealed with particular clarity when disability occurs. Cross-culturally, disability tends to raise questions about both humanness and personhood. Infants whose bodies differ from the expected have often been viewed with apprehension and skepticism, and sometimes even neglected or killed; and physical impairment often renders it difficult for an individual to be recognized as a full person.[12] Based on research conducted on the Thai-Cambodian border, for instance, Lindsay French (1994) describes how amputees' status as persons was drastically diminished as a result of their loss of physical capacity. Drawing on observations made in the United States, Irving Zola (1982) and Robert Murphy (1987) have shown how disabled people tend to be infantilized and devalued. And Gail Landsman (1998) offers vivid accounts of the ways in which North American mothers of disabled children struggle against the devaluing of their children and insist on their personhood. In an effort to counter the prejudice and discrimination that people with disabilities often face, disability scholars and activists across the world insist on the value and rights of the disabled, maintaining that the problems associated with disability are located not in the body of the disabled person, but in the society that fails to accommodate and appreciate human difference. As a consequence of this activism, and in reaction to the disturbing memories of twentieth-century eugenics programs, public discourse in the Western world generally claims acceptance of all individuals, insisting on equal citizenship rights.[13]

In Hanoi, I found, public discourses set forth other views of disability, emphasizing the limitations that physical or mental impairments tend to place on individual lives. Stories appearing on television and in newspapers often drew a contrast between two kinds of disabled individuals: those who lived in helpless dependency on others, and the exceptional few who managed to "overcome their fates" (*vượt qua số phận*), attaining a job, an income, and a family. People with disabilities are, these stories indicated—referring to a statement made by Hồ Chí Minh—infirm but not useless (*tàn nhưng không phế*); given the right conditions, they can still contribute to society. In one article published in *Family and Society,* for instance, a young mobility-impaired woman named Phương was quoted as saying to her mother, "Mum, I will not stay at the hospital anymore. I want to go home to work, so that I am useful to my family. . . . In this life, one must do something in order to be useful" (Lê Xuân Khiêm 2005:6). In another article, Huy, an eighteen-year-old man whose legs were lame, said, "I don't want to waste time any more. To live without being able to work means to simply exist. I must find a way to get an occupation so that I can support myself." The journalist concluded the article about Huy by expressing the hope that, with help from the community, people like him would be able to live according to what it means to be "a human being" (*với đúng nghĩa của một "con người"*) (Thanh Thúy 2009:10). These media stories, then, defined certain kinds of life as problematic and in need of intervention, while also setting norms and standards for personhood and proper conduct.

In day-to-day lives in Hanoi, similar expectations and attitudes were often expressed. Personhood, people suggested, hinges on the ability of the individual to take active part in social cycles of reciprocity and exchange. When talking about the suffering that childhood disability entails, people would often emphasize that severely disabled children spend their lives "lying in one place" (*nằm một chỗ*) whereas full personhood requires an ability to take up a position within local social communities, a capacity to place oneself in appropriate ways among others, addressing them correctly, answering to their demands, returning what they have given. To be a full person one must, people suggested, be able to contribute to the collective. In a very literal sense, therefore, "lying in one place" renders a child unable to enact socially valued roles, placing it in an agonizing position of nonbelonging. The reflections offered by Ông Kiêm, the maternal grandfather of a twelve-year-old mobility-impaired girl named Linh, may serve as an example of these concerns about personhood. Ông Kiêm and his wife lived in a semiurban community on the outskirts of Hanoi, and Linh had lived with them since she was born. Linh's mother had become pregnant out of wedlock. In an attempt to avoid the stigma associated with premarital pregnancies, she had tried to induce an abortion by taking an overdose of medication that she bought in the local pharmacy. She failed; and when Linh turned out to have trouble walking, people speculated that this must be due to her mother's unsuccessful abortion attempt. A few years later, Linh's mother got married and moved into her husband's household, while Linh stayed with her maternal grandparents. In 1999, when she reached the age of six, local authorities did not yet allow disabled children to go to school. Ông Kiêm therefore himself bought schoolbooks and taught Linh how to read and write. By the time I met them, however, he expressed doubts about whether his granddaughter—who had trouble walking and was slow in learning—would ever become a person. What kind of future, he asked, was his granddaughter headed toward? Ông Kiêm distinguished between human beings and persons in this way:

> To be a human being (*làm người*) means that you live, but you do not have an occupation. To become a *person* (*thành người*), you must have awareness and have an occupation. If you are able to produce something for society, then you are a person. To become a person you must make a contribution (*cống hiến*) to society. Only then can you say that you have achieved a place in the world (*thành đạt*). Being human merely means that you have a human body, but you don't have awareness, you don't produce anything for society, you don't contribute anything to society.

In the course of fieldwork, I met many other people who questioned the personhood of a disabled family member. One of them was Thanh, the mother of two boys. Her older son, nine-year old Vũ, was born with a curved spine that made him hunchbacked. The household income of the family was relatively modest; Thanh was a trader in their local market, and her husband did temporary work in the construction sector. Like many other parents I met, Thanh and her husband expressed the hope that their children would grow up to lead lives more comfortable and economically stable than their own. Thanh watched her boys closely, encouraging them to do their homework carefully and to try to do well at school. But thinking of her son's future, she felt, she said, utterly distressed. Even though he was a good and hardworking pupil, she doubted that he would ever attain a life like others. His physical deficiencies placed him, she explained, in a position of inherent disadvantage (*thiệt thòi*) that would be difficult for him to overcome. While Vũ played with his friends outside in the alley, she told Hằng and me about how she and her husband had struggled to enhance his life prospects: "Compared to other children," she said, "he has lost out. We have to accept that. I have tried to have him operated on, so that he could become a proper person (*một người hẳn hoi*), a decent person (*một người tử tế*). But the operations have failed. So we must accept our fate. . . . But as soon as I get home and see my son like this, I feel so sad." The operations that Vũ had undergone had been costly, but Thanh still felt burdened by the thought that perhaps they could have done more. Even though her neighbors did not say anything directly, she felt sure that they were blaming her and her husband for failing to ensure that their eldest son grew up to "become a person." Talking to people such as Vũ's mother, I was often overwhelmed by the hopelessness and moral pain they conveyed; many parents of disabled children expressed absolute certainty that their child's bodily deficiencies excluded him or her from ever attaining full personhood. Even in cases where the child's disability seemed relatively minor to me, parents often expressed deep sorrow and desperation (see Gammeltoft 2008a). The cultural concept of *công* (merit or work) was, I found, at the heart of such parental emotions.

The notion of *công* is, as Kate Jellema (2005:233) notes, "a polysemic idea close to the heart of Vietnamese morality." Integrating the multi-stranded spiritual beliefs and moral philosophies that constitute Vietnamese cosmologies, the concept of *công* defines social relationships as ties created out of work or favors (*ơn*) done for other people: the person who benefits from someone's efforts accrues moral debt, and this debt must be answered.[14] Social relations are, in other words, built up through work. Within the family, such work includes the love, care, and protection that parents give their children, including the food they provide them and the sacrifices they make for them. In return, children are expected to offer their parents loyalty, care, and support, particularly in their old age. In the communities that I came to know in Hanoi, the expectations placed on children were often captured in the concept of *hiếu*, filiality, a moral ideal that the social researcher Phạm Kim Ngọc (2006:32) describes as a key human virtue in Vietnamese lives and "the standard value to judge a person." When Phương's family went through with her wedding the day after her grandfather's death (chapter 5), it was the moral principle of filiality that they violated; they failed to show him the love, gratitude, and respect that was to be expected. When Oanh feared that her child might be born disabled (chapter 3), her fears were animated by her awareness that the children she had were not just hers. They belonged to the larger kin group, and moral principles of filiality obliged her as a daughter and daughter-in-law to produce children who would carry on and reciprocate the work done by family elders. In Oanh's family, as in other families in Hanoi, children were incessantly reminded of the gratitude they owed their parents and were told in numerous ways that they must reciprocate the gift of life they had received by respecting and caring for their elders (cf. Lainez 2012).

In official rhetoric, such moral expectations of reciprocity were often expressed as demands to "return moral favors and reciprocate goodness" (*đền ơn đáp nghĩa*) and to "remember the source when drinking water" (*uống nước nhớ nguồn*). These exhortations are ubiquitous in

Vietnamese society; they are painted in large letters on the walls of public buildings and frequently cited in schoolbooks, newspaper articles, and official speeches. Moral debts to parents, teachers, officials, and other benefactors, people are told, must be acknowledged and repaid.[15] In return for the life and upbringing they have been given, official exhortations suggest, citizens have a duty to contribute to family and society—whether by taking part in national defense, in mass campaigns for health care or family planning, or in the eradication of social evils such as drug use and prostitution. In many of the homes I visited in and around Hanoi, the walls were adorned with framed official certificates that recognized the contributions made by household members to national projects. These certificates read "has merit with the nation" (*có công với nước*) and were usually awarded for participation in war efforts or community activities. While celebrating individual accomplishments, such official statements also seemed to tell people that it is the capacity to repay moral debts and contribute to the collective that turns individuals into morally valuable persons.

It was within this ethical universe, then, that childhood disability came to be seen as a moral tragedy. As shown earlier, when people pondered where to draw the line between severe and mild disabilities, a decisive question was whether the prospective child was likely to grow up to be able to contribute to family and society. Parents who bring up a disabled child, people sometimes said, bring it up for nothing (*nuôi không*). In the words of Nga, the twenty-seven-year old mother of a nondisabled toddler: "If the child can be treated or operated so that it becomes a normal person who is useful for society, then I don't think one should terminate the pregnancy. . . . But children who are not normal are burdens for society. They cannot help their parents and society, and psychologically it is very hard for the parents." Severe disability was, in other words, seen as such because it was assumed to render the child forever dependent on others, cutting him or her off from the mutual relations of reciprocity that constitute everyday existence.[16] Severely disabled children cannot but fail morally: they will never be able to return what they have been given, never attain a place in intergenerational cycles of reciprocal exchanges.

At stake, however, when a child is born disabled is not only the child's but also its parents' moral existence. Listening to prospective parents' accounts, I was often struck by the ways in which they merged their child's pain with their own. Pondering how to act on a prenatal diagnosis, parents-to-be would often conclude by stating: "My child would suffer and I would suffer with it." Similarly, when describing the lives of families with a disabled child, they often depicted suffering as a painful state of being that was shared by parents and children. A child's suffering body was, they indicated, always intimately connected with the bodies of its parents; a defective child body places parents, too, in a situation of vulnerability and exposure. When the prospects that a child will ever attain full social belonging are bleak, therefore, its parents are placed in a position of permanent moral pain. This child belongs to them as a debt (*nợ*) and an obligation, but they remain powerless to fulfill their responsibility as parents by attaching the child to a larger community of others.

BEING AS BAD CONSCIENCE: COSMOLOGICAL IMPLICATIONS OF CHILDHOOD DISABILITY

"This year my son is twenty-two years old, but I feel very sad. I think there is no hope that he will become a person." In the prologue to this book I describe the sadness with which Tuyết's father talked about his son, Phúc. In many respects, this elderly man's account of his son's impairment resembles the stories I heard from other parents of disabled children. I noticed three common aspects in particular: first, the force of the feelings of love, pity, and sadness that parents expressed; second, their enormous persistence in struggling to turn their child into a person; and third, the loneliness of this endeavor. Phúc was born, his parents told me, suffering from curved bones. His father described his condition using metaphors of wild organic growth: "All the bones in his entire body are sticking out. They bend, like the branches of a pomelo tree heavy with fruit that bend to the ground. . . . His face is deformed, and his bones are sticking out in many places. Like a tree with branches coming out everywhere."

Telling us about their son's life, Tuyết's father emphasized the efforts that he and his wife had made to turn him into a person. When he was three years old, they took him to Hanoi in the hope that an operation could solve the health problems that he was suffering from. But the doctors sent them home, telling them that there was nothing they could do to help. When Phúc reached the age of six, his parents wanted him to go to school like other children. Every day, his father would take time off from work in the fields to ride him to school on the back of his bike, picking him up again at noon. But when Phúc reached grade six, he did not pass his exams, and his parents gave up. Now, he spent his days at home, rarely venturing outside. When communal village events were organized and when weddings and funerals were held, his parents encouraged him to come along. But he refused, uncomfortably aware of his difference from his peers and his inferiority in the eyes of others.

Like Phúc's parents, numerous other parents of disabled children told us how they had spent years, and sometimes fortunes, searching for medication that might help their child. Many had also struggled to help the child attain an education at a time when inclusive education had not yet been introduced in Vietnam and disabled children were not welcomed in schools; and they had fought for the child to become integrated in their local community, a participant in local social events. Telling us their children's life stories, these parents conveyed intense feelings of love and duty, sadness and frustration. Despite all their efforts, they said, they doubted whether their children would ever become persons. As parents, they were constantly "put-in-question" and "put to the question" (Levinas 1998b [1985]:144)—by people in their community who always seemed to expect them to do more for their child, and by the child itself, to whose demands they felt unable to respond. When they claimed that "my child would suffer and I would suffer with it," prospective parents seemed to evoke the pain of living in a situation where one is constantly called into question. Having a disabled child, they suggested, means a life lived in powerlessness and bad conscience. It means being called upon, but being unable to respond.

When women and their relatives described how they had come to their abortion decisions, they often referred directly to the plights of people they knew who were struggling to turn their children into persons. Living in a social environment where parental responsibilities were incessantly stressed, parents-to-be knew that they were held responsible for the fate of the child they were expecting. They knew also that no matter how hard they struggled, *if* their child did indeed turn out severely disabled, they could—like the child itself—only fail. Telling us about how their family had reached the decision to end Tuyết's pregnancy, her father said: "We were not concerned about the economic expenses of turning this fetus into a person. For sure, seeking treatment for it would be very expensive, but we are not scared of expenses. Our concern is that the child would remain sick. It would not become a complete person. Our elders use the expression 'losing money, but keeping the disease' (*tiền mất, tật mang*). If you make every effort to find treatment for someone who still fails to become a person, who does not recover, then you lose money but keep the disease."

During fieldwork, I was often struck by the insistence with which people claimed that it is the obligation of parents, and parents alone, to ensure that a child grows up to become a person.[17] A child, they implied, belongs to its mother and father; it binds its parents morally, demanding love, care, and protection. If the child turns out to have special needs, it is the obligation of parents to fulfill them; this is not a task that they can expect relatives, community members, or social authorities to undertake. When Phương's infant son was diagnosed with Down syndrome, for instance, her mother remarked that although she herself intended to help her daughter, Phương's parents-in-law were unlikely to offer support: "If a child is born sick or weak," she said, "the mother will have to care for it. Parents must bring up their own children. If the child is complete, they can be happy. If the child is sick, they cannot shift responsibility to the grandparents; it's their own responsibility." In everyday lives in villages and urban neighborhoods, moral expectations regarding parental roles were vivid, explicit, and omnipresent. If people found that parents did not live up to their responsibilities, this would elicit strong moral condemnation and intense gossip. As if in an effort to defend themselves against the criticism that they might otherwise meet, parents of disabled children seemed to always emphasize the efforts they were making in bringing up their children, telling others of their hard work to turn the child into a person and reminding the child of the sacrifices they were making for her or him.[18]

In the previous chapter I describe how reproductive mishaps were often interpreted in cosmological terms and taken as indications of moral transgressions. When people talked about the implications of childhood disability for parental lives, their reflections often seemed to rest on similar assumptions, evoking the spiritual and sacred connotations that childbearing holds.[19] By bringing up children who hold the potential to contribute to family and society, people suggested, parents tie themselves into families, communities, and the nation through the practical work they perform; but they also engage in a process of spiritual engagement that cuts across time and space, placing themselves within a wider community of ancestors and descendants. To attain a place within this larger world, parents depend on their children: only by having complete children who will, in turn, have other children is it possible to attain full social belonging. Parent-child relations of reciprocity are, in this sense, not a simple exchange between individuals of two generations, but an engagement with a larger social and spiritual world of affectivity and mutuality. Telling me about her aunt's hard life as the mother of a disabled boy, Thu, the veterinarian, asserted in a firm voice: "Children contribute *a lot* to the completion of their parents' lives." The tragedy faced by her aunt, she implied, was that her son's failure to become a person would render her own life forever incomplete; because of his defective body, her aunt would never attain the full social belonging that the parenting of a nondisabled child would have granted her. Conversely, when parents have successfully brought up their children to adulthood and married them off, people will say that they have now fulfilled their obligations (*hoàn thành nhiệm vụ*): by administering in proper ways the heavenly mandate of parenthood, they have completed the most sacred task that confronts human beings in this world, fulfilling obligations not only to their children but also to the larger social whole of which they are part. In deciding to terminate an affected pregnancy, prospective parents were, in short, striving to belong—to family, community, and nation, to people of this world and of the other. The incomplete body of the child they expected indexed moral failure in a cosmological sense while also threatening to render parents' lives socially and spiritually incomplete.

KNOWLEDGE AND BELONGING

By terminating problematic pregnancies, the pregnant women I met in Hanoi contributed to state goals of enhancing population quality, making the decisions that physicians and other state officials found appropriate. Yet what compelled them to act as they did was neither the pursuit of national development goals nor dreams of perfect children. Rather, they were striving to lead moral lives (cf. Kleinman 2006), seeking to place themselves and their children within larger sociomoral communities of mutual belonging.

This chapter shows that although abortion decisions were usually made on a relatively rudimentary biomedical basis, few women seemed to consider this diagnostic uncertainty problematic. This could be explained in several ways—by women's lack of scientific literacy, which made the medical world seem foreign and opaque to them, or by the social distance between patients and providers, which rendered it difficult for women to express demands for more information. This ethnographic material suggests, however, that matters of another nature were at issue too. In my search for a biomedical diagnosis of the fetal condition, I was taking what Bourdieu (2000:133) calls a "typically scholastic viewpoint on the body from outside." Pregnant women and their husbands, in contrast, were immersed in a social relation, engaging from inside with the fetus and the child it might become. They were, in Bourdieu's (2000:142) words, *disposed* because they were *exposed*. Living in a social world where defective infant bodies signal moral collapse, they knew what vulnerabilities life with a disabled child entails. Prereflexively, through all the density of their being (Levinas 1996 [1951]:4), they sensed that if born, this child would undo them, placing them in a situation of constant suffering and moral torment. They did not ask for more biomedical information, because they knew something that was more important: first, that they were tied into relations of obligation to this child-to-be, and second, that if the child was indeed, as indicated by physicians, severely impaired, this would give them a responsibility that was too large to bear. No matter how hard they struggled, they would never be able to fulfill this child's demands. The best way in which they could enact their love for their child was, therefore, by ending its life; *because* this child belonged to them, they had to sever their connections to it. The problem of the other, they realized, is not only that of building connections but also of suffering separation (cf. Das 2010). Abortions for fetal anomaly were, in short, actions of love and sacrifice. They were ways in which women sought to respond to the demands placed on them by others, including their child-to-be itself, thereby attaining a place in social worlds that they longed to belong to. In this realm of high-tech pregnancy care, then, party-state efforts to enhance population quality fed on deeply felt moral orientations and dispositions, resonating with people's visceral sense of what personhood, humanity, morality, and responsibility entail.

CHAPTER 7

Questions of Conscience

QUÝ: "MY DECISION DEPENDS ON MEDICAL
EXPERTISE"

When I first met her, Quý was forty-one years old and lived in a village
in Sóc Sơn district, northwest of Hanoi. On January 7, 2005, my colleague Hiệp and I went to visit her and her husband, Hinh. Their house
was new and well kept, and the yard outside it meticulously swept.
Hinh invited us in. After seating us in the heavy wooden chairs in the
main room of their house, he served us steaming-hot boiled corn "to
keep you warm on this chilly day." Telling us that their floor was cold
at this time of the year, he placed two pairs of plastic slippers in front of
us, insisting that we wear them. When I looked up, I noticed that, as in
most homes, the ancestral altar was placed at the center of the room, on
top of it a plate of fruit, a pot with incense sticks, and framed photographs of family elders. To one side of the room was another, smaller
altar of the kind that people build for those who have suffered an early
and untimely death. Two photographs of young men were hanging over
this altar, one old and faded, another of a recent date.

To begin with, Quý spoke very slowly and with an expression of
intense sorrow. She told us that in 2002, at the age of sixteen, their son
had suddenly died from a kidney disease. This had made Quý regret
that she had acceded to her husband's wishes to keep their family small:
Hinh was a local official and a party member and it had been important
for him to comply with the national family planning policy. Despite

194

Quý's wish to have a third child, therefore, he had insisted that they stop at two. The unexpected death of their son caused a family crisis. Hinh was the only man of childbearing age in their kin group; with his son's death, there was no one to carry on the lineage. When Hinh died, the entire family line would perish. Quý felt too old to have another child, but her parents-in-law insisted, putting her and Hinh under intense pressure to produce another son. Four months into her pregnancy, Quý went to the district health center for an ultrasound scan. The fetus was found to be male, but the physician also informed her that it was abnormal. Hearing this, Hinh drove her immediately on the back of his motorbike to the obstetrics hospital in Hanoi. Here, the physician told Quý that there were large amounts of fluid on the brain of her fetus and advised her to terminate the pregnancy. But her parents-in-law were of a different opinion. In Quý's words:

> My elders said, "This fetus is still small. It is only a couple of months old, so how can we know about its brain?" "Don't be ridiculous (*vớ vẩn*)," they said; "it is still in the womb, so we cannot know for sure." So I did not have an abortion. You see, in Vietnam, when you are married, you must follow your husband's family (*theo nhà chồng*). So how could I make my own decision (*làm sao mình quyết định cho riêng mình được*)? Our elders said, "Some people want to have children but cannot have them. Now that you are pregnant, you should appreciate that." They said, "If we see flowers, we appreciate flowers; if we see buds we appreciate buds." Our entire family was happy that I was pregnant again, so they thought that I should keep this child. People who understand about science would have opted for an abortion, but our elders do not understand about science, so they encouraged me to keep it. If I had been able to decide on my own, I would have trusted the experts. . . . I'm a rural person, so I am ignorant (*dốt nát*), but I do trust science and the experts. When I went for the scan, the doctor asked, "Given this problem, what will you decide?" I said: "My decision depends on medical expertise. I cannot know. If you tell me to keep it, I will keep it. If you tell me to have a C-section, I will have a C-section. If you tell me to have an abortion, I will have an abortion." But in the end, I decided to keep it because of what my husband's family said. I did understand that according to science, it would be acceptable to give it up. But my husband's family did not agree, and I feared that later on, they might criticize us, saying, "They had a child, but they gave it up." If that happened, life would become very difficult for me.

To avoid a conflict with her elders, Quý elected to keep her pregnancy. At eight months' gestation, she went into labor. When she and Hinh reached Hanoi's Obstetrics and Gynecology Hospital, the doctors told them that the child suffered from hydrocephalus and that they had to do a Caesarean section. Two days after his birth, their son died. Quý never saw him.[1]

ETHICAL MOMENTS

In human life, there are certain situations in which it is not immediately clear to us what is right or wrong, where we have to ponder where we stand and who we are or want to be. Jarrett Zigon (2009:262) describes these as *ethical moments* that occur "when some event or person intrudes into the everyday life of a person and forces her to consciously reflect upon the appropriate ethical response." When a fetal problem was found, parents-to-be in Hanoi found themselves in such morally challenging situations. Quý and her husband, for instance, felt caught between their elders' insistence on the value of the child they expected and health professionals' claims that this fetus carried flaws that made an abortion the most appropriate response. On the one hand, Quý explained, they felt attached to their child-to-be, sharing their elders' inclination to keep it; on the other, they feared that the birth of a defective child would place enormous caregiving obligations on them and that it might be wiser to follow the doctors' advice. Like this couple, all parents-to-be I met felt caught in a bewildering moral dilemma when an adverse diagnosis was made. Some compared this situation to the very different conditions under which their parents and grandparents had their children. In a poignant remark, for instance, Bích claimed that living in today's world had thrown her and her husband into "a world of action" that their elders had never known. "In the past," she said,

> women would simply give birth. Later, when they realized that their child did not understand anything, they found out [that the child was disabled]. But we have found out before birth. This gives us the opportunity to choose, to either give birth or give it up. . . . This has a good side, but it also has a bad side. It pushes us into doing something tormenting (*dằn vặt*). If one gives birth naturally without having any examinations, one simply has to accept the result. But this has pushed us into a world of action. Until the day we die, we will feel pained, miserable about this.

Like Bích, parents-to-be often described the decision regarding whether or not to keep this pregnancy as a tormenting one that they wished they had never had to make. Listening to their accounts, I was struck by their insistence that in these morally tense situations, they were not only considering their own innermost values but also, and perhaps primarily, responding to ethical demands placed on them by others. Quý put this in rhetorical terms when she exclaimed, "How could I make my own decision?" Like her, practically all the prospective parents I met described the agonizing process of decision making they went through in terms of collectivity, obligation, and shared social deliberation. Rather than looking inward to find out what kind of child they would be able to assume responsibility for, it seemed, they looked outward, seeking to comport themselves ethically in relation to significant others.

In this chapter, I explore the social relations of authority, obligation, and love out of which hard reproductive decisions were forged. I begin by investigating how women interacted with physicians and the system of biomedical expertise they represented. Next, I describe the ways in which women drew family members—husbands, parents, in-laws, and siblings—into their decision-making processes, sounding out possibilities by listening to their opinions. As we shall see, Quý's case was unique in one respect: she was the only woman I met who found herself caught in a conflict between the demands made on her by physicians and by family members. In all other cases, there was agreement between the suggestions for action laid out by relatives and health professionals. This alignment, however, did not seem to diminish the moral pain that women and their husbands felt. As the last section of this chapter shows, after having their pregnancies terminated, all the women I spoke to reported overwhelming feelings of remorse. Despite the rightness of their decision, they suggested, they felt haunted by questions of conscience, feeling that this avenue of action, though in principle right, was also acutely wrong. To account for these ambivalent emotions, I suggest, we must bring into consideration a third kind of moral other with whom women and their husbands interacted, namely the child-to-be that they expected.[2] As earlier chapters show, all women in our sample were pregnant with children they had wanted to have and to whom they enacted attachment and love from the first days of their pregnancy. At issue therefore was, as Mây expressed it, not only their own heart but also that of the fetus. "Why did we do this?" she asked. "The heart of our child was still beating. I don't know how we had the heart to do this." In the last section of the chapter I examine the fraught relations of love and regret, attachment and detachment that unfolded between abortion-seeking couples and the fetus that they lost. These pregnancy terminations raised, as we shall see, questions about human identity in a double sense, compelling prospective parents to consider not only who their fetus was but also who they themselves were.

"I COULD NEVER HAVE DECIDED ON MY OWN": BIOMEDICAL ENCOUNTERS

"If I had been able to decide on my own," Quý claimed, "I would have trusted the experts." Quý's proclamation of trust in biomedicine was echoed by practically everyone I met: most couples made it clear that in this situation of reproductive disruption, they placed their faith in health care professionals. Although most prospective parents expressed skepticism and disbelief when first informed that their fetus was abnormal, the vast majority eventually complied with the authority of biomedical opinion. By placing trust in science, it seemed, they also sought to define themselves as modern and knowledgeable individuals. Liên, for instance, the twenty-four-year-old journalist who lived in central Hanoi, explicitly associated her decision to resort to an abortion with an urban and educated attitude toward life. As if trying to make her decision more clear-cut and simple than it had seemed when she made it, she said: "Some parents still keep the fetus even if it is not normal. I think they lack awareness. . . . In rural areas they don't have ultrasound scans, so they always simply think that their children are normal. In Hanoi, it is different. People like us can find out such things at an early stage, and we solve the problem immediately."

Statements such as this indicate that biomedicine plays a critical role not only in shaping people's concepts of health and illness but also in forming their self-perceptions. In subtle ways, as Rose (1999) has observed, medical practices advance norms and values that compel individuals to think and act upon themselves in certain ways, tying people into intimate relations with certain truths and authorities. From this perspective, counseling encounters can be seen as intensifiers of ethicality, as sites in which processes of moral self-formation are particularly dense. At first glance, the interactions between pregnant women and physicians that I witnessed at the obstetrics hospital in Hanoi appeared to confirm this thesis; biomedical experts played important roles, it seemed, in shaping women's subjectivities, helping to set certain standards for modern womanhood. But the norms and relations that were enacted in Hanoi differed significantly from those described in the context of advanced liberal societies where, it is argued, subjectivity has come to be associated with personal choice and a continual exercise of freedom. Rather than expecting to make their own autonomous decisions, I found, prospective parents in Hanoi placed themselves—and were placed by their relatives—in the hands of others (cf. Klingberg-Allvin et al. 2008).

When talking to women who came for routine ultrasound scans at Hanoi's Obstetrics and Gynecology Hospital, I noticed that most women placed mutual moral obligation, rather than self-determination, at the center of the health care expectations they expressed. The duties they evoked worked both ways: on the one hand, they addressed the obligation of doctors to care properly for their patients, and, on the other, they spoke of pregnant women's duty to follow their physician's advice. Women would often define directive advice as an integral part of the package of care they expected to receive: health care technologies, as they defined them, included not only pregnancy tests and ultrasounds but also professional guidance and support. When we asked new mothers how they imagined they would have reacted if the ultrasound scan had found a fetal problem, the answer was practically always the same: they would have turned to the physicians for help. In Huyền's words: "First, I would want the doctor to offer explanations and advice. Second, I hope that the doctors would console me, making me feel calmer. If I go to a hospital, it means that I rely upon, and expect something, from the doctors." In a similar vein, Thảo said, "I would ask the doctor. This means that I would put myself entirely in the hands of the doctor. Whatever he encouraged me to do, I would do that. I would trust that this was best for my child." The final decisions regarding pregnancy outcomes, women held, must be made by mothers-to-be in consultation with their relatives. But to reach their decisions, they needed professional advice.

As we saw earlier, the counseling offered by physicians in this maternity hospital could be characterized as directive. When a fetal problem was found, the doctor would usually tell the pregnant woman in relatively straightforward terms whether or not she should keep her pregnancy. When we talked to them later, women and their relatives would often emphasize that they *needed* this advice; rather than interpreting it as an improper interference, they welcomed doctors' attempts to "steer" their decisions. Mây, for instance, described her relations with physicians in terms that indicated firm confidence that they would care for her in the best possible way: "When I was told that I could not keep my pregnancy, I felt very scared and shocked. My entire family felt like that. The doctors advised me and helped me to decide because they are the experts. Before saying or advising anything, they investigated the problem very carefully. They know that giving up a living human being is a serious matter. . . . We needed their advice, because we do not know much about medicine, and I could never have decided on my own."

Deciding to terminate a planned and wanted pregnancy on the basis of biomedical advice that she had trouble understanding, Mây placed herself in the hands of medical professionals, trusting that what they told her was correct. This enactment of trust took place in face-to-face interactions with physicians, but it also involved larger political questions of citizenship and national belonging.

ACTS OF TRUST: ENACTING NATIONAL BELONGING

Ultrasound scan results often seemed opaque and incomprehensible to people. Therefore, the first and most basic question that women and their relatives had to confront was, "Can we trust what the doctors tell us?" When physicians suggested to a pregnant woman that it was best for her to opt for an abortion, they also placed enormous moral demands on her, asking her to offer the ultimate proof of trust in modern medicine: the life of her (potential) child.

When we talked to them after an abortion had been performed, women and their relatives would nearly always express firm conviction that in following expert advice, they had done the right thing, saving their child from suffering. Beneath these declarations of certainty, however, doubts often seemed to linger. After the abortion, family elders would usually take a close look at the body of the fetus, comparing it to the scan. If inconsistencies were found, this produced intense unease. In Ngọc's case, for instance, the fetus was found to be suffering not only from hydrops but also from an umbilical hernia that the scan had not detected. When we met her after the abortion, she kept talking about this, as if this diagnostic imprecision had brought the entire abortion endeavor into question. In contrast, when the body of the fetus resembled the one that physicians had described to them, people's relief was palpable. For instance, telling us about how members of their family had brought the fetal body home from the hospital after the abortion, Hồng's mother said, "When they got here, I went to see if it was correct what they had said about the child. We were afraid that it was wrong. We did not entirely believe it, so we opened [the casket] to see if it was correct. It was, and so we knew that this had saved the child and our family from suffering. We were lucky that the state had examined this fetus so that we could allow it to leave this world, to go somewhere else."

The women in our sample who expressed the deepest distress were those who did not receive clear instructions from physicians regarding what to do. Loan had, as we saw in chapter 6, been informed that her fetus was suffering from a heart defect, but she had received no advice about how to act on this message. When Hiệp and I met her a few days after her 3D scan, she told us that she felt totally at a loss. The primary question that troubled her, she said, was whether this medical information could be trusted. Leafing through a pile of papers with the different scanning results she had received, she exclaimed: "We are afraid that the result is wrong; that's what we are all thinking about. It is very good that we have modern science now and can detect problems like this. But it all requires that the physicians are skilled and the machines good, so that they can come to precise conclusions. If they conclude correctly, it is very good. But if they are not precise, it creates extreme psychological distress and a lot of worry." In pondering the possibility of a medical error, Loan emphasized that her doubts concerned *only* the scanning equipment: "You see, I am scared that the machines we have in Vietnam are not so good. I am sure that the *people* who operate them are very skilled, that is, the doctors are skilled, but I am not sure that the *machines* are very precise. So that's what I am very worried about." In expressing doubts about the reliability of her scan result, then, Loan clearly made an effort to emphasize that she did *not* question the skills of health professionals or the medical-political system that they represented. Similarly, it seemed to be very important for Quý to state that she *herself* certainly *did* trust science and the experts, though her parents-in-law did not. This rhetorical commitment to science was reiterated in many other stories I heard: although they hesitated before the decision they had to make, people emphasized, they certainly *did* trust the experts. Often, I noticed, the lingering uncertainties regarding the reliability of biomedicine that always seemed to haunt abortion decisions remained strikingly unspoken. Very few individuals would openly question the authority of science, and Quý was the only woman in our sample who went directly against the guidance she received from physicians. What then made the question of medical trustworthiness so vitally important to women and yet, in most cases, so understated in the stories they told us?

Trust in biomedical knowledge was, our conversations indicated, also a question of trust in the socialist state. When women sought antenatal care at the obstetrics hospital, they knew that they were entering a domain of the state. The question of whether or not a scan result was reliable was, therefore, also a question of whether or not the state was trustworthy. When Hồng's mother said that the state had examined their fetus, her words pointed to the close linkages drawn in socialist

Vietnam between modernity, biomedicine, and the state. Since its introduction, induced abortion has been associated in official rhetoric with a
modern and educated attitude toward life, while moral doubts regarding this procedure have been relegated to the realm of backwardness
and superstition.[3] In declaring her willingness to "solve the problem
immediately," therefore, Liên also claimed allegiance to the socialist
state and its modernization agenda. By undergoing an induced abortion, she defined herself as a modern, enlightened, and progressive
citizen dedicated to state-led collective strivings for health. Sometimes,
the language in which people described abortion experiences explicitly
evoked these political connotations. Telling us about how his family
had reached a decision regarding Tuyết's pregnancy, for instance,
her father-in-law said that hospital staff had mobilized (*vận động*)
them to terminate the pregnancy. In using this term, he placed Tuyết's
abortion in the context of national history, associating the family's
reproductive decision with previous collective efforts to enhance the
health of the people (cf. chapter 2). Similarly, Mai's seventy-six-year-
old grandmother expressed her confidence in state-sanctioned science
when she said:

> Everyone in our family agreed on terminating the pregnancy. To tell you the
> truth, we do not have long educations. But science is skillful. We have to
> recognize that. . . . If we did not believe in the state (*nhà nước*), in the doc-
> tors, we would not have consented. But now we feel at ease. . . . The state is
> clever. It has helped our child [the fetus] escape suffering. If we did not have
> the state, we would have been worried to hear the doctor tell us [that some-
> thing was wrong]. But now we do not worry. In the feudal times [if a disa-
> bled child was born], we were scared to death. How would we take care of
> it? Would it die soon so we would be released, or would it just keep lying
> there? It was very scary. In the past, disabilities could not be cured. We had
> no science. That's why now we have to put our trust in science. To be hon-
> est, if we do not trust people of science, who can we trust?

In short, the reproductive choices that women confronted were
located within a larger and politically fraught terrain of health mobilization and nation-building; within this terrain, questions of the reliability of biomedical facts articulated larger questions of citizenship and
national belonging.[4] By following expert advice, people also claimed
loyalty to the socialist state and defined themselves as good and conscientious citizens, as members of a national collective engaged in shared
projects of health improvement and livelihood enhancement. Despite
this sense of commitment and direction, however, all couples wrestled
with the questions of conscience that Bích and Mây articulated so

succinctly. The decision they confronted, they claimed, had such far-reaching social and moral implications that they had to draw their relatives into it.

ACTS OF KINSHIP

In her account of the violence that accompanied the partition of Pakistan and India, Das (2007:218) shows how women's subjectivities emerged through processes of ordinary living. "Self-creation on the register of the everyday," she suggests, "is a careful putting together of life—a concrete engagement with the tasks of remaking that is mindful of both terms of the compound expression: *everyday* and *life*" (emphasis in original). In Hanoi, the detection of a fetal anomaly pushed women out of the realm of the ordinary into a state of medical emergency, but they all handled their predicament by placing themselves back into everyday networks of kin. The cases of Lan and Hồng illustrate how reproductive decisions became sites for the enactment of family belonging.

In chapter 5 we met Lan and Anh, whose fetus was diagnosed at 37 weeks' gestation with hydrocephalus. At the family meeting that their elders convened, Anh's father took the lead in the conversation, emphasizing the moral weight of the decision that confronted them. "Whatever we do," he said, "we must discuss this carefully. If the fetus is normal and intact (*nguyên vẹn*) and not in any kind of trouble, then we think that Lan should give birth. But if something is wrong, it is better to give up the child. The children [Lan and Anh] and our families all agree on that." Although we would rarely intervene directly in decision-making processes, in this situation, my colleague Hạnh seemed to feel that she had to comment on the family's plans. "Lan is nine months pregnant," she exclaimed. "If the delivery is induced now, the child may survive. Then what will you do?" There was a long silence. Then Anh's mother replied, almost whispering, "Once the child is born, once you have seen the child, then no one has the heart . . . Who would have the heart? . . . You are right. She was so close to the due date before we found out about this. So now we just don't know what to do." In a resolute tone, Anh's father said: "Now, we plan to ask the doctors if they can overcome this so that our child becomes a complete human being." At noon, when Hạnh and I departed, the family had not yet reached a decision. But in the afternoon, Anh called and asked us to meet them at the obstetrics hospital; they had decided to have the pregnancy terminated.

As Hạnh and I drove on her motorbike toward the hospital in the hectic afternoon traffic, I wondered how Lan felt about this decision. To what extent did she feel that it was hers? Did she herself feel ready to go along the path laid out by her elders? When we arrived at the hospital's courtyard, we found Lan surrounded by a group of around ten people: her own and Anh's parents and siblings and the spouses of those siblings. Lan's relatives went to the hospital's reception desk to register her for an abortion, and soon after a nurse led her down the corridor toward the delivery department. Hạnh and I went for coffee in the café outside. A few hours later, Anh passed by to inform us that the hospital's board of directors had denied Lan an abortion; her pregnancy was too advanced. Instead, they had asked her to stay at the hospital to wait for the delivery to occur naturally. Four weeks later, the contractions began. Due to the size of the child's head, the doctor on duty that night decided to perform a C-section, and on March 18 the son of Lan and Anh was born. They named him An (Peace).

During a visit to their family a few months later, the conversation turned to the last days of Lan's pregnancy, and I asked Lan how she had felt when her family decided to have her pregnancy terminated. Looking slightly surprised, she made it clear to me that I had misunderstood what was happening. What to me had appeared to be a group of senior males making a life-and-death decision on behalf of a younger woman was, as Lan saw it, a joint family discussion that only aimed to support her. "They did not decide," she emphasized; "Anh and I did. Our parents gave us the right to decide, and we did. We listened to the opinions of our parents and then we made our decision."

In Hồng's case, too, I found, the couple's relatives played a significant role in decision-making processes. Hồng's fetus was diagnosed in week 26 with anencephaly (vô sọ), a condition incompatible with life. Yet she and her husband left the hospital believing that if they kept the pregnancy, their child might yet live. They therefore went through a protracted process of deliberation before deciding to opt for an abortion. When I asked Hồng how she had come to this decision, she said: "I discussed it with my family, and my family decided on an abortion. It was best not to keep this child." Sitting next to her, her husband's elder brother Chính, who was the lineage head, then made an elaborate speech in which he took upon himself the responsibility for a decision that everyone in the family had found immensely painful:

> I was the one who presided over this entire matter. On the day when Hồng went for the abortion, I was busy, so I asked her eldest brother to

accompany her. On the maternal side of the family (*bên ngoại*), he is responsible. We looked at the scan result and discussed it carefully—I, my mother, and our siblings on both sides. On the basis of that I said, "I will decide." No one wants this to happen. But this is fate. No one can lie to science. No one can keep anything secret from science. In our family we analyzed this together and the decision caused no conflict between the two sides of the family. We just thank science that we were allowed to know about this in time. We felt shocked at the thought of having a child like the one in our village, the one with a brain problem. Even our elders felt scared, so they too agreed to the abortion.

Hearing this, my colleague Hằng—whose research interests were family hierarchies and gender inequalities—reacted promptly. "When your family discussed this," she asked Hồng, "who *exactly* made the final decision that you must go into hospital?" Hồng replied by emphasizing that this decision had been a communal endeavor: "Our entire family decided about this together (*cả nhà cùng quyết định làm*)," she said. "There was not one person deciding. We all agreed."

The vast majority of women I met suggested that finding themselves in this morally and emotionally excruciating situation, they needed and appreciated their relatives' support. Women who, like Lan and Hồng, lived in extended families placed particular emphasis on the fact that the decision they faced was not theirs alone, but one that must be made collectively. Other women said that they had made up their minds together with their husbands first, and only afterward ensured that their parents and siblings agreed. The women in the latter group usually lived in urban areas, separately from their parents-in-law, and had incomes that made them relatively independent of their families financially. One of them was Mây. When Hiệp asked her if she and her husband had discussed the abortion with their families, Mây replied:

> In making our decision, we first listened to the doctors, then discussed it with each other, and then decided. When I informed my family, I told them that the doctors had recommended an abortion. My mother said, "If that is what the doctors say, then we must follow that." When we told my husbands' parents, they said that they did not know anything about medicine. And my husband's grandparents simply said, "Oh, if that is what they say, then it must be like that." Our elders are a bit superstitious. They think that if this is the child's fate, then we must accept that.

In most cases, if the prospective parents opted to follow the physicians' advice, their parents and siblings would concur with this decision, feeling, like Mây's relatives, that they were not in a position to question expert opinion. But in a few cases where the couple decided to opt for an abortion, their elders objected. Bích, for instance, described her mother-in-law as a person staunchly opposed to any kind of induced abortion. When we met Bích after she had had her pregnancy terminated, she told us that it had been very difficult to convince her mother-in-law that a termination was necessary. What I found particularly striking in her account was the underlying premise that family consensus *must* be achieved: rather than simply obtaining the abortion, Bích and her husband put considerable effort into convincing this elderly woman of its necessity. They knew, it seemed, how hard it is to continue life in a close-knit family if disagreements about vital matters are not resolved in ways that enable people to continue living together:

> My mother-in-law never wanted us to give up this fetus. Really, she agreed to this only because we pressured her. All my husband's siblings supported us, so eventually my mother-in-law had to accept what we all said. We told her that this child was suffering from brain damage. If it were born, it would suffer. Therefore, an abortion was the best solution. But my mother-in-law still felt it was immoral. She felt that once you have a child, you must take care of it until it dies naturally. Everyone told her that it was impossible to know if this child would die. If it lived forever, how would we care for it? Then eventually my mother-in-law left it to us to decide. She realized that for sure, she was not going to live longer than we do, so she would not be able to care for our child. She said, "I cannot care for this child, and if I force you, it will only cause suffering." So, together with our siblings, we made our decision.

By turning pregnancy decision making into a joint endeavor, then, women also defined themselves as members of local communities of kin, framing their own existence as intimately bound up with that of others. They enacted attachment and belonging, placing themselves and the child they were expecting within a shared social world of sisters, brothers, aunts, uncles, parents, and grandparents. They used, in other words, this dramatic situation of choice and moral conflict to reconstitute and reaffirm relations of kinship, love, and obligation.

Nearly all the women in our sample enacted these relations of attachment within a situation of detachment, in that most of them experienced a reproductive loss of some kind. Some had an abortion, others lost their child at birth, and still others gave birth to a child whose anomalous body shattered their dreams of normal motherhood. When a pregnancy ended in an induced abortion, however, the loss that women suffered was inflected also by guilt and doubt: this was a chosen loss for which they felt painfully responsible and intensely remorseful.[5] The physical experience of having the fetus torn from their bodies

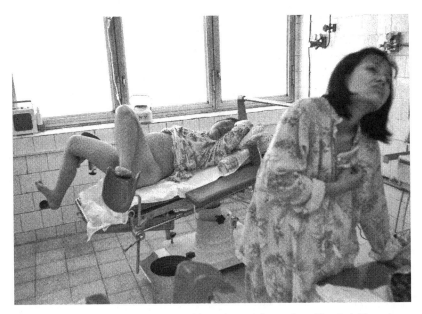

FIGURE 9. Birthing women at Hanoi's Obstetrics and Gynecology Hospital. Photo by Ditte Bjerregaard, 2000.

played an important part, women suggested, in shaping this experience of loss. Although both women and men described these pregnancy terminations as difficult and troubling experiences, women's stories conveyed a particularly acute pain that seemed to be grounded in the physical ruptures caused by the abortion. One of the women who offered a detailed account of her abortion experience was Mây. The termination of her pregnancy took place on October 28, 2004, in Hanoi's Obstetrics and Gynecology Hospital.

THE LIMITS OF LIFE ITSELF: SECOND-TRIMESTER ABORTION AS MORAL EXPERIENCE

Like other women who told us their abortion stories, Mây described the termination of her pregnancy as a harrowing experience, one that haunted her:

> At about 9 o'clock in the evening, I felt a terrible abdominal pain and it continued until 4 or 5 in the morning. Then my waters broke and I did not feel pain anymore. I could not feel anything. I just felt very tired. Dr. Lan came, and she said that there was no other way. I had to do this; if not, it

would be very harmful to my health. She examined me and looked for the head of the fetus. I did not have any contractions, so they gave me some injections. But I still did not have contractions. Then they said that there was only one thing to do. They had to cut the child into pieces and take it out bit by bit. . . . I did not agree to that. A mother's conscience cannot allow that. I could not allow my child to die in that way. My mother fainted. Seeing how much blood I was losing, she felt sorry for her child. My husband said, "Saving the mother is most important." He knew that at that point, the child had died. It died in my womb. People in the room said, "We have already lost the child, we cannot accept losing the mother too." My husband said, "We have to do this, no matter by what method." In the end, my husband, my mother, my father-in-law, my husband's brother, everyone said, "We must save the mother." They all agreed to cut up the child. After the delivery I did not look down. They had put a box there, but I could not look at it. I was very weak. I felt as if I died.[6]

Undergoing this medical intervention, Mây suggested, brought her up against the limits of life itself; she entered a liminal zone of nothingness where the pain she felt exceeded the words she had to describe it. Hà also suggested that this termination of a wanted pregnancy had been an experience that was painful beyond words. To her, pregnancy loss was nothing new: prior to this pregnancy, she had suffered three miscarriages. But this fourth loss was, she said, by far the most difficult. She described the emptiness she felt when the child she had looked forward to holding in her arms was suddenly gone:

I heard my child giving two cries. It cried "ọ ọe." I felt so pained. Since then I have felt full of sorrow, especially at the moment when the milk came. It is very sad to give birth but not to have a child. To tell you the truth, since I came home I have been lying in bed, crying. My mother keeps telling me to stop, she says, "My child, you did not cause this child to suffer." My younger sister says that according to Buddhist scriptures, this was a morally good deed (nhân đức), and I should not think about it anymore. But I keep thinking that the other three times, they [the fetuses] abandoned me. This time I managed to keep the fetus for seven months, and then I had to give it up. I feel so sad and remorseful (ân hận) because I could not keep it.

Remorse, Levinas (1990:65) writes, is "the painful expression of a radical powerlessness to redeem the irreparable." As if in an effort to cope with this powerlessness, women and their relatives insisted that by ending this pregnancy, they had protected their child-to-be against suffering. Casting the abortion in these terms made it possible for women to maintain an image of themselves as good mothers: the pregnancy termination could then be regarded as a gesture of love, care, and protection. In their efforts to come to terms with abortion decisions, moreover, women and their relatives often drew a moral boundary between an unborn and a newborn child. In ethical terms, they claimed, ending the life of a fetus is different from killing or abandoning an infant.

THE FACE: "HUMAN CONSCIENCE ALWAYS COMES FIRST"

The moral difference between a fetus and an infant, people in Hanoi said, stems from the fact that one meets the infant, but not the fetus, face-to-face. Although all women had seen the face of their fetus in the 3D scan image, they seemed to feel that this mediated encounter was categorically different from one that took place directly face-to-face.[7] The face-to-face meeting, they suggested, establishes an enduring relationship of affectivity and moral responsibility between a new child and those whose life it enters. The first meeting with a newborn's face was therefore charged with profound ethical importance; at this moment, people suggested, the child comes into being as a moral other. In the family meeting that Lan's elders convened, for instance, her father-in-law seemed to be struggling to justify the decision that they were headed toward. He described the moral difference between an unborn and a newborn child in these words: "If one gives birth to a child, then, whatever that child is like, human conscience does not allow one to throw it away. This would torment one's conscience. Human conscience always comes first. . . . But this child has not yet been born. It is still a fetus, lying in its mother's womb." Once a child is there, looking at one, this elderly man suggested, one has to care for it. But a fetus is different from a newborn infant; it has not yet "seen the light of day."

Throughout our conversations, people often emphasized the responsibility that one bears for a child once it has been born. As soon as it has entered this world, they suggested, a new child imposes its existence on people, intervening in their lives, placing demands on them. By then, they cannot turn their backs on it; they have to take charge of it. Therefore, people explained, the choices that one can make before a child is born no longer exist after its birth.[8] Describing the plight of a woman of her own generation who had her children before prenatal screening was available, Thảo's mother-in-law said, "If a child is born disabled, there is no way that you can give it up. You are forced to accept the situation. I once knew a woman who had three disabled children. They all suffered from brain damage. They would simply lie there, and she was forced to take care of them. One child died when it was five, one when it was six, and one when it was eight years old. Until then, she took care of them. She did not abandon them." Although stories such as this were often told, everyone knew that in reality, if a child is born severely impaired, there *are* ways that parents can give it up; such children are often left behind at the hospital after the delivery or given over to an orphanage. In practice, care for a disabled infant is a highly contingent matter, a responsibility that parents may or may not take upon themselves. Yet the moral obligation to care for the child, people suggested, is there, regardless of whether or not its parents live up to it. *Before* birth, the situation is different. When a fetus is still lying inside the womb, and one has not yet met it face-to-face, it is morally possible to give it up.

Despite this social consensus that a fetus is morally different from an infant, all the women who had their pregnancies terminated told us that they felt devastated by this experience, haunted by a feeling of having done wrong. Although they did not meet their child-to-be face-to-face, they still felt attached to it, describing it as a sentient other who placed moral demands on them, expecting care and protection, telling them not to kill it. Experientially, the face of their fetus, while not-yet-there in concrete and material terms, was still there. Levinas refers to this as a proximate exposure to the other: "The other haunts our ontological existence and keeps the psyche awake, in a state of vigilant insomnia. Even though we are ontologically free to refuse the other, we remain forever accused, with a bad conscience" (Levinas and Kearney 1986:28).[9] Despite its ambiguous status, then, in experiential terms, the fetus was an emergent human being to whom prospective parents felt attached and responsible. They had wanted this child, and if they had been able, they would have carried the pregnancy to term. Within local moral worlds, however, the social status of this fetus was contested. A doubly liminal creature, the impaired fetus was human and yet not fully human; it existed in this world and yet it did not. After the abortion, its liminality tripled; now it was dead, but not completely so. Its soul, people maintained, was still there. How to care for this soul often generated greater controversies within families than the decision to terminate the pregnancy had done.

"THIS WAS MY CHILD, NOT A THING": RITUAL DILEMMAS

Mai's grandmother looked me in the eye and proclaimed, "They *forced* us to take it home." Two weeks had passed since Mai had had her abortion, and Hằng and I were on our way to visit her. Entering the family's compound, the first person we met was her husband's grand-mother. The old woman was squatting on the ground, preparing vege-tables to sell in the market. When she saw us, she got up and invited us into Mai's house. She told us, looking deeply distressed, that the family, being unable to afford the fee demanded by the hospital, had had to take the body of the fetus home with them and bury it in the cemetery outside their village:

> My son said that it was best to leave the body at the hospital's morgue and people would take it somewhere. But they asked 500,000 *đồng* for that. We are poor. We did not have so much money. So we brought it home with us. But I did not want to take it home. I wanted to end it. There was no reason to take it home. It was a *monstrous* fetus (*cái thai quái vật*). This was not a premature delivery or an ordinary abortion. This was a *monstrous* fetus, so it was best to leave it there so that it did not come back. After abortions, fetuses very often return (*lộn vào*). Perhaps monstrous fetuses are even more likely to return. That's why they asked for so much money.[10]

A while later Mai came home, holding her two-year-old son by the hand. Her grandmother picked up her vegetables, heading to the mar-ket. After she had left, Mai told us that the question of how to handle the fetal remains had created a huge family controversy. Feeling attached to her fetus, she had wanted to ensure that it was decently buried. But her elders had been concerned that if she showed her love for it, the fetal spirit might keep haunting her, waiting for a chance to reincarnate in her next pregnancy:

> I wanted to take the fetus home and give it a decent burial (*chôn cất đàng hoàng*). When people die, we usually take them home and bury them prop-erly, decently (*tử tế*). This was my child, not a thing. I had given birth to it, and I wanted to give it a decent burial. So I said to my grandmother, "Bury-ing it properly is a way of generating merit." But she was very scared, and my elder sisters too. They said that bringing it home with us meant that I would remember it. Even if I stopped loving it, it would still love me. It would follow me everywhere. If I got pregnant again, it would jump into me. So I did get scared. Normally, people would leave it [at the hospital] so that it didn't get entangled [in the family]. But I took it home. I felt attached to it. This means that it will remember me, it will enter me again. I do feel scared. Perhaps it would have been better to throw it away. But I took it home; I felt sorry for it.

"Remembering," Linda Layne (2003:232) writes, "is one of the few maternal acts that bereaved mothers can engage in." In her work on pregnancy loss in North America, Layne describes how, prior to the advent of the pregnancy-loss support movement, women's mourning was made difficult because the body of the fetus would be taken away and disposed of by the hospital. Yet for bereaved parents, she claims, active remembrance is important and is considered an enactment of love and care and "an honorable, moral choice" (Layne 2003:217).[11] In a similar vein, writing about how villagers in Hà Mỹ and Mỹ Lai live with their losses thirty years after the massacres during the Second Indochina War, Heonik Kwon (2006) interprets people's sense of memorial obligation to the dead as a moral response to bereavement and as a claim to justice. For abortion-seeking women in Hanoi, however, the moral challenges posed by the death they were confronting were more complicated. They felt an urge to care for their fetus by offering it a proper funeral; but they also feared that if they did this, this fetus might stay attached to them forever, reentering their lives in uncanny ways. They had to find ways, therefore, of remembering the fetus while also forgetting it. This moral quandary must be seen in the context of the ways in which deaths are usually handled in Vietnam.

Everyone I know in Vietnam holds that the human world is divided into two realms: the domain of the living (cõi dương) and that of the dead (cõi âm), or the visible and the invisible world. When a person dies, his or her soul must make the passage from this to the other world. If all goes well, the deceased will take up a new life in the other world as an ancestral spirit who remains tied to the living in reciprocal relations of love and obligation. Through offerings presented at ancestral altars, people nourish the spirits of their dead, while the dead, from their side, watch over and gently support (phù hộ) the living. In rites of commemoration held at death anniversaries and other important days, the dead are invited home to eat, drink, and socialize with their descendants; incense is burnt to call them home and to transport people's prayers to them. As Kwon (2006:63) points out, "Vietnamese popular culture emphasizes the supreme importance of remembering the dead, but its emphasis is on the dead person's *living* presence rather than the memory of this person" (emphasis in original). Some deaths, however, do not fit easily into this scheme of ideal reciprocal relations between the living and the dead. Death rituals for children take other forms than those held for adults: the child is usually buried as quickly as possible and ritual acts are kept modest and held in private.[12] When a child dies, his or her parents are not allowed to participate in the funeral; their relatives perform the rites required to send the child off to the other world. When I asked why this is so, my colleague Hiệp pointed to the moral breakdown that the death of a child entails: "We are of the opinion that when parents die, the children must see them off (*đưa đi*). The duty (*nghĩa vụ*) of children is to send them off. In the unhappy event that the child leaves before the parents, the parents will have to stay at home. They cannot take their child to the grave. In order to be filial (*có hiếu*), the young must send off the old." In offering this explanation, Hiệp placed Vietnamese practices in the context of Confucian moral tradition: Confucian ideology discourages downward commemoration of persons to whom one does not owe ritual obligation.[13] Unable to reciprocate what their parents have given them, individuals who lose their lives at a young age cannot fulfill their most important moral obligations. This ethical failure comes into expression most graphically at funerals: if parents have to bury their own child, this brings into painful public exposure the inability of the child to enact and reaffirm its love and gratitude to its parents by sending them off properly to the other world. Child deaths, in other words, are not only emotionally taxing but also morally and genealogically disorderly; they violate fundamental ethical orders.

The souls of deceased infants, people told me, do not pass over to the other world to live as ancestral spirits. Rather, their bones soft and their spirits powerful (*thiêng*), they will hang around (*luẩn quẩn*) for a while before returning to this world, being born again (*đầu thai*) either to the same or to another woman. Under some circumstances, such a rebirth may be welcomed. Mai, for instance, told me that her younger sister had recently experienced her son's return. She had given birth to a beautiful boy who died shortly after birth. Three months later, she became pregnant again: her son, Mai said, came back to her, and this time he survived. Yet when an impaired child is born—whether at full term or through an induced abortion—the situation is more complicated. As Mai told me, even though she loved the child that she had lost as much as her sister had loved hers, she did not want it to return to her. "If one suffers a spontaneous abortion and the child is complete," she said, "one will take it home and hope that it comes back next time one gets pregnant. But this one suffered from this . . . so I feel scared." The return of this fetus might, Mai suggested, place her in an uncanny predicament where she would be giving birth to one unviable child after the other—something that she had seen happen to other women.[14] The spirit of a deceased fetus or child, people explained, may hover around its parents for a long time. Like other souls of the deceased, such spirits are capable of either supporting or destroying (*phá*) the living. If they bear grudges (*oán*) against them, they may return to their parents, troubling their lives and those of their living children in numerous ways.

Women who kept their pregnancies but lost their children shortly after birth also feared that this child might keep returning to them. When a child dies, they explained, powerful emotional bonds of anger or affection, or both, can tie its spirit to the family. As an example, Châu told us her sister's story: "My sister's child was stillborn. After she had given birth, she heard her child cry every night. So she prayed, saying: 'My child, please go home, don't make life so difficult for me.' You see, people are scared that children who die may come back to harass one's other children. They may keep hanging around, keep following their parents. . . . The soul follows the parents. It haunts them." Due to their association with superstition, however, fears of ghostly child returns were usually expressed with considerable ambivalence and voiced most explicitly by people of the older generation. Alluding to the socialist state's disapproval of superstitious practices, for instance, Hồng's grand-mother said, "The state is not superstitious, but I am: I'm afraid that it will be difficult for Hồng to have children. We had to bury it in another place, so that it would go to another house, so that it would not keep returning to us." Trâm's grandmother expressed the conviction that due to their good connections in the other world, the spirit of the fetus that Trâm had lost would not do their family any harm: "In our house, we have never had anyone coming back. No silly things dare come to our house. In the other world we have people who deal with these things, people in high positions, so there is no way that anyone can drop in at all. That's why, during the war, we had eight people drafted and they all came back intact." Few people, however, shared this elderly woman's certainty: practically all couples who lost a fetus or a neonate expressed anxiety that its soul might keep haunting them, edging itself into their lives—either in a mental form, as a ghostly apparition troubling their lives and minds, or in a material form, embodied in their next child. These anxieties were expressed with particular intensity by the couples who opted for a pregnancy termination.

Ethnographic studies from other East Asian countries have docu-mented how women deal ritually with the risk that the angered spirits of aborted fetuses may return to haunt them and their families. The Japanese *mizuko kuyo* ritual is particularly well described.[15] Through this ritual, performed in Buddhist pagodas, women ask the fetus they have lost for forgiveness. Similarly, some of the women I met in Hanoi addressed the soul of their deceased fetus, pleading with it to understand and bear with them. Khanh, for instance, who terminated a twin pregnancy, said: "'Children, please forgive me.' That's what I say in my heart. 'Forgive your mother. I'm not like that at all. Heaven did not allow you to become persons, so please bear with your mother.' Whenever I miss my children, that's what I say. . . . I ask my children to accept their fates, to bear with and forgive their mother, because this was not something that I wanted to happen." Yet one distinct difference between the *mizuko kuyo* rituals described in the ethnographic literature and ritual practices in Hanoi was that, in Japan, the ethical problems surrounding abortion seem to be placed squarely within the mother-child nexus: at issue are a (potential) mother's relations to her (potential) child. When an impaired fetus was aborted in Hanoi, in contrast, the relatives of the prospective parents would always enter into the mother-child relationship, taking over responsibility for ritual precautions.

EXORCISING CHILD-SPIRITS FROM THE FAMILY BODY

When family members sought to prevent a deceased fetus or newborn child from haunting its parents, face-to-face encounters emerged, once more, as key sites of ethicality. The first precaution that people took was ensuring that the prospective parents did not see their fetus/child face-to-face: when an abortion was over, or when a child died at birth, either physicians or relatives would immediately remove the body from the delivery room.[16] A direct encounter with the face of the fetus/child, people asserted, might tie its parents permanently to it, leaving a mental imprint on their minds that would never be erased. In Châu's words, "Everyone thinks that if you give birth to a child that dies, and you see the child's face, then the soul of the little one may keep following you forever. It may disturb the lives of the children that you have later. People say that the soul follows you. It haunts you (*nó ám ảnh*)." Listening to these stories, I was struck, again, by the ways in which women represented other people's interventions in their reproductive lives as gestures of protection and care. When Quý's newborn son died, for instance, the doctors immediately took away his body. Her relatives brought it home with them and conducted the funeral, while Quý herself did not get to see her child. When I asked her how she had felt about this, she replied in terms that expressed confidence in the health professionals who had cared for her: "I think they weigh the pros and cons together with the relatives, and the doctor decides what is best for the patient. They are uncertain about how seeing the child may affect the health of the patient. I am not sure how much energy I had. I was very weak. They made this decision and I trust it was for the best. . . . With a big child like this, it is very painful."

The second precaution that people took to prevent this potentially restless spirit from haunting its parents concerned the disposal of its body. When a pregnancy ended in an induced abortion, the question of what to do with the fetal remains was always a painfully open one. Unlike a child who dies accidentally at birth, this fetus had been intentionally rejected. Yet simply discarding its body, people indicated, would compromise the humanity of both the fetus and themselves. On the other hand, if a conventional funeral were held, it would tie a potentially angry and dangerous child-spirit to the household. As a way out of this moral quandary, physicians offered families the option of leaving the fetal body at the hospital, the 500,000 *đồng* fee serving to cover the costs of the funeral at Hanoi's Văn Điển graveyard. As one doctor told Châu, "Don't worry. We will put it in a small coffin and bury it carefully, so that it will not bear any grudges against you." Approximately half of the families opted for this solution, leaving the body in the hands of hospital staff. Bích's family was one of them. Feeling doubtful about how to handle this situation, Bích asked her mother-in-law, "Do we take the child home?" to which her mother-in-law replied, "No, let us leave it at the hospital, so that it can be together with the other children there, so that it is not alone, so that it has some friends. Our child will feel sad if it comes with us and sees that its siblings are all healthy." Bích concurred. At issue, she explained, was not only her own desire to remember her child but also her child's need to forget her:

> I want it to be free (*siêu thoát*). I don't want it to exist anymore. I don't want it to suffer. . . . You see, the soul can still hang around in the house and support its children and grandchildren. But this child was so small and it was also disabled and miserable, so I want it to leave and be together with the other children at the hospital. It is best to let it be entirely free so that it does not exist anymore. . . . I will *never* forget my child. But I want my child to forget me. That's why I did not want to take it home. If I had done that, it would have kept hanging around me, and so it would have suffered. I want it to forget me.

By leaving her child's body at the hospital, Bích suggested, she was trying to sever her relations with it completely, thereby setting it free.

Other women, in contrast, expressed deep moral unease at the thought of leaving the body of their fetus at the hospital. Ngọc, for instance, said: "My relatives brought it home. I think it would have been a pity (*tội nghiệp*) to leave it there. A small one like this, what would they do with it? I felt uneasy at the thought that they might simply throw it into the garbage can. My conscience did not feel at ease. So my relatives took the fetus to our home province (*mang về quê*)." When people brought the fetal body home with them, it was usually buried at the same site as the graves of other family members. A modest funeral was held, and flowers, incense, and prayers were offered at the grave—but always, in accordance with tradition, without the participation of the parents. Mai described how her relatives had addressed the fetus at the funeral, pleading with it to stay away from their family: "My relatives brought clothes, food, and other things to offer it to eat. After presenting the offerings, they prayed, asking it to go somewhere else. 'Please don't come back to our house,' they said; 'that would only cause suffering. Please go to the pagoda or to the Buddha. There will be people there to help you, to feel sorry for you. Please don't come back here.'" Mai was happy to know, she said, that her fetus was buried at the site where other family graves were placed, so that the spirits of her elders could care for it: "It would have been wrong to leave it at the hospital. Knowing that we took it home and buried it properly makes me feel more at ease. I do love my child. I feel more at ease knowing that our elders are looking after it. It is not alone. There are many people around it out there. Our elders will see how small it is, and they will look after it."

The last precaution that people took in dealing with the spirit of the fetus/child concerned ritual commemoration. If a person dies young, a separate altar is often established to worship him or her. When her son died at two years of age, for instance, Lan's relatives established a small altar for him close to their ancestral altar. When presenting offerings to the deceased at such altars, people usually address them by calling out their names. In this ritual sphere as in other contexts, then, personal names are important elements in the forging of personhood and social connections. Yet when individuals die very young, or have not yet been born, names become a more complicated matter. To name a child is, as Barbara Bodenhorn and Gabriele Vom Bruck (2006:3) note, an enactment of social attachment: "Because others usually name us, the act of naming has the potential to implicate infants in relations through which they become inserted into and, ultimately will act upon, a social matrix. Individual lives thus become entangled—through the name—in the life histories of others." During their pregnancies, few women in our sample named their children-to-be. Those who did denamed the fetus after the abortion, thereby making another effort to detach it from their family. Combining her husband's and her own family name, for instance, Mây had called her child-to-be Nguyễn Hoàng Đức; yet at the funeral her relatives placed a note with his name in the coffin, thereby burying the name along with the body. Vân and her husband had also named their child-to-be, but when they found out that they could not keep it, they stopped using the name. Bích had wanted to call her child Bắc if it was a boy and Ngọc Anh if it was a girl. Yet her fetus did not get either of these names. Instead, trying to prevent it from haunting their family, her mother-in-law named it Từ Biệt (Farewell Forever).[17]

With one exception, none of the couples I met burnt incense at home when they lost a fetus or a newborn child. This child, they said, did not yet belong to their family (chưa phải là người nhà). Instead, as Mây explained, they would try to release or "kill" its spirit, telling it to stay away in the future. "At the grave," Mây said,

> my family burnt the things we had collected for the child. That was all. We did not want it to stay with us, so we did not make an altar. My elders were scared that the next time I got pregnant, my first child would be angry and it would follow me and enter me again. Therefore, they did not allow me to make an altar and bring incense and offerings. At the grave, my parents made the offerings, and then they untied it or what we call killed (hóa kiếp) it in order to send it to another house. They said to it, "Our house is poor, so do go to another and wealthier house." They did not want me to keep being preoccupied with it.

Like Mây's parents, women's relatives would always emphasize to the spirit of the fetus/child that the funeral marked the end of their involvement with it: with this ritual, they untied it, thereby putting their engagement with this threatening creature to an end. With this second death, they hoped to have exorcised the spirit forever from the family body, allowing it to be released (siêu thoát) and vanish.

Only one person in our sample burnt incense at home. Chung's husband, Đạt, told us that after their infant daughter had died, he had gone to the hospital's morgue to collect her body. Here, the caretaker had asked him how many children he had. Hearing that this was his first child, he sent him away, telling him, "If this is your first child, you must be very cautious or the child will return to you. It is better that you go home, and don't go to the cemetery either." Their relatives had then picked up the body and conducted the funeral the same night. When I talked to him later, Đạt commented, "Actually, I am not superstitious at all. But if everyone tells me to do something, I do it, that's all. I want to visit the grave of our child, but our elders don't allow me to, so I have not seen the grave yet." After being sent away by the morgue caretaker, Đạt left the hospital feeling sad and lonely. Their relatives living in a rural province, he and Chung shared a one-room apartment in the center of Hanoi. When he came home to the empty apartment, he made a small altar and burnt incense for their child. A few days later, when some of his neighbors saw it, they told him to remove the altar immediately and throw the bowl for incense sticks into the neighborhood lake: "People in the area told me that there was no reason to burn incense. If I burnt incense to remember it, there was a risk that it would return. It would haunt my heart and my thoughts. I would keep thinking of our little child. . . . So I must try to push it away. They say that the child probably does not want to stay with us anyway because we are poor. Of course, they say that to help me to forget, to prevent me from being haunted."

In Đạt's case, I was again struck by the ways in which actions that I would tend to see as subtle or not-so-subtle pressures on young couples to handle their loss in certain ways were described by women and men themselves as gestures of love, care, and protection. But the efforts that women and their relatives made to cope with the threats posed by fetal specters, I contend, not only illustrate the communal character of day-to-day lives and people's interventions in each other's existence. They also point us to the moral solitude that prospective parents experienced.

GHOSTS AND GRIEVANCES

Over the past decade, a surge in ghost talk has taken place in Vietnam. When people get together, nearly everyone has a story to tell about bodies and buildings plagued by spirits of the dead. These stories are recounted in the academic literature too: Kwon (2008) writes about the ghosts that linger after the wartime massacres in central Vietnam; Mai Lan Gustafsson (2009), about ghosts that haunt citizens of present-day Hanoi.[18] Angry, hungry, and restless, these spirits of the dead haunt and disturb the living, causing illness and other forms of misfortune. Observers often link this proliferation of ghosts to Vietnam's history of war. The lingering spirits that inhabit the country, they suggest, are enraged by the bad deaths they have suffered and by the failure of the living to care properly for them. Ghosts, then, articulate not merely the dramas of past events but also, and perhaps primarily, present-day problems of

FIGURE 10. Hạnh burning incense for Lan's son. In the mirror, Lan. Photo by the author, 2006.

conscience. There are, people in Vietnam hold, good deaths and bad deaths, deaths that can be justified and deaths that cannot. From my first fieldwork in a Red River delta village I recall that, when an old person's death approached, his or her family would summon relatives and neighbors to come and sit at the bedside. Often, the atmosphere would be lively; children playing and adults chatting, enmeshing the dying person in the sounds of bustling human activity. This, in essence, is what people in Hanoi consider a good death: to die at home, in old age, peacefully surrounded by relatives. A bad death, in contrast, takes place away from home, prematurely, and under violent circumstances. The morality of death is, moreover, understood not only in spatial and temporal but also in legal terms: to be good, a death must be just, occurring in accordance with preordained cosmic cycles of life and death (cf. Kwon 2006:123). An unjust death (chết oan) is wrongful and disorderly; it indexes the precariousness of human worlds and the capriciousness of higher powers.

When abortions for fetal anomaly were performed, this was not only a birth but also a death, and one that was bad in all senses of this term: it was violent, premature, and took place away from home (cf. Gammeltoft 2010). A key, yet often subdued, question in our conversations with women and their relatives was therefore, Could this death be justified? Had they come to a proper and right decision—or had they in an immoral and brutal way denied their child a life? Was this death in alignment with the meaning of things and the intentions of higher powers? To these questions, everyone answered yes—yes, the violent ending of this pregnancy was in accordance with the intentions of higher powers. It was somehow preordained. Prospective parents and their relatives often seemed to find comfort in the thought that the course their lives had taken was embedded within larger cosmological schemes over which they themselves had little control. They did only what they had to do, they indicated, completing a process that higher powers had set in motion for them. This intervention was painful, but just and right. As seen in chapter 5, people's claims of confidence in science and medicine would often coalesce with expressions of faith in higher powers such as Heaven or fate. Pondering how to act on the medical message she had received, for instance, Lê collapsed biomedical and Heavenly authority: "What kind of mother has the heart to do this?" she asked. "But the doctors explained very clearly to me that if I kept the child, I would never be able to raise it. . . . This means doing something wrong, but I have to accept that (phải chịu tội thôi). I do want my child to become a human being like myself. But Heaven did not allow this, so I am forced to accept that." Similarly, reflecting on their family's decision to terminate Hồng's pregnancy, her brother-in-law suggested that they had complied with higher powers: "Of course this was not something that we wanted to happen. Emotionally we found it very painful. We felt so sorry for the child. Our family felt very troubled. . . . But sometimes one cannot escape a difficult fate."

Despite these declarations of moral certainty, people's anxieties that the spirit of their dead fetus would keep haunting its parents seemed to make manifest the deep moral ambivalence inherent in their predicament. Although miscarried fetuses and children who die accidentally may also return to haunt their parents, the risk of the fetal spirit hovering around its parents in restlessness and anger seemed to heighten in this situation of deliberate loss. In this context, the notion of fate was, several women said, an idea that they themselves mobilized in order to assuage the remorse that they felt. In Châu's words: "To feel better, my husband and I try to console each other by saying that it was not its fate to be with us. It was not its fate to live. But in reality we did decide to give it up. We just try to console each other. That's all." The spectral fetuses that people feared, I suggest, index moral anxiety. As Stephan Feuchtwang (2003:94) points out, the presence of ghosts indicates that wrongs have been committed, that deaths have occurred in untimely or immoral ways. "Stories of ghosts," he notes, "are a permissive sanction for what is repressed and fantastic. They are a way of transmitting and collecting melancholia, and therefore they are potent figures for the transmission of grievance." Prospective parents' fears that the memory of their lost fetus/child would keep haunting them, that intrusive thoughts and unbidden images would unsettle their future lives, bring to the surface more complicated aspects of the subjectivity formation that took place when pregnancy decisions were made. In opting for a pregnancy termination, women suggested, they did the right thing, saving their child, themselves, and their families from suffering. By making this decision, they contributed to the collectivities they were part of, demonstrating loyalty to national projects and commitment to family and kin, thereby defining themselves as good citizens and dutiful family members. Nevertheless, they were haunted by doubts and bad conscience. Mây described the moral doubts suffusing her abortion experience in particularly succinct terms: "Everyone told me that according to scientific expertise, this was good for me and for my child too. This solution was the most appropriate. It was better to set the fetus free, to release it and free it from suffering. But I feel that what we did was wrong. In my heart I feel troubled. Our child was alive and we were heartless enough to give it up. I feel it was cruel (*nhẫn tâm quá*)."

Women's fears of a ghostly fetal return can, then, be seen as moral commentaries on impossibly hard reproductive choices. Although decisions to keep or to terminate a pregnancy were always made through collective processes of shared deliberation, the ultimate moral responsibility, women and their husbands suggested, must be carried individually. Bích put this moral loneliness into words when she described the conscience questions with which she struggled after the abortion: "I feel tormented, I feel at a loss. I miss my child very much. I keep imagining that I have a child to carry. I feel so lonely, even though I know that there are many people in this situation. . . . Thinking about my child makes me scared. It haunts me. In my conscience I do feel tormented. I am afraid that this will pain me forever." While Bích's decision to terminate her pregnancy allowed her to place herself within larger communal worlds, affirming social attachments to nation and kin, it severed other relational possibilities, forcing her to ignore the moral demands placed on her by the child that she did not have. The dilemmas of conscience that she struggled with could not, she suggested, be shared. They were hers to bear alone.

Conclusion

Toward an Anthropology of Belonging

In this book I define childbearing as a site where subjectivities are forged, arguing that by framing reproductive decision making as a matter of belonging rather than of freedom, we may attain new understandings of human lives, aspirations, and interconnections. I have made this claim on the basis of ethnographic material from Vietnam that suggests that people handle existentially extreme situations by responding to the demands that others place on them, thereby claiming and enacting social attachment and commitment. Such attachment is, as the preceding pages show, inherently contingent and tenuous, making for a shifting and unstable moral accomplishment rather than a given property of social relations.

To conclude, I briefly summarize the key arguments that I make through the chapters of this book. I proceed in three steps. First, I sketch the systems of subjectivation within which the women and men I met in Hanoi defined themselves as certain kinds of persons. These systems postulated modes of belonging, and they were vocally articulated by the party-state, particularly in its representations of the pasts and futures of Vietnamese nationhood. Second, I examine the strivings for belonging that were expressed in day-to-day lives, strivings that intensified in situations of reproductive crisis. Belonging is more than a product of discursive practices; it is also an urge and a social force, one generated from day-to-day interactions. Although the quests for belonging that people voiced and enacted in everyday lives drew upon state narratives of national and familial belonging, they also indexed doubts and uncertainties that remained subdued in state discourse. Third, I focus on the shadow side of belonging, on that which is repressed and excluded in both state discourses and everyday lives—on the losses, absences, and acts of willed forgetting that underlie state narratives and local practices of belonging. Belonging is enacted, the preceding pages suggest, in the presence of ghosts, specters of social figures that have been lost or set aside yet continue to hover, haunting and troubling people. In short, in this concluding chapter I consider belonging as state discourse, belonging as social practice, and belonging as loss. These three themes represent central analytical avenues along which an anthropology of belonging may proceed. But first I return to Tuyết and Huy, whose story opened this book.

QUYẾT TIẾN VILLAGE, JANUARY 18, 2006

"My brother died this winter," Tuyết whispered, slipping her arm under mine as we stepped over the wooden doorstep that separated the sun-filled courtyard outside from the cool and dark interior of her parents' house. It was a bright January day, the sun was out for the first time in weeks, and in the branches of the pomelo tree that threw its shade over the yard, songbirds warbled. As we entered the house, I noticed a small wooden altar hanging on the wall opposite the large ancestral altar in the middle of the room, half-burnt-down incense sticks reaching toward the ceiling.

Nearly two years had passed since Tuyết's abortion 29 weeks into her pregnancy. As we walked down the village lanes toward her parents' house, my colleague Hạnh and I recalled the pain, confusion, and doubt that had suffused the atmosphere in her family when we first visited. When we arrived, Tuyết's mother offered us tea, and her father immediately began telling us about his son's death. "People may say, 'Why couldn't you save your child?'" he said, looking intensely sad. "But with this disease, there was nothing we could do to save him. We knew that all along. I don't know much about medicine, but I brought up this child, and I knew all the time that we could not save him." The death of Tuyết's brother was, her father suggested, a loss they had anticipated. His disease had been a habituated part of the family's life for years, and they had foreseen that he would die young. The loss of Tuyết's pregnancy, in contrast, had been a sudden and unpredicted event, one that had shattered the entire family. When her father had finished the story about his son, Tuyết's mother immediately took over, telling us again about that night at the obstetrics hospital when Tuyết could have lost her life and the doctor on duty refused to assist her. "We called her, but she did not come," Tuyết's mother said, in the same tone of disbelief in which she had spoken two years earlier. "We could have sued her, but we decided not to. But I told her: 'Next time, whether people pay a little or they pay a lot, you must do your duty. That's your obligation.'" Tuyết added, "Doctors should be like gentle mothers. They always say that on television. But what kind of mother treats others like this?"

Tuyết cried as she told us how scared and abandoned she had felt during the abortion. "This was not a normal delivery at all," she said; "it was much more painful. I lost a lot of blood, my entire body trembled, and I felt so weak and cold. I was just lucky not to hemorrhage. . . . The next days I could not stop crying." Trying to protect his wife, Huy had insisted that they rent a private room for her in the hospital, one that she had to share with only one other person, thereby escaping the crowded wards where two or three patients often had to share the same bed. "My wife must have a place where she can lie down and rest," he had said. "Even though we can't afford it, I want to ensure that my wife has a decent (tử tế) place to be. This procedure must take place in a decent manner." Ironically, however, Huy's efforts to maintain moral dignity led to a life-threatening delivery that pained the family for years. Since they had rented an expensive room, the doctor on duty that night assumed that this was a family with access to economic resources. When they paid her only a small under-the-table fee, she ignored their calls, leaving the family to manage the delivery on their own. "When the child came out, it gave two cries," Tuyết's mother said. "The woman in the other bed said, 'Grandmother, the child has died. It cried, so you should cry for it.' But I was so perplexed. I could not cry yet."

By demanding that Tuyết's relatives cry for their child, the other woman in the room told them that the child belonged to them; it was theirs to love and to mourn for. Yet the child's attachment to their kin group was, Tuyết and her relatives suggested, questionable and contentious. "Did you burn incense for the little one?" I asked, nodding at the incense sticks on the altar above us. "No," Tuyết said. "When I came home, my elders told me not to think about it anymore. If I think about it, it will return to me next time I get pregnant. So they told me to stop caring about it, to forget about it." Her father added in a firm tone: "She had to forget about it immediately. . . . It was too small. A small child has the right to be born again, and therefore people don't worship it. If it is put in a coffin, they will make holes in it so that it can get out. One has to let it go wherever it wants to go." The room fell silent. Then

Tuyết said, her eyes dark, her voice low: "But how could I forget? My elders try to console me, that's all. Maybe they think I have forgotten. But I still remember. How can I forget?"

The story that Tuyết and her relatives told us was about expectations and demands. It was a story about Tuyết's expectations that others would care for her; about her family's demands that the doctor on duty would assume responsibility for the birthing women in her ward; and about a fellow patient's expectations that the child that Tuyết gave birth to would be recognized as a human being and a family member. It was, moreover, a story of belonging and of its contingency. What I found most striking in the family's account of that night at the hospital was their firm expectation that the state, embodied by the physician on duty, must reciprocate the commitment they had shown to it. Through active participation in party-state projects of warfare, production, and reproduction, this family had consistently, over several generations, defined themselves as loyal and dutiful members of the socialist nation-state. Having served for more than fifteen years in the armed forces, the fathers of both Huy and Tuyết were war veterans, their wounds still visible. During the socialist years, family members had taken active part in party-led mass movements for collectivization and modernization. But when they needed it most, the state had let them down. The attachment that they had assumed to exist could not, this episode revealed, be taken for granted. Similarly, although the child that Tuyết gave birth to did, in one sense, belong to their family and lineage, embodying their past and their future, it did not necessarily belong at all. Its place within networks of social relations was fragile and contentious, a product of social negotiations rather than a stable and given position.

In the course of research, I often found that the reflections on lives, habits, and decisions that people such as Tuyết and her relatives set forth were strikingly consonant with official views on social relations; in both state and everyday discourse, emphasis was placed on interhuman sentiments, obligations, and attachments. In the following section I briefly sum up how Vietnamese state discourses placed human reproduction at the core of notions of nation and kin.

SYSTEMS OF SUBJECTIVATION: STATE-SANCTIONED STRUCTURES OF BELONGING

When a 3D scan found fluid on the brain of the child they expected, Tuyết and Huy appealed to physicians and to senior relatives for help, expressing trust in the moral authority of state representatives and kin. By making the decision to terminate Tuyết's pregnancy, they demonstrated loyalty to a national project of biomedical advancement and reproductive control, and trust in the wisdom of family elders. The identity-making they undertook in this situation was, in other words, located within long-standing normative frameworks, within systems of subjectivation that defined what it means to be a son, daughter, father, mother, community member, or citizen. Practically all couples I met during fieldwork traveled along similar decision-making paths, thereby engaging with powerful models for belonging articulated by the Vietnamese state. In Vietnam, as in many other societies, two interrelated ideologies of belonging are set forth with particular vigor: one defines the parameters of kinship, and the other sets boundaries for the nation-state. Childbearing is placed at the intersection of these two ideologies; it is through the bearing of children, state discourses claim, that people come to take up their places in networks of kin, and through the creation of families that they contribute to making the nation. The bodies of kin and nation are, in this sense, articulated as one, tied together through reproductive practices. While ideologies of family and nation have numerous social effects, what interests me in this book is mainly their power to render the subject in particular ways.

Over the past decades, anthropological approaches to kinship have shifted. From being regarded mainly as a matter of classification and organization, kinship has come to be seen as a contingent enactment of forms of relatedness that may have little to do with reproductive biology. As articulated in twenty-first-century Vietnamese official discourse, however, kinship is strikingly biology-centered. Communities of ancestors and descendants are, party-state rhetoric claims, generated through biological substances: by combining the seed provided by men with the gestational work done by women, kin bodies are produced. A person's belonging to the existential-biological community constituted by family and kin hinges, therefore, on his or her capacity to produce a child who will continue the family line. Seen against this background, it is not surprising that marriage is nearly universal in Vietnam; in a society where successful reproduction is officially defined as a crucial precondition for social belonging, not marrying and having children means placing oneself outside the vital social communities that sustain individuals. Since there is hardly any position that the subject can occupy outside the family, failed childbearing brings a person's entire existence into question. Seen in this light, selective reproduction becomes a project of social attachment, a tool that people use in an effort to attain social membership and value.

Besides being a structure of differentiation and belonging in itself, kinship is also an important idiom through which the national body is brought into being rhetorically. By representing the Vietnamese nation as a family writ large, the party-state defines the nation as an intimate moral-genealogical community to which people are expected to feel attachment, loyalty, and love. This places childbearing at the center of the state's efforts to produce a sense of nationness; if the nation is a family writ large, then national belonging, too, hinges on the production of children, and parental labor and love become acts of patriotism. In official rhetoric, reproductive responsibilities are centrally placed, and the cultural integrity and survival of the Vietnamese nation is envisioned as depending directly on the ability of individuals to fulfill their social responsibilities within family and community. These social responsibilities are, as shown earlier, suffused by cosmology; the visions of happy and harmonious families that state discourses project are animated by long-standing cultural ideologies that define complete infant bodies as signs of moral-political order.

In the current era of global capitalist integration, the reproductive achievements of Vietnam's citizens are measured by new moral standards. Enhancing the quality of reproduction, state rhetoric claims, increases the nation's chances of development and growth. This turns selective reproduction into an important political tool, as citizens are expected to produce children whose bodies hold the potential to strengthen Vietnam's position on the global economic scene. Although people are not mobilized to partake in projects of selective reproduction in the systematic manner that they were summoned to take part in the family planning movement in the 1990s, official messages are clear: in the twenty-first century, responsible parenthood demands attention to children's quality, to their wholesomeness and bodily completeness. This political quest is animated by public awareness of the plights of the country's Agent Orange victims. Agent Orange, this ethnographic material suggests, is a specter of death and disability that continues to haunt Vietnam decades after the war ended. The politics of Agent Orange draws our attention to the affective dimensions of state discourse, to the ways in which public representations of human suffering and bodily disintegration can become part of political projects that aim to generate a collective sense of unity and coherence.

Although state policies and classification schemes are neither monolithic nor necessarily perceived in a unitary manner, then, they do nevertheless project important cultural ideals and set certain frameworks for the organization of experience (cf. Borneman 1992). As the preceding chapters show, the normative frameworks that the Vietnamese party-state articulates in the realm of reproduction define subjectivity as a product of a person's position within networks of biologically related kin, within a kin group that, in its extended sense, comprises the entire nation. This turns participation in state-led projects of selective reproduction into a question of kinship duties and national loyalties; by screening children-to-be for defects, prospective parents also define themselves as responsible mothers and fathers and as conscientious citizens of the Vietnamese state. When Huy drove Tuyết from their rural commune to Hanoi's Obstetrics and Gynecology Hospital for a 3D scan, both of them knowing that the end result of this trip to the capital city might be a pregnancy termination, their journey was also a gesture of belonging, an expression of confidence in the state and its health care policies. Even so, this trip was suffused by anxieties and uncertainties; rather than a linear movement toward a goal, it was a hesitant and doubtful quest for knowledge and certainty. While the subject positions that Tuyết and Huy were offered by social authorities were relatively unitary and clear-cut, the practices through which they took up these positions seemed more complicated. Comprehending how people came to take up the possibilities for action and reflection that they were offered requires, the preceding pages suggest, that we attend closely to day-to-day social practice within local moral worlds.

BELONGING AS SOCIAL PRACTICE

Anthropologists have long been skeptical of cultural and political assertions of belonging. Projects of national unity and integrity are always also projects of exclusion, and dominant kinship models often tend to deny alternative ways of cultivating relations and living together. The conventional anthropological approach to belonging has therefore been to deconstruct and denaturalize it, to take apart the cultural ideologies that underpin it. My aim with this book has not been to add to this literature of skepticism, but rather to point to the existential importance that communal belonging holds for people. Underlying strivings for solidarity and belonging, as Jackson (2002:108) writes, "lies a universal human assumption that each person's individual being not only *is* but *must be* embedded in collective fields of being that outrun it in both space and time, such that the actions, words, and energies of everyone are consummated in his or her relations with the many" (emphasis in original). There is reason, this book suggests, for anthropology to take such human quests for belonging seriously. To comprehend how individuals come to project their labor and love in specific directions, forming communities, making sacrifices, and enduring pain, we must place strivings for belonging at the center of analysis. Yet belonging is, as noted earlier, a fragile, contingent, and temporary achievement. Belonging's contingency becomes particularly evident in moments of crisis: when routines are suspended, social orientations are shattered, and given frames of life are questioned, social memberships and loyalties are brought into question too. The reproductive crisis in which couples such as Tuyết and Huy found themselves was one such moment—a point in time when they were forced to reconsider in very fundamental ways their own identities and attachments. With whom were they connected? To whom were they obliged?

In Vietnam, most people I know define the family and the kin group as their most vital communities of belonging. The emphasis that official ideology places on biological membership in a larger social group is reiterated in day-to-day lives. The forging of kinship through childbearing is often characterized as giving human life its very meaning, as *the* central activity through which people constitute themselves as social beings. In Vietnam, as elsewhere, the realization of kinship demands day-to-day enactment and commitment. The product of purposeful social activity, kinship is built out of mundane everyday acts of caring for, feeding, and paying attention to one another. I have often been moved by the ways in which such care unfolds across the boundary of death, as when ancestral souls are called home to share a meal with their relatives, or a plate of newly purchased fruit is placed on the altar for deceased parents or grandparents to eat first. Through these gestures of care, it seems, people embed their own existence within larger communities of moral being, drawing together past, present, and future social lives. Kinship practices often tend to find their most passionate expression in parent-child relations. Children are cared for out of love and obligation, but childcare also has a performative dimension: it is a terrain in which parents demonstrate moral commitment to others—to the child itself and to those whose labor has made their own lives and that of the child possible. A child embodies the past and the future: by fulfilling parental obligations, people continue the work that their ancestors have done while also weaving their own existence into future human lives. Childbearing is, in this sense, a way for people to commit themselves to one another, claiming social positions and attachments—through the practical, humdrum, day-to-day social connections of talk, mutual help, and sharing of anxieties and frustrations that childcare brings with it, and through the cross-generational links that childbearing builds.

But the belonging that childbearing affords is inherently precarious. In Rupert Stasch's apt formulation, "Belonging, as an ideal of kin relatedness, travels with and by its resistances" (2009:133). At the heart of people's practices of belonging, I found, was deep ambivalence, uncertainty, and contingency. Women often described this uncertainty in particularly acute terms, expressing keen awareness that their belonging to their husbands' kin groups and to local village communities depended directly on their capacity to fulfill their roles as wives, daughters-in-law, and mothers in a satisfactory manner. Having married into their husbands' families, they did not belong to their household of residence in any taken-for-granted way; their belonging was contingent on their ability to live up to social expectations. In this context, childbearing was a critical moral test. In Vietnam, as the preceding pages have shown, a complete child body affirms the capacities of parents (particularly mothers) for practical care, while also attesting to their moral integrity in a cosmological sense, indicating that they and their ancestors have lived in proper ways. Compromised childbearing, therefore, places parents in a situation of deep moral vulnerability, exposing them to other people's assessments, comments, and accusations.

It was within this matrix of precarious relations of kinship and community that practices of prenatal screening unfolded. When pregnancies developed as expected, ultrasound scans seemed to intensify women's feelings of love for their child-to-be while also holding out promises of closer attachment to families and kin groups. The detection of a fetal problem, however, revealed the contingency of these social bonds, bringing the prospective child's belonging to its parents and the parents' attachment to their kin group into doubt. If severely disabled, prospective parents assumed, their child would remain unable to take an active part in the reciprocal exchanges out of which day-to-day social relations were forged. No matter how hard they strove, they would never be able to answer to this child's demands or to realize their responsibilities as parents by turning their son or daughter into a socially acknowledged person. This powerlessness would, in turn, render them unable to fulfill familial and kinship obligations by continuing the life projects of their predecessors. The birth of a severely disabled child would, in short, place the child's parents in a state of constant bad conscience, rendering them unable to return what they had been given, incapable of answering to moral demands, outside cosmologically mediated cycles of moral reciprocity. When an adverse diagnosis was made, prospective parents handled this moral threat by holding on to their kin group, locating the decision they had to make within it. Hồng's formulation was typical: *Cả nhà cùng quyết định,* "the entire family decided together." Prenatal screening became, in this way, more than a tool used to assess the quality of fetuses; when a fetal problem was found, this moral rupture was taken as an opportunity to reaffirm intimate relations, to articulate and enact social belonging. In most cases, as we have seen, affected pregnancies were terminated. Aware of the difficulties of parenting a disabled child in this low-income setting, most couples made the painful decision to sever their connections to the fetus, accepting that they must end its life. This brings us to the third aspect of social belonging that this book addresses: the setting of limits that belonging entails, the loss that is always involved.

GHOSTS: BELONGING AS LOSS

In the evening of the February day in 2004 when I first met Tuyết and Huy, the words in which Huy characterized their plight kept echoing in my mind. "This," he said, "is a question of conscience. No matter what we do, this decision will haunt us forever." Problems of conscience point us to the ways in which we participate in each other's existence, exposing one another to demands that are sometimes painfully irreconcilable. While Tuyết and Huy expressed no hesitancy in defining reproductive choice as a question of belonging, the social realization of this belonging was, as Huy suggested, a morally complex, contentious, and divisive matter. By enacting one form of belonging, he and his wife sacrificed another, cutting their connections to the fetus that could have become their child. Integral to belonging was loss, a permanent and painful loss of the child and the family they could have had. It was in an effort to soften the moral pain of this experience that Tuyết's father urged her not to commemorate her fetus. She must, he counseled, push this child-to-be out of the zones of memory within which deceased kin members are usually cared for with affection, love, and respect. With this gesture, this elderly man also seemed to tell his daughter and son-in-law that the shared social lives that people treasure and struggle to attain are always and invariably haunted and conditioned by loss, solitude, and separation.

Throughout this book, I place fetuses at the center of attention. With this, as should by now be clear, I do not seek to impose an essential humanness on fetuses; rather, I want to emphasize the roles played by the inchoate, the invisible, the not fully articulated in human lives. Perhaps more than any other social figure, the fetus embodies the possible, the tentative, that which is not yet fully there; it exists and yet it does not, it affects others without being tangible or visible to the eye. Fetuses that have been put deliberately to death must, people in Vietnam told me, be handled with caution, or they will keep hovering, registering past violence and reminding the living of what could have been. To an even greater extent than other kinds of ghosts, fetal specters draw our attention to that which lies beyond the borders of established social orders, that which is omitted from official histories and socially shared narratives. The enactment of belonging, such ghosts tell us, always relies on exclusions; social experiences of unity and connection arise only through (sometimes painful) denials and willed forgetting. The ghosts that plague Vietnam at present—specters of fetuses and children, of victims of accidents and wars—testify to such lapses of memory and attention. Within families, the spirits of those who died untimely and violent deaths often roam, restless, calling on the living in anger and frustration; and the unity and coherence of the nation is brought into question by the seething presence of ghosts of Vietnamese soldiers who died fighting on the "wrong" side and who therefore remain uncommemorated in the public domain. To capture the range of human experience, then, anthropology must attend not only to official identity claims or to people's everyday efforts to create a social world to which they can belong, but also to such subdued universes of unrealized human being and relating. Anthropologies of belonging are also anthropologies of lives *in potentia:* investigations into not-fully-realized identities and relational possibilities, into lives that could have unfolded but did not.

Core Cases

Pseudonym	Age	Gestational week at involvement in the research	Main fetal problem	Pregnancy outcome	Occupation	Family form	Residence
Mai	22	20	Dilated ventricles	Abortion	Farmer	Nuclear	Từ Liêm, Hanoi
Liên	24	14	Abdominal anomaly	Abortion	Journalist	Nuclear	Hoàn Kiếm, Hanoi
Lý	25	23	Hydrops fetalis	Abortion	Factory worker	Nuclear	Cầu Giấy, Hanoi
Trâm	22	19	Prune belly syndrome	Abortion	Farmer	Nuclear	Vĩnh Tường, Vĩnh Phúc
Khanh	41	15	Twins with a shared spine	Abortion	Trader	Nuclear	Gia Lâm, Hanoi
Bích	30	19	Dilated ventricles	Abortion	Factory worker	Nuclear	Gia Lâm, Hanoi
Thu	27	23	Cleft lip	Abortion	Army official	Extended	Thanh Xuân, Hanoi
Huyền	22	29	Dilated ventricles	Abortion	Factory worker	Extended	Hoa Lư, Ninh Bình
Tuyết	25	28	Dilated ventricles	Abortion	Farmer	Extended	Quốc Oai, Hà Tây
Ngọc	28	23	Hydrops fetalis	Abortion	Factory worker	Extended	Hoàn Kiếm, Hanoi
Hà	33	28	Abdominal hernia	Abortion	Tailor	Nuclear	Từ Liêm, Hanoi
Châu	26	17	Dilated ventricles	Abortion	Factory worker	Nuclear	Đông Anh, Hanoi
Nga	27	34	Dilated ventricles	Abortion	Office assistant	Extended	Gia Lâm, Hanoi
Hồng	30	26	Anencephaly	Abortion	Teacher	Nuclear	Đông Anh, Hanoi
Vân	23	20	Hydrops fetalis	Abortion	Student	Extended	Ba Đình, Hanoi
Mây	26	19	Hydrops fetalis	Abortion	Economist	Nuclear	Thanh Xuân, Hanoi
Xuyến	24	22	Umbilical hernia	Abortion	Café owner	Extended	Từ Liêm, Hanoi
Chúc	27	36	Curved legs	Birth	Farmer	Extended	Phúc Thọ, Hà Tây

(continued)

Pseudonym	Age	Gestational week at involvement in the research	Main fetal problem	Pregnancy outcome	Occupation	Family form	Residence
Oanh	25	34	Dilated ventricles	Birth (child died at birth)	Secretary	Nuclear	Từ Liêm, Hanoi
Lộc	24	34	Abdominal anomaly	Birth	Farmer	Nuclear	Đan Phượng, Hà Tây
Phương	20	35	Dilated ventricles	Birth	Farmer	Extended	Vĩnh Tường, Vĩnh Phúc
Lê	41	29	Dilated ventricles	Birth (child died at birth)	Trader	Nuclear	Hai Bà Trưng, Hanoi
Lan	25	37	Dilated ventricles	Birth	Trader	Extended	Từ Liêm, Hanoi
Hạnh	35	38	Anencephaly	Birth (child died at birth)	Farmer	Nuclear	Thạch Thất, Hà Tây
Thuý	32	33	Curved arms	Birth	Trader	Extended	Thạch Thất, Hà Tây
Mai Chi	23	30	Heart defect	Birth	Farmer	Nuclear	Thạch Thất, Hà Tây
Hoa	23	38	Umbilical hernia	Birth (child died 7 days after birth)	Factory worker	Nuclear	Gia Lâm, Hanoi
Chung	25	21	Abdominal hernia	Birth (child died 4 days after birth)	Office assistant	Nuclear	Tây Hồ, Hanoi
Loan	44	23	Heart defect	Birth	Teacher	Nuclear	Hà Đông, Hà Tây
Quý	41	32	Dilated ventricles	Birth (child died 2 days after birth)	Farmer	Nuclear	Sóc Sơn, Hanoi

Notes

1. Except for the names of my Vietnamese colleagues, all personal names given in this book are pseudonyms.

2. In accordance with conventional usage, in this book I define first-trimester abortions as pregnancy terminations conducted up to week 12, second-trimester abortions as terminations in weeks 13–28, and third-trimester abortions as terminations in week 29 and later.

3. Some Americans did know. The use of herbicide dioxins in Vietnam was publicly questioned and criticized on several occasions. For instance, in March 1964 the Federation of American Scientists issued a statement that read (in part): "We are concerned with reports of the field use of chemical weapons in Vietnam. . . . These charges give rise to the broader implication that the U.S. is using the Vietnamese battlefield as a proving ground for chemical and biological warfare. We . . . feel that such experimentation involving citizens of other countries compounds the moral liability of such actions" (D. Fox 2007:239). On the use of Agent Orange in Vietnam, see chapters 1 and 2.

4. The late president Hồ Chí Minh once stated that a good doctor should be "like a loving mother" (*lương y như từ mẫu*) (see chapter 2). In today's Vietnam, many people use this expression with an ironic twist, since the rampant corruption in the health care sector tends to place doctors in positions quite far from that of the idealized gentle mother. Yet to some people the analogy between mothers and health professionals seems to hold lasting moral value.

INTRODUCTION

1. As human beings we are, as Michael Jackson (2012:3) puts it, always both a part of and apart from other people's lives: "While human existence is

profoundly social (*comprising relationships with others*), it always entails a sense of our own singularity and aloneness (a *relationship with oneself*)" (emphasis in original).

2. The term *selective reproductive technology* (SRT) was coined by my colleague Ayo Wahlberg and refers to technologies used to prevent or allow the birth of certain kinds of children. For a review of anthropological research on SRTs, see Wahlberg and Gammeltoft (forthcoming).

3. In the category of Western societies, I include Europe, North America, and Oceania. Of the world's total 2010 population of 6.9 billion, only 14.1 percent lived in the West. The population of Asia was 4.2 billion or 60.4 percent of the world's population (United Nations 2011).

4. Rose uses the term *advanced liberal* to characterize contemporary societies in which government works through freedom, by inducing individuals to govern themselves. "Freedom is seen as autonomy, the capacity to realize one's desires in one's secular life, to fulfil one's potential through one's own endeavours, to determine the course of one's own existence through acts of choice" (1999:84). Rayna Rapp's research (1999) on amniocentesis in New York City, Rose (2001:19) observes, offers an exemplary illustration of the ways in which responsibility is enacted in this advanced liberal ethics.

5. Over the past two decades, the anthropology of reproduction has grown into a dynamic research area. Whereas previous anthropological work in this field often took a more descriptive approach, offering empirically based ethnographic studies of pregnancy and childbirth across cultures, this new anthropology of reproduction approaches human procreation as a transnational terrain of power and politics (cf. Ginsburg and Rapp 1991; see also Ginsburg and Rapp 1995b; Inhorn and Birenbaum-Carmeli 2008; Browner and Sargent 2011a). This book is in conversation with several bodies of work in this field. First, the analysis I present is indebted to feminist studies of reproductive technologies. With the development of a range of new biomedical technologies used to assist or enhance reproduction, childbearing has become an area of deliberation and achievement in historically unprecedented ways. This has led to an increase in social science research exploring how assisted reproductive technologies (ARTs) and selective reproductive technologies (SRTs) are implicated in the formation of specific ways of thinking and enacting morality, sociality, relatedness, responsibility, and choice. Monographs on SRTs include Rothman 1993 [1986]; Rapp 1999; Franklin and Roberts 2006; Khanna 2010; edited volumes taking up questions pertaining to selective reproduction include Ginsburg and Rapp 1995a; Franklin and Ragoné 1998; Lock and Kaufert 1998; Layne 1999; Inhorn 2009 [2007]; Bauer and Wahlberg 2009; Inhorn and Birenbaum-Carmeli 2009; Whittaker 2010; and Browner and Sargent 2011b.

Second, this book is in conversation with the growing body of anthropological work that explores social processes of parenting, investigating how people turn themselves into particular kinds of mothers and fathers in daily lives and in moments of crisis (see, for example, Scheper-Hughes 1992; M. Weiss 1994; Layne 2003; Einarsdóttir 2004; Landsman 2009; useful edited collections are Scheper-Hughes and Sargent 1998; Layne 1999; Ragoné and Twine 2000; J. Taylor et al. 2004). A subset of the literature on parenting comprises a growing body of studies conducted in East Asia on the mothering of fetal spirits (see chapter 7). Following the lead of scholars who contend that research on human reproduction must include attention to disability, in this book I draw particularly on studies of parenthood that explore how people deal with the complicated social, moral, and political questions of difference that arise when children are born disabled. I take "disability" to be a way of organizing social difference, a socially constructed cognitive category equivalent to categories such as gender or race (see Ingstad and Whyte 1995, 2007; Linton 1998). For research on the intersections between childbearing and disability, see Ginsburg and Rapp 1999; Rapp 2000; Rapp and Ginsburg 2001, 2007; Landsman 2009.

6. In writing this book, I have found inspiration in the expanding anthropological literature on the use of sonographic imaging in pregnancy. Obstetrical ultrasonography is the topic of monographs based on research conducted in Canada (L. Mitchell 2001); Tanzania (Müller-Rockstroh 2007); the United States (J. Taylor 2008); and India (Khanna 2010). On the use of this technology in low- and middle-income countries, see Tautz et al. 2000; Bashour et al. 2005; Ranji and Dykes 2012.

7. When used according to established guidelines, ultrasound is considered to pose minimal risk to the fetus and the woman (Whitworth et al. 2010). Yet some uncertainties regarding safety do remain, as studies have shown that ultrasounds may affect fetal neurological development (Marinac-Dabic et al. 2002; Torloni et al. 2009).

8. Fetal conditions that can be detected through ultrasonography include hydrocephalus, anencephaly, spina bifida, congenital heart defects, limb anomalies, diaphragmatic hernias, kidney abnormalities, and other structural malformations (Powell 2000; see also Green and Statham 1999). Ultrasound screenings in pregnancy have become increasingly sensitive, and this poses new clinical dilemmas concerning whether or not to follow up with more invasive tests (Getz and Kirkengen 2003).

9. In 2011, 50 percent of the world's countries permitted abortion for fetal impairment, including 38 percent of "developing" and 86 percent of "developed" countries (United Nations 2013). Termination of pregnancy after the first trimester was permitted on different grounds in different countries, depending on the type of impairment, gestational age, and abortion legislation (see Statham 2002; United Nations 2013). Studies in Europe and North America show that termination rates after prenatal diagnosis vary widely across countries and fetal conditions (see Mansfield et al. 1999; Statham 2002).

10. In some countries fetal surgery has been attempted, but with limited success (see Casper 1998).

11. See Belizan 1998 for the WHO guidelines; J. Taylor 1998 on U.S. guidelines; and Ministry of Health 2002 for the Vietnamese guidelines. In Vietnam, official policy changed when new national guidelines for reproductive health care were issued in 2009; these guidelines recommend three scans in each pregnancy (Ministry of Health 2009).

12. Comparison is integral to the discipline of anthropology. This comparative intention, however, raises the question of what exactly it is that we compare. Few anthropologists today feel comfortable comparing one "culture" to

another, and yet cultural differences do demand our attention (see Robbins 2013). When I hold practices of selective reproduction in Vietnam up against those described in literature from the Western world, I do so with an eye to the challenge that always confronts anthropological work: how do we capture cultural differences without essentializing them? In this context I take notions such as choice, care, and responsibility to be "embedded concepts" in Talal Asad's sense: "What is distinctive about modern anthropology is the comparison of embedded concepts (representations) between societies differently located in time or space. The important thing in this comparative analysis is not their origin (Western or non-Western), but the forms of life that articulate them, the powers they release or disable" (Asad 2003:17). In my analysis of ethnographic findings from Vietnam, I have tried to acknowledge complexity and the ambiguities of forms of life by paying close attention to the social processes through which specific incidents unfold (see the section on fieldwork in this chapter).

13. Parliamentary Decision on Prenatal Diagnosis, May 15, 2003 (Schwennesen 2011:12). Denmark was the first Nordic country to implement a publicly funded first-trimester prenatal screening program that covers all pregnant women regardless of risk status. The program is free of charge and participation is estimated to be 90–95 percent (Schwennesen et al. 2010).

14. From a historical perspective, this position is rather new: when prenatal screening was first introduced, it was part of a public health agenda that explicitly aimed to prevent the birth of children with disabilities (see Chadwick 1999; Petersen 1999).

15. Many scholars have pointed out that in practice nondirective counseling is difficult to implement and perhaps not even desirable (see, for instance, Petersen 1999; Williams et al. 2002c).

16. On the consequences of this eugenic past for present-day reproductive sensibilities, see Paul 1998; Rapp 1999:56–62; Koch 2004.

17. See, for instance, Press and Browner 1997; Rapp 1998b; Remennick 2006; Kelly 2009; Markens et al. 2009; Gupta 2010a; France et al. 2011; Teman et al. 2011.

18. See, for instance, Green et al. 1993; Press et al. 1998; Rapp 1999:129–164; Gupta 2010a.

19. See Sandelowski and Jones 1996; Rapp 1999: 220–262; Statham 2002; Sandelowski and Barroso 2005; Gammeltoft 2007a; Gupta 2010a; Kato 2010b; Choi et al. 2012; France et al. 2012; Pilnick and Zayts 2012.

20. Margaret Lock, for instance, writes: "Today, unlike in the past, interventions that may result in a neoeugenics are usually masked by a rhetoric very different from that of the early twentieth century, one in which individual choice is dominant and in which the role of government is rendered invisible" (2007:190). See also Wertz 1998; Duster 2003; Taussig et al. 2003.

21. As Lene Koch (2004) has shown, the notion of eugenics often tends to become a projection screen for present-day anxieties rather than an index of actual historical events. In a similar vein, Diane Paul (1998:97) observes that "to assert that a policy with undesirable effects is also 'eugenics' does not add anything substantive to the accusation. What it does add is emotional charge."

22. For reflections on the problems associated with the notion of reproductive choice, see, for instance, Ginsburg and Rapp 1991, 1995b; Gregg 1995; Van Hollen 2003; Paxson 2004; Kaufman and Morgan 2005; Mol 2008. For a compelling ethnographic account of how choice is socially and culturally conditioned at the end of human life, see Kaufman 2005.

23. Landsman 2009:47. See also Press and Browner 1997; Layne 2003:243.

24. See Battaglia 1999; Lippman 1999a; A. Robertson 1999. In an effort to think beyond conventional notions of subjectivity and autonomy, feminist philosophers have introduced the concept of *relational autonomy* (e.g., Sherwin 1998). The problem with this term is, however, that it tends to maintain the idea of subjectivity as something bounded, thereby rendering it difficult to capture the ways in which we are open to and opened by each other.

25. Researching prenatal risk assessments in Denmark, for instance, Nete Schwennesen and her colleagues found that nondirective counseling gave pregnant women a feeling of being left to themselves, "in limbo and with a very limited space for action" (Schwennesen et al. 2010:213). Women were, they note, reluctant to take on the choice; instead they sought to reinstall authority in medical experts. See also Lippman 1991, 1999a; Rapp 1999; Kerr 2003; Sandelowski and Barroso 2005; Schwennesen and Koch 2012.

26. Much has been written on China's efforts to enhance population quality. See, for instance, Hairong 2003; Anagnost 2004; Greenhalgh and Winckler 2005; Kipnis 2007; Sigley 2009. These scholars show that political strivings to improve population quality have become central to the dynamics of governance in present-day China, though they differ in their interpretations of the linkages that exist between quality discourse and governance.

27. For Asia, the exceptions include research conducted in China (Sleeboom-Faulkner 2010, 2011); Hong Kong (Pilnick and Zayts 2012); India (Gupta 2000, 2010a, 2010b; Khanna 2010); Japan (Lock 1998; Ivry 2006, 2009, 2010; Kato 2010a, 2010b; Tsuge 2010); Sri Lanka (Simpson 2009, 2010); and my own research in Vietnam.

28. The category of the subject differs from concepts of individual, self, and person by linking social being directly with the workings of power; inspired by the work of Michel Foucault, scholarship on subjectivity explores how subjects are constituted through language, knowledge, and normative regulations. Individuals become subjects, according to Foucault, by being subjected: "There are two meanings of the word 'subject': subject to someone else by control and dependence, and tied to his own identity by a conscience or self-knowledge. Both meanings suggest a form of power that subjugates and makes subject to" (Foucault 2003c:130). For anthropological reflections on notions of subjectivity, see, for instance, Ortner 2005; Biehl et al. 2007; Das 2007; Whyte 2009.

29. See, for instance, Weir 1996; Lupton 1999; Greenhalgh 2010; Bridges 2011.

30. In an article written for expatriates living in Vietnam, Lady Borton (n.d.:2) defines the concept of belonging as central to Vietnamese administrative assumptions: "Viet Nam has created its own cultural norms that have evolved over the centuries from a base in Confucianism. The concept of 'belonging'—expressed by the word '*của*' in Vietnamese—begins in this long history but has

changed through years of socialism. 'Belonging' indicates Right Relationship and the primary channel of responsibility. NGOs, for instance, 'belong' to the People's Aid Coordinating Committee (PACCOM). An expatriate company 'belongs' to its partner in their joint venture. 'Belonging' in terms of NGO work is partnership."

31. Levinas's philosophy is inspired by Jewish thought and by the horrors of World War II. Levinas was appalled by Heidegger's 1933 commitment to National Socialism, and much of his work is written in implicit or explicit polemic with Heidegger. Where Heidegger gives Being priority over the human, Levinas seeks to develop a "humanism of the other"; the presence of the other, he claims, is a crucial precondition for subjectivity (see Cohen 2006). For accounts of Levinas's work and life, see Cohen 2006; Critchley 2002; for anthropological work inspired by Levinas's thought, see, for instance, Scheper-Hughes 1992; A. Garcia 2010; Geissler and Prince 2010; Throop 2010.

32. For humorous observations of the ways in which elderly Hanoians intervened in the daily life of an anthropologist, see Oosterhoff 2008:19–20. I recall the first time I brought my then-six-month-old daughter to Hanoi. It was early December, and I took her for a walk in the stroller. As soon as I stepped onto the street, an elderly woman, a stranger to me, tapped my shoulder and demanded: "*Where* is the child's hat? It is cold today; she will get sick!" My attempts to explain that compared to what we were used to, this was not a cold day at all did not impress her, and I ended up succumbing to grandmotherly authority, feeling mildly annoyed and strangely cared for.

33. One example of this that I have encountered particularly often is people's inclination to keep the death of a newborn secret from the mother. If an infant dies at birth, relatives often try to protect the mother against emotional and physical shock by delaying the bad news, telling her that her child is sick and undergoing hospital treatment. Chung, one of the women I got to know in Hanoi, lost her child shortly after birth, but her relatives did not reveal the death to her until several days later. Telling me about this, Chung said that she thought her relatives did the right thing: "At that moment I was quite weak, so they were afraid that I would hemorrhage because of the shock. It is common that people hemorrhage if they feel very sad. Therefore they had to keep it secret so that I could recover first."

34. While conducting this fieldwork, in other words, I too was engaged in practices of parenting. Even though they took more dramatic forms, the moral challenges described by parents and parents-to-be in Hanoi often resonated with my own experiences at this time of my life; like the women I met, I was trying to turn myself into a particular kind of mother, striving to live up to demands and to tie myself into social collectives. With Jackson, we may see these experiential correspondences as indications of a shared humanity; "all human beings, while never exactly the same," he notes, "tend to share similar differences" (1998:2). Having spent substantial amounts of time in Vietnam, moreover, I may have come to adopt some of the social expectations and moral intuitions that people in Hanoi were oriented toward, my own existence and aspirations being transformed in the encounter with Vietnamese social life. As Cecilia Van Hollen (2003:220) notes, "Just as there is always an autobiograph-

ical bent to how ethnography is conceived and written, so, too, autobiography becomes punctuated by ethnography."

35. While conducting this research, I was also involved in the Vietnamese-Danish research project REACH (Strengthening Reproductive Health Research in Vietnam) (1999–2011). REACH aimed to enhance reproductive health research capacity in Vietnam through twinning arrangements involving Vietnamese and Danish researchers. The project offered master's and PhD training for Vietnamese students at the University of Copenhagen and a series of short courses on medical anthropology and public health held in Hanoi. It was through REACH that I came to know most of the Vietnamese researchers who worked with me on the present project on selective reproduction. The research was conducted under the auspices of REACH and five of the researchers on our team have been enrolled, either prior to or after this fieldwork, as master's or PhD students at the University of Copenhagen.

36. Each of the Vietnamese researchers was responsible for the publication of one article in a local peer-reviewed journal. The articles were published in the journals *Khoa Học Về Phụ Nữ* (Journal of Women's Studies), *Tạp Chí Y Tế Công Cộng* (Journal of Public Health), *Tạp Chí Nghiên Cứu Y Học* (Journal of Medical Research), and *Tạp Chí Y Học Thực Hành* (Journal of Practical Medicine). The fact that four of our female team members were pregnant and gave birth during the course of the research enriched our opportunities for participant observation.

37. According to hospital statistics, in 2004, 11,381 abortions and 83,313 ultrasounds were performed in this hospital, and there were 15,098 deliveries.

38. In many cases, the women expressed expectations that we could offer them answers to the questions they struggled with—questions about what to do, about the cause of the fetal malformation, about how to prevent recurrence in subsequent pregnancies, and for women who carried their pregnancies to term, about how to care for the child after birth. We rarely intervened directly in the decisions that women and their relatives confronted, but listened to their concerns and did our best to offer them the information they asked for. Although several researchers on our team were medical doctors, the women's need for information often exceeded our own knowledge. In some cases, therefore, we accompanied them to the Department for Medical Biology and Genetics at Hanoi Medical University, the National Hospital of Obstetrics and Gynecology, or the National Hospital of Pediatrics, for further assistance.

39. This commission was originally named National Committee for Population and Family Planning (NCPFC). It was founded in 1984 to take charge of the implementation of Vietnam's family planning policies and served as the counterpart institution for the REACH project. The VCPFP has now merged with the Ministry of Health and is called the Government Office for Population and Family Planning (GOPFP).

1. SONOGRAPHIC IMAGING AND SELECTIVE REPRODUCTION IN HANOI

1. Readers may ask whether there was any concern for privacy. None of the women I talked to brought up privacy concerns. This can be explained in

several ways. First, since urban health facilities are generally overcrowded, being the only patient in a consultation room is a very rare occurrence and this experience probably shaped women's expectations of the services they received. Second, it was my impression that many women appreciated the presence of other women in the room while their ultrasound was conducted. In Vietnam, scientific expertise and technology are ideologically celebrated, and patient-provider relationships tend to be quite hierarchical (see chapter 4). The presence of other antenatal care clients, it seemed, provided reassurance by softening these medical hierarchies and creating a sense of sharing and camaraderie among the women. In 2004, the U.S. anthropologist Victoria H. Luong conducted fieldwork in the delivery department at Hanoi's Obstetrics and Gynecology Hospital. Regarding privacy she notes: "Women do not seem to be bothered by the lack of privacy or all the staff walking in and out of the delivery room. I asked women how they felt about the impersonal nature of the delivery room and they reported that they liked the fact that many people were walking about. It gave them a sense of comfort since they could flag anyone's attention when they needed help" (V. Luong 2007:136).

2. During my first fieldwork in Vietnam, Bà Chính, the elderly woman who hosted me, would often recount stories of this day, telling me about how, in a joyous atmosphere, she and her fellow villagers walked barefoot from their village in Hà Tây province into Hanoi, feeling certain that their country was at the threshold of an epochal change for the better.

3. On đổi mới in Vietnam, see Turley and Selden 1993; and Fforde and de Vylder 1996. For an excellent account of political life in Vietnam, see Gainsborough 2010.

4. Despite this overall economic progress, many people in Vietnam have incomes very close to the poverty line and are vulnerable to falling back into poverty as a result of economic shocks caused by job loss, accidents, illness, or death (World Bank 2012). On the growing economic disparities in Vietnam, see P. Taylor 2004b; Lê Bạch Dương et al. 2005; World Bank 2007, 2012.

5. One day, for instance, a woman gave birth to a girl in the maternity ward. Her husband was furious and threatened to sue the hospital, as repeated ultrasounds had shown the child to be a boy. This news, which not only questioned the authority of science but also resonated with provider fears of committing medical mistakes, rippled through the entire hospital within a few hours after the delivery.

6. The questions regarding safety that women raised concerned mainly whether the "electric waves" (sóng điện) through which they assumed ultrasound worked could be harmful to mother or fetus (see Gammeltoft 2007b).

7. The physicians I talked to rarely remembered exactly who had donated the first machines; among the donors they mentioned were the governments of France and Holland, the Japanese manufacturer Aloka, a Japanese hospital, and the World Health Organization.

8. Vietnam's health sector is plagued by many different kinds of corruption, including insurance fraud, bribes related to licensing, overtreatment of patients, and informal payments to providers (Vian et al. 2011). Such informal payments, also known as envelopes (phong bì), constitute a significant proportion

of health care fees and are an important source of revenue for poorly paid health care staff. In many medical settings, priority is given to patients who offer thick envelopes; these practices are known to intensify when people are critically ill or injured. Even if they have health insurance, therefore, there is no guarantee that the country's poorest will receive appropriate health care services. In maternity care as well, informal payments are routine practices. Rather than seeing this as corruption (*tham nhũng*), however, most women I met during fieldwork represented informal payments as a natural and habituated part of interactions with health staff, as an extra cost that one simply has to calculate when seeking medical care in the public health care system. Among the people in our sample, only Tuyết and her relatives recounted a situation where patient and provider expectations collided and modest and morally acceptable extra payments slid into unacceptable corruption (see the last chapter of this book).

9. Political efforts have recently been made to protect the most vulnerable citizens through redistributive means such as fee exemptions and health insurance plans (see London 2008). Nevertheless, health care costs often exceed the financial means of Vietnam's poorest households, and ill health can have dire economic consequences (see Wagstaff 2007; Thanh et al. 2010).

10. Economic arrangements whereby public health facilities lease equipment from their own staff are becoming increasingly common; the 3D scanning machine at Hanoi's Obstetrics Hospital being a case in point (see London 2008).

11. See Johansson et al. 1996:103; Wolf et al. 2010:155. The first national population policy was issued in 1963, encouraging couples to have no more than two or three children, spaced five years apart (see Vũ Quý Nhân 1992).

12. On May 1, 2003, the National Assembly issued a Population Ordinance (Pháp Lệnh Dân Số) that broke with years of state-set limitations on childbearing, stipulating that people were now allowed to have the number of children they desired. In the years that followed, however, the government registered a rise in the number of third births, and in December 2008 the National Assembly revised the Population Ordinance, reverting to the two-child limit on childbearing (Bùi Kim Chi 2010).

13. In 2003, a government decree made it illegal for health providers to inform women of the sex of their fetuses. Most pregnant women are, however, eager to know whether their fetus is male or female, and health providers fear that if they do not offer this information, women will turn to other clinics (UNFPA 2011b). Many physicians therefore inform women of the sex in subtle terms, saying for instance "This one looks like its father" or "This one will wear a dress." The commercialization of health care in Vietnam, in other words, renders it difficult to implement legislation against sex determination. When information about fetal sex has been obtained, the woman can seek a pregnancy termination on the basis of social or economic difficulties; being legal up to week 22, second-trimester abortions are not difficult for women to access. Although most people I talked to condemned the use of ultrasonography for sex selection, finding it morally wrong to terminate a pregnancy due to fetal sex, this intervention too was defined as an example of scientific progress. A commune leader cited in a United Nations Population Fund (UNFPA) report, for instance, said: "Nowadays science has advanced. People can have two sons and then they stop

[bearing children]. If the first child is a daughter, people may terminate the second pregnancy if they find out it is a female baby" (UNFPA 2011b:41). On son preference and sex-selection in Vietnam, see also Trần Minh Hằng 2011.

14. In the Kovac's procedure, a condom-covered catheter with saline solution is introduced into the uterine cavity, thereby inducing labor. Until around 2002, this was the principal method used for second-trimester abortion in Vietnam. Since the Kovac's method was associated with serious complications, including uterine rupture, hemorrhage, and sepsis, medical abortion performed through administration of misoprostol has become the preferred method of pregnancy termination after week 18 in Hanoian hospitals. At the time of this fieldwork, medical abortion was in principle also available for pregnancy terminations earlier than week 18, but this method was rarely used. On second-trimester abortion procedures in Vietnam, see Gallo and Nghia 2007; Hoang et al. 2008; Bélanger and Oanh 2009.

15. The term *feticide* refers to acts aiming to induce fetal death before abortion. In some countries, feticide is performed in abortions after 21 weeks and 6 days' gestation: to prevent a live birth, the fetus is injected with medication that stops its heart (Royal College of Obstetricians and Gynaecologists 2011).

16. Playing a core role in the government's efforts to control population growth, induced abortion has been sanctioned by the socialist party-state for decades, and no organized anti-abortion movements exist in Vietnam. In a conversation that we had in June 2004, Dr. Lương reflected explicitly on the private nature of abortion skepticism in Vietnam. During our talk, I told him about a Danish colleague of mine who had commented that the country's high abortion rates must be a sign that Vietnamese people "do not respect life." I knew Dr. Lương as a calm and gentle man, but this remark seemed to upset his equilibrium. "Just because abortion rates are high, you *cannot* say that people do not respect life. They have a deep respect for life," he exclaimed, banging his hand on the table between us.

> I think that if they were allowed to, many people in Vietnam would actually *support* legislation against abortion. They think that abortions are wrong . . . because it means to kill a human soul. Abortion rates are high because people do not have access to or information about contraceptive methods, not because they want to have abortions. If you go to our abortion department, you will see that nine out of ten women are crying after the abortion. They are very sad, and they only opt for the abortion because they can see no other way. . . . The reality is that women feel very pained and full of regret when having abortions.

The regret that Dr. Lương described has recently become articulated in new public fora: Internet sites have emerged where women establish online graves and burn virtual incense for aborted fetuses, some of them as young as two weeks old. On these sites, women name their fetuses, apologize to them, and appeal to them for understanding and forgiveness (see http://www.nhomai. vn/forum/showthread.php?t=1598; accessed March 28, 2013). On moral experiences of abortion in Vietnam, see Johansson et al. 1998; Gammeltoft 2006; Trần Minh Hằng 2011.

17. See Lê Bạch Dương et al. 2005; Lê Bạch Dương et al. 2008; Rydstrøm 2010; Mont and Cuong 2011; Nguyen Thi Xuan Thuy 2011; Palmer et al.

2012. In response to this situation, in 2010 a new Disability Law was issued. Influenced by international disability rights language, this law focuses explicitly on stigma and discrimination. Whereas previous official documents tended to represent disability as a problem inherent in individual bodies, the new law emphasizes the social barriers that prevent people with disabilities from becoming fully integrated members of society.

18. One of the few people I met who questioned the benevolence of prenatal screening was Nam, a lab technician and the father of a ten-year-old girl with cerebral palsy. During our talk on October 17, 2004, in his home in a dusty and densely populated neighborhood, Nam shared his thoughts on selective reproduction with me:

> This is a question of feelings, of being humane. Our society will become very utilitarian if everyone thinks that if something is difficult we can just discard it. People may say that if a child like this is born, it will be harmful for the family's economy, or it will not be of any benefit for society. But I think that there are other social evils that are much more dangerous, such as drug use or prostitution. . . . We have this child, and of course we are at a disadvantage in many ways. But I think that our child has a lot of feelings and she is very loveable. This is how I feel, even though I know that when other people look at us they think we are deeply miserable.

19. Grassroots organizations formed by people with disabilities began to emerge in Vietnam's urban areas already in the 1980s, but it was not until the 1990s, after a 1993 government decree permitted the establishment of civil society organizations, that disability groups became a common social phenomenon (Vasiljev 2003). For an analysis of the disability network the Bright Future Group as a civil society organization, see Wells-Dang 2011.

20. According to James Clary, a defoliation program scientist, the military was aware of the harm that dioxin contamination can do: "When we initiated the herbicide program in the 1960s, we were aware of the potential for damage due to dioxin contamination in the herbicide. We were even aware that the 'military' formulation had a higher dioxin concentration than the 'civilian' version due to the lower cost and speed of manufacture. However, because the material was to be used on the 'enemy,' none of us were overly concerned" (Waugh 2010:3). For resource and teaching materials on Agent Orange, see the War Legacies Project webpage: http://www.agentorangerecord.com/home/ (accessed March 28, 2013).

21. In its 2009 report on veterans and Agent Orange, the U.S. Institute of Medicine points to the need for more research on the possible transgenerational effects of Agent Orange exposure: "Developing understanding of epigenetic mechanisms leads this committee to conclude that it is considerably more plausible than previously believed that exposure to the herbicides sprayed in Vietnam might have caused paternally-mediated transgenerational effects" (Institute of Medicine 2009:11).

22. On the human health consequences of exposure to Agent Orange, see Le Cao Dai 2000; Le and Johansson 2001; Ngo et al. 2006; D. Fox 2007. For a sensitive and nuanced ethnographic account of the life experiences of people in Vietnam who suffer from health problems and disabilities that are assumed to stem from Agent Orange exposure, see D. Fox 2007. For literary accounts of victims' plight, see Waugh and Lien 2010.

23. As Peter H. Schuck points out (1986:9), dioxin's diffuse, latent toxicity is difficult to prove, and lawsuits concerning mass toxic injury always entail huge uncertainties: "Often the pathways of causation are difficult to detect, the time periods extend over decades, and the effects are not readily isolated or scientifically understood."

24. In 2002, the United States and Vietnam agreed on a framework for joint research on the environmental and human health consequences of exposure to dioxin. But since it turned out to be impossible to reach agreement on study protocols, the research was not conducted (Martin 2009:6). In 2012, a U.S.-funded $43 million program to clean up environmental contamination was initiated at Danang International Airport, where dioxin concentrations in the soil are particularly high. Among people in Vietnam this program is appreciated, yet it is also seen as inadequate compared to the overall damage done. In the words of Ngô Quang Xuân, a former Vietnam ambassador to the UN, "It's a big step. But in the eyes of those who suffered the consequences, it's not enough" (Fuller 2012).

25. The contrast between the results of this lawsuit and the settlement attained by U.S. veterans is striking. In the latter case, too, proof was lacking. As Judge Weinstein said in 1984, "It is likely that even if plaintiffs as a class could prove that they were injured by Agent Orange, no individual class member would be able to prove that his or her injuries were caused by Agent Orange" (Schuck 1986:185). The 2005 court ruling was appealed to the United States Court of Appeals for the Second Circuit in New York City. On February 22, 2008, this court upheld the decision of the district court. The plaintiffs later filed a petition with the U.S. Supreme Court requesting a reconsideration of the case, but the Supreme Court decided not to review it.

26. In September 2010, I visited Phạm Kim Ngọc in CGFED's office, where she showed me stacks of photographs of Agent Orange victims taken by CGFED staff. I include one of them in chapter 1; a photo of a "three-generation Agent Orange family" (figure 3). The husband of Nguyệt (the elderly woman) was exposed to Agent Orange during military service from 1965 to 1967. Today their son and two grandchildren suffer from physical and mental health problems that the family attributes to Agent Orange. Nguyệt's daughter-in-law Hoa (in the striped shirt) characterizes her mother-in-law's life in these words: "She has cared for three handicapped generations. She took care of her husband for twenty years, she has been taking care of her son for thirty years, and her granddaughter has suffered for more than twenty years. She has never enjoyed a happy life" (CGFED n.d.). Thảo, another CGFED researcher, commented: "It seems that the war never finished in this family."

27. For examples of such Agent Orange photographs, see Đoàn Đức Minh n.d.; Griffiths 2003, 2005.

28. The term *cultured family* (*gia đình văn hóa*) is used to designate families that have been certified as living in accordance with officially promulgated moral values, maintaining "happy and harmonious" family relations, supporting neighbors, implementing family planning, and undertaking other citizenship duties. If assessed by their local People's Committees to have attained these goals, families are awarded a certificate that affirms their status as cultured (see Drummond 2004; Leshkowich 2012).

29. Policy documents, however, often expressed an intention to promote the use of genetic health care services. An official document accompanying the 2003 Population Ordinance, for instance, states: "Examinations for hereditary diseases have immense importance for each individual, each family, and for the entire society. Our ability to perform these examinations is still restricted by a lack of equipment. Still, it is necessary to set regulations for this problem in order to step-by-step make people used to health examinations, in order to contribute to a reduction of the rate of people with congenital malformations" (Ủy Ban Dân Số, Gia Đình và Trẻ Em 2003:53). During the first decade of this century, however, amniocentesis became more widely practiced, and it is now an integral part of the pregnancy care offered at maternity hospitals in Hanoi.

30. According to historical studies, the preoccupation in Japan with population quality began considerably earlier than this; there was a vibrant eugenics movement in the late nineteenth and early twentieth centuries, and in 1940 a National Eugenics Law was passed (see J. Robertson 2002, 2005; Frühstück 2003).

31. In general, I find, anthropological studies have all too often reified the state, treating it as a bounded object with set social functions and unified goals (see Gal and Kligman 2000; Gammeltoft 2008b). A more productive mode of approaching the state may proceed through investigations of the actions and imaginings of those who embody it. As I discuss in more detail in chapter 4, placing state actors at the center of inquiry enables us to examine the involvement of people in making the state and to draw into analysis the sentiments and sensibilities that animate state policies.

32. The responses of these policy makers can be seen as exemplary illustrations of the trends in modern governance identified by Didier Fassin (2012). Humanitarian government, Fassin proposes, is a form of government that draws on moral sentiments. Emphasizing human suffering, empathetic engagement, and compassion, this form of government tends to result in a masking of important social realities, particularly structural inequalities and violence. Seen in this perspective, the social realities that Agent Orange discourse can be said to hide are the increasing inequalities in Vietnamese society itself; inequalities that manifest with particular force when people are sick or disabled. When unsettling mass media stories of suffering Agent Orange victims capture the public's attention, calling for U.S. responsibility and justice, the Vietnamese government's own responsibilities for addressing the increasing social disparities within the country are easily overlooked.

33. In calling for counseling of Agent Orange victims to convince them of the futility of their hopes, Phương placed herself within a long tradition in Vietnam of community mobilization for health, a tradition that I discuss in more detail in chapters 2 and 4.

2. A COLLECTIVIZING BIOPOLITICS

1. On the ways in which human reproduction is tied into national imaginaries, see, for instance, Das 1995; Paxson 1997; Gal and Kligman 2000; Kanaaneh 2002; J. Robertson 2002; Phạm and Eipper 2009.

2. Writing about population policies in China, for instance, Susan Greenhalgh and Edwin A. Winckler suggest that "the quality project has been a major site for the creation of the sorts of self-regulating, 'autonomous,' neoliberal subjects assumed by both the marketizing capitalist economy and the slimmed down neoliberalizing state" (2005:217).

3. For critiques of the interpretive overemphasis of neoliberalism and processes of individuation in social science research on East Asia, see Kipnis 2007, 2011; Nonini 2008; Gainsborough 2010; Leshkowich 2012; Schwenkel and Leshkowich 2012.

4. See Ong 2006; Kipnis 2007; Sigley 2009; Harms 2012; Pashigian 2012.

5. This is in line with Martin Gainsborough's (2010) observation that despite twenty years of reform that has involved considerable engagement with neoliberal actors such as the World Bank, the state in Vietnam has changed little in terms of its practices and political philosophy.

6. See Phinney 2005, 2008; Barbieri and Bélanger 2009; Pashigian 2009; Leshkowich 2011.

7. On the history of family planning in socialist Vietnam, see Vũ Quý Nhân 1992; Gammeltoft 1999. V.H. Luong (2007) offers a nuanced ethnographic description of the ways in which such mobilization campaigns continue to be carried out in Hanoi in the twenty-first century.

8. For critical discussions of the happy family as a political figure, see Gammeltoft 2001; Pettus 2003; Drummond 2004; Phinney 2005, 2008; Leshkowich 2012.

9. While limiting family size to two children, most couples also aim to have at least one son—hence the skewed sex ratio at birth in Hanoi.

10. For a vivid account of how images of severe disability are presented to pregnant women in Israel, see Ivry 2010:51–58.

11. As Michael M.J. Fischer (2007) observes, communities of memory offer key support for the constitution of personhood and subjectivity. For ethnographic accounts of the ways in which the past is selectively remembered in contemporary Vietnam, see, for instance, Hue-Tam Ho Tai 2001; Malarney 2001, 2011; Jellema 2005; Kwon 2006, 2008; Leshkowich 2008; Schwenkel 2009; Werner 2009.

12. I cite the Declaration reprinted in H.V. Luong (1992:129–130). I prefer to translate the term *nòi giống* or *giống nòi* as "stock" rather than, as here, "race," as the connotations that the term *race* holds in English differ significantly from those held by the term *giống nòi* in Vietnamese. According to my Vietnamese dictionary, *giống nòi* refers to "people with a shared ancestral origin, many generations following each other; often used to refer to a people (*dân tộc*)" (Hoàng Phê 1994).

13. See Malarney 2002. Political efforts to construct the nation as one and indivisible have a long history in Vietnam. Patricia Pelley (1998) has shown that postcolonial Vietnamese scholars made concerted efforts to write a history of Vietnam that represented the country as one "unified bloc" (*khối thống nhất*).

14. Hồ's address can be found at http://vnthuquan.net/diendan/tm. aspx?m=90505 (accessed September 25, 2012). In Vietnam, bionationalist ideas are often set forth in literature on Sino-Vietnamese medicine (known as *thuốc ta* [our medicine]). Vietnamese people, local pharmacists often claim, possess

specific biologies and pathologies that differ from those of other people (see Monnais et al. 2012).

15. A detailed discussion of the diversity of kinship in Vietnam is beyond the scope of this book. Both among ethnic minorities and among the ethnic majority Kinh, a variety of different kin practices exist. In the southern parts of the country, many researchers note, kinship carries more bilateral traits than in the northern regions (see, for instance, Guilmoto 2012).

16. In principle, according to Vietnamese law, daughters too can carry on family names and inherit their parents' property (UNFPA 2011b). Yet powerful cultural ideologies posit that only sons can continue family lines, and son preference is strong in the country. Daughters, people hold, can perform most of the tasks that sons can (earning an income, caring for parents in their old age, worshipping the ancestors), but they cannot carry on the lineage. Despite rhetorical party-state critiques of the patriarchal family, limited efforts have been made to challenge the idea that family lines are continued through men or to encourage alternatives to patrilocal living arrangements.

17. The importance placed on biological motherhood is reflected in the 1986 Law on Marriage and the Family, which states that the state shall assist women "in fulfilling their noble tasks of motherhood." As Harriet Phinney (2005) notes, this is usually taken to imply that all women, including those who are single, have a state-sanctioned right to bear a child. The significance of pregnancy is also expressed in Vietnamese legislation on the use of assisted reproductive technologies that defines gestation as more important than genetics in determining to whom a child belongs (see Pashigian 2009).

18. Hồ Chí Minh (1988) quoted in Malarney 2002:55. On the emergence of the term *individual* (*cá nhân*) in Vietnam in the first decades of the twentieth century, see Marr 2000.

19. "Tôi chỉ có một sự ham muốn, ham muốn tột bậc là làm sao cho nước ta được hoàn toàn độc lập, dân ta được hoàn toàn tự do, đồng bào ai cũng có cơm ăn, áo mặc, ai cũng được học hành." Practically everyone I have heard quote this statement has done so with approval and appreciation. Shaun Malarney's reflections (1997:907) on the centrality of Hồ in day-to-day political lives resonate with my fieldwork experiences: "It is difficult to describe the prominence of Hồ in northern Vietnamese life without appearing completely credulous. Hồ's portrait, maxims, and biography are ubiquitous in social life. . . . Hồ still remains a defining image or symbol of political morality for both the people and the party in northern Viet Nam."

However, opinions are divided regarding the present government's treatment of Hồ's thoughts: some people claim that today's state policies are in line with his visions (though there is still a long way to go before they are realized), while others complain that the political elite abuses Hồ Chí Minh's legacy in an attempt to gain legitimacy.

20. Hairong Yan, for instance, claims that "the phantasmatic production of suzhi is a new valuation of human subjectivity specific to China's neoliberal reforms" (2003:497; see also Anagnost 2004).

21. As many observers have noted, these efforts have not been particularly successful. Despite a rhetorical commitment to equity and despite some government

initiatives aimed at bridging the gap between rich and poor, large segments of Vietnam's population experience deepening vulnerability in the current era of market economic liberalization. These groups include, in particular, poor farmers, urban migrants, and people with disabilities. In many situations, the social inequalities and exclusions that characterize present-day Vietnam make a mockery of party-state discourse on equity and inclusion. As P. Taylor (2004c:25) observes, "The Vietnamese state's response to inequality-based disputes and its commitment to poverty reduction suggests that its concern is less to attain social equity than to minimize the risks that overt forms of social exclusion might pose to its underlying quest for a strong nation, a cohesive society, and a coherent ideological mandate" (see also Lê Bạch Dương et al. 2005; World Bank 2007, 2012; Barbieri and Bélanger 2009).

22. This blending of languages of justice and compassion in Vietnam's Agent Orange case illustrates the point made by Fassin (2007:509) that in today's world, politics and humanitarianism tend to merge (see also D. Fox 2007:251).

23. For ethnographic accounts of how people in present-day Vietnam live with divisive memories of war, see Kwon 2006, 2008; Leshkowich 2008; Schwenkel 2009.

24. Other scholars have argued that continuous exposure to images of violence and destruction may desensitize and disengage viewers (see Sontag 1977; Kleinman and Kleinman 1997).

3. PRECARIOUS MATERNAL BELONGING

1. Although some epidemiological studies have found associations between congenital abnormalities and common cold in early pregnancy, in statistical terms the risk is modest (e.g., Zhang and Cai 1993). Fears that a maternal cold might harm the fetus did, however, loom large in the pregnancy stories I heard in Hanoi, and were, it seemed, exacerbated by the popular pregnancy handbooks that many women resorted to. In a study conducted in three provinces of Vietnam, Maria Gallo and Nguyen C. Nghia (2007:1819) found that some women opted for a second-trimester abortion out of fears that influenza in early pregnancy might have damaged the fetus.

2. The term tử tế, which can be translated as "good," "decent," or "upright," collapses bodily and moral qualities. Like the word complete (lành lặn or hoàn chỉnh), this term points to the moral-cosmological connotations that birth defects carry, a theme that I return to in chapters 4 and 5.

3. See, for instance, Bashour et al. 2005; Gammeltoft and Nguyễn 2007; Ranji and Dykes 2012.

4. See, for instance, Rapp 1998a; J. Taylor 1998; Tautz et al. 2000; Garcia et al. 2002; Harris et al. 2004; Tsuge 2010.

5. See Tsing 1990; Morgan 1997; Mitchell and Georges 1997; Landsman 1998; Paxson 2004; V. Luong 2007; Ivry 2009; Sleeboom-Faulkner 2011.

6. See Rapp 1998a; Lupton 1999; Harris et al. 2004.

7. The vast majority of Hanoi's population belongs to the ethnic majority Kinh. On kinship among the Kinh, see, for instance, H.V. Luong 1989; Gammeltoft 1999; Phạm Văn Bích 1999; Rydstrøm 2003; Jellema 2007; Pashigian

2009. H. V. Luong (1989) points out that although male-oriented kinship is normatively emphasized in Vietnam, this model coexists with more bilateral forms of kinship.

8. Similarly, as a contemporary political construct, the figure of the happy family seems to feed on older cosmological fears and is animated by the long-standing moral connotations that reproductive successes and failures carry.

9. In Vietnamese, the term *ơi* is used to attract people's attention in a manner that communicates intimacy and trust. In her essay "*An Ode to 'Ơi,'*" erin Khuê Ninh (2011) reflects on this "untranslatable but meaningful" term, calling it "the most heartaching word in Vietnamese language."

10. Numerous studies have documented how ultrasound scans come to serve as sites for the formation of fetal subjects: by claiming to offer a neutral and objective view of the fetus, the ultrasound helps to construct it as a person, a social actor, a baby (see, for instance, Mitchell 2001; Layne 2003; Han 2009). In many societies, the routinization of new reproductive technologies seems to be accompanied by a tendency to attribute personhood to children-to-be at increasingly early stages of their lives.

11. This resonates with Tsipy Ivry's observations in Japanese medical settings. With reference to feminist critiques of the erasure of women in ultrasonography, Ivry (2010:182) notes that in Japan, "the fetus can never be imagined as a free-floating being alone, and mothers can never be reduced to black outer space. Babies can be imagined only *as part* of a maternal-child interactive bond, without which the child could not have won life in the first place" (emphasis in original). In Hanoi, sonographers explained that when they asked the woman how many children she had already, this was also an attempt to prevent sex-selective abortions: if the woman answered that she had two daughters, and if she looked nervous, they considered her a likely candidate for sex-selective abortion.

12. See, for instance, Statham 2002; Mitchell 2004; Ivry 2010:110–111; Tsuge 2010. In Israel, in contrast, Ivry (2009:207) found that risks of reproductive catastrophe loomed large when scans were performed. "The powerful scheme of thinking through the paradigm of threat," she argues, "makes Israeli experiences of pregnancy considerably more vulnerable to terrorization."

13. When conjuring risks of anomalies, both women and health care providers seemed to pay particular attention to the brain and the face of the fetus. Problems with the brain were generally considered to be very serious; if the brain of a fetus was found to differ from the normal, many women asserted, then an abortion was undoubtedly the best solution. While physical impairments may be remedied after birth, they claimed, this is not possible in cases of mental disabilities. Thuý, for instance, said: "A child who is mentally impaired will never be able to develop properly. It will have no future. It will not be able to learn, to grow up and live a life like normal people." The face of the fetus seemed to be considered important because it was held to be emblematic of the person (see the introduction to this book); a disfigured face, in other words, indexes flawed personhood. Further, in Vietnam congenital disabilities are traditionally associated with moral defects in the family; if a child is born disabled or disfigured, therefore, this is often taken as a sign that its parents or grandparents have lived immorally (see chapter 5). A facial anomaly such as a cleft lip

and palate is particularly obvious and difficult to hide; it lays bare the morality of the family before the world. As the child's face is split open, so the family is opened and exposed to moral questioning and critique. This moral terrain turned facial anomalies such as cleft lips into grave problems in social and experiential terms, in spite of the fact that both women and health professionals considered them relatively negligible from a biomedical perspective.

14. On the subjunctive aspects of images, see Barthes 1993 [1977]; Zelizer 2004; Gammeltoft 2013.

15. According to the historian Toàn Ánh, the idea that a mother's thoughts can affect her fetus directly is an old one in Vietnam and related to long-standing concepts of fetal education (*thai giáo*): "Right from the moment when we are still fetuses in the wombs of our mothers, we receive education from our mothers. This is fetal education. Fetal education is very important for us, partly for the sake of the mother's health and partly because all the mother's thoughts and behaviors can affect the fetus in the womb" (Toàn Ánh 1992:36). In China, prescriptions for prenatal care have a long history (see Furth 1995). The concept of fetal education (*taijiao*), which is rooted in classical Confucian teachings, has had a social and political revival since the 1980s in parallel with the increasing political interest in population quality (see Dikötter 1998; Nie 2005).

16. It is important to emphasize that these were pregnancies that the women had wanted and, in many cases, had planned for years. Their visions of the fetus were clearly shaped by the social circumstances of its emergence: this was a child-to-be that they longed to bring into being.

17. In a U.S. context, Judith L.M. McCoyd (2007:43) observes, the polarized abortion debates render this moral tension difficult to grasp: "The prochoice group cannot accept the love the woman feels for the entity she calls her 'baby'; the pro-life group cannot condone the woman's willingness to terminate the pregnancy."

18. In spite of Vietnam's liberal abortion legislation, 11.5 percent of maternal deaths are attributed to unsafe abortion (Hoang et al. 2008).

19. Women's inclination to define abortion as an immoral act must be seen in the context of Buddhist indictments against harming living beings and Confucian ideologies that stress people's obligations to continue the family line (see chapter 5). The women I talked to, however, also often underscored the need for empathy (*thông cảm*) with those who have to terminate their pregnancies. Hiền, for instance, explained that women resort to abortion only when they have no alternative (*bất đắc dĩ*).

20. In Vietnam, children are considered to be one year old at birth, as the "nine months and ten days" in the womb count as the first year of life (*tuổi mụ*). The concept of the fetus as a moral subject is, my interlocutors said, an old one in Vietnam: in the pre-revolutionary era, a spiritual approach to life prevailed in which fetuses were regarded as human beings (*sinh linh*) from an early age of gestation, and abortion was considered a severe moral transgression (*tội*). When grandmothers took part in our conversations, they often emphasized that according to people of their generation, any abortion, regardless of the stage of gestation, is morally wrong and may bring the anger of Heaven (*Ông Trời*) upon the family. Thảo's mother-in-law, for instance, told us how opinions had

clashed when she got pregnant with her fifth child in 1978: "People encouraged me to have an abortion. But my father-in-law said no: 'When you have become pregnant, you must give birth. Only people from immoral households (*nhà vô phúc*) would do something like that.' So I gave birth to my fifth child, a very pretty girl."

4. "LIKE A LOVING MOTHER"

1. In this endeavor, I build on earlier anthropological studies that have approached biomedicine as a social enterprise shaped by the institutional structures, political ideologies, and cultural values of a given society. See, for instance, Lock and Gordon 1988.

2. See, for instance, Gail Kligman's (1998) study of Ceaucescu's draconian anti-abortion regime; Greenhalgh and Winckler's (2005) research on China's heavy-handed population policies; or Van Hollen's (2003) account of state-mandated IUD insertions in India.

3. On the history of health care in socialist Vietnam, see, for instance, Wahlberg 2006, 2009; London 2008; Deolalikar 2009; Monnais et al. 2012. Although there is ample evidence that significant health care achievements were made between 1954 and the late 1980s, more critical accounts point out that in practice, socialist Vietnam struggled with persistent health problems and with numerous health system inefficiencies and shortcomings (see, for instance, Fforde and de Vylder 1996). Nevertheless, Vietnam's vital health indicators are comparable to those of much wealthier countries, an achievement that most observers ascribe to the socialist past.

4. In an article written during the Second Indochina war, for instance, Nguyễn Văn Hương (1970:19) observed: "Hygiene activists, first-aid assistants, midwives, nurses, assistant physicians, doctors, and hospital employees, all have rendered great services to the country. In carrying out their mission, they have all shown revolutionary heroism, working selflessly under enemy fire to save their patients. . . . By daily practice and research work, our health service has made a worthy contribution to the victory of our entire people."

5. On Japan's history of eugenics, see, for instance, Norgren 2001; J. Robertson 2002, 2005; Frühstück 2003.

6. There is a parallel here to Nancy Press and Carole H. Browner's (1997) research on maternal serum alpha fetoprotein (MSAFP) testing in California: this new test was easily accepted, they found, because it was absorbed under the label of uncontroversial antenatal care.

7. The concerns set forth by these physicians resonate with Dorothy C. Wertz and John C. Fletcher's (2004:17) reflections on global inequities in genetic services. Regarding developing countries, they write: "Parents in these countries are cheated in three ways: unequal access to reliable contraceptives, unequal access to prenatal diagnosis and safe abortion, and inadequate health and education services for children with Down syndrome."

8. In today's Vietnam, reproductive health disparities are large, and women's access and use of high-quality antenatal care vary considerably depending on their economic status and place of residence (see Knowles et al. 2010;

Tran et al. 2011). Knowles et al. (2010) found, however, that this inequality decreased significantly between 1992 and 2006.

9. See Williams et al. 2002a–2002d; Farsides et al. 2004; van den Heuvel et al. 2008. As Rapp (1999:97) has shown, however, despite a declared adherence to principles of nondirective counseling, American counselors tend to convey information in ways that take ethnic and class differences into account: "Nondirectiveness is easiest to practice when patients direct themselves."

10. See, for instance, Wertz 2000; Williams et al. 2002a–2002d; Wahlberg 2008.

11. See, for instance, Fan 1997; Renzong 1999; Fagan 2004.

12. For social science critiques of bioethics, see, for instance, R. Fox and Swazey 1984; Das 1999; Kleinman 1999; Petryna 2005; Hamdy 2012. Based on Japanese historical material, J. Robertson (2005) offers an incisive critique of the notion of a singular and monolithic "East Asian bioethics."

13. This description of Bích's first 3D ultrasound scan is based on field notes taken by my colleague Chi.

14. The unease expressed by these physicians resembles that described by Jing-Bao Nie (2005:169) in his research among ob-gyns in China: like their counterparts in Hanoi, these physicians tried to dissuade women from abortions that they considered unnecessary from a medical point of view. On health provider skepticism toward abortion, see also Rivkin-Fish 2005:102–105.

15. Women were, doctors told us, significantly more likely to opt for an abortion for cleft lip-palate if the fetus was female. The marital chances for a girl child, prospective parents felt, would be severely jeopardized by a cleft lip-palate, while those of a boy would not. On the differential values attached to the bodies of boys and girls in Vietnam, see Rydstrøm 2003, 2010.

16. In her PhD thesis on sex-selective abortions in Hanoi, Trần Minh Hằng (2011:215) describes how health providers in Hanoi resort to rituals performed at Buddhist pagodas in order to alleviate their feelings of moral unease over second-trimester pregnancy terminations.

17. For accounts of similar problems in Vietnamese reproductive health care counseling, see Nguyễn M.H. et al. 2007; Nguyễn-võ 2008:98–106. Also my Vietnamese co-researchers were struck by the limitations of the care that women received. Several of them published articles in Vietnamese peer-reviewed journals focusing on these problems (see, for instance, Đỗ Thị Thanh Toàn et al. 2005). Heightened professional vulnerabilities in the realm of obstetrics and gynecology are, however, not unique to Vietnam. In a study of maternity care in South Africa, for instance, Rachel Jewkes and her colleagues draw linkages between such professional vulnerabilities and providers' tendencies to humiliate and abuse their patients: "Part of the vulnerability of Kwazola midwives stemmed from the inherently unpredictable nature of birthing, complications can rapidly develop during an apparently normal pregnancy or birth. . . . This may have been a factor underlying the preoccupation in the Kwazola midwife interviews with controlling the workplace and patients" (Jewkes et al. 1998:1789).

18. See, for instance, Jewkes et al. 1998 on South Africa; Van Hollen 2003:130 on India; Dalsgaard 2004:152 on Brazil; and Rivkin-Fish 2005:73 on Russia.

19. Due to the considerable revenues generated by informal patient payments (see chapter 1), there are strong incentives for physicians to seek employment at the major urban hospitals that serve the wealthier segments of the population.

20. The atmosphere in the 3D scanning room was strikingly different. Since the fee for 3D scans was relatively high, ample time was allocated for each scan. Moreover, the room was quite small and a maximum of seven women were allowed to wait inside; if more women entered, the nurse would ask them to wait outside, "otherwise we cannot breathe in here." The tone in which health staff working in the 3D scanning room talked to women was markedly different from the one I sometimes overheard in the antenatal care rooms; in the scanning room, providers would usually address women courteously, often taking time to ask questions about their family or their general state of health. Since the health providers working in the antenatal care rooms and in the 3D scanning room were sometimes the same individuals, and the patient groups similar, I take this difference in tone as an indication that the working conditions of staff were a key factor shaping patient-provider interactions and quality of care in this hospital. On the consequences of overcrowdedness in health care facilities for quality of care, see also Van Hollen 2003:126; V.H. Luong 2007:135–136.

21. Existing anthropological research shows that genetic testing does not necessarily eliminate ambiguity; in some respects it tends to intensify clinical uncertainties (e.g., Rapp 1999). Soon after I conducted this fieldwork, amniocentesis was made available at the hospital. When I visited in 2009, an entire department for prenatal screening had been established, offering 2D, 3D, and 4D ultrasounds as well as genetic testing and counseling.

22. Physicians insisted, however, that despite the fact that they were not always able to establish a diagnosis of the fetal condition, they did have the experience required to ensure that abortions were medically justified. Autopsies were not performed, but doctors always examined the fetal body after the pregnancy termination, comparing the prenatal assessment of the problem to the condition observed post-abortion.

23. An emergent literature points to the existence of alternative ethics also in Western contexts. Drawing on fieldwork in Danish clinical settings, for instance, Nete Schwennesen and Lene Koch note that the ethics of nondirective counseling and autonomous decision making coexists with professional moral ideals that stress more active care and intervention: "Such modes of doing good care express an ethics of being locally accountable for the ways in which programmes of prenatal testing inevitably intervene in pregnant women's lives and of taking responsibility for the entities and phenomena that emerge through such knowledge production" (Schwennesen and Koch 2012:295).

5. "HOW HAVE WE LIVED?"

1. A rich anthropological literature examines reproductive disruptions caused by infertility, pregnancy loss, abortions, maternal deaths, and unexpected pregnancy outcomes (see, for instance, Layne 2003; Inhorn 2009 [2007]). In this chapter, however, I focus on misfortune rather than disruption.

Following Susan R. Whyte (1997), I see reproductive problems as one among many categories of misfortune—understood as "failures of the good life"—with which human beings have to deal. Misfortune reveals, as Whyte points out, the uncertain and indeterminate nature of life, demanding intellectual, spiritual, and practical responses.

2. The literature on religious and spiritual practice in Vietnam has expanded considerably over the past decade, in parallel with the increasing official acceptance of people's engagements with the other world. See, for instance. P. Taylor 2004a, 2007; DiGregorio and Salemink 2007; Norton 2009.

3. Today's state-sector labor market is politicized in a similar manner: an individual's career opportunities will be severely constrained if his or her family record (lý lịch) shows a history of collaboration with enemy forces.

4. Hue-Tam Ho Tai 1985:27. On practices and interpretations of Buddhism in contemporary Vietnam, see Soucy 2000; Malarney 2002; P. Taylor 2004a, 2007; Leshkowich 2006.

5. In her study of medical texts of late imperial China, Charlotte Furth (1995) notes that adulthood was achieved only when men and women had moved "from birth to birth" by marrying and having their own children, thereby contributing to the cycle linking generations; it was through successful biological reproduction that social maturity within the family was attained.

6. See French 1994; Mrozik 2007. On the roles played by notions of karma in genetics and prenatal screening, see Kato 2010a; Simpson 2007, 2010.

7. See O'Flaherty 1980; M. G. Weiss 1980; Wadley 1983. M. G. Weiss writes that some Buddhist texts ascribe defects in offspring to the behaviors of the parents, "with no mention of the child's karma" (1980:100). For discussions of intergenerational karmic linkages in Vietnamese contexts, see Pashigian 2009; Phạm and Eipper 2009.

8. Khuyết tật is, however, preferred over tàn tật by disability organizations, as the former term suggests that the disabled person still possesses skills and capacities.

9. These cosmological connotations differ markedly from those that the terms disability and handicap bear in Western discourse, where, as Susan R. Whyte and Benedicte Ingstad (1995:7–8) point out, these terms have connotations of competition and efforts to create equality.

10. In Hanoi, Caesarean section rates have risen sharply over the past few years. Women seem to find this intervention attractive, partly because of the assumed greater safety of the birth and partly due to the possibility of timing it astrologically.

11. See D. Fox 2007; Johansson 2007.

12. This account of Liên's experiences in the hospital is based on field notes taken by my colleague Toàn.

13. A report on occupational health in Vietnam notes: "Due to the market economic mechanism, many farmers have abused pesticides in agriculture . . . in vegetable-grow[ing] areas out[side] of Hanoi, many farmers even used forbidden pesticides such as Methamidophos. . . . Farmers also tend to use pesticides that are cheap and have strong effect regardless of safety. Furthermore, farmers do not use personal protective equipment during spraying pesticides. Many

users of agriculture products have therefore engaged pesticide poisoning" (Nguyen T.H.T. et al. 2004:13–14).

14. For anthropological studies of (reproductive) health damage done by chemical contamination, see Das 1995; Layne 2001; Petryna 2002.

15. The fact that the consequences of congenital disabilities reach beyond the affected individual, impacting also the future life chances of other family members, seems to be one of the reasons why people in Vietnam tend to consider congenital disabilities to be more severe than impairments acquired later in life.

16. For other ethnographic observations of the ways in which the domains that people label scientific and supernatural, respectively, merge in realms of high-tech reproduction, see Simpson 2004, 2009; Bharadwaj 2006a, 2006b; Paxson 2006; Pashigian 2009; Kato 2010a; Roberts 2012.

6. BEYOND KNOWLEDGE

1. See, for instance, Rapp 1999; Statham et al. 2000; McCoyd 2007.

2. Women who had abortions for fetal anomaly were placed in the hospital's department for reproductive disorders. So were women who had experienced pregnancy complications, but ended up giving birth to a live child. Since hospital facilities were overcrowded, it was not possible to offer these two groups of patients separate rooms, just as it was often not possible to offer women separate beds. Private rooms required payment of an extra fee that not all women could afford.

3. This resembles the decision-making processes that Rapp (1999:226) has described. Decisions made on the basis of a positive prenatal diagnosis, she found, reflected "the prior knowledge, attitudes, and beliefs that pregnant women and their supporters hold about specific disabling conditions, as well as about childhood disability in general" (see also Lippman 1999b; Statham 2002; France et al. 2011, 2012).

4. Dũng died in 2010 at the age of nine. Carrying him in his arms, his eighty-six-year-old grandfather stumbled and fell as he stepped out of their house. The old man's weight, Dũng's mother told us, crushed all the bones in the boy's body.

5. Several studies conducted in Vietnam have documented the social and financial difficulties experienced by families in which one or more persons are disabled. See, for instance, Lê Bạch Dương et al. 2008; Mont and Cuong 2011. As in many other countries, taking care of disabled family members is a highly gendered task, much of the labor being undertaken by women.

6. Given the strong son preference that prevails in Vietnam, it was probably no coincidence that all thirteen children were male.

7. To cope with this situation, two parents had to leave their home to take on higher-paying migrant work: Phương left her infant son in the care of her mother, engaging in trade on the border between China and Vietnam, and Lan's husband, Anh, left their village in order to work at a factory in another town.

8. Previous studies of prenatal screening have come to similar conclusions, finding that the choice that people face when receiving an adverse diagnosis is largely theoretical. See, for instance, Green and Statham 1999.

9. In the years that have passed since this fieldwork was conducted, however, the tone of the Vietnamese mass media has changed, and public attention is now often drawn to the barriers that discriminatory attitudes place on disabled people's full participation in society (see Nguyen Thi Xuan Thuy 2011).

10. In a few cases, people of the elder generation would suggest that a damaged fetus was not a human being. Encouraging Mai to terminate her pregnancy, for instance, her grandmother asserted: "This is not a human being, it's a monstrous fetus" (*nó không là người, nó là quái thai*).

11. See Strathern 1992; Whyte and Ingstad 1995; Conklin and Morgan 1996; Landsman 2009.

12. See Scheper-Hughes 1992; M. Weiss 1994; Whyte and Ingstad 1995; Morgan 1996; Einarsdóttir 2004.

13. Needless to say, despite these claims of acceptance, disabled people living in the Western world continue to meet prejudice and discrimination and often lack social and financial support (see Rapp and Ginsburg 2001; Landsman 2009).

14. On the conditioning of Vietnamese moralities by relations of reciprocity, see Soucy 2000; P. Taylor 2004a:224; Jellema 2005, 2007. The notion of intergenerational moral debt is an important cultural concept throughout East Asia (see, for instance, Stafford 1995; Oxfeld 2010).

15. When the Vietnamese state distributes disability support, this also takes place on the basis of principles of moral reciprocation. As mentioned in chapter 1, only a minority of Vietnam's disabled population receives support from the state, but if the impairment stems from military service for the revolutionary cause, a monthly allowance is granted. This allowance is, then, offered not merely on the basis of the biomedical problem at issue but also as a moral gesture of reciprocity and gratitude.

16. Notably, one of the terms for "complete" that people often used to characterize nondisabled people—*hoàn chỉnh*—in itself connotes reciprocity; *hoàn* means "to return," while *chỉnh* can be translated as "right," "straight," or "correct."

17. In her study of China's late imperial period, Furth (1995:177) notes that in Confucian doctrine, children were considered to belong to parents. Commenting on images of children in early Chinese art, Wu Hung (1995:82) makes similar observations. There was, he writes, a "belief that only the bond between parent and child was reliable; all other kin and nonkin relationships were to be treated with suspicion. But the problem was that the parent/child tie was inevitably challenged and conditioned by death." In Vietnam, official discourses on citizenship and child socialization place similar emphasis on parental responsibilities. The mutual obligations between parents and children are enshrined in article 64 of Vietnam's 1992 Constitution: "Parents are duty bound to bring up and educate their children into useful citizens of society. Children have an obligation to respect and care for their grandparents and parents." In the current era of market reform, the parent-child nexus seems to be invested with increasing moral-political importance. In a typical statement, an official publication on the challenges faced by today's Vietnamese family declares that "the Vietnamese family lives for its children. The upbringing of children truly is both the duty and the function of the family. The bad things, the faults in children are often

created by the family, therefore 'children are spoilt by their mother, grandchild-ren are spoilt by their grandmother' (*con hư tại mẹ, cháu hư tại bà*)" (Uỷ Ban Dân Số, Gia Đình và Trẻ Em 2004:69). Like many other official statements, this publication emphasized the gendered nature of parental civic obligations, placing special responsibilities on the shoulders of women.

18. Mothers, in particular, often stressed their own sacrifices on behalf of their children. This is not unique to parents of disabled children. As Alexander Soucy (2000:193) observes, "A great deal of women's energy is spent cultivat-ing these moral debts (*ơn*) in their husbands and especially in their children, for it is these debts that give them a platform on which they can build capital within family relations." See also Gammeltoft 1999, 2008a.

19. As one official publication states, "The family has many functions, but the greatest and the most sacred (*thiêng liêng*) is that of moral instruction (*giáo dục*). The family must have children . . . and must teach the children so that they become persons (*thành người*)" (Vũ Ngọc Khánh 2008:14–15).

7. QUESTIONS OF CONSCIENCE

1. Half a year later, Quý got pregnant again. At 4:50 in the morning of April 11, 2006, she called my colleague Hiệp to say that she and Hinh were on their way to the obstetrics hospital for the delivery. Hiệp and I found them later that day in the maternity ward, beaming. Their son weighed three kilos and had been declared entirely healthy. His picture is on the front cover of this book.

2. Drawing mainly on ethnographic material from the United States, an important branch of feminist literature has shown how the personhood of fetuses is socially and politically produced, with far-ranging consequences for reproductive medicine and women's lives (see, for instance, Petchesky 1984; Casper 1998; Morgan and Michaels 1999; Mitchell 2001). In this chapter I build on these insights, basing my account on the assumption that there is rea-son to pay close ethnographic attention to the specific ways in which fetuses are brought into being in different social contexts. As Laury Oaks (1999:193) observes: "A valuable feminist project would be to make fetuses more visible— not in the independent, free-floating way that pro-life images do—but in richly textured ways that recognize different fetuses in specific women's bodies at dif-ferent stages in women's lives."

3. See Gammeltoft 2002. Numerous ethnographic studies have shown how biomedical interventions are associated with a modern, educated attitude to life. See, for instance, Van Hollen 2003; V.H. Luong 2007.

4. For reflections on the ways in which people tie themselves into—or untie themselves from—social and political collectives through intimate acts of loy-alty or betrayal, see Thiranagama and Kelly 2010.

5. On such chosen losses, see Rapp 1999:225–228; Layne 2003; Sandelowski and Barroso 2005.

6. This technique of dismembering the fetus was rarely used at the hospital. In Mây's case doctors resorted to it only to avoid a Caesarean section. Due to the risk of uterine rupture, women in Vietnam are usually not allowed to have more than two C-sections in a reproductive lifetime. For women such as Mây

who do not yet have children, the consequence of an abortion performed through C-section can therefore be that they can have only one child, as their next pregnancy may also end in a C-section. When Mây's labor did not proceed as expected, therefore, the physicians attending to her recommended dismemberment of the fetus in order not to compromise her future childbearing.

7. Some women, however, commented that meeting the fetus through the 3D scanning image made them feel more attached to it. Lý, for instance, said: "The first two times I did not see anything. But this time I think it will take a long time for me to forget, because I have seen the fetus in the 3D scanning picture."

8. Vietnam differs from other countries with a strong preference for sons, such as India and China, in that there is no tradition of female infanticide. The skewed sex ratio at birth did not arise until ultrasounds in combination with abortion became widely available in the country at the beginning of the twenty-first century.

9. Levinas claims that the face is not a concrete object of perception; rather, access to the face is a question of proximity: "The relation with the face can surely be dominated by perception, but what is specifically the face is what cannot be reduced to that" (1985b [1982]:85–86).

10. As we have seen, Mai's grandmother insisted that this fetus had not been a human being, but an evil spirit (con quỷ). In all other families we visited, the child-to-be was defined as a human life (một đời người or, in Buddhist terms, một kiếp người) and a potential family member.

11. Previous research on abortion for fetal anomaly has found that questions of how to treat the deceased fetal body often pose significant moral and emotional challenges to parents (Sandelowski and Barroso 2005). For discussions of the politics involved when fetal remains are produced and disposed of, see Morgan 2002, 2009.

12. Like the souls of adults, child-spirits are expected to pass over into an existence in the other world. But if a child dies very young, its relatives do not always try to tie it to their households. Instead, its spirit may be encouraged to go to another house or to a pagoda, where monks or nuns will care for it. The ethnographic literature offers numerous accounts of "spirit children" who hover between this and the other world; see, for instance, Scheper-Hughes 1992:430; Montgomery 2009:87–95.

13. Kwon (2006:71) writes that survivors of the Mỹ Lai and Hà Mỹ massacres still commemorated their war-killed children but that such practices were considered strictly private.

14. In Vietnam's recent past, infant death rates were high and some women would lose one child after another. When this happened, people often suspected that it was the same child who kept coming back to the woman. To determine if this was the case, they would mark the deceased infant's body with ink (đánh dấu); this treatment, people hoped, would ensure that the fetal spirit was born into another household in its next incarnation.

15. See, for instance, LaFleur 1992; Oaks 1994; Hardacre 1997; Moskowitz 2001. Feminists have criticized the Japanese mizuko rituals for placing responsibility for reproductive misfortune on women and for exploiting them financially.

16. This contrasts with current health care practices in the United States and Europe, where emphasis is placed on allowing the parents of deceased infants and fetuses to hold and mourn the fetus they have lost (see Layne 2003; Sandelowski and Barroso 2005).

17. Layne's ethnographic account of the importance that parents in the United States place on the naming of stillborn children offers an interesting point of comparison to the Vietnamese case. Through naming, Layne notes, "the baby is being constructed as part of the collective identity of the family" (2003:225).

18. Ann Marie Leshkowich (2008:34) shows that ghost metaphors are used in postwar southern Vietnam to capture struggles over economic resources and social status. The image of ghosts, she argues, "alludes to fragments of the past that cannot be incorporated into publicly voiced, shared representations."

Bibliography

Allen, Lori A.

    2009   Martyr Bodies in the Media: Human Rights, Aesthetics, and the Politics of Immediation in the Palestinian Intifada. *American Ethnologist* 36(1):161–180.

Anagnost, Ann

    2004   The Corporeal Politics of Quality (*Suzhi*). *Public Culture* 16(2):189–208.

Aretxaga, Begoña

    2003   Maddening States. *Annual Review of Anthropology* 32:393–410.

Asad, Talal

    2003   *Formations of the Secular: Christianity, Islam, Modernity.* Stanford: Stanford University Press.

Bao Ninh

    1993   *The Sorrow of War.* English version by Frank Palmos. Vo Bang Thanh, Phan Thanh Hao, with Katerina Pierce, trans. London: Secker and Warburg.

Barbieri, Magali, and Danièle Bélanger, eds.

    2009   *Reconfiguring Families in Contemporary Vietnam.* Stanford: Stanford University Press.

Barthes, Roland

    1993   [1977] The Third Meaning. In *Image, Music, Text.* Stephen Heath, trans. Pp. 52–68. London: Fontana Press.

Bashour, Hyam, Raghda Hafez, and Asmaa Abdulsalam

    2005   Syrian Women's Perceptions and Experiences of Ultrasound Screening in Pregnancy: Implications for Antenatal Policy. *Reproductive Health Matters* 13(25):147–54.

Battaglia, Debbora
     1999   Toward an Ethics of the Open Subject: Writing Culture in Good
            Conscience. In *Anthropological Theory Today*. Henrietta Moore,
            ed. Pp. 114–150. Cambridge: Polity Press.
Bauer, Susanne, and Ayo Wahlberg
     2009   *Contested Categories: Life Sciences in Society.* Farnham, Surrey:
            Ashgate.
Bélanger, Danièle, and Khuat Thi Hai Oanh
     2009   Second-Trimester Abortions and Sex-Selection of Children in Hanoi,
            Vietnam. *Population Studies* 63(2):163–171.
Belizan, J.
     1998   *Ultrasound for Fetal Assessment in Early Pregnancy: RHL Com-
            mentary* (Last Revised, 22 September 1998). The WHO Reproduc-
            tive Health Library. Geneva: World Health Organization.
Bharadwaj, Aditya
     2006a Sacred Conceptions: Clinical Theodicies, Uncertain Science, and
            Technologies of Procreation in India. *Culture, Medicine, and Psychi-
            atry* 30(4):451–465.
     2006b Sacred Modernity: Religion, Infertility, and Technoscientific Con-
            ception around the Globe. *Culture, Medicine, and Psychiatry*
            30(4):423–425.
Bích Thuận
     2005   Nước Mỹ Phải Có Trách Nhiệm (The U.S. Must Take Responsibil-
            ity). *Hà Nội Mới* (New Hanoi), March 30:4.
Biehl, João, Byron Good, and Arthur Kleinman
     2007   *Subjectivity: Ethnographic Investigations.* Berkeley: University of
            California Press.
Bộ Y Tế (Ministry of Health)
     2008   Nâng Cao Chất Lượng Dân Số Việt Nam Giai Đoạn 2008–2020.
            Bản Thảo (Strengthening Vietnam's Population Quality in the 2008–
            2020 Period. Draft). Hanoi.
Bodenhorn, Barbara, and Gabriele vom Bruck
     2006   "Entangled in Histories": An Introduction to the Anthropology of
            Names and Naming. In *The Anthropology of Names and Naming.*
            Gabriele vom Bruck and Barbara Bodenhorn, eds. Pp. 1–30. Cam-
            bridge: Cambridge University Press.
Borneman, John
     1992   *Belonging in the Two Berlins: Kin, State, Nation.* Cambridge: Cam-
            bridge University Press.
Borton, Lady
     n.d.   *Learning to Work in Vietnam.* New York: U.S.-Indochina Recon-
            ciliation Project.
Bourdieu, Pierre
     1977   *Outline of a Theory of Practice.* Richard Nice, trans. Cambridge:
            Cambridge University Press.
     2000   *Pascalian Meditations.* Richard Nice, trans. Stanford: Stanford
            University Press.

Bridges, Khiara
    2011   *Reproducing Race: An Ethnography of Pregnancy as a Site of Racialization.* Berkeley: University of California Press.
Broberg, Gunnar, and Nils Roll-Hansen, eds.
    2005   *Eugenics and the Welfare State: Sterilization Policy in Denmark, Sweden, Norway, and Finland.* East Lansing: Michigan State University Press.
Browner, Carole H., and Carolyn F. Sargent
    2011a Introduction: Toward Global Anthropological Studies of Reproduction: Concepts, Methods, Theoretical Approaches. In *Reproduction, Globalization, and the State: New Theoretical and Ethnographic Perspectives.* Carole H. Browner and Carolyn F. Sargent, eds. Pp. 1–17. Durham, NC: Duke University Press.
    2011b (eds.) *Reproduction, Globalization, and the State: New Theoretical and Ethnographic Perspectives.* Durham, NC: Duke University Press.
Bùi Kim Chi
    2010   Reproductive Choices among HIV Positive Women in Northern Vietnam. PhD Dissertation. Faculty of Health Sciences, University of Copenhagen.
Casper, Monica J.
    1998   *The Making of the Unborn Patient: A Social Anatomy of Fetal Surgery.* New Brunswick, NJ: Rutgers University Press.
CGFED (Research Center for Gender, Family and Environment in Development)
    n.d.   The U.S. Must Accept Full Responsibility for the Consequences of Dioxin Spraying on Vietnamese Territory! Pamphlet.
Chadwick, Ruth
    1999   Genetics, Choice, and Responsibility. *Health, Risk and Society* 1(3): 293–300.
Chánh Công Phan
    1993   The Viêtnamese Concept of the Human Souls and the Rituals of Birth and Death. *Southeast Asian Journal of Social Science* 21(2):159–198.
Choi, H., M. Van Riper, and S. Thoyre
    2012   Decision Making Following a Prenatal Diagnosis of Down Syndrome: An Integrative Review. *Journal of Midwifery and Women's Health* 57(2):156–164.
Cohen, Richard A.
    2006   Introduction: Humanism and Anti-humanism—Levinas, Cassirer, and Heidegger. In *Emmanuel Levinas: Humanism of the Other.* Nidra Poller, trans. Pp. vii-xliv. Urbana: University of Illinois Press.
Conklin, Beth A., and Lynn M. Morgan
    1996   Babies, Bodies, and the Production of Personhood in North America and a Native Amazonian Society. *Ethos* 24(4):657–694.
Craig, David
    2002   *Familiar Medicine: Everyday Health Knowledge and Practice in Today's Vietnam.* Honolulu: University of Hawai'i Press.

Critchley, Simon

2002   Introduction. In *The Cambridge Companion to Levinas*. Simon Critchley and Robert Bernasconi, eds. Pp. 1–32. Cambridge: Cambridge University Press.

Dalsgaard, Anne Line

2004   *Matters of Life and Longing: Female Sterilisation in Northeast Brazil*. Copenhagen: Museum Tusculanum Press.

Đặng Cảnh Khanh

2009   Đi Tìm Những Đặc Trưng Của Gia Đình Việt Nam Truyền Thống (Searching for the Characteristics of the Traditional Vietnamese Family). In *Nghiên Cứu Gia Đình và Giới Thời Kỳ Đổi Mới* (Research on Family and Gender in the Đổi Mới Era). Nguyễn Hữu Minh and Trần Thị Vân Anh, eds. Pp. 128–165. Hanoi: Nhà Xuất Bản Khoa Học Xã Hội (Social Sciences Publishing House).

Das, Veena

1995   *Critical Events: An Anthropological Perspective on Contemporary India*. Delhi: Oxford University Press.

1999   Public Good, Ethics, and Everyday Life: Beyond the Boundaries of Bioethics. *Daedalus* 128(4):99–133.

2007   *Life and Words: Violence and the Descent into the Ordinary*. Berkeley: University of California Press.

2010   The Life of Humans and the Life of Roaming Spirits. In *Rethinking the Human*. J. Michelle Molina and Donald K. Swearer, eds. Pp. 31–50. Cambridge, MA: Center for the Study of World Religions, Harvard Divinity School.

Das, Veena, and Renu Addlakha

2001   Disability and Domestic Citizenship: Voice, Gender, and the Making of the Subject. *Public Culture* 13(3):511–531.

Deolalikar, Anil

2009   Health Care and the Family in Vietnam. In *Reconfiguring Families in Contemporary Vietnam*. Magali Barbieri and Danièle Bélanger, eds. Pp. 75–94. Stanford: Stanford University Press.

Dewey, John

1929   *The Quest for Certainty: A Study of the Relation of Knowledge and Action*. New York: Minton, Balch and Company.

1968   [1916] *Democracy and Education*. New York: Free Press.

DiGregorio, Michael, and Oscar Salemink

2007   Living with the Dead: The Politics of Ritual and Remembrance in Contemporary Vietnam. *Journal of Southeast Asian Studies* 38(3):433–440.

Dikötter, Frank

1998   *Imperfect Conceptions: Medical Knowledge, Birth Defects and Eugenics in China*. New York: Columbia University Press.

Đỗ Thị Thanh Toàn, Nguyễn Thị Thúy Hạnh, Nguyễn Huy Bạo, and Tine Gammeltoft

2005   Tư Vấn Trong Thời Kỳ Mang Thai: Một Việc Làm Thiết Thực Cho Những Hoàn Cảnh Thai Bất Thường (Pregnancy Counseling: An

Urgent Task When a Fetus Is Not Normal). *Tạp Chí Nghiên Cứu Y Học* (Journal of Medical Research) 39(6):90–96.

Đoàn Đức Minh
    n.d.   *Suffering and Smiles*. New York: Cosmos Communications.

Dow Chemical Company
    2013   Agent Orange. http://www.dow.com/sustainability/debates/agentor-ange/. Accessed March 23, 2013.

Drummond, Lisa
    2004   The Modern "Vietnamese Woman": Socialization and Women's Magazines. In *Gender Practices in Contemporary Vietnam*. Lisa Drummond and Helle Rydstrøm, eds. Pp. 158–178. Singapore: Singapore University Press.

Duster, Troy
    2003   *Backdoor to Eugenics*. New York: Routledge.

Einarsdóttir, Jónína
    2004   *Tired of Weeping: Mother Love, Child Death, and Poverty in Guinea-Bissau*. Madison: University of Wisconsin Press.

Erikson, Susan
    2007   Fetal Views: Histories and Habits of Looking at the Fetus in Germany. *Journal of Medical Humanities* 28:187–212.
    2011   Global Ethnography: Problems of Theory and Method. In *Reproduction, Globalization, and the State: New Theoretical and Ethnographic Perspectives*. Carole H. Browner and Carolyn F. Sargent, eds. Pp. 23–37. Durham, NC: Duke University Press.

Evens, T. M. S.
    2006   Some Ontological Implications of Situational Analysis. In *The Manchester School: Practice and Ethnographic Praxis in Anthropology*. T. M. S. Evens and Don Handelman, eds. Pp. 49–63. New York: Berghahn Books.

Fagan, Andrew
    2004   Challenging the Bioethical Application of the Autonomy Principle within Multicultural Societies. *Journal of Applied Philosophy* 21(1):15–31.

Fan, Ruiping
    1997   Self-Determination vs. Family-Determination: Two Incommensurable Principles of Autonomy. *Bioethics* 11(3–4):309–322.

Farsides, Bobbie, Clare Williams, and Priscilla Alderson
    2004   Aiming Towards "Moral Equilibrium": Health Care Professionals' Views on Working within the Morally Contested Field of Antenatal Screening. *Journal of Medical Ethics* 30(5):505–509.

Fassin, Didier
    2007   Humanitarianism as a Politics of Life. *Public Culture* 19:(3):499–520.
    2012   *Humanitarian Reason: A Moral History of the Present*. Berkeley: University of California Press.

Ferguson, James, and Akhil Gupta
    2002   Spatializing States: Toward an Ethnography of Neoliberal Governmentality. *American Ethnologist* 29(4):981–1002.

Feuchtwang, Stephan

    2003   An Unsafe Distance. In *Living with Separation in China: Anthropological Accounts*. Charles Stafford, ed. Pp. 85–112. London: Routledge.

Fforde, Adam, and Stefan de Vylder

    1996   *From Plan to Market: The Economic Transition in Vietnam*. Boulder, CO: Westview Press.

Fischer, Michael M. J.

    2007   Epilogue: To Live with What Would Otherwise Be Unendurable: Return(s) to Subjectivities. In *Subjectivity: Ethnographic Investigations*. João Biehl, Byron Good, and Arthur Kleinman, eds. Pp. 423–446. Berkeley: University of California Press.

Foucault, Michel

    2003a On the Genealogy of Ethics: An Overview of Work in Progress. In *The Essential Foucault*. Paul Rabinow and Nikolas Rose, eds. Pp. 102–125. New York: The New Press.

    2003b The Ethics of the Concern of the Self as a Practice of Freedom. In *The Essential Foucault*. Paul Rabinow and Nikolas Rose, eds. Pp. 25–42. P. Aranov and D. McGrawth, trans. New York: The New Press.

    2003c The Subject and Power. In *The Essential Foucault*. Paul Rabinow and Nikolas Rose, eds. Pp. 126–144. New York: The New Press.

Fox, Diane Niblack

    2003   Chemical Politics and the Hazards of Modern Warfare: Agent Orange. In *Synthetic Planet: Chemical Politics and the Hazards of Modern Life*. Monica Casper, ed. Pp. 73–90. New York: Routledge.

    2007   "One Significant Ghost": Agent Orange Narratives of Trauma, Survival, and Responsibility. PhD dissertation. Department of Anthropology, University of Washington.

Fox, Renée C., and Judith P. Swazey

    1984   Medical Morality Is Not Bioethics: Medical Ethics in China and the United States. *Perspectives in Biology and Medicine* 27(3): 336–360.

France, Emma F., Sally Wyke, Sue Ziebland, Vikki A. Entwistle, and Kate Hunt

    2011   How Personal Experiences Feature in Women's Accounts of Use of Information for Decisions about Antenatal Diagnostic Testing for Foetal Abnormality. *Social Science and Medicine* 72(5):755–762.

France, E. F., L. Locock, K. Hunt, S. Ziebland, K. Field, and S. Wyke

    2012   Imagined Futures: How Experiential Knowledge of Disability Affects Parents' Decision-Making about Fetal Abnormality. *Health Expectations* 15(2):139–156.

Franklin, Sarah, and Helena Ragoné, eds.

    1998   *Reproducing Reproduction: Kinship, Power, and Technological Innovation*. Philadelphia: University of Pennsylvania Press.

Franklin, Sarah, and Celia Roberts

    2006   *Born and Made: An Ethnography of Preimplantation Genetic Diagnosis*. Princeton: Princeton University Press.

French, Lindsay

1994   The Political Economy of Injury and Compassion: Amputees on the Thai-Cambodia Border. In *Embodiment and Experience: The Existential Ground of Culture and Self.* Thomas Csordas, ed. Pp. 69–99. Cambridge: Cambridge University Press.

Frühstück, Sabine

2003   *Colonizing Sex: Sexology and Social Control in Modern Japan.* Berkeley: University of California Press.

Fuller, Thomas

2012   4 Decades On, U.S. Starts Cleanup of Agent Orange in Vietnam. *New York Times,* August 10:A4.

Furth, Charlotte

1995   From Birth to Birth: The Growing Body in Chinese Medicine. In *Chinese Views of Childhood.* Anne Behnke Kinney, ed. Pp. 157–191. Honolulu: University of Hawai'i Press.

Gainsborough, Martin

2010   Present but not Powerful: Neoliberalism, the State, and Development in Vietnam. *Globalizations* 7(4):475–488.

Gal, Susan, and Gail Kligman

2000   *The Politics of Gender after Socialism: A Comparative-Historical Essay.* Princeton: Princeton University Press.

Gallo, Maria, and Nguyen C. Nghia

2007   Real Life Is Different: A Qualitative Study of Why Women Delay Abortion until the Second Trimester in Vietnam. *Social Science and Medicine* 64(9):1812–1822.

Gammeltoft, Tine

1999   *Women's Bodies, Women's Worries: Health and Family Planning in a Vietnamese Rural Community.* Richmond, Surrey: Curzon Press.

2001   "Faithful, Heroic, Resourceful": Changing Images of Women in Vietnam. In *Vietnamese Society in Transition: The Daily Politics of Reform and Change.* John Kleinen, ed. Pp. 265–280. Amsterdam: Het Spinhuis.

2002   Between "Science" and "Superstition": Moral Perceptions of Induced Abortion among Young Adults in Vietnam. *Culture, Medicine, and Psychiatry* 26:313–338.

2006   Beyond Being: Emergent Narratives of Suffering in Vietnam. *Journal of the Royal Anthropological Institute* (N.S.) 12(3):589–605.

2007a   Prenatal Diagnosis in Postwar Vietnam: Power, Subjectivity, and Citizenship. *American Anthropologist* 109(1):153–163.

2007b   Sonography and Sociality: Obstetrical Ultrasound Imaging in Urban Vietnam. *Medical Anthropology Quarterly* 21(2):133–153.

2008a   Childhood Disability and Parental Moral Responsibility in Northern Vietnam: Towards Ethnographies of Intercorporeality. *Journal of the Royal Anthropological Institute* 14(4):825–842.

2008b   Figures of Transversality: State Power and Prenatal Screening in Contemporary Vietnam. *American Ethnologist* 35(4):570–587.

2010   Between Remembering and Forgetting: Maintaining Moral Motherhood after Late-Term Abortion. In *Abortion in Asia: Local*

Dilemmas, Global Politics. Andrea Whittaker, ed. Pp. 56–77. New York: Berghahn Books.

2013   Potentiality and Human Temporality: Haunting Futures in Vietnamese Pregnancy Care. *Current Anthropology* 54(S7):S159–S171.

Gammeltoft, Tine, and Nguyễn Thị Thúy Hạnh

2007   The Commodification of Obstetric Ultrasound Scanning in Hanoi, Viet Nam. *Reproductive Health Matters* 15(29):163–171.

Garcia, Jo, Leanne Bricker, Jane Henderson, Marie-Anne Martin, Miranda Mugford, Jim Nielson, and Tracy Roberts

2002   Women's Views of Pregnancy Ultrasound: A Systematic Review. *Birth* 29(4):225–250.

Garcia, Angela

2010   *The Pastoral Clinic: Addiction and Dispossession along the Rio Grande.* Berkeley: University of California Press.

Geertz, Clifford

1993   [1973] *The Interpretation of Cultures: Selected Essays.* London: Fontana Press.

Geissler, Paul Wenzel, and Ruth Jane Prince

2010   *The Land Is Dying: Contingency, Creativity and Conflict in Western Kenya.* New York: Berghahn Books.

Gender and Society Research Center

2012   Petition Demanding the American Pharmaceutical Companies to Take Responsibility for the Alleviation of the Impact from Dioxin Agent Orange. http://gas.hoasen.edu.vn/en/gas-page/petition-demanding-american-pharmaceutical-companies-take-responsibility-alleviation-impact. Accessed March 23, 2013.

Getz, Linn, and Anne Luise Kirkengen

2003   Ultrasound Screening in Pregnancy: Advancing Technology, Soft Markers for Fetal Chromosomal Aberrations, and Unacknowledged Ethical Dilemmas. *Social Science and Medicine* 56(10):2045–2057.

Ginsburg, Faye D., and Rayna Rapp

1991   The Politics of Reproduction. *Annual Review of Anthropology* 20:311–343.

1995a (eds.) *Conceiving the New World Order: The Global Politics of Reproduction.* Berkeley: University of California Press.

1995b Introduction: Conceiving the New World Order. In *Conceiving the New World Order: The Global Politics of Reproduction.* Faye D. Ginsburg and Rayna Rapp, eds. Pp. 1–17. Berkeley: University of California Press.

1999   Fetal Reflections: Confessions of Two Feminist Anthropologists as Mutual Informants. In *Fetal Subjects, Feminist Positions.* Lynn M. Morgan and Meredith W. Michaels, eds. Pp. 279–295. Philadelphia: University of Pennsylvania Press.

Gluckman, Max

2006   [1959] Ethnographic Data in British Social Anthropology. In *The Manchester School: Practice and Ethnographic Praxis in Anthropology.* T. M. S. Evens and Don Handelman, eds. Pp. 13–22. New York: Berghahn Books.

Government of Vietnam

1994 Ordinance on Preferential Treatment of Revolutionary Activists, Fallen Heroes and their Families, War Invalids, Diseased Soldiers, Resistance Activists and People with Meritorious Services to the Revolution. *Official Gazette* 22:5.

2006 *National Action Plan to Support People with Disabilities: 2006–2010.* Hanoi.

Green, Josephine M., Claire Snowdon, and Helen Statham

1993 Pregnant Women's Attitudes to Abortion and Prenatal Screening. *Journal of Reproductive and Infant Psychology* 11(1):31–39.

Green, Josephine, and Helen Statham

1999 Psychosocial Aspects of Prenatal Screening and Diagnosis. In *The Troubled Helix: Social and Psychological Implications of the New Human Genetics.* Theresa Marteau and Martin Richards, eds. Pp. 140–163. Cambridge: Cambridge University Press.

Greenhalgh, Susan

2010 *Cultivating Global Citizens: Population in the Rise of China.* Cambridge, MA: Harvard University Press.

Greenhalgh, Susan, and Edwin A. Winckler

2005 *Governing China's Population: From Leninist to Neoliberal Biopolitics.* Stanford: Stanford University Press.

Gregg, Robin

1995 *Pregnancy in a High-Tech Age: Paradoxes of Choice.* New York: New York University Press.

Griffiths, Philip Jones

2003 *Agent Orange: "Collateral Damage" in Viet Nam.* London: Trolley.

2005 Agent Orange in Viet Nam. *Critical Asian Studies* 37(1):141–160.

Guilmoto, Christophe Z.

2012 Son Preference, Sex Selection, and Kinship in Vietnam. *Population and Development Review* 38(1):31–54.

Gupta, Jyotsna Agnihotri

2000 *New Reproductive Technologies, Women's Health and Autonomy: Freedom or Dependency?* New Delhi: Sage.

2010a Exploring Indian Women's Reproductive Decision-Making Regarding Prenatal Testing. *Culture, Health, and Sexuality* 12(2):191–204.

2010b Private and Public Eugenics: Genetic Testing and Screening in India. In *Frameworks of Choice: Predictive and Genetic Testing in Asia.* Margaret Sleeboom-Faulkner, ed. Pp. 43–64. Amsterdam: Amsterdam University Press.

Gustafsson, Mai Lan

2009 *War and Shadows: The Haunting of Vietnam.* Ithaca, NY: Cornell University Press.

Hà Anh

2009 Sàng Lọc Trước Sinh và Sơ Sinh ở Hà Nội: Kết Quả Chưa Cao (Prenatal and Neonatal Screening in Hanoi: Not Yet Good Results). *Gia Đình và Xã Hội* (Family and Society) September 28:6.

Hà Thư

2009a   Công Tác DS-KHHGĐ Trong Giai Đoạn Tới: Khó Khăn Bội Phần
(Population and Family Planning Work in the Coming Stage: Great
Difficulties). *Gia Đình và Xã Hội* (Family and Society) August 21:6.

2009b   Mô Hình 'Tư Vấn Và Kiểm Tra Sức Khỏe Tiền Hôn Nhân': Giảm
Thiểu Tỉ Lệ Dị Tật Bẩm Sinh (Counseling and Health Examinations
Prior to Marriage: Reducing the Rate of Congenital Malformations).
Gia Đình và Xã Hội (Family and Society) September 9:6.

2010a   Dị Tật Bẩm Sinh Và Những Nỗi Đau: Mẹ Chủ Quan, Con Dị Tật
(Congenital Malformations and Feelings of Pain: When Mothers
Don't Care, Children are Born Disabled). *Gia Đình và Xã Hội*
(Family and Society), August 11:6.

2010b   Dị Tật Bẩm Sinh Và Những Nỗi Đau: Phủ Sóng Nhận Thức (Congenital Malformations and Feelings of Pain: Inadequate Parental
Knowledge). *Gia Đình và Xã Hội* (Family and Society) August 18:6.

2010c   Dị Tật Bẩm Sinh Và Những Nỗi Đau: Sàng Lọc Tới 95% Hội Chứng
Down (Congenital Malformations and Feelings of Pain: Screening
up to 95% of Down Syndrome Cases). *Gia Đình và Xã Hội* (Family
and Society) August 16:6.

2010d   Dị Tật Bẩm Sinh Và Những Nỗi Đau: Thủ Phạm Giấu Mặt (Congenital Malformations and Feelings of Pain: The Hidden Perpetrator).
Gia Đình và Xã Hội (Family and Society) August 13:6.

Hà Thư and Hồng Sơn

2009   Những Trái Tim vì Cộng Đồng (Having a Heart for the Community).
Gia Đình và Xã Hội (Family and Society) July 10:7.

Hairong, Yan

2003   Neoliberal Governmentality and Neohumanism: Organizing Suzhi/
Value Flow through Labor Recruitment Networks. *Cultural Anthropology* 18(4):493–523.

Hamdy, Sherine

2012   *Our Bodies Belong to God: Organ Transplants, Islam, and the Struggle
for Human Dignity in Egypt.* Berkeley: University of California Press.

Han, Sallie

2009   Seeing Like a Family: Fetal Ultrasound Images and Imaginings of
Kin. In *Imagining the Fetus: The Unborn in Myth, Religion, and
Culture.* Vanessa R. Sasson and Jane Marie Law, eds. Pp. 275–290.
Oxford: Oxford University Press.

Hardacre, Helen

1997   *Marketing the Menacing Fetus in Japan.* Berkeley: University of
California Press.

Harms, Erik

2012   Neo-Geomancy and Real Estate Fever in Postreform Vietnam. *positions: east asia cultures critique* 20(2):405–434.

Harris, Gillian, Linda Connor, Andrew Bisits, and Nick Higginbotham

2004   "Seeing the Baby": Pleasures and Dilemmas of Ultrasound Technologies for Primiparous Australian Women. *Medical Anthropology
Quarterly* 18(1):23–47.

Henshaw, Stanley K., Susheela Singh, and Taylor Haas
    1999   The Incidence of Abortion Worldwide. *International Family Planning Perspectives* 25 (Supplement):S30-S38.

Hồ Chí Minh
    1988   *Về Tư Cách Người Đảng Viên Cộng Sản* (On the Behavior of Communist Party Members). Hanoi: Nhà Xuất Bản Sự Thật (Truth Publishing House).

Hoang, Tuyet T.D., Thuy Phan, and Trang Huynh N.K.
    2008   Second Trimester Abortion in Vietnam: Changing to Recommended Methods and Improving Service Delivery. *Reproductive Health Matters* 16(31 Supplement):145–150.

Hoàng Bá Thịnh
    2006   Families of Agent Orange/Dioxin Victims of the Third Generation. *Anthropology Review* 1(8):101–110.

Hoàng Đình Cầu, Nguyễn Tuấn Anh, and Phùng Trí Dũng
    2001   Ảnh Hưởng Của Chất Độc Hoá Học Trong Chiến Tranh Đến Chất Lượng Dân Số (The Influence of Wartime Toxic Chemicals on Population Quality). *Dân Số và Phát Triển* (Population and Development) 9:7–8.

Hoàng Phê
    1994   *Từ Điển Tiếng Việt* (Vietnamese Language Dictionary). Hanoi: Nhà Xuất Bản Khoa Học Xã Hội (Social Sciences Publishing House).

Hue-Tam Ho Tai
    1985   Religion in Vietnam: A World of Gods and Spirits. In *Vietnam: Essays on History, Culture and Society.* David W.P. Elliott, Gerald Canon Hickey, Nguyen Ngoc Bich, Hue-Tam Ho Tai, and Alexander Woodside, eds. Pp. 22–39. New York: Asia Society.
    2001   Introduction: Situating Memory. In *The Country of Memory: Remaking the Past in Late Socialist Vietnam.* Hue-Tam Ho Tai, ed. Pp. 1–17. Berkeley: University of California Press.

Humphrey, Caroline
    2008   Reassembling Individual Subjects: Events and Decisions in Troubled Times. *Anthropological Theory* 8(4):357–380.

Hung, Wu
    1995   Private Love and Public Duty: Images of Children in Early Chinese Art. In *Chinese Views of Childhood.* Anne Behnke Kinney, ed. Pp. 79–110. Honolulu: University of Hawai'i Press

Ingstad, Benedicte, and Susan Reynolds Whyte, eds.
    1995   *Disability and Culture.* Berkeley: University of California Press.
    2007   *Disability in Local and Global Worlds.* Berkeley: University of California Press.

Inhorn, Marcia C., ed.
    2009   [2007] *Reproductive Disruptions: Gender, Technology, and Biopolitics in the New Millennium.* New York: Berghahn Books.

Inhorn, Marcia C., and Daphna Birenbaum-Carmeli
    2008   Assisted Reproductive Technologies and Culture Change. *Annual Review of Anthropology* 37:177–196.

2009   (eds.) *Assisting Reproduction, Testing Genes: Global Encounters with New Biotechnologies*. New York: Berghahn Books.
Institute of Medicine
2009   *Veterans and Agent Orange: Update 2008*. Washington, DC: National Academies Press.
Ivry, Tsipy
2006   At the Back Stage of Prenatal Care: Japanese Ob-Gyns Negotiating Prenatal Diagnosis. *Medical Anthropology Quarterly* 20(4): 441–468.
2009   The Ultrasonic Picture Show and the Politics of Threatened Life. *Medical Anthropology Quarterly* 23(3):189–211.
2010   *Embodying Culture: Pregnancy in Japan and Israel*. New Brunswick, NJ: Rutgers University Press.
Jackson, Michael
1998   *Minima Ethnographica: Intersubjectivity and the Anthropological Project*. Chicago: University of Chicago Press.
2002   *The Politics of Storytelling: Violence, Transgression and Intersubjectivity*. Copenhagen: Museum Tusculanum Press.
2007   *Excursions*. Durham, NC: Duke University Press.
2012   *Between One and One Another*. Berkeley: University of California Press.
James, Wendy R.
2000   Placing the Unborn: On the Social Recognition of New Life. *Anthropology and Medicine* 7(2):169–189.
Jellema, Kate
2005   Making Good on Debt: The Remoralisation of Wealth in Post-Revolutionary Vietnam. *Asia Pacific Journal of Anthropology* 6(3):231–248.
2007   Everywhere Incense Burning: Remembering Ancestors in Đổi Mới Vietnam. *Journal of Southeast Asian Studies* 38(3):467–492.
Jewkes, Rachel, Naeemah Abrahams, and Zodumo Mvo
1998   Why Do Nurses Abuse Patients? Reflections from South African Obstetric Services. *Social Science and Medicine* 47(11):1781–1795.
Johansson, Annika
2007   "The Agent Orange Family": Reflections on Consequences of the Wartime Use of Agent Orange in Vietnam for Reproductive Health and Rights. Paper presented at the Annual Conference of the Association for Asian Studies, Boston, March 22–25.
Johansson, Annika, Le Thi Nham Tuyet, Nguyen The Lap, and Kajsa Sundström
1996   Abortion in Context: Women's Experience in Two Villages in Thai Binh Province, Vietnam. *International Family Planning Perspectives* 22(3):103–107.
Johansson, Annika, Nguyen Thu Nga, Tran Quang Huy, Doan Du Dat, and Kristina Holmgren
1998   Husbands' Involvement in Abortion in Vietnam. *Studies in Family Planning* 29(4):400–413.
Jordan, Brigitte
1997   Authoritative Knowledge and Its Construction. In *Childbirth and Authoritative Knowledge: Cross-Cultural Perspectives*. Robbie E.

Davis-Floyd and Carolyn F. Sargent, eds. Pp. 55–79. Berkeley: University of California Press.

Kanaaneh, Rhoda Ann
  2002   *Birthing the Nation: Strategies of Palestinian Women in Israel.* Berkeley: University of California Press.

Kato, Masae
  2010a   Cultural Notions of Disability in Japan: Their Influence on Prenatal Testing. In *Frameworks of Choice: Predictive and Genetic Testing in Asia.* Margaret Sleeboom-Faulkner, ed. Pp. 125–144. Amsterdam: Amsterdam University Press.
  2010b   Quality of Offspring? Socio-cultural Factors, Pre-natal Testing and Reproductive Decision-Making in Japan. *Culture, Health, and Sexuality* 12(2):177–189.

Kaufman, Sharon R.
  1997   Construction and Practice of Medical Responsibility: Dilemmas and Narratives from Geriatrics. *Culture, Medicine, and Psychiatry* 21(1):1–26.
  2005   . . . *And a Time to Die: How American Hospitals Shape the End of Life.* Chicago: University of Chicago Press.

Kaufman, Sharon R., and Lynn M. Morgan
  2005   The Anthropology of the Beginnings and Ends of Life. *Annual Review of Anthropology* 34:317–341.

Kelly, Susan E.
  2009   Choosing Not to Choose: Reproductive Responses of Parents of Children with Genetic Conditions or Impairments. *Sociology of Health and Illness* 31(1):81–97.

Kerr, Anne
  2003   Rights and Responsibilities in the New Genetics Era. *Critical Social Policy* 23(2):208–226.

Khanna, Sunil K.
  2010   *Fetal/Fatal Knowledge: New Reproductive Technologies and Family-Building Strategies in India.* Belmont, CA: Wadsworth Cengage Learning.

Khổng Diễn
  2006   Damaging Effects of Agent Orange/Dioxin: The Pain of Many Communities, Families and Generations. *Anthropology Review* 1(8):72–80.

Kinney, Anne Behnke
  2004   *Representations of Childhood and Youth in Early China.* Stanford: Stanford University Press.

Kipnis, Andrew
  2007   Neoliberalism Reified: *Suzhi* Discourse and Tropes of Neoliberalism in the People's Republic of China. *Journal of the Royal Anthropological Institute* (N.S.) 13(2):383–400.
  2011   Subjectification and Education for Quality in China. *Economy and Society* 40(2):289–306.

Kleinman, Arthur
  1999   Moral Experience and Ethical Reflection: Can Ethnography Reconcile Them? A Quandary for "The New Bioethics." *Daedalus* 128(4):69–97.

2006   *What Really Matters: Living a Moral Life amidst Uncertainty and Danger*. Oxford: Oxford University Press.

Kleinman, Arthur, and Joan Kleinman
1997   The Appeal of Experience, the Dismay of Images: Cultural Appropriations of Suffering in Our Times. In *Social Suffering*. Arthur Kleinman, Veena Das, and Margaret Lock, eds. Pp. 1–23. Berkeley: University of California Press.

Kligman, Gail
1998   *The Politics of Duplicity: Controlling Reproduction in Ceausescu's Romania*. Berkeley: University of California Press.

Klingberg-Allvin, Marie, Nguyen Binh, Annika Johansson, and Vanja Berggren
2008   One Foot Wet and One Foot Dry: Transition into Motherhood among Married Adolescent Women in Rural Vietnam. *Journal of Transcultural Nursing* 19(4):338–346.

Knowles, James C., Sarah Bales, Le Quang Cuong, Tran Thi Mai Oanh, and Duong Huy Luong
2010   *Health Equity in Vietnam: A Situational Analysis Focused on Maternal and Child Mortality*. Hanoi: UNICEF.

Koch, Lene
2004   The Meaning of Eugenics: Reflections on the Government of Genetic Knowledge in the Past and the Present. *Science in Context* 17(3): 315–331.

Kohrman, Matthew
2005   *Bodies of Difference: Experiences of Disability and Institutional Advocacy in the Making of Modern China*. Berkeley: University of California Press.

Kwon, Heonik
2006   *After the Massacre: Commemoration and Consolation in Ha My and My Lai*. Berkeley: University of California Press.
2008   *Ghosts of War in Vietnam*. Cambridge: Cambridge University Press.

LaFleur, William R.
1992   *Liquid Life: Abortion and Buddhism in Japan*. Princeton: Princeton University Press.

Lainez, Nicolas
2012   Commodified Sexuality and Mother-Daughter Power Dynamics in the Mekong Delta. *Journal of Vietnamese Studies* 7(1):149–180.

Landsman, Gail
1998   Reconstructing Motherhood in the Age of "Perfect" Babies: Mothers of Infants and Toddlers with Disabilities. *Signs* 24(1):69–99.
2009   *Reconstructing Motherhood and Disability in the Age of "Perfect" Babies*. New York: Routledge.

Layne, Linda L.
1999   (ed.) *Transformative Motherhood: On Giving and Getting in a Consumer Culture*. New York: New York University Press.
2001   In Search of Community: Tales of Pregnancy Loss in Three Toxically Assaulted U.S. Communities. *Women's Studies Quarterly* 29(1–2): 25–50.

2003   *Motherhood Lost: A Feminist Account of Pregnancy Loss in America.* New York: Routledge.

Lê Bạch Dương, Đặng Nguyễn Anh, Khuất Thu Hồng, Lê Hoài Trung, and Robert Leroy Bach
2005   *Social Protection for the Most Needy in Vietnam.* Hanoi: Thế Giới Publishers.

Lê Bạch Dương, Đặng Nguyễn Anh, and Nguyễn Đức Vinh
2008   *People with Disabilities in Vietnam. Findings from a Social Survey at Thai Binh, Quang Nam, Da Nang, and Dong Nai.* Hanoi: National Political Publishing House.

Le Cao Dai
2000   *Agent Orange in the Viet Nam War: History and Consequences,* Diane Niblack Fox, trans. Hanoi: Vietnam Red Cross Society.

Lê Thi
2007   Vietnamese Women and Children Facing the Effects of Agent Orange. *Anthropology Review* 1(8):47–56.

Le Thi Nham Tuyet, and Annika Johansson
2001   Impact of Chemical Warfare with Agent Orange on Women's Reproductive Lives in Vietnam: A Pilot Study. *Reproductive Health Matters* 9(18):156–164.

Lê Thị Thu
2004   The Vietnamese Family in the Cause of National Industrialization and Modernization. *Population, Family and Children,* September–October:4–5.

Lê Xuân Khiêm
2005   Người Thắp Lửa (People Who Light the Fire). *Gia Đình và Xã Hội* (Family and Society), February 26:6.

Leshkowich, Ann Marie
2006   Woman, Buddhist, Entrepreneur: Gender, Moral Values, and Class Anxiety in Late Socialist Vietnam. *Journal of Vietnamese Studies* 1(1–2):277–313.
2008   Wandering Ghosts of Late Socialism: Conflict, Metaphor, and Memory in a Southern Vietnamese Marketplace. *Journal of Asian Studies* 67(1):5–41.
2011   Making Class and Gender: (Market) Socialist Enframing of Traders in Ho Chi Minh City. *American Anthropologist* 113(2): 277–290.
2012   Rendering Infant Abandonment Technical and Moral: Expertise, Neoliberal Logics, and Class Differentiation in Ho Chi Minh City. *positions: east asia cultures critique* 20(2):497–526.

Levinas, Emmanuel
1985a   [1982] Responsibility for the Other. In *Ethics and Infinity: Conversations with Philippe Nemo.* Richard A. Cohen, trans. Pp. 93–101. Pittsburgh: Duquesne University Press.
1985b   [1982] The Face. In *Ethics and Infinity: Conversations with Philippe Nemo.* Richard A. Cohen, trans. Pp. 85–92. Pittsburgh: Duquesne University Press.

1990   Reflections on the Philosophy of Hitlerism. *Critical Inquiry* 17(1):62–71.

1996   [1951] Is Ontology Fundamental? Peter Atterton, trans. In *Emmanuel Levinas: Basic Philosophical Writings*. Adriaan T. Peperzak, Simon Critchley, and Robert Bernasconi, eds. Pp. 1–10. Bloomington: Indiana University Press.

1998a   [1985] Diachrony and Representation. In *Entre Nous: On Thinking-of-the-Other*. Michael B. Smith and Barbara Harshav, trans. Pp. 159–178. New York: Columbia University Press.

1998b   [1983] From the One to the Other. In *Entre Nous: On Thinking-of-the-Other*. Michael B. Smith and Barbara Harshav, trans. Pp. 133–153. New York: Columbia University Press.

1998c   [1982] Useless Suffering. In *Entre Nous: On Thinking-of-the-Other*. Michael B. Smith and Barbara Harshav, trans. Pp. 91–101. New York: Columbia University Press.

2000   [1981] *Otherwise Than Being or Beyond Essence*. Alphonso Lingis, trans. Pittsburgh: Duquesne University Press.

2006   [1970] No Identity. In *Collected Philosophical Papers*. Alphonso Lingis, trans. Pp. 141–151. Pittsburgh: Duquesne University Press.

Levinas, Emmanuel, and Richard Kearney

1986   Dialogue with Emmanuel Levinas. In *Face to Face with Levinas*. Richard Cohen, ed. Pp. 13–33. Albany: State University of New York Press.

Linton, Simi

1998   *Claiming Disability: Knowledge and Identity*. New York: New York University Press.

Lippman, Abby

1991   Prenatal Genetic Testing and Screening: Constructing Needs and Reinforcing Inequities. *American Journal of Law and Medicine* 17(1–2):15–50.

1999a   Choice as a Risk to Women's Health. *Health, Risk and Society* 1(3):281–291.

1999b   Embodied Knowledge and Making Sense of Prenatal Diagnosis. *Journal of Genetic Counseling* 8(5):255–274.

Lock, Margaret

1998   Perfecting Society: Reproductive Technologies, Genetic Testing, and the Planned Family in Japan. In *Pragmatic Women and Body Politics*. Margaret Lock and Patricia Kaufert, eds. Pp. 206–239. Cambridge: Cambridge University Press.

2007   Genomics, Laissez-Faire Eugenics, and Disability. In *Disability in Local and Global Worlds*. Benedicte Ingstad and Susan Reynolds Whyte, eds. Pp. 189–211. Berkeley: University of California Press.

2009   Globalization and the State: Is an Era of Neo-eugenics in the Offing? In Embodiment and the State: Health, Biopolitics and the Intimate Life of State Powers. Giovanni Pizza and Helle Johannessen, eds. Special issue, *AM Rivista della Società Italiana di Antropologia Medica* 27–28:261–296.

Lock, Margaret, and Deborah Gordon
    1988   *Biomedicine Examined*. Dordrecht: Kluwer Academic Publishers.
Lock, Margaret, and Patricia A. Kaufert, eds.
    1998   *Pragmatic Women and Body Politics*. Cambridge: Cambridge University Press.
London, Jonathan D.
    2008   Reasserting the State in Viet Nam: Health Care and the Logics of Market-Leninism. *Policy and Society* 27:115–128.
Luong, Hy Van
    1989   Vietnamese Kinship: Structural Principles and the Socialist Transformation in Northern Vietnam. *Journal of Asian Studies* 48(4):741–756.
    1992   *Revolution in the Village: Tradition and Transformation in North Vietnam, 1925–1988*. Honolulu: University of Hawaii Press.
Luong, Victoria H.
    2007   In Pursuit of Modernity: The Making of "Modern Mothers" in Northern Vietnam. PhD dissertation. University of California, Irvine.
Lupton, Deborah
    1999   Risk and the Ontology of Pregnant Embodiment. In *Risk and Sociocultural Theory: New Directions and Perspectives*. Deborah Lupton, ed. Pp. 59–85. Cambridge: Cambridge University Press.
Maarse, Anneke
    2000   "The Whole Leaf Shall Support the Damaged One": Interfaces within a CBR Project. MA thesis, Wageningen University.
Mahmood, Saba
    2005   *Politics of Piety: The Islamic Revival and the Feminist Subject*. Princeton: Princeton University Press.
Malarney, Shaun Kingsley
    1997   Culture, Virtue, and Political Transformation in Contemporary Northern Viet Nam. *Journal of Asian Studies* 56(4):899–920.
    2001   "The Fatherland Remembers Your Sacrifice": Commemorating War Dead in North Vietnam. In *The Country of Memory: Remaking the Past in Late Socialist Vietnam*. Hue-Tam Ho Tai, ed. Pp. 46–76. Berkeley: University of California Press.
    2002   *Culture, Ritual and Revolution in Vietnam*. Honolulu: University of Hawai'i Press.
    2011   Living with the War Dead in Contemporary Vietnam. In *Everyday Life in Southeast Asia*. Kathleen M. Adams and Kathleen A. Gillogly, eds. Pp. 237–246. Bloomington: Indiana University Press.
Mansfield, C., S. Hopfer, and T. M. Marteau
    1999   Termination Rates after Prenatal Diagnosis of Down Syndrome, Spina Bifida, Anencephaly, and Turner and Klinefelter Syndromes: A Systematic Literature Review. *Prenatal Diagnosis* 19(9):808–812.
Marinac-Dabic, Danica, Cara J. Krulewitch, and Roscoe M. Moore
    2002   The Safety of Prenatal Ultrasound Exposure in Human Studies. *Epidemiology* 13(3S):S19–S22.

Markens, Susan, Carole H. Browner, and Mabel H. Preloran

2009 Interrogating the Dynamics between Power, Knowledge and Pregnant Bodies in Amniocentesis Decision-Making. *Sociology of Health and Illness* 32(1):37–56.

Marr, David

2000 Concepts of "Individual" and "Self" in Twentieth-Century Vietnam. *Modern Asian Studies* 34(4):769–796.

Martin, Michael F.

2009 Vietnamese Victims of Agent Orange and U.S.-Vietnam Relations. Congressional Research Service 7–5700.

McCoyd, Judith L. M.

2007 Pregnancy Interrupted: Loss of a Desired Pregnancy after Diagnosis of Fetal Anomaly. *Journal of Psychosomatic Obstetrics and Gynecology* 28(1):37–48.

McHale, Shawn

2004 *Print and Power: Confucianism, Communism, and Buddhism in the Making of Modern Vietnam*. Honolulu: University of Hawai'i Press.

Merleau-Ponty, Maurice

1964 [1960] *Signs*. Richard C. McCleary, trans. Evanston, IL: Northwestern University Press.

Michaels, Meredith W., and Lynn M. Morgan

1999 Introduction: The Fetal Imperative. In *Fetal Subjects, Feminist Positions*. Lynn M. Morgan and Meredith W. Michaels, eds. Pp. 1–9. Philadelphia: University of Pennsylvania Press.

Minh Thịnh

2004 Bước Nhảy Vọt của Kỹ Thuật Siêu Âm Trong Chẩn Đoán (The Great Advance of Ultrasound Scanning in Diagnosis). *Khoa Học và Đời Sống* (Science and Life) December 17:9.

Ministry of Health

2002 *National Standards and Guidelines for Reproductive Health Care Services*. Hanoi.

2009 *National Guidelines for Reproductive Health Care Services*. Hanoi.

Mitchell, Lisa M.

2001 *Baby's First Picture: Ultrasound and the Politics of Fetal Subjects*. Toronto: University of Toronto Press.

2004 Women's Experiences of Unexpected Ultrasound Findings. *Journal of Midwifery and Women's Health* 49(3):228–234.

Mitchell, Lisa M., and Eugenia Georges

1997 Cross-Cultural Cyborgs: Greek and Canadian Women's Discourses on Fetal Ultrasound. *Feminist Studies* 23(2):373–401.

Mol, Annemarie

2008 *The Logic of Care: Health and the Problem of Patient Choice*. London: Routledge.

Monnais, Laurence, C. Michele Thompson, and Ayo Wahlberg, eds.

2012 *Southern Medicine for Southern People: Vietnamese Medicine in the Making*. Newcastle upon Tyne: Cambridge Scholars Publishing.

Mont, Daniel, and Nguyen Viet Cuong
    2011   Disability and Poverty in Vietnam. *World Bank Economic Review* 25(2):323–359.

Montgomery, Heather
    2009   *An Introduction to Childhood: Anthropological Perspectives on Children's Lives.* Oxford: Wiley-Blackwell.

Morgan, Lynn M.
    1996   When Does Life Begin? A Cross-Cultural Perspective on the Personhood of Fetuses and Young Children. In *Talking about People: Readings in Contemporary Cultural Anthropology.* 2nd Edition. William A. Haviland and Robert J. Gordon, eds. Pp. 24–34. Mountain View, CA: Mayfield.
    1997   Imagining the Unborn in the Ecuadoran Andes. *Feminist Studies* 23(2):323–350.
    2002   "Properly Disposed of": A History of Embryo Disposal and the Changing Claims on Fetal Remains. *Medical Anthropology* 21(3–4): 247–274.
    2009   *Icons of Life: A Cultural History of Human Embryos.* Berkeley: University of California Press.

Morgan, Lynn M., and Meredith W. Michaels, eds.
    1999   *Fetal Subjects, Feminist Positions.* Philadelphia: University of Pennsylvania Press.

Moskowitz, Marc L.
    2001   *The Haunting Fetus: Abortion, Sexuality, and the Spirit World in Taiwan.* Honolulu: University of Hawai'i Press.

Mrozik, Susanne
    2007   *Virtuous Bodies: The Physical Dimensions of Morality in Buddhist Ethics.* Oxford: Oxford University Press.

Murphy, Robert Frances
    1987   *The Body Silent: The Different World of the Disabled.* New York: Henry Holt.

Müller-Rockstroh, Babette
    2007   Ultrasound Travels: The Politics of a Medical Technology in Ghana and Tanzania. PhD dissertation. Maastricht University.

National Committee for Population and Family Planning
    2001   *Study on Major Matters concerning Population Quality in Vietnam (2001–2010).* Hanoi: National Committee for Population and Family Planning.

Nelkin, Dorothy
    2003   Foreword: The Social Meanings of Risk. In *Risk, Culture, and Health Inequality: Shifting Perceptions of Danger and Blame.* Barbara Herr Harthorn and Laury Oaks, eds. Pp. vii–xiii. Westport, CT: Praeger Publishers.

Ngo, Anh D., Richard Taylor, Christine L. Roberts, and Tuan V. Nguyen
    2006   Association between Agent Orange and Birth Defects: Systematic Review and Meta-Analysis. *International Journal of Epidemiology* 35:1220–1230.

Nguyễn Bá Thuỷ

    2007   Nâng Cao Chất Lượng Dân Số Đã Trở Thành Đòi Hỏi Cấp Bách (Enhancing Population Quality Has Become an Urgent Demand). *Gia Đình và Trẻ Em. Số đặc biệt tháng* 2:7. (Family and Children. Special issue, February: 7).

Nguyễn Mỹ Hương, Tine Gammeltoft, and Vibeke Rasch

    2007   Situation Analysis of Quality of Abortion Care in the Main Maternity Hospital in Hải Phòng, Viet Nam. *Reproductive Health Matters* 15(29):172–182.

Nguyễn Quốc Triệu

    2009   Việt Nam Trong Tiến Trình Hội Nhập và Phát Triển (Vietnam in the Process of Integration and Development). In *Toàn Cảnh Y Tế Việt Nam Giai Đoạn Đầu Hội Nhập WTO* (Outline of Vietnam's Health Sector in the Initial Stage of Integration into the WTO). Pp. 10–12. Hanoi: Nhà Xuất Bản Y Học (Medical Publishing House).

Nguyễn Thị Hoàn

    2006   Sàng Lọc Sơ Sinh Nhằm Mục Tiêu Nâng Cao Chất Lượng Dân Số (Neonatal Screening with the Aim of Improving Population Quality). *Gia Đình và Trẻ Em* (Family and Children). September.

Nguyen Thi Hong Tu, Nguyen Thi Lien Huong, and Nguyen Bich Diep

    2004   Globalization and Its Effects on Health Care and Occupational Health in Vietnam. Draft paper prepared for the RUIG/UNRISD project on Globalization, Inequality, and Health. Geneva.

Nguyen Thi Xuan Thuy

    2011   Policy, Power, and the Paradigm Shift in the Vietnamese Discourses of Disability and Inclusion. PhD dissertation. Department of Integrated Studies in Education, McGill University.

Nguyễn Văn Đức, Nông Thúy Ngọc, and Nguyễn Ninh Hải

    2003   *Thai Nghén, Sinh Đẻ và Chăm Sóc Em Bé* (Pregnancy, Delivery, and Care for the Little One). Hanoi: Nhà Xuất Bản Thanh Niên (Youth Publishing House).

Nguyễn Văn Hương

    1970   Twenty-Five Years of Health Activities in the DRVN. *Vietnamese Studies* 25:7–20.

Nguyễn Văn Huyền

    2004   Hồ Chí Minh's Thought about Humanity. *Tạp Chí Cộng Sản* (Communist Review), January 16. http://tapchicongsan.org.vn/data/tcc/Html_Data/So_52.html. Accessed December 10, 2013.

Nguyễn-võ Thu-hương

    2008   *The Ironies of Freedom: Sex, Culture, and Neoliberal Governance in Vietnam.* Seattle: University of Washington Press.

Nguyễn Xuân Hoài

    2005   Nỗi Đau Mang Tên Da Cam (A Pain Bearing the Name Orange). *Gia Đình và Xã Hội* (Family and Society). January 20:6.

Nie, Jing-Bao

    2005   *Behind the Silence: Chinese Voices on Abortion.* Oxford: Rowman and Littlefield.

Ninh, erin Khuê
　2011　An Ode to "Ơi." *Diacritics*, December 11. http://diacritics.org/2011/erin-ninh-an-ode-to-%C6%A1i. Accessed September 28, 2013.

Nonini, Donald
　2008　Is China Becoming Neoliberal? *Critique of Anthropology* 28(2): 145–176.

Norgren, Tiana
　2001　*Abortion before Birth Control: The Politics of Reproduction in Postwar Japan*. Princeton: Princeton University Press.

Norton, Barley
　2009　*Songs for the Spirits: Music and Mediums in Modern Vietnam*. Urbana: University of Illinois Press.

Oaks, Laury
　1994　Fetal Spirithood and Fetal Personhood: The Cultural Construction of Abortion in Japan. *Women's Studies International Forum* 17(5):511–523.
　1999　Irish Trans/national Politics and Locating Fetuses. In *Fetal Subjects, Feminist Positions*. Lynn M. Morgan and Meredith W. Michaels, eds. Pp. 175–198. Philadelphia: University of Pennsylvania Press.

O'Flaherty, Wendy Doniger
　1980　Karma and Rebirth in the Vedas and Puranas. In *Karma and Rebirth in Classical Indian Traditions*. Wendy Doniger O'Flaherty, ed. Pp. 3–37. Berkeley: University of California Press.

Ong, Aihwa
　2006　*Neoliberalism as Exception: Mutations in Citizenship and Sovereignty*. Durham, NC: Duke University Press.

Oosterhoff, Pauline
　2008　Pressure to Bear: Gender, Fertility and Prevention of Mother-to-Child Transmission of HIV in Vietnam. PhD dissertation. University of Amsterdam.

Ortner, Sherry
　2005　Subjectivity and Cultural Critique. *Anthropological Theory* 5(1): 31–52.

Oxfeld, Ellen
　2010　*Drink Water, but Remember the Source: Moral Discourse in a Chinese Village*. Berkeley: University of California Press.

Palmer, Michael G., Nguyen Thi Minh Thuy, Quach Thi Ngoc Quyen, Dang Sy Duy, Hoang Van Huynh, and Helen L. Berry
　2012　Disability Measures as an Indicator of Poverty: A Case Study from Viet Nam. *Journal of International Development* 24(S1):S53-S68.

Pang, Mei-che Samantha
　1999　Protective Truthfulness: The Chinese Way of Safeguarding Patients in Informed Treatment Decisions. *Journal of Medical Ethics* 25(3): 247–253.

Pashigian, Melissa
　2009　The Womb, Infertility, and the Vicissitudes of Kin-Relatedness in Vietnam. *Journal of Vietnamese Studies* 4(2):34–68.

2012 Counting One's Way onto the Global Stage: Enumeration, Accountability, and Reproductive Success in Vietnam. *positions: east asia cultures critique* 20(2):529–558.

Paul, Diane

1998 *The Politics of Heredity: Essays on Eugenics, Biomedicine, and the Nature-Nurture Debate.* Albany: State University of New York Press.

Paxson, Heather

1997 Demographics and Diaspora, Gender and Genealogy: Anthropological Notes on Greek Population Policy. *South European Society and Politics* 2(2):34–56.

2004 *Making Modern Mothers: Ethics and Family Planning in Urban Greece.* Berkeley: University of California Press.

2006 Reproduction as Spiritual Kin Work: Orthodoxy, IVF, and the Moral Economy of Motherhood in Greece. *Culture, Medicine, and Psychiatry* 30(4):481–505.

Pelley, Patricia

1998 "Barbarians" and "Younger Brothers": The Remaking of Race in Postcolonial Vietnam. *Journal of Southeast Asian Studies* 29(2):374–391.

Petchesky, Rosalind Pollack

1987 Fetal Images: The Power of Visual Culture in the Politics of Reproduction. *Feminist Studies* 13(2):263–292.

Petersen, Alan

1999 Counselling the Genetically "At Risk": The Poetics and Politics of "Non-Directiveness." *Health, Risk and Society* 1(3):253–265.

Petryna, Adriana

2002 *Life Exposed: Biological Citizens after Chernobyl.* Princeton: Princeton University Press.

2005 Ethical Variability: Drug Development and Globalizing Clinical Trials. *American Ethnologist* 32(2):183–197.

Pettus, Ashley

2003 *Between Sacrifice and Desire: National Identity and the Governing of Femininity in Vietnam.* New York: Routledge.

Phạm Kim Ngọc

2006 Thảm Hoạ Mất Quyền Sinh Sản Và Huỷ Hoại Sức Khoẻ Sinh Sản (Disastrous Loss of Reproductive Rights and Damaged Reproductive Health). *Dân Tộc Học* (Anthropology Review) 1(139):31–34.

Phạm Quỳnh Phương and Chris Eipper

2009 Mothering and Fathering the Vietnamese: Religion, Gender, and National Identity. *Journal of Vietnamese Studies* 4(1):49–83.

Phạm Văn Bích

1999 *The Vietnamese Family in Change: The Case of the Red River Delta.* Richmond, Surrey: Curzon Press.

Phinney, Harriet

2005 Asking for a Child: The Refashioning of Reproductive Space in Post-War Northern Vietnam. *Asia Pacific Journal of Anthropology* 6(3):215–230.

2008   Objects of Affection: Vietnamese Discourses on Love and Emancipation. *positions: east asia cultures crtique* 16(2):329–358.

Pilnick, Alison, and Olga Zayts
2012   "Let's Have It Tested First": Choice and Circumstances in Decision-Making Following Positive Antenatal Screening in Hong Kong. *Sociology of Health and Illness* 34(2):266–282.

Powell, Cynthia M.
2000   The Current State of Prenatal Genetic Testing in the United States. In *Prenatal Testing and Disability Rights*. Erik Parens and Adrienne Asch, eds. Pp. 44–53. Washington, DC: Georgetown University Press.

Press, Nancy, and Carole H. Browner
1997   Why Women Say Yes to Prenatal Diagnosis. *Social Science and Medicine* 47(7):979–989.

Press, Nancy, Carole H. Browner, Diem Tran, Christine Morton, and Barbara Le Master
1998   Provisional Normalcy and "Perfect Babies": Pregnant Women's Attitudes Toward Disability in the Context of Prenatal Testing. In *Reproducing Reproduction: Kinship, Power, and Technological Innovation*. Sarah Franklin and Helena Ragoné, eds. Pp. 46–65. Philadelphia: University of Pennsylvania Press.

Ragoné, Helena, and Frances Winddance Twine, eds.
2000   *Ideologies and Technologies of Motherhood: Race, Class, Sexuality, Nationalism*. New York: Routledge.

Ranji, A., and A.K. Dykes
2012   Ultrasound Screening during Pregnancy in Iran: Women's Expectations, Experiences, and Number of Scans. *Midwifery* 28(1):24–29.

Rapp, Rayna
1998a   Real-Time Fetus: The Role of the Sonogram in the Age of Monitored Reproduction. In *Cyborgs and Citadels: Anthropological Interventions in Emerging Sciences and Technologies*. Gary Lee Downey and Joseph Dumit, eds. Pp. 31–48. Santa Fe: School of American Research Press.
1998b   Refusing Prenatal Diagnosis: The Meanings of Bioscience in a Multicultural World. *Science, Technology, and Human Values* 23(1):45–70.
1999   *Testing Women, Testing the Fetus: The Social Impact of Amniocentesis in America*. New York: Routledge.
2000   Extra Chromosomes and Blue Tulips: Medico-familial Interpretations. In *Living and Working with the New Medical Technologies*. Margaret Lock, Allan Young, and Alberto Cambrosio, eds. Pp. 184–208. Cambridge: Cambridge University Press.

Rapp, Rayna, and Faye D. Ginsburg
2001   Enabling Disability: Rewriting Kinship, Reimagining Citizenship. *Public Culture* 13(3):533–556.
2007   Enlarging Reproduction, Screening Disability. In *Reproductive Disruptions: Gender, Technology, and Biopolitics in the New Millennium*. Marcia C. Inhorn, ed. Pp. 98–121. New York: Berghahn Books.

Remennick, Larissa

    2006   The Quest for the Perfect Baby: Why Do Israeli Women Seek Prenatal Genetic Testing? *Sociology of Health and Illness* 28(1):21–53.

Renzong Qiu

    1999   Cultural and Ethical Dimensions of Genetic Practices in China. In *Chinese Scientists and Responsibility: Ethical Issues of Human Genetics in Chinese and International Contexts.* Ole Döring, ed. Pp. 213–238. Hamburg: Institut für Asienkunde.

Rivkin-Fish, Michele

    2005   *Women's Health in Post-Soviet Russia: The Politics of Intervention.* Bloomington: Indiana University Press.

Robbins, Joel

    2013   Beyond the Suffering Subject: Toward an Anthropology of the Good. *Journal of the Royal Anthropological Institute* 19(3):447–462.

Roberts, Elizabeth F. S.

    2012   *God's Laboratory: Assisted Reproduction in the Andes.* Berkeley: University of California Press.

Robertson, Ann

    1999   Health Promotion and the Common Good: Theoretical Considerations. *Critical Public Health* 9(2):117–133.

Robertson, Jennifer

    2002   Blood Talks: Eugenic Modernity and the Creation of New Japanese. *History and Anthropology* 13(3):191–216.

    2005   Dehistoricizing History: The Ethical Dilemma of "East Asian Bioethics." *Critical Asian Studies* 37(2):233–250.

Rose, Nikolas

    1999   *Powers of Freedom: Reframing Political Thought.* Cambridge: Cambridge University Press.

    2001   The Politics of Life Itself. *Theory, Culture & Society* 18(6):1–30.

    2007   *The Politics of Life Itself: Biomedicine, Power, and Subjectivity in the Twenty-First Century.* Princeton: Princeton University Press.

Rothman, Barbara Katz

    1993   [1986] *The Tentative Pregnancy: How Amniocentesis Changes the Experience of Motherhood.* New York: W. W. Norton.

Royal College of Obstetricians and Gynaecologists

    2011   *The Care of Women Requesting Induced Abortion.* Evidence-Based Clinical Guideline Number 7. London: Royal College of Obstetricians and Gynaecologists.

Rydstrøm, Helle

    2003   *Embodying Morality: Growing Up in Rural Northern Vietnam.* Honolulu: University of Hawai'i Press.

    2010   Having "Learning Difficulties": The Inclusive Education of Disabled Girls and Boys in Vietnam. *Improving Schools* 13(1):81–98.

Sandelowski, Margarete, and Julie Barroso

    2005   The Travesty of Choosing after Positive Prenatal Diagnosis. *Journal of Obstetric, Gynecologic, and Neonatal Nursing* 34(3): 307–318.

Sandelowski, Margarete, and Linda Corson Jones
  1996   "Healing Fictions": Stories of Choosing in the Aftermath of the Detection of Fetal Anomalies. *Social Science and Medicine* 42(3): 353–361.
Saxton, Martha
  2006   Disability Rights and Selective Abortion. In *The Disability Studies Reader.* 2nd Edition. Lennard J. Davis, ed. Pp. 105–116. New York: Routledge.
Schechter, Arnold, and John D. Constable
  2006   Commentary: Agent Orange and Birth Defects in Vietnam. *International Journal of Epidemiology* 35(5):1230–1232.
Schechter, Arnold, Le Cao Dai, Le Thi Bich Thuy, Hoang Trong Quynh, Dinh Quang Minh, Hoang Dinh Cau, Pham Hoang Phiet, Nguyen Thi Ngoc Phuong, John D. Constable, Robert Baughman, Olaf Päpke, J.J. Ryan, Peter Fürst, and Seppo Räisänen
  1995   Agent Orange and the Vietnamese: The Persistence of Elevated Dioxin Levels in Human Tissue. *American Journal of Public Health* 85(4):516–522.
Scheper-Hughes, Nancy
  1992   *Death without Weeping: The Violence of Everyday Life in Brazil.* Berkeley: University of California Press.
Scheper-Hughes, Nancy, and Carolyn Sargent, eds.
  1998   *Small Wars: The Cultural Politics of Childhood.* Berkeley: University of California Press.
Schuck, Peter H.
  1986   *Agent Orange on Trial: Mass Toxic Disasters in the Courts.* Cambridge, MA: Belknap Press of Harvard University Press.
Schwenkel, Christina
  2009   *The American War in Contemporary Vietnam. Transnational Remembrance and Representation.* Bloomington: Indiana University Press.
Schwenkel, Christina, and Ann Marie Leshkowich
  2012   How Is Neoliberalism Good to Think Vietnam? How Is Vietnam Good to Think Neoliberalism? *positions: east asia cultures critique* 20(2):379–401.
Schwennesen, Nete
  2011   Practicing Informed Choice: Inquiries into the Redistribution of Life, Risk and Relations of Responsibility in Prenatal Decision Making and Knowledge Production. PhD dissertation. Faculty of Health Sciences, University of Copenhagen.
Schwennesen, Nete, and Lene Koch
  2012   Representing and Intervening: "Doing" Good Care in First Trimester Prenatal Knowledge Production and Decision-Making. *Sociology of Health and Illness* 34(2):283–298.
Schwennesen, Nete, Mette Nordahl Svendsen, and Lene Koch
  2010   Beyond Informed Choice: Prenatal Risk Assessment, Decision-Making, and Trust. *Clinical Ethics* 5(4):207–216.

Sedgh, Gilda, Stanley K. Henshaw, Susheela Singh, Akinrinola Bankole, and Joanna Drescher
  2007   Legal Abortion Worldwide: Incidence and Recent Trends. *International Family Planning Perspectives* 33(3):106–116.
Sherwin, Susan
  1998   A Relational Approach to Autonomy in Health Care. In *The Politics of Women's Health: Exploring Agency and Autonomy*. The Feminist Health Care Ethics Research Network. Susan Sherwin, coordinator. Pp. 19–47. Philadelphia: Temple University Press.
Sigley, Gary
  2009   *Suzhi*, the Body, and the Fortunes of Technoscientific Reasoning in Contemporary China. *positions: east asia cultures critique* 17(3):537–566.
Simpson, Bob
  2004   Impossible Gifts: Bodies, Buddhism and Bioethics in Contemporary Sri Lanka. *Journal of the Royal Anthropological Institute* 10(4):839–859.
  2007   On Parrots and Thorns: Sri Lankan Perspectives on Genetics, Science, and Personhood. *Health Care Analysis* 15(1):41–49.
  2009   We Have Always Been Modern: Buddhism, Science and the New Genetic and Reproductive Technologies in Sri Lanka. *Culture and Religion* 10(2):137–157.
  2010   A "Therapeutic Gap": Anthropological Perspectives on Prenatal Diagnostics and Termination in Sri Lanka. In *Frameworks of Choice: Predictive and Genetic Testing in Asia*. Margaret Sleeboom-Faulkner, ed. Pp. 27–42. Amsterdam: Amsterdam University Press.
Sleeboom-Faulkner, Margaret
  2010   Eugenic Birth and Fetal Education: The Friction between Lineage Enhancement and Premarital Testing among Rural Households in Mainland China. *China Journal* 64:121–141.
  2011   Genetic Testing, Governance, and the Family in the People's Republic of China. *Social Science and Medicine* 72(11):1802–1809.
Sontag, Susan
  1977   *On Photography*. New York: Farrar, Straus and Giroux.
Soucy, Alexander
  2000   The Problem with Key Informants. *Anthropological Forum* 10(2):179–199.
Stafford, Charles
  2005   *The Roads of Chinese Childhood: Learning and Identification in Angang*. Cambridge: Cambridge University Press.
  2009   Numbers and the Natural History of Imagining the Self in Taiwan and China. *Ethnos* 74(1): 110–126.
Stasch, Rupert
  2009   *Society of Others: Kinship and Mourning in a West Papuan Place*. Berkeley: University of California Press.
Statham, Helen
  2002   Prenatal Diagnosis of Fetal Abnormality: The Decision to Terminate the Pregnancy and the Psychological Consequences. *Fetal and Maternal Medicine Review* 13(4):213–247.

Statham, Helen, Wendy Solomou, and Lyn Chitty
    2000   Prenatal Diagnosis of Fetal Abnormality: Psychological Effects on Women in Low-Risk Pregnancies. *Baillière's Clinical Obstetrics and Gynaecology* 14(4):731–747.

Stellman, Jeanne Mager, Steven D. Stellman, Richard Christian, Tracy Weber, and Carrie Tomasallo
    2003   The Extent and Patterns of Usage of Agent Orange and Other Herbicides in Vietnam. *Nature* 422:681–687.

Stone, Richard
    2007   Agent Orange's Bitter Harvest. *Science* 315(5809):176–179.

Strathern, Marilyn
    1992   *Reproducing the Future: Anthropology, Kinship and the New Reproductive Technologies.* Manchester: Manchester University Press.

Sức Khoẻ và Đời Sống (Health and Life)
    2004   Quan Tâm Hơn Nữa Đối Với Người Tàn Tật (Pay More Attention to Disabled People). December 3:3–4.

Taussig, Karen-Sue, Rayna Rapp, and Deborah Heath
    2003   Flexible Eugenics: Technologies of Self in the Age of Genetics. In *Genetic Nature/Culture: Anthropology and Science beyond the Two-Culture Divide.* Alan H. Goodman, Deborah Heath, and M. Susan Lindee, eds. Pp. 58–76. Berkeley: University of California Press.

Tautz, Siegrid, Albrecht Jahn, Imelda Molokomme, and Regina Görgen
    2000   Between Fear and Relief: How Rural Pregnant Women Experience Foetal Ultrasound in a Botswana District Hospital. *Social Science and Medicine* 50(5):689–701.

Taylor, Janelle S.
    1998   Image of Contradiction: Obstetrical Ultrasound in American Culture. In *Reproducing Reproduction: Kinship, Power, and Technological Innovation.* Sarah Franklin and Helena Ragoné, eds. Pp. 15–45. Philadelphia: University of Pennsylvania Press.
    2008   *The Public Life of the Fetal Sonogram: Technology, Consumption, and the Politics of Reproduction.* New Brunswick, NJ: Rutgers University Press.

Taylor, Janelle S., Linda L. Layne, and Danielle F. Wozniak, eds.
    2004   *Consuming Motherhood.* New Brunswick, NJ: Rutgers University Press.

Taylor, Philip
    2004a   *Goddess on the Rise: Pilgrimage and Popular Religion in Vietnam.* Honolulu: University of Hawai'i Press.
    2004b   (ed.) *Social Inequality in Vietnam and the Challenges to Reform.* Singapore: Institute of Southeast Asian Studies (ISEAS).
    2004c   Introduction: Social Inequality in a Socialist State. In Philip Taylor, ed. *Social Inequality in Vietnam and the Challenges to Reform.* Pp. 1–40. Singapore: Institute of Southeast Asian Studies (ISEAS).
    2007   (ed.) *Modernity and Re-enchantment: Religion in Post-revolutionary Vietnam.* Singapore: Institute of Southeast Asian Studies (ISEAS).

Teerawichitchainan, Bussarawan, and Sajeda Amin
    2009   The Role of Abortion in the Last Stage of Fertility Decline in
           Vietnam. Working Paper No. 15. New York: Population Council.
Teman, E., T. Ivry, and B. A. Bernhardt
    2011   Pregnancy as a Proclamation of Faith: Ultra-Orthodox Jewish Women
           Navigating the Uncertainty of Pregnancy and Prenatal Diagnosis.
           American Journal of Medical Genetics 155A(1):69–80.
Thanh, Nguyen Xuan, Curt Löfgren, Ho Dang Phuc, Nguyen Thi Kim Cuc, and
    Lars Lindholm
    2010   An Assessment of the Implementation of the Health Care Funds for
           the Poor Policy in Rural Vietnam. *Health Policy* 98(1):58–64.
Thanh Thúy
    2009   Ước Mong của Người "Sống Nằm" (The Longings of People Who
           "Live Lying Down"). *Gia Đình và Xã Hội* (Family and Society),
           August 14:10.
Thảo Nguyên
    2006   Cho Ngày "Mãn Nguyệt Khai Hoa" [For the Day "When Pregnancy
           Ends"]. *Gia Đình và Trẻ Em* (Family and Children). December:14.
Thiranagama, Sharika, and Tobias Kelly, eds.
    2010   *Traitors: Suspicion, Intimacy, and the Ethics of State-Building*.
           Philadelphia: University of Pennsylvania Press.
Throop, Jason C.
    2010   *Suffering and Sentiment: Exploring the Vicissitudes of Experience
           and Pain in Yap*. Berkeley: University of California Press.
Thùy Hương
    2009   Nạo Phá Thai: Những Giọt Nước Mắt Muộn Mằn (Abortion:
           Belated Tears). *Gia Đình và Trẻ Em* (Family and Children)
           August:20–21.
Toàn Ánh
    1992   *Nếp Cũ Con Người Việt Nam* (Old Ways of Life among Vietnamese
           People). Ho Chi Minh City: Nhà Xuất Bản Thành Phố Hồ Chí Minh
           (Ho Chi Minh City Publishing House).
Torloni M.R., N. Vedmedovska, M. Merialdi, A.P. Betrán, T. Allen, R.
    González, L.D. Platt (ISUOG-WHO Fetal Growth Study Group)
    2009   Safety of Ultrasonography in Pregnancy: WHO Systematic Review
           of the Literature and Meta-Analysis. *Ultrasound in Obstetrics and
           Gynecology* 33(5):599–608.
Trần Chí Liêm
    2009   Investment in Technical Infrastructure to Serve the Cause of
           Tending and Protecting People's Health. In *Toàn Cảnh Y Tế
           Việt Nam Giai Đoạn Đầu Hội Nhập WTO* (Outline of Vietnam's
           Health Sector in the Initial Stage of Integration into the WTO).
           Pp. 50–53. Hanoi: Nhà Xuất Bản Y Học (Medical Publishing
           House).
Trần Minh Hằng
    2011   Global Debates, Local Dilemmas: Sex-Selective Abortion in
           Contemporary Vietnam. PhD thesis. Australian National University.

Trần Quốc Long
    2009   Chuẩn Bị Làm Mẹ—Hãy Cảnh Giác với Rubella (When Preparing to Become a Mother, Be on Guard against Rubella). *Sức Khoẻ và Đời Sống* (Health and Life) online. March 7. http://suckhoedoisong.vn/20093611403067I p45c5I/chuan-bi-lam-mehay-canh-giac-voi-rubella.htm. Accessed September 28 2011.

Trần Thị Trung Chiến
    2005   *Một Số Yếu Tố Liên Quan Đến Chất Lượng Dân Số Việt Nam* (Some Factors Related to Vietnam's Population Quality). Hanoi: Uỷ Ban Dân Số, Gia Đình và Trẻ Em (Commission for Population, Family, and Children).

Tran, Toan K., Chuc T.K. Nguyen, Hinh D. Nguyen, Bo Eriksson, Goran Bondjers, Karin Gottvall, Henry Ascher, and Max Petzold
    2011   Urban-Rural Disparities in Antenatal Care Utilization: A Study of Two Cohorts of Pregnant Women in Vietnam. *BMC Health Services Research* 11:120.

Trần Tuấn
    1995   *Historical Development of Primary Health Care in Vietnam: Lessons for the Future.* Research Paper no. 102. Takemi Program in International Health, Harvard School of Public Health.

Trần Văn Tiến, Hoàng Thị Phượng, Inke Mathauer, and Nguyễn Thị Kim Phượng
    2011   *A Health Financing Review of Viet Nam with a Focus on Social Health Insurance.* Hanoi: World Health Organization.

Tsing, Anna Lowenhaupt
    1990   Monster Stories: Women Charged with Perinatal Endangerment. In *Uncertain Terms: Negotiating Gender in American Culture.* Faye Ginsburg and Anna Lowenhaupt Tsing, eds. Pp. 282–299. Boston: Beacon Press.

Tsuge, Azumi
    2010   How Japanese Women Describe Their Experiences of Prenatal Testing. In *Frameworks of Choice: Predictive and Genetic Testing in Asia.* Margaret Sleeboom-Faulkner, ed. Pp. 109–124. Amsterdam: Amsterdam University Press.

Tu Wei-Ming
    1985   *Confucian Thought: Selfhood as Creative Transformation.* Albany: State University of New York Press.

Turley, William S., and Mark Selden, eds.
    1993   *Reinventing Vietnamese Socialism: Doi Moi in Comparative Perspective.* Boulder, CO: Westview Press.

UNFPA (United Nations Population Fund)
    2011a   *People with Disabilities in Viet Nam: Key Findings from the 2009 Viet Nam Population and Housing Census.* Hanoi.
    2011b   *Son Preference in Viet Nam: Ancient Desires, Advancing Technologies.* Qualitative Research Report to Better Understand the Rapidly Rising Sex Ratio at Birth in Viet Nam. Hanoi.

United Nations
    2011   World Population Prospects: The 2010 Revision. Department of Economic and Social Affairs, Population Division. http://esa.un.org/wpp/index.htm. Accessed May 21, 2013.
    2013   World Abortion Policies 2013. Department of Economic and Social Affairs, Population Division. http://www.un.org/en/development/desa/population/publications/policy/world-abortion-policies-2013.shtml. Accessed May 21, 2013.

Uỷ Ban Dân Số, Gia Đình và Trẻ Em (Commission for Population, Family, and Children)
    2003   *Những Nội Dung Chủ Yếu Của Pháp Lệnh Dân Số* (Key Contents of the Population Ordinance). Hanoi: Nhà Xuất Bản Lao Động Xã Hội (Labor and Social Affairs Publishing House).
    2004   *Thực Trạng và Những Vấn Đề Đặt Ra Đối Với Gia Đình Việt Nam Hiện Nay* (The Actual Situation and Some Problems Facing the Vietnamese Family Today). Hanoi.

Van den Heuvel, Ananda, Lyn Chitty, Elizabeth Dormandy, Ainsley Newson, Zuzana Deans, and Theresa M. Marteau
    2008   Informed Choice in Prenatal Testing: A Survey among Obstetricians and Gynaecologists in Europe and Asia. *Prenatal Diagnosis* 28(13): 1238–1244.

Van der Geest, Sjaak, and Kaja Finkler
    2004   Hospital Ethnography: Introduction. *Social Science and Medicine* 59(10):1995–2001.

Van Hollen, Cecilia
    2003   *Birth on the Threshold: Childbirth and Modernity in South India.* Berkeley: University of California Press.

Vasiljev, Ivo
    2003   The Disabled and Their Organizations: The Emergence of New Paradigms. In *Getting Organized in Vietnam: Moving in and around the Socialist State.* Ben J. Tria Kerkvliet, Russell H.K. Heng, and David W.H. Koh, eds. Pp. 126–152. Singapore: Institute of Southeast Asian Studies.

Vian, Taryn, Derick W. Brinkerhoff, Frank G. Feeley, Matthieu Salomon, and Nguyen Thi Kieu Vien
    2011   *Confronting Corruption in the Health Sector in Vietnam: Patterns and Prospects.* Boston: Center for Global Health and Development, Boston University School of Public Health.

Vietnam Courier
    1979   Interview with Mrs Dinh Thi Can. In *Mother and Infant Welfare in Vietnam.* Pp. 9–19. Hanoi: Foreign Languages Publishing House.

Vũ Dung, Vũ Thúy Anh, and Vũ Quang Hào
    1993   *Từ Điển Thành Ngữ và Tục Ngữ Việt Nam* (Dictionary of Vietnamese Idioms and Proverbs). Hanoi: Nhà Xuất Bản Giáo Dục (Education Publishing House).

Vũ Ngọc Khánh
    2008   *Văn Hóa Gia Đình Việt Nam* (Vietnamese Family Culture). Hanoi: Nhà Xuất Bản Văn Hóa Thông Tin (Culture and Information Publishing House).

Vũ Quý Nhân
    1992   Population Policies and Development in Vietnam. In *The Challenges of Vietnam's Reconstruction*. Neil L. Jamieson, Nguyen Manh Hung, and A. Terry Rambo, eds. Pp. 40–54. Fairfax, VA: Indochina Institute, George Mason University.

Wadley, Susan S.
    1983   Vrats: Transformers of Destiny. In *Karma: An Anthropological Inquiry*. Charles F. Keyes and E. Valentine Daniel, eds. Pp. 147–162. Berkeley: University of California Press.

Wagstaff, Adam
    2007   The Economic Consequences of Health Shocks: Evidence from Vietnam. *Journal of Health Economics* 26(1):82–100.

Wahlberg, Ayo
    2006   Bio-politics and the Promotion of Traditional Herbal Medicine in Vietnam. *Health* 10(2):123–147.
    2008   Reproductive Medicine and the Concept of "Quality." *Clinical Ethics* 3(4):189–193.
    2009   Bodies and Populations: Life Optimization in Vietnam. *New Genetics and Society* 28(3): 241–251.

Wahlberg, Ayo, and Tine M. Gammeltoft
Forthcoming. Selective Reproductive Technologies. *Annual Review of Anthropology* (2014 volume).

Waugh, Charles
    2010   Introduction. In *Family of Fallen Leaves: Stories of Agent Orange by Vietnamese Writers*. Charles Waugh and Huy Lien, eds. Pp. 1–16. Athens: University of Georgia Press.

Waugh, Charles, and Huy Lien
    2010   *Family of Fallen Leaves: Stories of Agent Orange by Vietnamese Writers*. Athens: University of Georgia Press.

Weir, Lorna
    1996   Recent Developments in the Government of Pregnancy. *Economy and Society* 25(3):373–392.

Weiss, Meira
    1994   *Conditional Love: Parents' Attitudes towards Handicapped Children*. Westport, CT: Bergin and Garvey.

Weiss, Mitchell G.
    1980   *Caraka Samhita* on the Doctrine of Karma. In *Karma and Rebirth in Classical Indian Traditions*. Wendy Doniger O'Flaherty, ed. Pp. 90–115. Berkeley: University of California Press.

Wells-Dang, Andrew
    2011   Informal Pathbreakers: Civil Society Networks in China and Vietnam. PhD dissertation. Department of Politics and International Studies, School of Government and Society, University of Birmingham.

Werner, Jayne
 2009 *Gender, Household and State in Post-Revolutionary Vietnam.* London: Routledge.
Wertz, Dorothy C.
 1998 Eugenics Is Alive and Well: A Survey of Genetic Professionals around the World. *Science in Context* 11(3–4):493–510.
 2000 Drawing Lines: Notes for Policymakers. In *Prenatal Testing and Disability Rights.* Erik Parens and Adrienne Asch, eds. Pp. 261–287. Washington, DC: Georgetown University Press.
Wertz, Dorothy C., and John C. Fletcher
 2004 *Genetics and Ethics in Global Perspective.* Dordrecht: Kluwer Academic Publishers.
Whittaker, Andrea, ed.
 2010 *Abortion in Asia: Local Dilemmas, Global Politics.* New York: Berghahn Books.
Whitworth M., L. Bricker, J. P. Neilson, and T. Dowswell
 2010 Ultrasound for Fetal Assessment in Early Pregnancy. *Cochrane Database of Systematic Reviews,* Issue 4.
WHO (World Health Organization
 2010 Dioxins and Their Effects on Human Health. Fact Sheet No. 225. http://www.who.int/mediacentre/factsheets/fs225/en/. Accessed September 29, 2012.
Whyte, Susan Reynolds
 1997 *Questioning Misfortune: The Pragmatics of Uncertainty in Eastern Uganda.* Cambridge: Cambridge University Press.
 2009 Health Identities and Subjectivities: The Ethnographic Challenge. *Medical Anthropological Quarterly* 23(1):6–15.
Whyte, Susan Reynolds, and Benedicte Ingstad
 1995 Disability and Culture: An Overview. In *Disability and Culture.* Benedicte Ingstad and Susan Reynolds Whyte, eds. Pp. 3–37. Berkeley: University of California Press.
Williams, Clare, Priscilla Alderson, and Bobbie Farsides
 2002a Dilemmas Encountered by Health Practitioners Offering Nuchal Translucency Screening: A Qualitative Case Study. *Prenatal Diagnosis* 22(3):216–220.
 2002b "Drawing the Line" in Prenatal Screening and Testing: Health Practitioners' Discussions. *Health, Risk and Society* 4(1):61–75.
 2002c Is Nondirectiveness Possible within the Context of Antenatal Screening and Testing? *Social Science and Medicine* 54(3):339–347.
 2002d Too Many Choices? Hospital and Community Staff Reflect on the Future of Prenatal Screening. *Social Science and Medicine* 55(5):743–753.
Wolf, Merrill, Phan Bich Thuy, Alyson Hyman, and Amanda Huber
 2010 Abortion in Vietnam: History, Culture and Politics Collide in the Era of Doi Moi. In *Abortion in Asia: Local Dilemmas, Global Politics.* Andrea Whittaker, ed. Pp. 149–174. New York: Berghahn Books.

World Bank

2007   *Vietnam Development Report 2008: Social Protection.* Hanoi.

2012   *2012 Vietnam Poverty Assessment: Well Begun, Not Yet Done: Vietnam's Remarkable Progress on Poverty Reduction and the Emerging Challenges.* Hanoi: World Bank in Vietnam.

Zelizer, Barbie

2004   The Voice of the Visual in Memory. In *Framing Public Memory.* Kendall R. Phillips, ed. Pp. 157–186. Tuscaloosa: University of Alabama Press.

Zhang, J., and Cai W. W.

1993   Association of the Common Cold in the First Trimester of Pregnancy with Birth Defects. *Pediatrics* 92(4):559–563.

Zigon, Jarrett

2009   Within a Range of Possibilities: Morality and Ethics in Social Life. *Ethnos* 74(2):251–276.

Zola, Irving Kenneth

1982   *Missing Pieces: A Chronicle of Living with a Disability.* Philadelphia: Temple University Press.

Index

Page numbers in *italics* indicate illustrations.